At Garlingho... ...ying more tha... ...s.

You're buying a history of exceptional cu... ...s...... ...a......

In addition to our experienced staff of sales professionals, The Garlinghouse Company maintains an expert staff of trained house design professionals to help guide you through the complex process of customizing your plans to meet all your needs and expectations.

We don't just want to sell you a plan, we want to partner with you in buildi... Some of the many services we offer our customers include:

Answers to Your Questions
If you have technical questions on any plan we sell, give us a call toll-free at 1-800-235-5700.

Customizing Your Stock Plan
Any plan we sell can be modified to become your custom home. For more information, see page 32 and page 407.

Information for Budgeting Your New Home's Construction
A very general cost of building your new home can be arrived at using the so-called National Average Cost to Build, which is $110 per square foot. Based on that average, a 2,400-square-foot home would cost $264,000, including labor and materials, but excluding land, site preparation, windows, doors, cabinets, appliances, etc.

For a more inclusive rough estimate, Garlinghouse offers a Zip Quote estimate for every plan we sell. Based on current prices in your zip code area, we can provide a rough estimate of material and labor costs for the plans you select. See page 408 to learn more.

However, for a more accurate estimate of what it will cost to build your new home, we offer a full materials list, which lists the quantities, dimensions, and specifications for the major materials needed to build your home including appliances. Available at a modest additional charge, the materials list will allow you to get faster, more accurate bids from your contractors and building suppliers—and help you avoid paying for unused materials and waste. Due to differences in regional requirements and homeowner or builder preferences, electrical, plumbing, and heating/air conditioning equipment specifications are not designed specifically for each plan. See page 406 for additional information.

Garlinghouse blueprints have helped create a nation of homeowners, beginning back in 1907. Over the past century, we've made keeping up with the latest trends in floor plan design for new house construction our business. We understand the business of home plans and the real needs and expectations of the home plan buyer. To contact us, call 1-800-235-5700, or visit us on the web at www.familyhomeplans.com.

the **Garlinghouse** company

For America's best home plans.
Trust, value, and experience. Since 1907.

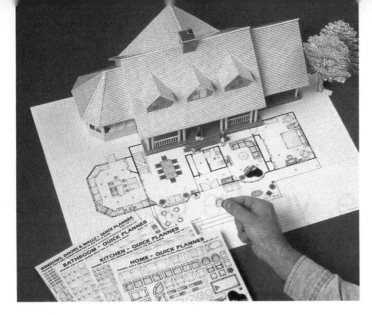

Design, Build and Decorate
Your New Home on Your Kitchen Table

Don't let the frustration of complicated home design software get between you and your dream. Visualize and test your ideas using our proven design systems.

HOME QUICK PLANNER

Design and Decorate Your New Home

Go ahead! Knock down walls and move cabinets, bathroom fixtures, furniture, windows and doors—even whole rooms. 700 pre-cut, reusable peel-and-stick furniture, fixture and architectural symbols. Includes 1/4-in. scale Floor Plan Grid, stairs, outlets, switches, lights, plus design ideas.

Regularly $22.95   Special Offer: $19.95

3-D HOME KIT

"Build" Your New Home

Construct a three-dimensional scale model home of up to 3,000 square feet. (For larger homes, order an extra kit.) A complete assortment of cardboard building materials—from brick, stone, clapboards, roofing and decking to windows, doors, skylights, stairs, bathroom fixtures, kitchen cabinets and more. Includes Floor Plan Grid, interior walls, special Scaled Ruler and Roof Slope Calculator, professional design notes and complete model building instructions.

Regularly $33.95   Special Offer: $29.95

the **Garlinghouse** company

Helping to build dreams since 1907

To order, call
1-800-235-5700

Monday - Friday 8 a.m. - 8 p.m. Eastern Time

Affordable
HOME PLANS

AN ACTIVE INTEREST MEDIA PUBLICATION

GARLINGHOUSE, LLC

General Manager	Steve Culpepper
Art Director	Christopher Berrien
Managing Editor	Debra Cochran
Art Production Manager	Debra Novitch
Production Artist	Cindy King

Exec. Director of Operations	Wade Schmelter
Senior Accountant	Angela West
Director of Home Plan Sales	Sue Lavigne
Director of Sales	Tom Valentino
Architectural Plan Reviewer	Jeanne Devins
Accounts Receivable/Payable	Monika Jackson
Telesales Manager	Helene Crispino
Telesales Team	Julianna Blamire
	Randolph Hollingsworth
	Renee Johnson
	Barbara Neal
	Carol Patenaude
	Robert Rogala
	Alice Sonski
Fulfillment Supervisor	Audrey Sutton
Fulfillment Support	Javier Gonzalez

Advertising Sales
Jerry Stoeckigt
1-800-279-7361

Newsstand Distributor
Curtis Circulation Company
730 River Road, New Milford, New Jersey 07646
Phone: 201-634-7400 Fax: 201-634-7499

For Plan Orders in Canada
The Garlinghouse Company
102 Ellis Street, Penticton, BC V2A 4L5
1-800-361-7526

For Designer's Submission Information,
e-mail us at dcochran@aimmedia.com
402 AFFORDABLE HOME PLANS
Library of Congress: 2004100833   ISBN: 1-893536-13-0

contents
affordable home plans

page 10

page 11

resources

Find thousands of plans on-line, visit our website
www.familyhomeplans.com

page 23

All Website
Credit Card
Transactions
Are Secure With
VeriSign Encryption

Exquisite Efficiency

above A wraparound covered porch and stacked gables give this thoroughly modern home a touch of traditional country appeal.

Practicality mixes with beauty in this well-designed two-story home punctuated with built-ins. A tiled entry with closet ushers guests into the formal dining room, where a built-in niche provides a place for a buffet or china cabinet. The great-room is ideal for gatherings. Light streams in through the bay window, while the two-sided fireplace sets a cozy atmosphere. Work space defines the efficient kitchen, which opens to the hearth room, where the fireplace casts its glow, and the window-lined breakfast room. The second floor is reserved for all four bedrooms. This home is designed with a basement foundation. Alternate foundation options available at an additional charge. Please call 1-800-235-5700 for more information.

Design 99457

Price Code	E
Total Finished	2,270 sq. ft.
First Finished	1,150 sq. ft.
Second Finished	1,120 sq. ft.
Basement Unfinished	1,150 sq. ft.
Garage Unfinished	457 sq. ft.
Dimensions	46'x48'
Foundation	Basement
Bedrooms	4
Full Baths	2
Half Baths	1

Please note: The photographed home may have been modified to suit homeowner preferences. If you order plans, have a builder or design professional check them against the photographs to confirm construction details.

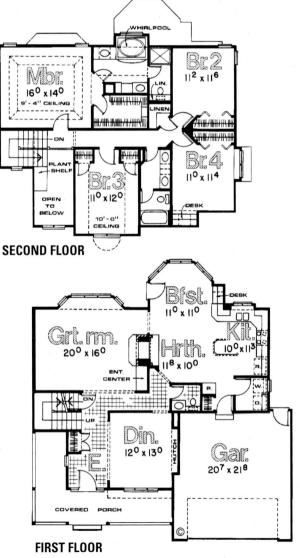

SECOND FLOOR

FIRST FLOOR

above This home attracts attention thanks to its country classic wraparound porch, second-floor stacked gables, and dormer.

SECOND FLOOR

STEPPED CEIL

MSTR BEDRM
17'-0" x 12'-0"

CL

CL

MSTR BATH

BATH #2

WICL

STORAGE ATTIC

CL

DN

BEDRM #3
10'-4" x 10'-0"

LIN

CL

BEDRM #2
11'-6" x 10'-0"

FIRST FLOOR

FAMILY RM
17'-0" x 10'-0"

OPT. MEDIA UNIT LOCATION

LAV

LAUN RM

UTIL

KITCHEN
13'-8" x 8'-0"

PANT

CL

UP UP

TWO CAR GARAGE
18'-0" x 20'-0"

LOCATION OF OPT BSMT STAIR

DINING RM
10'-4" x 11'-0"

CL

FOY

OPT. FIREPLACE

9'-4" CEIL

LIVING RM
11'-6" x 16'-0"

METER & TRASH CAN ALCOVE

PLANTER

COV. PORCH

Optional Details

Perfect for a narrow lot, this home's layout lines up its rooms in the most livable manner. The entry opens to a hexagonal foyer where columns mark entrances to the living and dining rooms. Down the hall, a work island separates the L-shape kitchen from the family room. The plan offers several additional options to make this the home of your dreams: a living room fireplace, a family room media unit, and stairs to the basement. On the second floor, two secondary bedrooms are toward the front and the master suite fills the rear. Storage and closet space abound. This home is designed with basement, slab, and crawlspace foundation options.

Please note: The photographed home may have been modified to suit homeowner preferences. If you order plans, have a builder or design professional check them against the photographs to confirm construction details.

Design 99689

Price Code	B
Total Finished	1,635 sq. ft.
First Finished	880 sq. ft.
Second Finished	755 sq. ft.
Basement Unfinished	880 sq. ft.
Porch Unfinished	403 sq. ft.
Dimensions	36'x54'4"
Foundation	Basement
	Crawlspace
	Slab
Bedrooms	3
Full Baths	2
Half Baths	1

above Simple country lines with just the right touch of detail enliven this traditional design.

Well-Divided Space

Inside this home is a clear separation of public and private areas. The front door opens into the living room, which is crowned by a tray ceiling. A wide opening connects the living room to the dining room, which is crowned with a stepped ceiling. A change in ceiling treatment and a center island define the kitchen boundaries. To the left, past the conveniently-located closet laundry, a short hall leads past a full bath and linen closet to the three bedrooms. The two secondary bedrooms overlook the front yard and include generous closet space. The master suite has a corner of windows, a walk-in closet, and its own bath. This home is designed with basement, slab, and crawlspace foundation options.

Please note: The photographed home may have been modified to suit homeowner preferences. If you order plans, you may wish to have a builder or design professional check them against the photographs to confirm construction details.

Design 99690

Price Code	A
Total Finished	1,097 sq. ft.
Main Finished	1,097 sq. ft.
Garage Unfinished	461 sq. ft.
Dimensions	56'x35'
Foundation	Basement
	Crawlspace
	Slab
Bedrooms	3
Full Baths	1
3/4 Baths	1

PATIO

MSTR BDRM · MSTR BATH · DN · DINING

BATH · CL · CL

HALL

OPTIONAL BASEMENT STAIR LOCATION

ALT GARAGE LOCATION 19'-6" X 20'-0"

PATIO

MSTR BEDRM 13'-0" X 15'-4" · MSTR BATH · UTIL RM · STEPPED CLG · DINING · KIT · DW · S

OPT TWO CAR GARAGE 22'-0" X 20'-0"

D · W · BATH · CL · DINING 15'-0" X 13'-4" · P · REF · UP

WIC

HALL

BEDRM #2 9'-0" X 11'-0" · LIN · BEDRM #3 9'-4" X 10'-0" · CL · TRAY CLG LIVING RM 15'-0" X 15'-4"

CL

PORCH · UP

MAIN FLOOR

above The smaller gable topping the entry complements the large gable to the left.

Country Home

Design 68187

Price Code	E
Total Finished	2,144 sq. ft.
Main Finished	2,144 sq. ft.
Garage Unfinished	504 sq. ft.
Porch Unfinished	341 sq. ft.
Dimensions	67'x52'
Foundation	Slab
Bedrooms	4
Full Baths	2

Please note: The photographed home may have been modified to suit homeowner preferences. If you order plans, have a builder or design professional check them against the photographs to confirm construction details.

Traditional shapes and forms dominate the design of this home, from the front porch, fan window transom, and sidelites, to the cheery gables that face the street. Inside the foyer, arched openings left and right lead to the dining room and study. A vaulted ceiling tops the large living room, which features a broad fireplace. Centering the shared spaces is the kitchen, which is open to the living room and the sizable breakfast nook, all of which wrap around a small rear porch. The master suite is contained in the right wing of the home. Three secondary bedrooms, each with a large closet, fill the left rear corner. This home is designed with a slab foundation. Alternative foundation options available at an additional charge. Please call 1-800-235-5700 for more information.

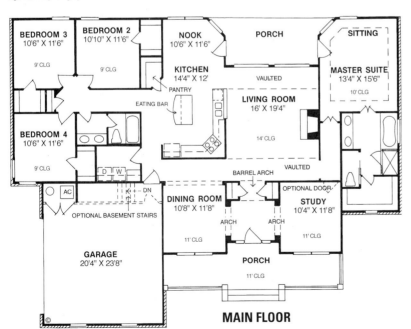

MAIN FLOOR

PHOTOGRAPHY: JOHN EHRENCLOU

Traditionally Pleasing

top   Three dormers and a gabled garage give this home a vintage look.

above   This house was built with a deck in place of the solar room and without the private patio off the master sitting area.

The entry to this classic home opens to the living room, which is distinctly separate from the other common areas. The dining room, however, opens to the kitchen, separated only by a snack bar. On the other side of the kitchen, a mudroom offers plenty of storage space and a closet laundry. A large storage space is accessible from the garage. To the left, the master suite is isolated in its own wing and includes a private patio. Two secondary bedrooms and a full bath make up the second floor. This home is designed with basement, slab, and crawlspace foundation options.

Please note: The photographed home may have been modified to suit homeowner preferences. If you order plans, have a builder or design professional check them against the photographs to confirm construction details.

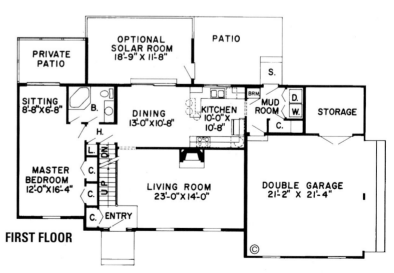

Design 10386

Price Code	B
Total Finished	1,738 sq. ft.
First Finished	1,164 sq. ft.
Second Finished	574 sq. ft.
Basement Unfinished	1,164 sq. ft.
Garage Unfinished	574 sq. ft.
Dimensions	63'6"x42'8"
Foundation	Basement
	Crawlspace
	Slab
Bedrooms	3
Full Baths	2

above A cheery array of windows and gables create a welcoming facade.

SECOND FLOOR

FIRST FLOOR

American Traditional

Attention to detail is evident from the outset. Inside the foyer, a tiled floor provides an attractive and easy-clean surface. A few steps up reveal the living room, that includes a fireplace and sloped, box-beam ceiling. To the left are the open kitchen and breakfast areas, with dining room and deck nearby. The 1,279-square-foot first floor also houses the master suite, which features a decorative ceiling in the bedroom and a luxurious skylit bath. On the 502-square-foot second floor, two mirror-image secondary bedrooms share the space with their own skylit bath, a cedar-lined closet, and a linen closet. This home is designed with a basement foundation.

Please note: The photographed home may have been modified to suit homeowner preferences. If you order plans, have a builder or design professional check them against the photographs to confirm construction details.

Design 20060

Price Code	C
Total Finished	1,781 sq. ft.
First Finished	1,279 sq. ft.
Second Finished	502 sq. ft.
Basement Unfinished	729 sq. ft.
Garage Unfinished	470 sq. ft.
Dimensions	43'x56'4"
Foundation	Basement
Bedrooms	3
Full Baths	1
3/4 Baths	1
Half Baths	1

PHOTOGRAPHY: JOHN EHRENCLOU

Thoughtful Spaces

above A simple, dormer-like second floor and an offset living/dining room wing create architectural appeal.

The quaint, covered porch draws family and friends into a floor plan that's just perfect for entertaining. The foyer leads directly into the open living and dining room area. It also leads straight ahead into the kitchen, which opens to the vast family room. Each area has its own special feature, such as a sloped ceiling, ample counter space, or a fireplace with wood storage. For privacy, three bedrooms share the second floor. Each one has ample closet space; an additional linen closet is in the hall, a step away from the full bath. This home is designed with basement, slab, and crawlspace foundation options.

Please note: The photographed home may have been modified to suit homeowner preferences. If you order plans, have a builder or design professional check them against the photographs to confirm construction details.

Design 34878

Price Code	C
Total Finished	1,838 sq. ft.
First Finished	1,088 sq. ft.
Second Finished	750 sq. ft.
Basement Unfinished	750 sq. ft.
Garage Unfinished	517 sq. ft.
Dimensions	50'x36'8"
Foundation	Basement
	Crawlspace
	Slab
Bedrooms	3
Full Baths	2
Half Baths	1

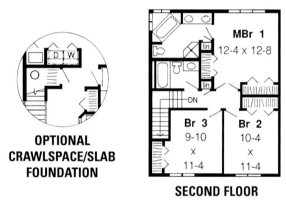

OPTIONAL CRAWLSPACE/SLAB FOUNDATION

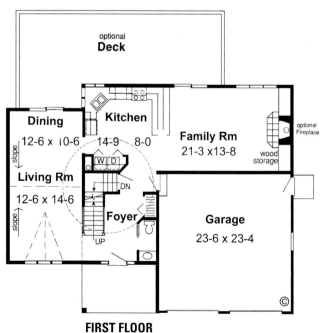

SECOND FLOOR

FIRST FLOOR

10

above The center gable nicely sets off the gabled garage. The covered porch and triple windows add curb appeal.

Design 99420

Price Code	B
Total Finished	1,694 sq. ft.
First Finished	1,298 sq. ft.
Second Finished	396 sq. ft.
Basement Unfinished	1,298 sq. ft.
Garage Unfinished	513 sq. ft.
Dimensions	54'x45'4"
Foundation	Basement
Bedrooms	3
Full Baths	2
Half Baths	1

Compact and Pleasing

The main entry leads directly into the formal dining room to the right, past the stairs leading to the second floor, and into the great-room. The breakfast room, with a built-in desk, shares a snack bar with the kitchen, which is surrounded by ample counters. The laundry room is a few steps away, beside the door to the spacious garage. In the opposite wing of the first floor is the master suite. The second floor is reserved for two secondary bedrooms and a full bath. A linen closet makes use of what could have been wasted space. This home is designed with a basement foundation. Alternate foundation options available at an additional charge. Please call 1-800-235-5700 for more information.

Please note: The photographed home may have been modified to suit homeowner preferences. If you order plans, have a builder or design professional check them against the photographs to confirm construction details.

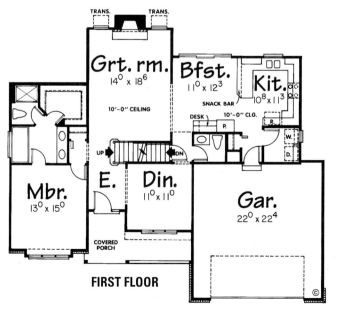

FIRST FLOOR

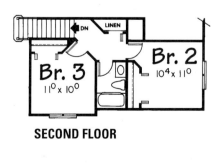

SECOND FLOOR

above This home's L-shape footprint and arched entrance create a courtyard effect around the main entrance.

Cordial & Comfortable

The arched entry is a cordial welcome to this Mediterranean-style, stucco home. Inside is just as friendly. The corner kitchen, convenient to the dining room and patio, has ample built-ins and an island for cooking and serving meals or snacks. The porch and patio offer more outdoor living space for family gatherings and barbecues. The skylight is a luxurious feature in the master bath. Meanwhile, secondary bedrooms enjoy the light of two large front-facing windows.

In addition to entertaining, this home is designed with storage needs in mind, offering plenty of closets and a separate storage room with built-in shelves. This home is designed with a crawlspace foundation.

Design 10643

Price Code	A
Total Finished	1,285 sq. ft.
Main Finished	1,285 sq. ft.
Garage Unfinished	473 sq. ft.
Dimensions	62'x40'
Foundation	Crawlspace
Bedrooms	3
Full Baths	1
3/4 Baths	1

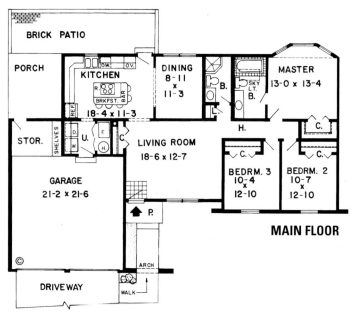

MAIN FLOOR

above This facade combines classic design elements such as a central gable, covered porch, and side-load garage.

All About Space

A long entry leads past a powder room and coat closet to the living room on the left, set off by half walls, and to the dining room ahead. Beside the dining area is the L-shape kitchen, whose pantry and work island add even more usefulness in addition to its ample counter space. A closet laundry is tucked into the corner of the attached breakfast nook.

The master suite features a linen closet, walk-in closet, and five-piece bath with whirlpool tub. The two secondary bedrooms each have a walk-in closet and share a full hall bath. Rounding out the second floor are 144 square feet of bonus space. This home is designed with basement, slab, and crawlspace foundation options.

SECOND FLOOR

- Master Br 13-5 X 15-6
- Walk-In Clos.
- Whirl-Pool
- Ledge
- Flat Clg. @ 11'-0"
- Attic Access
- Linen
- DN
- Br 2 13-5 X 10-11
- Linen
- Br 3 12-0 X 12-0
- Bonus Rm 11-5 X 11-8

FIRST FLOOR

- Covered Porch 13-7 X 19-5
- Dining Rm 11-6 X 13-6
- Kitchen 9-0 X 13-6
- Brkfst 10-7 X 13-6
- Island
- Living Rm 13-7 X 19-5 Flat Clg. @ 10'
- 1/2 wall
- UP
- DN
- Pantry
- Entry
- Furn
- Garage 22-5 X 22-11
- Porch

Crawl Space Access

OPTIONAL CRAWLSPACE/SLAB FOUNDATION

Please note: The photographed home may have been modified to suit homeowner preferences. If you order plans, have a builder or design professional check them against the photographs to confirm construction details.

Design 24665

Price Code	C
Total Finished	1,944 sq. ft.
First Finished	988 sq. ft.
Second Finished	956 sq. ft.
Bonus Unfinished	144 sq. ft.
Basement Unfinished	976 sq. ft.
Garage Unfinished	532 sq. ft.
Dimensions	50'4"x47'
Foundation	Basement Crawlspace Slab
Bedrooms	3
Full Baths	2
Half Baths	1

PHOTOGRAPHY: SUSAN GILMORE

Clean Lines

above Windows on the porch allow in only low, soft light, while the double-hung windows above allow direct sunlight into the two-story great-room.

Constructed with the basic elements of design—one larger rectangle and two smaller rectangles topped by triangular gables—this home is attractive and cost-effective to build. Soaring ceilings, open spaces, and carefully positioned windows work together to make this home seem larger than it is. The front porch welcomes guests into an air-lock vestibule, which maintains inside heat during cold weather and air conditioning during hot weather. The vestibule opens to the great-room, which has a cathedral ceiling and a prominent fireplace. The great-room is large enough to accommodate a dining area and opens to the sunroom on one side and kitchen on the other. Stairs lead down from this area to the bedrooms on the walk-out lower floor. Stairs also lead up to the master suite, which includes a private study. This home is designed with a basement foundation.

below Pocket doors lead from the master bedroom to a private study, which together form the ideal master suite retreat.

above The sunny two-story great-room is warmed by a fireplace, tall windows, and light from the adjoining sunroom. The staircase leads down to the two lower-level bedrooms and up to the master suite.

Please note: The photographed home may have been modified to suit homeowner preferences. If you order plans, have a builder or design professional check them against the photographs to confirm construction details.

Design 32056

Price Code	D
Total Finished	1,988 sq. ft.
First Finished	968 sq. ft.
Second Finished	510 sq. ft.
Lower Finished	510 sq. ft.
Basement Unfinished	840 sq. ft.
Garage Unfinished	672 sq. ft.
Dimensions	81'x52'
Foundation	Basement
Bedrooms	3
Full Baths	2

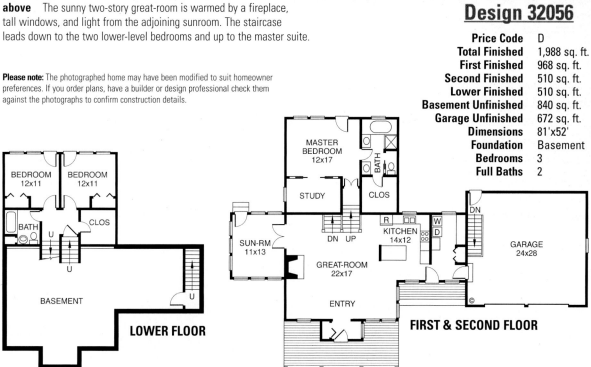

LOWER FLOOR

FIRST & SECOND FLOOR

PHOTOGRAPHY: JAMES YOCHUM PHOTOGRAPHY

Farmhouse Favorite

above The covered porch and center gable add a touch of tradition to the front of this home.

below Large closets flank the short hall that connects the master bedroom to its bath.

All the right spaces in all the right places are packed into this efficient beauty, including formal and informal living spaces as well as three bedrooms—all in just 1,550 square feet. A simple footprint makes the design extremely cost-efficient to build. The front porch (not shown on the floor plan) lines the living room, which feels more spacious because it opens to the dining room. The U-shape kitchen maximizes space and seems larger because it opens into the breakfast area and den (which can include a fireplace). A laundry area, closet, and powder room complete the 775-square-foot first floor. On the second floor, double doors open to the master suite, and two secondary bedrooms share a full hall bath. This home is designed with a basement foundation.

Design 32229

Price Code	B
Total Finished	1,550 sq. ft.
First Finished	775 sq. ft.
Second Finished	775 sq. ft.
Basement Unfinished	775 sq. ft.
Deck Unfinished	112 sq. ft.
Porch Unfinished	150 sq. ft.
Dimensions	25'x37'
Foundation	Basement
Bedrooms	3
Full Baths	1
3/4 Baths	1
Half Baths	1

above The angled sink is lit by two corner windows, creating a comfortable, well-lit workplace.

above right An open plan allows the living room to flow freely into the adjacent dining room.

Please note: The photographed home may have been modified to suit homeowner preferences. If you order plans, have a builder or design professional check them against the photographs to confirm construction details.

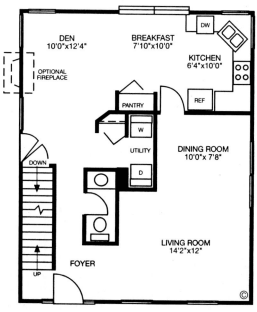

FIRST FLOOR

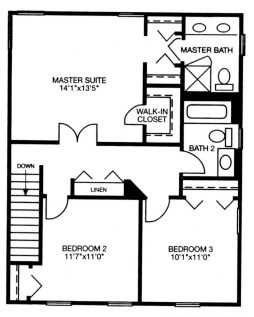

SECOND FLOOR

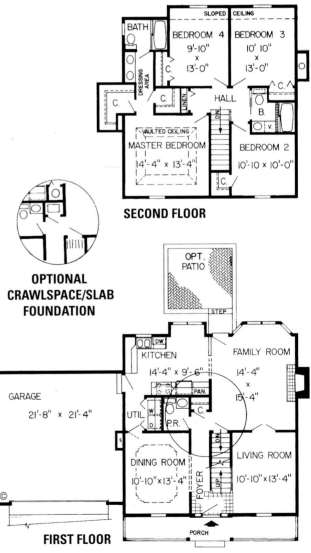

PHOTOGRAPHY: JOHN EHRENCLOU

above Simple rooflines rise above this home's comfortable covered porch.

Classic Design

An inviting porch graces the house, shading the front rooms. Beside the foyer is the open dining room, which is topped by a decorative ceiling and linked to the rear kitchen through a utility hall. A bay window illuminates the family room, which has its own fireplace for cold winter nights. The living room beside the staircase enjoys a view of the porch. On the 1,000-square-foot second floor, the master bedroom rests beneath a vaulted ceiling, while a special dressing area leads to a secluded private bath. This home is designed with basement, slab, and crawlspace foundation options.

Please note: The photographed home may have been modified to suit homeowner preferences. If you order plans, have a builder or design professional check them against the photographs to confirm construction details.

SECOND FLOOR

OPTIONAL CRAWLSPACE/SLAB FOUNDATION

FIRST FLOOR

Design 34027

Price Code	C
Total Finished	1,960 sq. ft.
First Finished	955 sq. ft.
Second Finished	1,005 sq. ft.
Basement Unfinished	930 sq. ft.
Garage Unfinished	484 sq. ft.
Dimensions	52'x31'
Foundation	Basement
	Crawlspace
	Slab
Bedrooms	4
Full Baths	2
Half Baths	1

18

above & top A tall gable adds an interesting architectural focal point to this home's classic colonial shape.

SECOND FLOOR

BEDROOM *2
10'-0"X11'-10"

B.*2

MASTER BEDROOM
15'-4"X15'-4"

UNFINISHED AREA

C.

L.

H.

DN.

C.

DRESSING

C.

BEDROOM *3
11'-8"X11'-8"

C.

MAST. BATH

FIRST FLOOR

D. W.

LAUN.

S.

C.

OVEN

KIT.
10'-0" X 11'-0"

DW

BRKFST.
10'-2"X10'-6"

PANTRY

H.

LAV.

BOOKS

FAMILY ROOM
20'-10"X15'-4"

UP

GARAGE
22'-8"X21'-8"

DINING ROOM
11'-8"X11'-8"

FOYER

C.

LIVING ROOM
11'-4"X17'-4"

PORCH

W.

Separate Formal Spaces

The tiled foyer leads to the private dining room on the left and to the formal living room on the right. Ahead is the large family room, which features a fireplace on one end and built-in bookshelves on the other. A left turn leads to the window-lined breakfast nook, which shares a peninsula snack bar with the kitchen. The handy laundry room is just steps away. On the second floor, two secondary bedrooms, each with walk-in closets, share a full bath. The master suite, with two walk-in closets and a full bath with dressing area, fills the right wing. An unfinished area to the left supplies 350 square feet of future space. This home is designed with basement, slab, and crawlspace foundation options.

Please note: The photographed home may have been modified to suit homeowner preferences. If you order plans, have a builder or design professional check them against the photographs to confirm construction details.

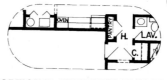

OVEN

PANTRY

H.

LAV.

C.

OPTIONAL CRAWLSPACE/SLAB FOUNDATION

Design 34825

Price Code	D
Total Finished	2,242 sq. ft.
First Finished	1,212 sq. ft.
Second Finished	1,030 sq. ft.
Bonus Unfinished	350 sq. ft.
Basement Unfinished	1,212 sq. ft.
Garage Unfinished	521 sq. ft.
Dimensions	55'x34'4"
Foundation	Basement Crawlspace Slab
Bedrooms	3
Full Baths	2
Half Baths	1

Details & Options

above This plan was modified so that the garage opens to the side, which keeps all attention focused on charming details such as the entry gable, porch, and bay window.

The covered porch keeps you keep dry during the rainy season and cool when it's sunny and hot. Inside, the foyer separates the dining room (which comes with optional decorative ceiling) from the breakfast area and kitchen. Placing the kitchen/breakfast area and dining room up front means the living room and bedrooms are at the rear of the home, where it's quieter and more private. A full bath is located between the living room and secondary bedrooms, both of which have large closets. The master suite has the entire right rear corner of the house and includes an optional decorative ceiling and skylight above the entrance to its private bath. The master bathroom has a large walk-in closet, double vanity, and separate water closet. For those who enjoy outdoor living, an optional deck is offered, accessible through sliding glass doors off the master bedroom. This home is designed with basement, slab, and crawlspace foundation options.

Please note: The photographed home may have been modified to suit homeowner preferences. If you order plans, have a builder or design professional check them against the photographs to confirm construction details.

OPTIONAL CRAWLSPACE/SLAB FOUNDATION

Design 34029

Price Code	B
Total Finished	1,686 sq. ft.
Main Finished	1,686 sq. ft.
Basement Unfinished	1,676 sq. ft.
Garage Unfinished	484 sq. ft.
Dimensions	61'x54'
Foundation	Basement Crawlspace Slab
Bedrooms	3
Full Baths	1
3/4 Baths	1

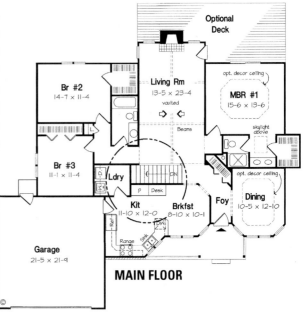

MAIN FLOOR

above Perfect for a narrow lot, the garage on this home is tucked into the rear, which prevents it from dominating the front facade.

Please note: The photographed home may have been modified to suit homeowner preferences. If you order plans, have a builder or design professional check them against the photographs to confirm construction details.

OPT. BONUS ROOM
19'-8" X 26'-8"

BONUS

GARAGE
20'-0" X 19'-8"

BENCH W/ STORAGE

GRILLING PORCH
8'-0" X 16'-8"
BEADED CEILING

LAU.
6'-0" X 8'-4"

KID'S NOOK

MASTER SUITE
13'-0" X 14'-8"
OPT. 10' BOXED CEILING

BRKFAST ROOM
10'-6" X 9'-0"

COMPUTER CENTER

LIN.

8' COLUMNS

DINING RM.
12'-8" X 12'-0"

KITCHEN
9'-6" X 14'-0"

DW   REF

PANTRY   REF

GLASS SHWR   KNEE SPACE

M.BATH
13'-0" X 15'-2"

WHP TUB

3' GAS FIREPLACE

GREAT ROOM
18'-10" X 17'-8"

BEDROOM 2
13'-0" X 11'-0"

OPT. STAIRS

8' COVERED PORCH
BEADED CEILING

12' COLUMNS

BED RM. 3 / STUDY
13'-0" X 11'-0"

MAIN FLOOR

Family Spaces

The porch opens directly into the great-room, which features a gas fireplace. Directly to the right of the entrance, a short hallway connects the two secondary bedrooms to a full bath. Past the great-room is the dining room and large kitchen/breakfast area. The kitchen, almost completely enveloped by counter space, holds a snack bar and built-in computer center. Off the breakfast room are a kid's nook featuring a bench with storage, a laundry room, and access to the grilling porch. The boxed-ceiling master suite takes up half of the right wing and features ample closet space and a luxurious bath with whirlpool tub. On the second floor are 1,191 square feet of bonus space. This home is designed with slab and crawlspace foundation options.

Design 82020

Price Code	C
Total Finished	1,845 sq. ft.
Main Finished	1,845 sq. ft.
Bonus Unfinished	1,191 sq. ft.
Garage Unfinished	496 sq. ft.
Porch Unfinished	465 sq. ft.
Dimensions	41'4"x83'8"
Foundation	Crawlspace
	Slab
Bedrooms	3
Full Baths	2

PHOTOGRAPHY: JOHN EHRENCLOU

Modern Classic

above This home presents a cozy and classic facade outside, but inside it's filled with all the modern amenities and details today's families require.

A traditional front porch shelters guests as they approach the entry, which opens into a wide-open space containing the living room and dining room. The large living room is visually separated into two distinct areas, each defined by different ceiling heights. A fireplace and built-ins enhance the space. Steps away from the dining room, the U-shape kitchen is open to the breakfast area, where a walk-in pantry and laundry room add to its usefulness. Secondary bedrooms fill the left wing of the 1,821-square-foot home, with a skylit full bath between them. On the right side of the design is the master suite. A tray ceiling crowns the bedroom; a vaulted ceiling caps its five-piece bath, which includes a whirlpool tub. In the rear, a deck provides additional room for extending living space in warmer months. The garage is placed discretely beneath the home. This home is designed with a basement foundation.

Please note: The photographed home may have been modified to suit homeowner preferences. If you order plans, have a builder or design professional check them against the photographs to confirm construction details.

Design 24651

Price Code	C
Total Finished	1,821 sq. ft.
Main Finished	1,821 sq. ft.
Basement Unfinished	742 sq. ft.
Garage Unfinished	1,075 sq. ft.
Dimensions	56'x42'
Foundation	Basement
Bedrooms	3
Full Baths	2

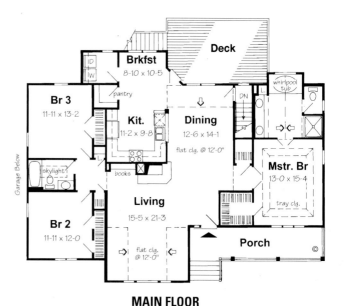

MAIN FLOOR

above Stacked gables topping a covered porch add an extra dimension of detail to this classic home.

Design 97476

Price Code	A
Total Finished	1,297 sq. ft.
First Finished	603 sq. ft.
Second Finished	694 sq. ft.
Bonus Unfinished	354 sq. ft.
Garage Unfinished	478 sq. ft.
Deck Unfinished	160 sq. ft.
Dimensions	42'x43'
Foundation	Basement
Bedrooms	3
Full Baths	2
Half Baths	1

Please note: The photographed home may have been modified to suit homeowner preferences. If you order plans, have a builder or design professional check them against the photographs to confirm construction details.

Lovely Balance

The front entry opens into a foyer designed for utmost efficiency, with its tiled floor and coat closet. From there you are lead into the fireplace-warmed living room, which has a bay window overlooking the front porch. A second closet on the 603-square-foot first floor is right outside a guest bath. Toward the rear, the U-shape kitchen opens to the dining room; both areas have access to the three-season porch. Two secondary bedrooms and the master suite share the 694-square-foot second floor with 354 square feet of bonus space. This home is designed with a basement foundation. Alternate foundation options are available at an additional charge. Please call 1-800-235-5700 for more information.

FIRST FLOOR

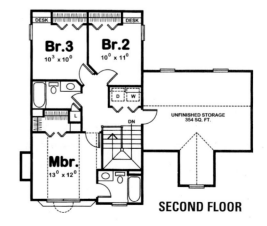

SECOND FLOOR

For thousands of home plans on-line, visit **www.family home plans.com**

A Hint of Tradition

above White-framed windows and a covered porch add extra appeal to this home's traditional facade.

Inside, the design is far from traditional. In the entry, a wide, angled staircase leads up to the living areas, while a second staircase leads down to the lower floor. To the right of the plan, the great-room, dining room, and kitchen blend together under a cathedral ceiling. The kitchen is full of counter space, including a snack bar that divides it from the dining room. A decorative ceiling and corner of windows enhance the master bedroom. A linen closet and full hall bath add more convenience. This home is designed with basement, slab, and crawlspace foundation options. Alternate foundation options available at an additional charge. Please call 1-800-235-5700 for more information.

Design 97916

Price Code	A
Total Finished	1,125 sq. ft.
Main Finished	1,125 sq. ft.
Garage Unfinished	458 sq. ft.
Dimensions	44'x26'
Foundation	Basement
	Crawlspace
	Slab
Bedrooms	3
Full Baths	1
3/4 Baths	1

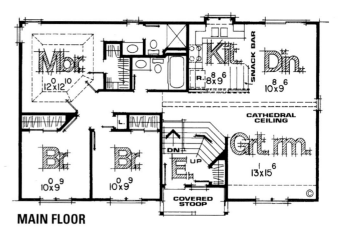

MAIN FLOOR

Please note: The photographed home may have been modified to suit homeowner preferences. If you order plans, have a builder or design professional check them against the photographs to confirm construction details.

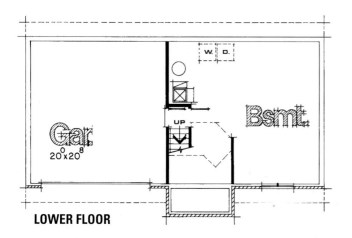

LOWER FLOOR

above Small details, such as French doors and arched windows with keystone caps, add style to this traditional ranch design.

Ranch Living

Design 20164

Price Code	A
Total Finished	1,456 sq. ft.
Main Finished	1,456 sq. ft.
Basement Unfinished	1,448 sq. ft.
Garage Unfinished	452 sq. ft.
Dimensions	50'x45'4"
Foundation	Basement
	Crawlspace
	Slab
Bedrooms	3
Full Baths	2

Guests enter through French doors and walk a long hallway that leads directly into the living room. The location of the home's bedrooms keeps private spaces separate from public spaces. Shared spaces include the living room with fireplace, large den (which could be converted into a third bedroom), dining room, and kitchen. Included in the kitchen/dining area are a built-in desk, pantry, closet, and laundry room. The master suite fills the rear of the bedroom wing. It features a decorative ceiling and a window that bumps out into the backyard. A garage and rear deck complete the plan. This home is designed with basement, slab, and crawlspace foundation options.

Please note: The photographed home may have been modified to suit homeowner preferences. If you order plans, have a builder or design professional check them against the photographs to confirm construction details.

MAIN FLOOR

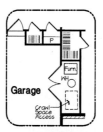

OPTIONAL CRAWLSPACE/SLAB FOUNDATION

above A smaller covered porch set back from the front of the home complements the larger front porch.

Sheltering Porches

A wide covered porch spans the front of the home, allowing just the right amount of light to filter in through the tall windows that open onto the family room and master bedroom. Inside, each room is clearly separated, allowing privacy throughout. The eat-in kitchen forms an "ell" off the main space and features plenty of counter space and a pantry for additional storage. The three bedrooms on the left side of the design share a well-appointed bath. This home is designed with a basement foundation.

Design 65395

Price Code	A
Total Finished	1,147 sq. ft.
Main Finished	1,147 sq. ft.
Dimensions	44'x30'
Foundation	Basement
Bedrooms	3
Full Baths	1

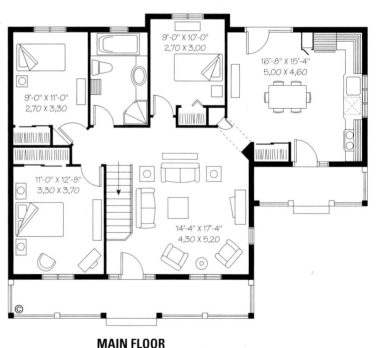

MAIN FLOOR

above A traditional covered porch is a nice complement to the architecturally interesting windows, rooflines, and gables.

Design 65396

Price Code	A
Total Finished	1,026 sq. ft.
Main Finished	1,026 sq. ft.
Dimensions	30'x36'
Foundation	Basement
Bedrooms	2
Full Baths	1

11'-0" X 10'-0"
3,30 X 3,00

17'-4" X 15'-0"
5,20 X 4,50

14'-4" X 15'-4"
4,30 X 4,60

11'-0" X 12'-0"
3,30 X 3,60

MAIN FLOOR

It's All There

In just over 1,000 square feet, this design is the perfect home for empty nesters or those just starting out. The entry, with large closet, opens directly into the family room, welcoming friends and family. A short hall leads into the kitchen area, where there is room for both casual or more formal dining. L-shape counters and cabinets provide the kitchen with plenty of work and storage space. The two bedrooms and a full bath, easily accessible from all parts of the home, fill the left wing. Each bedroom has generous closet space. This home is designed with a basement foundation.

PHOTOGRAPHY: MICHAEL PARTENIO

Made for Real Life

above The large combination family and dining room is flooded with natural light from three sides.

below A two-tier peninsula separates the kitchen and dining area. The raised breakfast bar serves three purposes: It provides a perfect spot to share a quick meal, extra counter space, and helps obscure the cooking and cleanup areas from diners.

With three levels and an emphasis on open spaces and storage, this home packs a lot of living into just over 1,600 square feet. One large area combines the window-lined dining and family areas, as opposed to the more formal tradition of isolated eating areas. The kitchen, which is lined with counters, has a peninsula counter to divide the spaces. A cozy secondary bedroom and a separate den round out the 1,022-square-foot first floor.

The entire 580-square-foot second floor is dedicated to the master suite. Storage space surrounds the bedroom, including built-in cedar cabinets, which are located in the exterior kneewalls. The master bath includes a window-lined soaking tub.

The lower floor was created for utility. The large two-car garage has additional space for storage or a workshop. The laundry is conveniently and discretely located at the bottom of the stairs. Another large rooms serves as a mechanical/storage area. This home is designed with a basement foundation.

above left & right Whether its the central gabled structure out front or the chimney on the side, symmetry dominates the design.

below The front French door and its surrounding windows flood the entryway with natural light.

SECOND FLOOR

FIRST FLOOR

LOWER LEVEL

Design 32385

Units	Single
Price Code	B
Total Finished	1,602 sq. ft.
First Finished	1,022 sq. ft.
Second Finished	580 sq. ft.
Basement Unfinished	473 sq. ft.
Garage Unfinished	547 sq. ft.
Dimensions	42'x28'
Foundation	Basement
Bedrooms	2
Full Baths	2

Please note: The photographed home may have been modified to suit homeowner preferences. If you order plans, have a builder or design professional check them against the photographs to confirm construction details.

Farmhouse Flavor

A tiled floor, coat closet, and powder room provide neighborly touches inside the entryway. The dining room, illuminated by a bay window, is just inside, easily accessible from the kitchen. A peninsula bar divides the two areas, offering additional work space or a casual place to dine. In the corner, a pantry and large laundry room provide additional storage. A wood stove warms the nearby living room. The master suite, featuring a walk-in closet and five-piece bath with linen closet, rounds out the floor. On the second floor, a skylit balcony connects a full bath to the two secondary bedrooms, each with a dormer window and walk-in closet. This home is designed with basement, slab, and crawlspace foundation options.

Design 10785

Price Code	C
Total Finished	1,907 sq. ft.
First Finished	1,269 sq. ft.
Second Finished	638 sq. ft.
Basement Unfinished	1,269 sq. ft.
Dimensions	47'x39'
Foundation	Basement
	Crawlspace
	Slab
Bedrooms	3
Full Baths	2
Half Baths	1

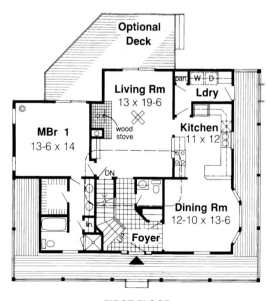

FIRST FLOOR

SECOND FLOOR

OPTIONAL CRAWLSPACE/SLAB FOUNDATION

above This home's extended garage provides privacy and shelter to the front entry.

Design 20062

Price Code	A
Total Finished	1,500 sq. ft.
Main Finished	1,500 sq. ft.
Basement Unfinished	1,500 sq. ft.
Garage Unfinished	482 sq. ft.
Dimensions	49'8"x44'4"
Foundation	Basement
	Crawlspace
	Slab
Bedrooms	3
Full Baths	2

MAIN FLOOR

Places to Gather

The design of this home makes a definite distinction between the gathering and private areas. A long tiled foyer, featuring a coat closet, branches off straight to the hallway that leads to all three bedrooms, a full hall bath, and a conveniently located laundry closet or to the shared spaces ahead. The living room with fireplace, dining room with large windows, and kitchen with plenty of counter space and a separate breakfast nook, blend together under a sloped ceiling. A rear deck rounds out the plan and extends living space outdoors. This home is designed with basement, slab, and crawlspace foundation options.

Quick and Easy Customizing
Make Changes to Your Home Plan in 4 Easy Steps

Here's an **affordable** and **efficient** way to make **custom changes** to your home plan.

1 Select the house plan that most closely meets your needs. Purchase of a reproducible master (vellum) is necessary to make changes to a plan.

2 Call 800-235-5700 to place your order. Tell the sales representative you're interested in customizing a plan. A $50 refundable consultation fee will be charged. Then you'll need to complete a customization checklist indicating all the changes you wish to make to your plan, attaching sketches if necessary. If you proceed with the custom changes, the $50 will be credited to the total amount charged.

3 Fax the completed customization checklist to our design consultant at 1-866-477-5173 or e-mail blarochelle@drummonddesigns.com. Within 24 to 48* business hours you will be provided with a written cost estimate to modify your plan. Our design consultant will contact you by phone if you wish to discuss any of your changes in greater detail.

4 Once you approve the estimate, a 75% retainer fee is collected and customization work gets underway. Preliminary drawings can usually be completed within 5 to10* business days. Following approval of these preliminary drawings, your design changes are completed within 5 to 10* business days. Your remaining 25% balance due is collected prior to shipment of your completed drawings. You will be shipped five sets of revised blueprints, or a reproducible master.

*Terms are subject to change without notice.

BEFORE

AFTER

Sample Modification Pricing Guide

CATEGORIES	AVERAGE COST
Adding or removing living space (square footage)	Quote required
Adding or removing a garage	$400—$680
Garage: Front entry to side load or vice versa	Starting at $300
Adding a screened porch	$280—$600
Adding a bonus room in the attic	$450—$780
Changing full basement to crawlspace or vice versa	Starting at $220
Changing full basement to slab or vice versa	Starting at $260
Changing exterior building material	Starting at $200
Changing roof lines	$360—$630
Adjusting ceiling height	$280—$500
Adding, moving, or removing an exterior opening	$55 per opening
Adding or removing a fireplace	$90—$200
Modifying a non-bearing wall or room	$55 per room
Changing exterior walls from 2"x4" to 2"x6"	Starting at $200
Redesigning a bathroom or a kitchen	$120—$280
Reverse plan right reading	Quote required
Adapting plans for local building code requirements	Quote required
Engineering stamping only	Quote required
Any other engineering services	Quote required
Adjust plan for handicapped accessibility	Quote required
Interactive Illustrations (choices of exterior materials)	Quote required
Metric conversion of home plan	$400

Note: Prices are subject to change according to plan size and style. Please remember that figures shown are average costs. Your quote may be higher or lower depending upon your specific requirements.

Design 65386

Units	Single
Price Code	A
Total Finished	784 sq. ft.
Main Finished	784 sq. ft.
Dimensions	28'x28'
Foundation	Slab
Bedrooms	1
Full Baths	1
Roof Framing	Stick

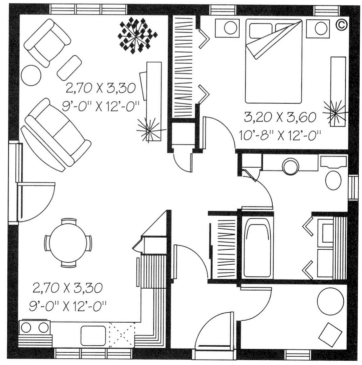

MAIN FLOOR

Units	Single
Price Code	A
Total Finished	786 sq. ft.
Main Finished	786 sq. ft.
Deck Unfinished	580 sq. ft.
Dimensions	46'x22'
Foundation	Crawlspace
Bedrooms	2
3/4 Baths	2
Main Ceiling	8'
Vaulted Ceiling	16'
Max Ridge Height	18'6"
Roof Framing	Truss
Exterior Walls	2x6

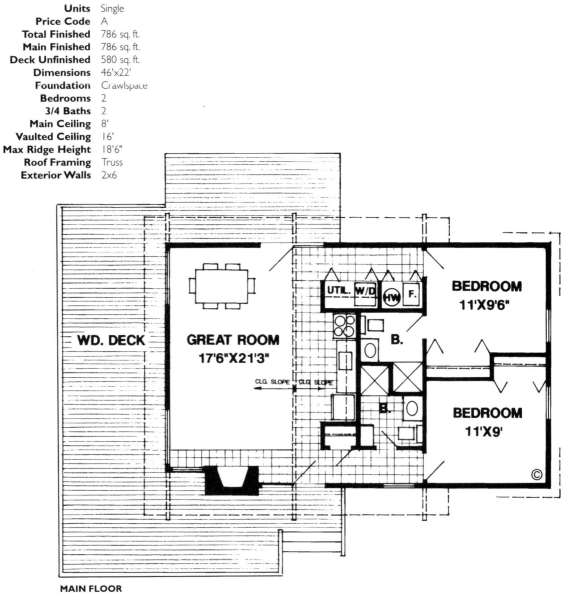

MAIN FLOOR

To order blueprints, call **800-235-5700** or visit us on the web, **familyhomeplans.com**

Design 65263

Units	Single
Price Code	A
Total Finished	840 sq. ft.
Main Finished	840 sq. ft.
Porch Unfinished	466 sq. ft.
Dimensions	33'x31'
Foundation	Basement
Bedrooms	1
Full Baths	1
Main Ceiling	8'
Max Ridge Height	22'11"
Roof Framing	Truss
Exterior Walls	2x6

4.80 X 4.80
16'-0" X 16'-0"

4.40 X 3.30
14'-8" X 11'-0"

2.70 X 3.90
9'-0" X 13'-0"

2.40 X 3.90
8'-0" X 13'-0"

3.60 X 3.50
12'-0" X 11'-8"

MAIN FLOOR

Design 65045

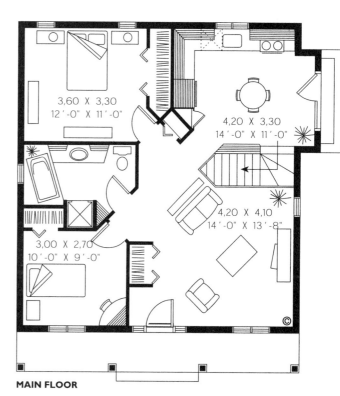

Units	Single
Price Code	A
Total Finished	860 sq. ft.
Main Finished	860 sq. ft.
Dimensions	30'x30'
Foundation	Basement
Bedrooms	2
Full Baths	1
Roof Framing	Stick

3.60 X 3.30
12'-0" X 11'-0"

4.20 X 3.30
14'-0" X 11'-0"

4.20 X 4.10
14'-0" X 13'-8"

3.00 X 2.70
10'-0" X 9'-0"

MAIN FLOOR

Units	Single
Price Code	A
Total Finished	880 sq. ft.
First Finished	572 sq. ft.
Second Finished	308 sq. ft.
Dimensions	22'x26'
Foundation	Crawlspace
Bedrooms	2
3/4 Baths	1
Max Ridge Height	20'
Roof Framing	Stick
Exterior Walls	2x6

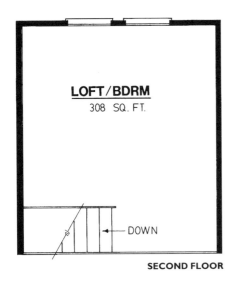

LOFT/BDRM
308 SQ. FT.

← DOWN

SECOND FLOOR

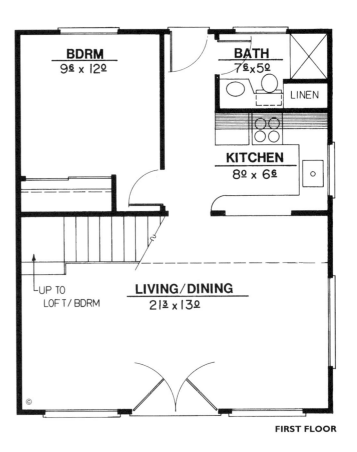

BDRM
9⁰ x 12⁰

BATH
7⁸ x 5⁰

LINEN

KITCHEN
8⁰ x 6⁸

UP TO
LOFT/BDRM

LIVING/DINING
21³ x 13⁰

FIRST FLOOR

Design 65006

Units	Single
Price Code	A
Total Finished	920 sq. ft.
Main Finished	920 sq. ft.
Porch Unfinished	152 sq. ft.
Dimensions	38'x28'
Foundation	Basement
Bedrooms	2
Full Baths	1
Main Ceiling	8'
Max Ridge Height	20'6"
Roof Framing	Truss
Exterior Walls	2x6

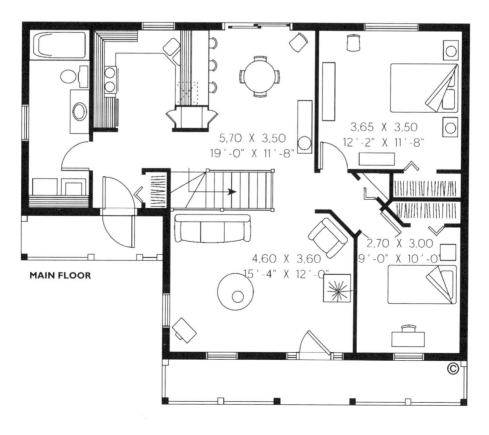

5,70 X 3,50
19'-0" X 11'-8"

3,65 X 3,50
12'-2" X 11'-8"

4,60 X 3,60
15'-4" X 12'-0"

2,70 X 3,00
9'-0" X 10'-0"

MAIN FLOOR

Design 65366

Units	Single
Price Code	A
Total Finished	923 sq. ft.
Main Finished	923 sq. ft.
Basement Unfinished	923 sq. ft.
Dimensions	30'x31'
Foundation	Basement
Bedrooms	2
Full Baths	1
Main Ceiling	8'
Max Ridge Height	22'1"

3,40 X 3,30
11'-4" X 11'-0"

4,40 X 4,70
14'-8" X 15'-8"

3,20 X 3,00
10'-8" X 10'-0"

3,50 X 4,20
11'-8" X 14'-0"

MAIN FLOOR

Design 65009

Units	Single
Price Code	A
Total Finished	947 sq. ft.
Main Finished	947 sq. ft.
Basement Unfinished	947 sq. ft.
Dimensions	34'x30'
Foundation	Basement
Bedrooms	2
Full Baths	1
Main Ceiling	8'2"
Max Ridge Height	16'10"
Roof Framing	Truss
Exterior Walls	2x6

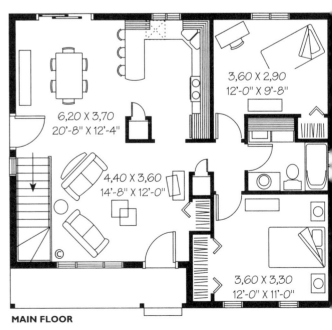

6,20 X 3,70
20'-8" X 12'-4"

3,60 X 2,90
12'-0" X 9'-8"

4,40 X 3,60
14'-8" X 12'-0"

3,60 X 3,30
12'-0" X 11'-0"

MAIN FLOOR

Design 65387

Units	Single
Price Code	A
Total Finished	948 sq. ft.
Main Finished	948 sq. ft.
Dimensions	30'x34'
Foundation	Basement
Bedrooms	2
Full Baths	1
Roof Framing	Stick

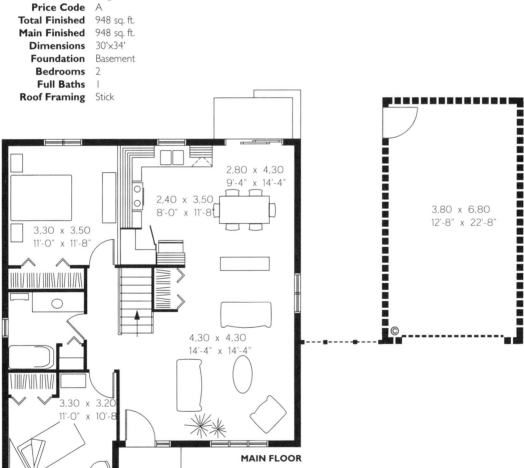

MAIN FLOOR

Merillat

Visit us at www.merillat.com

Units	Single
Price Code	A
Total Finished	972 sq. ft.
Main Finished	972 sq. ft.
Basement Unfinished	972 sq. ft.
Dimensions	30'x35'
Foundation	Basement
Bedrooms	2
Full Baths	1
Main Ceiling	8'
Max Ridge Height	18'7"
Roof Framing	Truss
Exterior Walls	2x6

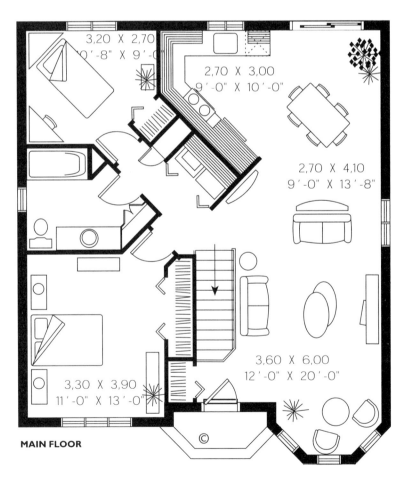

MAIN FLOOR

Design 65003

Units	Single
Price Code	A
Total Finished	976 sq. ft.
First Finished	593 sq. ft.
Second Finished	383 sq. ft.
Basement Unfinished	593 sq. ft.
Dimensions	22'8"x26'8"
Foundation	Crawlspace
Bedrooms	2
Full Baths	I
3/4 Baths	I
First Ceiling	8'
Second Ceiling	8'
Max Ridge Height	22'8"
Roof Framing	Truss
Exterior Walls	2x6

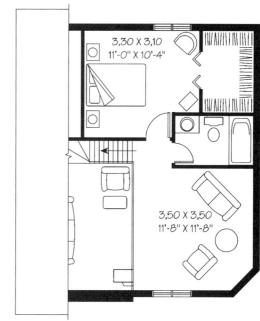

3,30 X 3,10
11'-0" X 10'-4"

3,50 X 3,50
11'-8" X 11'-8"

SECOND FLOOR

2,80 X 3,10
9'-4" X 10'-4"

2,40 X 4,30
8'-0" X 14'-4"

3,00 X 7,20
10'-0" X 24'-0"

3,90 X 3,60
13'-0" X 12'-0"

FIRST FLOOR

Design 65643

Units	Single
Price Code	A
Total Finished	984 sq. ft.
Main Finished	984 sq. ft.
Dimensions	33'9"x43'
Foundation	Crawlspace
	Slab
Bedrooms	2
Full Baths	1
3/4 Baths	1
Max Ridge Height	26'
Exterior Walls	2x6

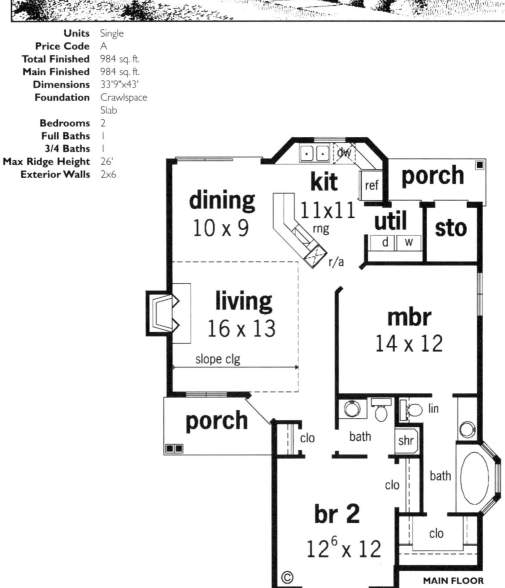

Design 24302

OPTIONAL BASEMENT STAIR LOCATION

Units	Single
Price Code	A
Total Finished	988 sq. ft.
Main Finished	988 sq. ft.
Basement Unfinished	988 sq. ft.
Garage Unfinished	280 sq. ft.
Dimensions	54'x28'
Foundation	Basement
	Crawlspace
Bedrooms	3
Full Baths	1
3/4 Baths	1
Main Ceiling	8'
Max Ridge Height	18'
Roof Framing	Stick
Exterior Walls	2x4

MAIN FLOOR

Design 65033

Units	Single
Price Code	A
Total Finished	994 sq. ft.
Main Finished	994 sq. ft.
Basement Unfinished	994 sq. ft.
Dimensions	38'x32'
Foundation	Basement
Bedrooms	2
Full Baths	1
Main Ceiling	8'
Max Ridge Height	18'6"
Roof Framing	Truss
Exterior Walls	2x6

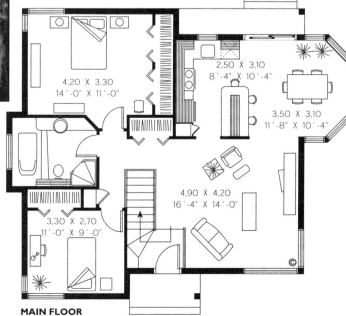

MAIN FLOOR

Design 65011

Units	Single
Price Code	A
Total Finished	996 sq. ft.
Main Finished	896 sq. ft.
Lower Finished	100 sq. ft.
Garage Unfinished	796 sq. ft.
Dimensions	28'x32'
Foundation	Slab
Bedrooms	2
3/4 Baths	1
Half Baths	1
Main Ceiling	8'2"
Max Ridge Height	26'10"
Roof Framing	Truss
Exterior Walls	2x6

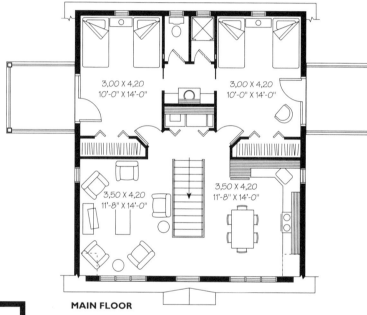

MAIN FLOOR

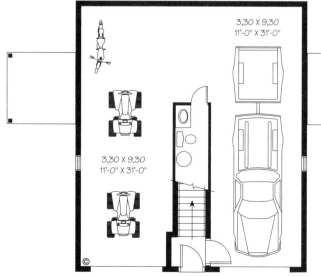

LOWER FLOOR

To order blueprints, call **800-235-5700** or visit us on the web, **familyhomeplans.com**

Design 92426

Units	Single
Price Code	A
Total Finished	997 sq. ft.
Main Finished	997 sq. ft.
Dimensions	49'6"x33'6"
Foundation	Crawlspace
Bedrooms	3
Full Baths	2
Max Ridge Height	16'
Roof Framing	Stick
Exterior Walls	2x4

DECK
14'0" x 11'8"

OPTIONAL BAY

MASTER BDRM
13'6" x 10'10"

FAMILY ROOM
14'0" x 20'0"

BRKFST
7'3" x 8'0"

KITCH
7'3" x 8'0"

WH

OPT. LAUNDRY

GARAGE
14'10" x 24'6"

BEDRM 2
9'6" x 9'6"

BEDRM 3
9'6" x 9'6"

PORCH
11'8" x 5'0"

MAIN FLOOR

OPT. BEDRM 3 EXPANSION

Units	Single
Price Code	A
Total Finished	998 sq. ft.
Main Finished	998 sq. ft.
Dimensions	48'x29'
Foundation	Crawlspace
	Slab
Bedrooms	3
Full Baths	1
Main Ceiling	8'
Max Ridge Height	26'
Roof Framing	Stick
Exterior Walls	2x4

MAIN FLOOR

To order blueprints, call **800-235-5700** or visit us on the web, **familyhomeplans.com**

Units	Single
Price Code	A
Total Finished	1,019 sq. ft.
First Finished	811 sq. ft.
Second Finished	208 sq. ft.
Dimensions	34'6"x28'
Foundation	Basement
	Crawlspace
	Slab
Bedrooms	2
Full Baths	1
3/4 Baths	1
First Ceiling	8'
Second Ceiling	8'
Max Ridge Height	27'
Roof Framing	Stick
Exterior Walls	2x4

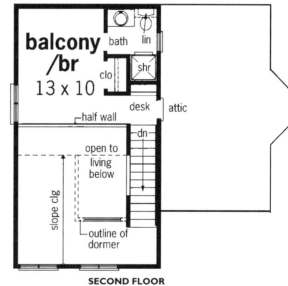

SECOND FLOOR

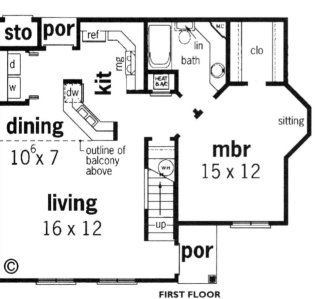

FIRST FLOOR

Visit us at www.merillat.com

Merillat.

Design 92400

Units	Single
Price Code	A
Total Finished	1,050 sq. ft.
Main Finished	1,050 sq. ft.
Garage Unfinished	261 sq. ft.
Dimensions	36'x42'
Foundation	Basement
	Slab
Bedrooms	3
Full Baths	2
Max Ridge Height	16'
Roof Framing	Stick
Exterior Walls	2x4

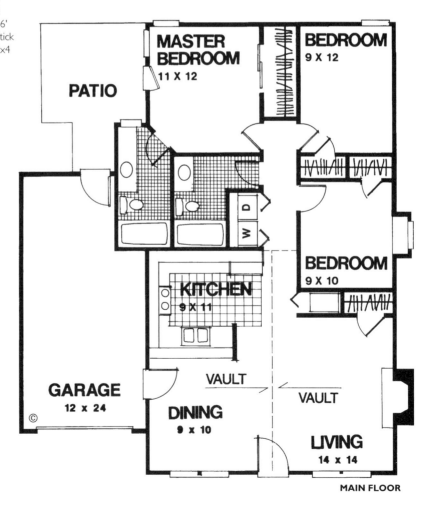

MAIN FLOOR

Design 65078

Units	Single
Price Code	A
Total Finished	1,059 sq. ft.
Main Finished	1,059 sq. ft.
Garage Unfinished	300 sq. ft.
Dimensions	38'x46'8"
Foundation	Basement
Bedrooms	2
Full Baths	1
Main Ceiling	8'
Max Ridge Height	17'1"
Roof Framing	Truss
Exterior Walls	2x6

390 X 3,30
13'-0" X 11'-0"

4,80 X 3,60
16'-0" X 12'-0"

3,30 X 3,00
11'-0" X 10'-0"

4,30 X 4,80
14'-4" X 16'-0"

4,30 X 6,20
14'-4" X 20'-8"

MAIN FLOOR

Design 65241

Units	Single
Price Code	A
Total Finished	1,068 sq. ft.
Main Finished	1,068 sq. ft.
Basement Unfinished	1,068 sq. ft.
Garage Unfinished	245 sq. ft.
Dimensions	30'8"x18'
Foundation	Basement
Bedrooms	2
Full Baths	1
Main Ceiling	8'
Max Ridge Height	22'1"
Roof Framing	Truss
Exterior Walls	2x6

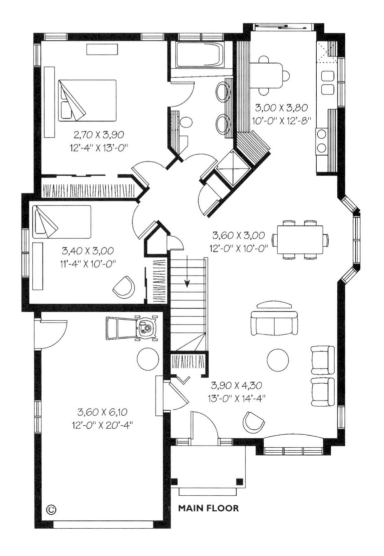

MAIN FLOOR

Design 65385

Units	Single
Price Code	A
Total Finished	1,079 sq. ft.
Main Finished	1,079 sq. ft.
Dimensions	34'x34'
Foundation	Basement
Bedrooms	2
Full Baths	1
Roof Framing	Stick

4,00 X 3,60
13'-4" X 12'-0"

5,70 X 3,60
19'-0" X 12'-0"

3,60 X 4,80
12'-0" X 16'-0"

3,30 X 3,00
11'-0" X 10'-0"

MAIN FLOOR

Units	Single
Price Code	A
Total Finished	1,081 sq. ft.
First Finished	814 sq. ft.
Second Finished	267 sq. ft.
Dimensions	28'x34'6"
Foundation	Basement
	Crawlspace
	Slab
Bedrooms	2
Full Baths	1
3/4 Baths	1
First Ceiling	8'
Second Ceiling	8'
Max Ridge Height	26'
Roof Framing	Stick
Exterior Walls	2x4

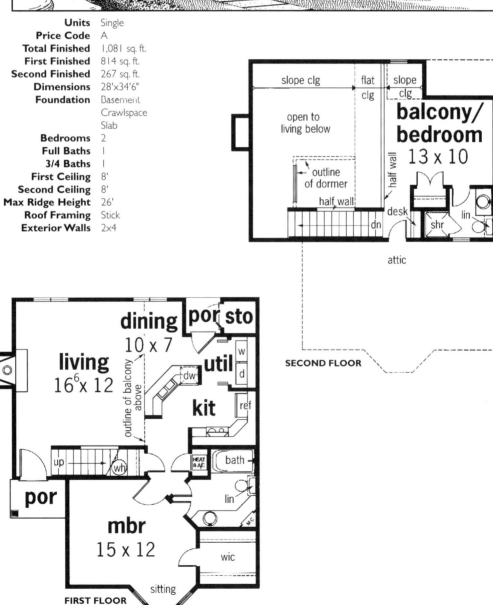

SECOND FLOOR

FIRST FLOOR

Design 52013

Units	Single
Price Code	A
Total Finished	1,085 sq. ft.
Main Finished	1,085 sq. ft.
Basement Unfinished	1,105 sq. ft.
Dimensions	48'x36'
Foundation	Basement
	Crawlspace
Bedrooms	3
Full Baths	2
Main Ceiling	9'
Max Ridge Height	21'
Roof Framing	Stick
Exterior Walls	2x4

CAD **FILES AVAILABLE**
For more information call
800-235-5700

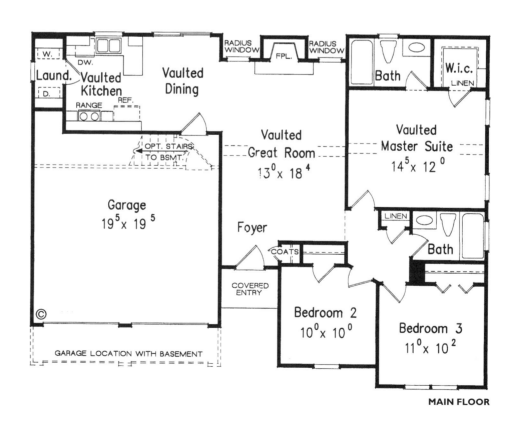

MAIN FLOOR

Design 65093

Units	Single
Price Code	A
Total Finished	1,087 sq. ft.
Main Finished	1,087 sq. ft.
Dimensions	46'×40'4"
Foundation	Basement
Bedrooms	2
Full Baths	1

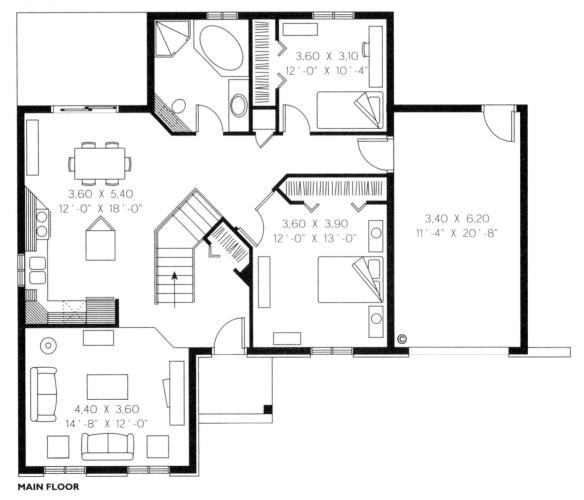

MAIN FLOOR

Units	Single
Price Code	A
Total Finished	1,088 sq. ft.
Main Finished	1,088 sq. ft.
Bonus Unfinished	580 sq. ft.
Dimensions	34'x44'
Foundation	Crawlspace
	Slab
Bedrooms	2
Full Baths	1
Main Ceiling	8'
Second Ceiling	8'
Max Ridge Height	30'
Roof Framing	Stick
Exterior Walls	2x6

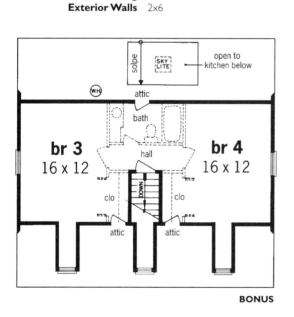

BONUS

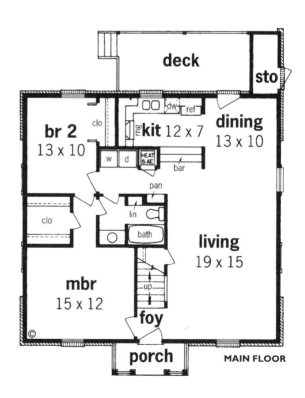

MAIN FLOOR

Units	Single
Price Code	A
Total Finished	1,092 sq. ft.
Main Finished	1,092 sq. ft.
Dimensions	42'x26'
Foundation	Basement
Bedrooms	3
Full Baths	1

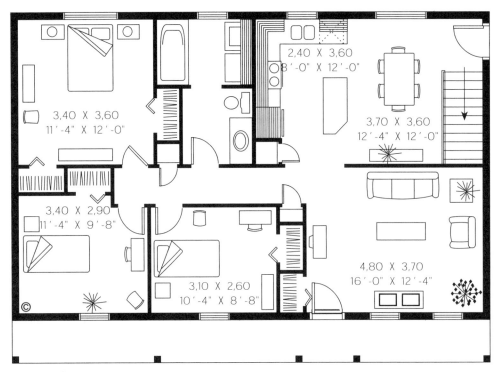

MAIN FLOOR

Design 91002

Units	Single
Price Code	A
Total Finished	1,096 sq. ft.
First Finished	808 sq. ft.
Second Finished	288 sq. ft.
Dimensions	24'x32'
Foundation	Crawlspace
Bedrooms	2
Full Baths	1
3/4 Baths	1
Max Ridge Height	25'
Roof Framing	Stick
Exterior Walls	2x6

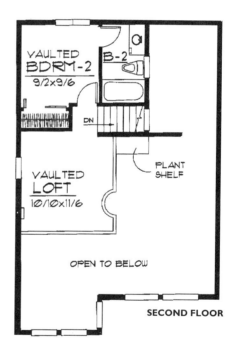

VAULTED BDRM-2 9/2x9/6

B-2

VAULTED LOFT 10/10x11/6

PLANT SHELF

DN

OPEN TO BELOW

SECOND FLOOR

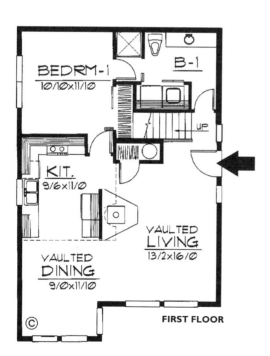

BEDRM-1 10/10x11/10

B-1

UP

KIT. 9/6x11/0

VAULTED LIVING 13/2x16/0

VAULTED DINING 9/0x11/10

FIRST FLOOR

Design 32122

PHOTOGRAPHY: JAMES SALOMON

Units	Single
Price Code	A
Total Finished	1,112 sq. ft.
Main Finished	1,112 sq. ft.
Basement Unfinished	484 sq. ft.
Deck Unfinished	280 sq. ft.
Porch Unfinished	152 sq. ft.
Dimensions	47'x45'6"
Foundation	Basement
	Crawlspace
Bedrooms	2
Full Baths	1
Main Ceiling	9'
Vaulted Ceiling	18'9"
Max Ridge Height	24'9"
Roof Framing	Stick
Exterior Walls	2x6

MAIN FLOOR

Please note: The photographed home may have been modified to suit homeowner preferences. If you order plans, have a builder or design professional check them against the photograph to confirm actual construction details.

Design 62096

Units	Single
Price Code	A
Total Finished	1,120 sq. ft.
Main Finished	1,120 sq. ft.
Garage Unfinished	430 sq. ft.
Porch Unfinished	288 sq. ft.
Dimensions	28'x69'6"
Foundation	Crawlspace
	Slab
Bedrooms	2
Full Baths	2
Main Ceiling	9'
Max Ridge Height	16'8"
Roof Framing	Stick
Exterior Walls	2x4, 2x6

GARAGE
19'-0" X 21'-0"

GRILLING PORCH
8'-0" X 8'-0"

LAU.
7'-0" X 6'-0"

BEDROOM 2
12'-6" X 12'-0"

KITCHEN
9'-10" X 10'-2"

BATH
6'-0"X 9'-10"

BATH
6'-0"X 10'-10"

DINING ROOM
14'-2" X 9'-6"

GREAT ROOM
14'-2" X 13'-0"

MASTER SUITE
12'-6" X 13'-0"

COVERED PORCH
28'-0" X 8'-0"

MAIN FLOOR

Units	Single
Price Code	A
Total Finished	1,120 sq. ft.
First Finished	587 sq. ft.
Second Finished	533 sq. ft.
Deck Unfinished	32 sq. ft.
Porch Unfinished	10 sq. ft.
Dimensions	26'8"x24'
Foundation	Slab
Bedrooms	2
Full Baths	1
Half Baths	1
First Ceiling	8'
Second Ceiling	8'
Max Ridge Height	23'10"
Roof Framing	Truss

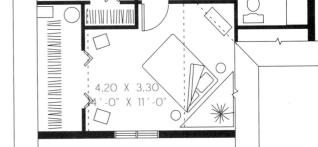

SECOND FLOOR

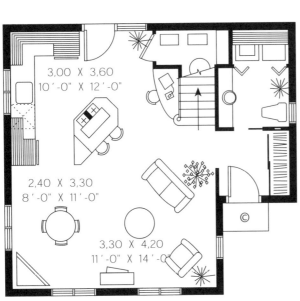

FIRST FLOOR

Design 96538

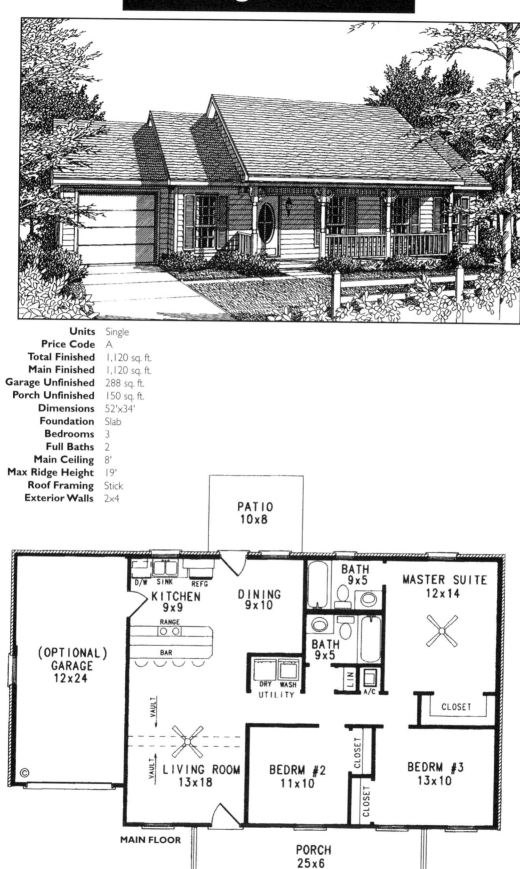

Units	Single
Price Code	A
Total Finished	1,120 sq. ft.
Main Finished	1,120 sq. ft.
Garage Unfinished	288 sq. ft.
Porch Unfinished	150 sq. ft.
Dimensions	52'x34'
Foundation	Slab
Bedrooms	3
Full Baths	2
Main Ceiling	8'
Max Ridge Height	19'
Roof Framing	Stick
Exterior Walls	2x4

PATIO
10x8

D/W SINK REFG

KITCHEN
9x9

RANGE

BAR

DINING
9x10

BATH
9x5

MASTER SUITE
12x14

(OPTIONAL)
GARAGE
12x24

BATH
9x5

DRY WASH
UTILITY

LIN

A/C

CLOSET

VAULT

VAULT

LIVING ROOM
13x18

BEDRM #2
11x10

CLOSET

CLOSET

BEDRM #3
13x10

MAIN FLOOR

PORCH
25x6

Design 32399

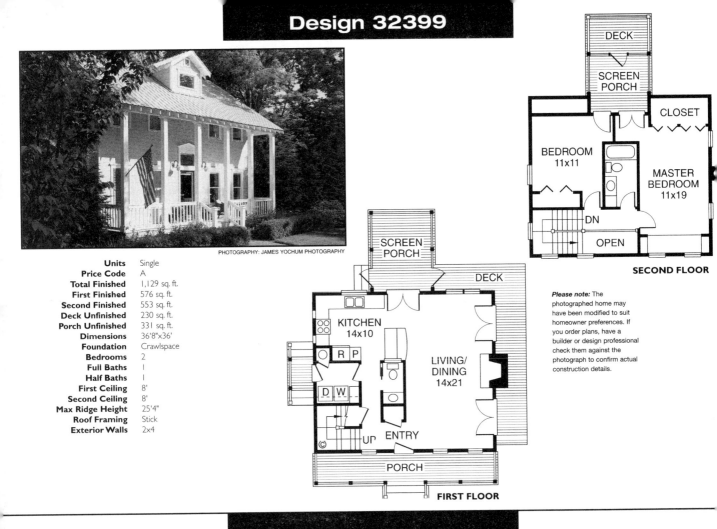

PHOTOGRAPHY: JAMES YOCHUM PHOTOGRAPHY

Units	Single
Price Code	A
Total Finished	1,129 sq. ft.
First Finished	576 sq. ft.
Second Finished	553 sq. ft.
Deck Unfinished	230 sq. ft.
Porch Unfinished	331 sq. ft.
Dimensions	36'8"x36'
Foundation	Crawlspace
Bedrooms	2
Full Baths	1
Half Baths	1
First Ceiling	8'
Second Ceiling	8'
Max Ridge Height	25'4"
Roof Framing	Stick
Exterior Walls	2x4

SECOND FLOOR

DECK
SCREEN PORCH
CLOSET
BEDROOM 11x11
MASTER BEDROOM 11x19
DN
OPEN

SCREEN PORCH
DECK
KITCHEN 14x10
LIVING/ DINING 14x21
R P
D W
UP
ENTRY
PORCH

FIRST FLOOR

Please note: The photographed home may have been modified to suit homeowner preferences. If you order plans, have a builder or design professional check them against the photograph to confirm actual construction details.

Design 65376

Units	Single
Price Code	A
Total Finished	1,142 sq. ft.
Main Finished	1,142 sq. ft.
Garage Unfinished	400 sq. ft.
Dimensions	46'x38'
Foundation	Basement
Bedrooms	2
Full Baths	1

3,70 X 3,00
12'-0" X 10'-0"

4,20 X 3,40
14'-0" X 11'-4"

4,20 X 3,30
14'-0" X 11'-0"

3,00 X 3,30
10'-0" X 11'-0"

4,50 X 7,40
15'-0" X 24'-8"

3,60 X 4,50
12'-0" X 15'-0"

MAIN FLOOR

Design 34003

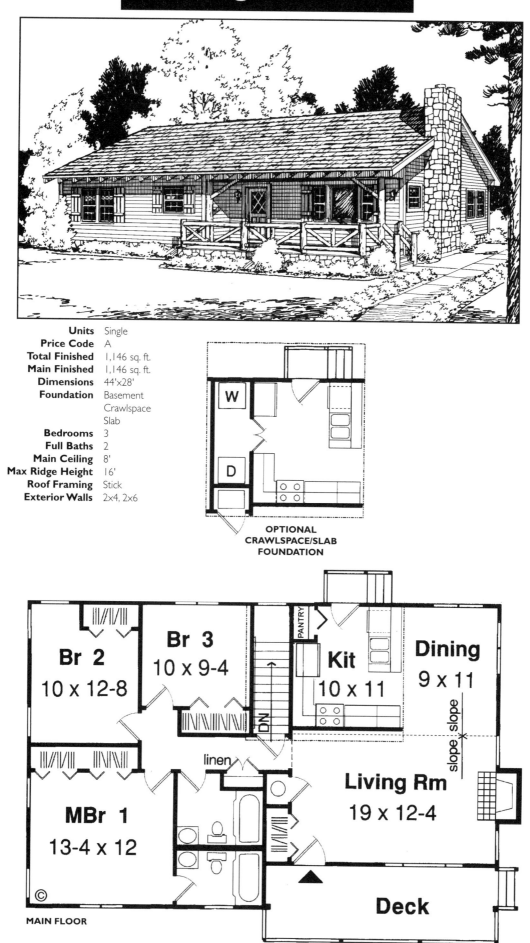

Units	Single
Price Code	A
Total Finished	1,146 sq. ft.
Main Finished	1,146 sq. ft.
Dimensions	44'x28'
Foundation	Basement
	Crawlspace
	Slab
Bedrooms	3
Full Baths	2
Main Ceiling	8'
Max Ridge Height	16'
Roof Framing	Stick
Exterior Walls	2x4, 2x6

OPTIONAL CRAWLSPACE/SLAB FOUNDATION

W

D

Br 2
10 x 12-8

Br 3
10 x 9-4

DN

PANTRY

Kit
10 x 11

Dining
9 x 11

slope slope

linen

MBr 1
13-4 x 12

Living Rm
19 x 12-4

Deck

MAIN FLOOR

Units	Single
Price Code	A
Total Finished	1,152 sq. ft.
First Finished	576 sq. ft.
Second Finished	576 sq. ft.
Dimensions	24'x24'
Foundation	Basement
Bedrooms	3
Full Baths	1
Half Baths	1

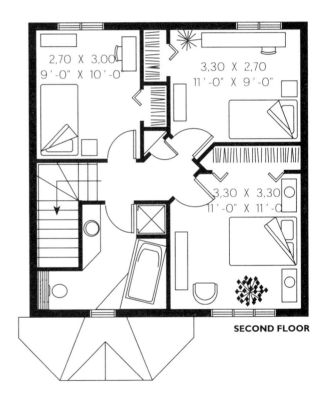

SECOND FLOOR

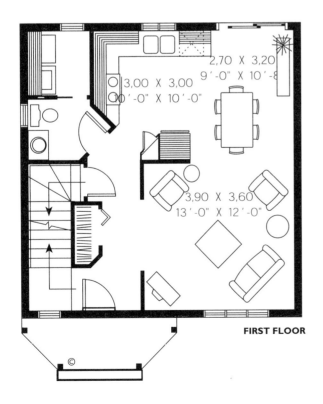

FIRST FLOOR

Design 32611

Units	Single
Price Code	B
Total Finished	1,170 sq. ft.
Main Finished	988 sq. ft.
Second Finished	182 sq. ft.
Dimensions	26'x38'
Foundation	Pier/Post
Bedrooms	2
Full Baths	2
Main Ceiling	8'
Second Ceiling	8'
Max Ridge Height	24'4"
Roof Framing	Stick
Exterior Walls	2x4

Please note: The photographed home may have been modified to suit homeowner preferences. If you order plans, have a builder or design professional check them against the photograph to confirm actual construction details.

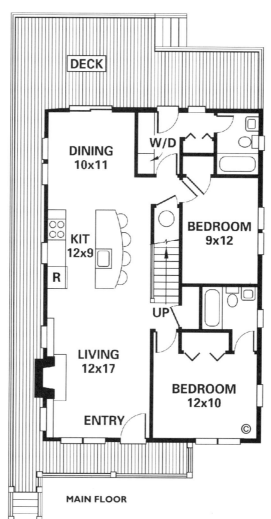

MAIN FLOOR

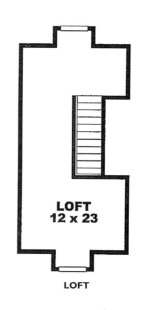

LOFT

Units	Single
Price Code	A
Total Finished	1,176 sq. ft.
Main Finished	1,176 sq. ft.
Basement Unfinished	1,176 sq. ft.
Garage Unfinished	401 sq. ft.
Porch Unfinished	110 sq. ft.
Dimensions	58'x28'
Foundation	Basement
Bedrooms	3
Full Baths	1
Max Ridge Height	18'10"
Roof Framing	Truss
Exterior Walls	2x6

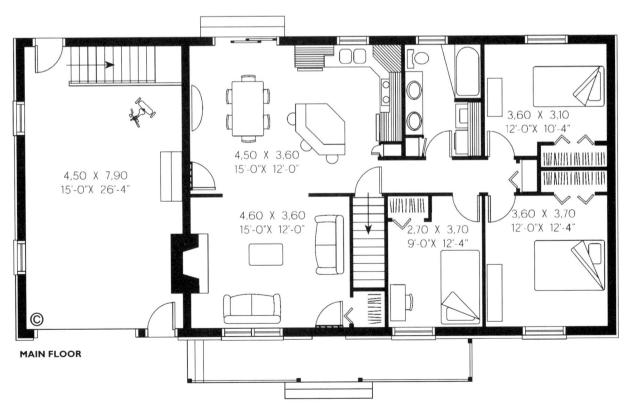

MAIN FLOOR

Units	Single
Price Code	A
Total Finished	1,189 sq. ft.
First Finished	615 sq. ft.
Second Finished	574 sq. ft.
Basement Unfinished	615 sq. ft.
Dimensions	36'x35'8"
Foundation	Basement
Bedrooms	3
Full Baths	2
Half Baths	1
Max Ridge Height	27'
Roof Framing	Truss
Exterior Walls	2x4

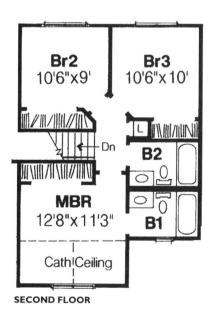

Br2 10'6"x9'

Br3 10'6"x10'

Dn

B2

MBR 12'8"x11'3"

B1

Cath Ceiling

SECOND FLOOR

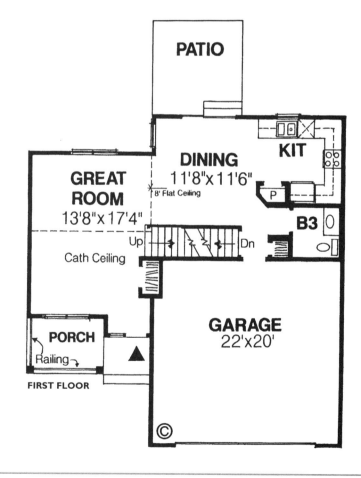

PATIO

KIT

DINING 11'8"x11'6"

GREAT ROOM 13'8"x17'4"

8' Flat Ceiling

Cath Ceiling

Up

Dn

B3

PORCH

Railing

FIRST FLOOR

GARAGE 22'x20'

©

PHOTOGRAPHY: ED GOHLICH

Units	Single
Price Code	A
Total Finished	1,200 sq. ft.
Main Finished	1,200 sq. ft.
Porch Unfinished	200 sq. ft.
Dimensions	51'4"x34'
Foundation	Crawlspace
Bedrooms	2
Full Baths	2
Main Ceiling	8'
Vaulted Ceiling	12'4"
Max Ridge Height	16'4"
Roof Framing	Stick
Exterior Walls	2x4

Please note: The photographed home may have been modified to suit homeowner preferences. If you order plans, have a builder or design professional check them against the photograph to confirm actual construction details.

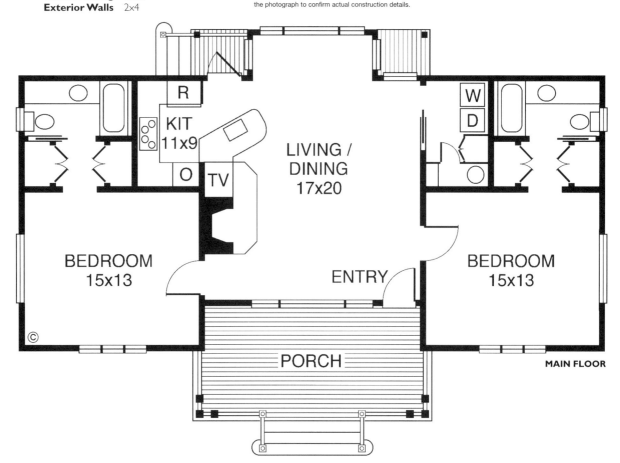

MAIN FLOOR

Units	Single
Price Code	A
Total Finished	1,208 sq. ft.
Main Finished	1,208 sq. ft.
Garage Unfinished	448 sq. ft.
Deck Unfinished	100 sq. ft.
Porch Unfinished	40 sq. ft.
Dimensions	48'x29'
Foundation	Basement
Bedrooms	3
Full Baths	2
Main Ceiling	8'
Max Ridge Height	17'
Roof Framing	Stick
Exterior Walls	2x6

MAIN FLOOR

Units	Single
Price Code	A
Total Finished	1,208 sq. ft.
Main Finished	1,208 sq. ft.
Basement Unfinished	728 sq. ft.
Garage Unfinished	480 sq. ft.
Deck Unfinished	100 sq. ft.
Porch Unfinished	40 sq. ft.
Dimensions	48'x29'
Foundation	Basement
Bedrooms	3
Full Baths	2
Max Ridge Height	17'10"
Roof Framing	Truss
Exterior Walls	2x4

Sundeck 10-0 x 10-0

Lin.

M. Bath

Bedroom 2

Opt. Plant Shelf Opeh To Bdrm.

Vaulted Ceil.

W. D.

Bath 2

Kitchen 8-0 x 10-0

Dw.

Ref.

Dining 10-4 x 10-0

Master Bedroom 11-6 x 14-6

Cts.

Down

Family Room 18-4 x 13-0

Vaulted Ceil.

Entry

Bedroom 3 11-0 x 10-0

MAIN FLOOR

Design 98925

Units	Single
Price Code	A
Total Finished	1,208 sq. ft.
Main Finished	1,208 sq. ft.
Basement Unfinished	760 sq. ft.
Garage Unfinished	448 sq. ft.
Deck Unfinished	100 sq. ft.
Porch Unfinished	40 sq. ft.
Dimensions	50'4"x29'
Foundation	Basement
Bedrooms	3
Full Baths	2
Max Ridge Height	25'
Roof Framing	Truss
Exterior Walls	2x4

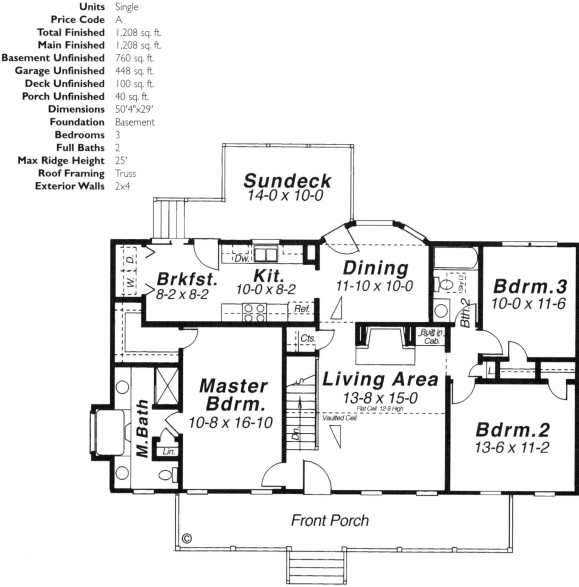

MAIN FLOOR

PHOTOGRAPHY: JAMES SALOMON

Units	Single
Price Code	A
Total Finished	1,214 sq. ft.
First Finished	1,114 sq. ft.
Second Finished	100 sq. ft.
Deck Unfinished	441 sq. ft.
Porch Unfinished	120 sq. ft.
Dimensions	48'4"x47'
Foundation	Crawlspace
Bedrooms	3
Full Baths	1
Vaulted Ceiling	17'
Max Ridge Height	20'4"
Roof Framing	Stick
Exterior Walls	2x6

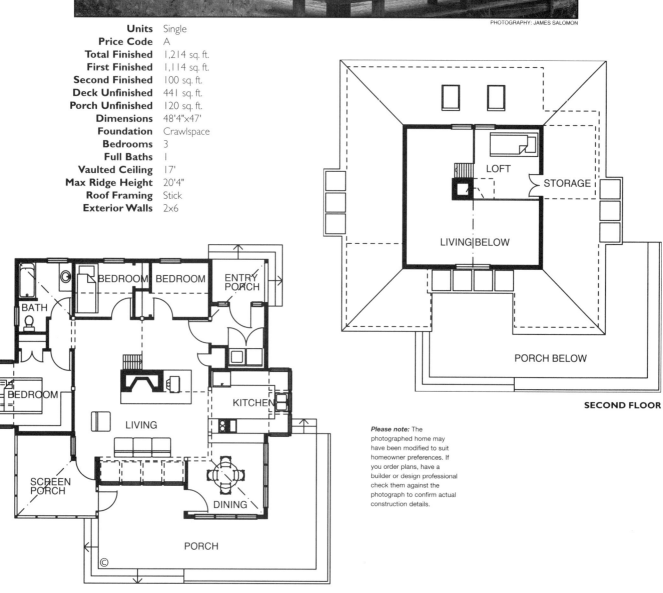

SECOND FLOOR

FIRST FLOOR

Please note: The photographed home may have been modified to suit homeowner preferences. If you order plans, have a builder or design professional check them against the photograph to confirm actual construction details.

Design 90682

Units	Single
Price Code	A
Total Finished	1,243 sq. ft.
Main Finished	1,243 sq. ft.
Basement Unfinished	1,103 sq. ft.
Garage Unfinished	490 sq. ft.
Dimensions	66'4"x30'4"
Foundation	Basement
	Slab
Bedrooms	3
Full Baths	2
Max Ridge Height	16'
Roof Framing	Stick
Exterior Walls	2x4

MAIN FLOOR

To order blueprints, call **800-235-5700** or visit us on the web, familyhomeplans.com

Units	Single
Price Code	A
Total Finished	1,244 sq. ft.
Main Finished	1,244 sq. ft.
Dimensions	44'x62'
Foundation	Crawlspace
	Slab
Bedrooms	3
Full Baths	2
Main Ceiling	8'
Max Ridge Height	26'
Roof Framing	Stick
Exterior Walls	2x6

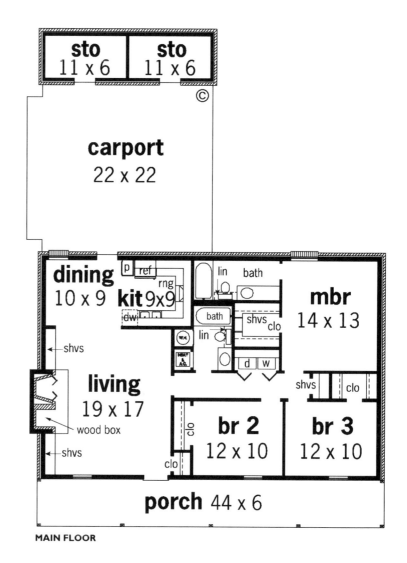

MAIN FLOOR

Design 96511

Units	Single
Price Code	A
Total Finished	1,247 sq. ft.
Main Finished	1,247 sq. ft.
Garage Unfinished	512 sq. ft.
Dimensions	43'×60'
Foundation	Crawlspace
	Slab
Bedrooms	3
Full Baths	2
Main Ceiling	8'
Max Ridge Height	19'
Roof Framing	Stick
Exterior Walls	2x4

Units	Single
Price Code	A
Total Finished	1,249 sq. ft.
First Finished	952 sq. ft.
Second Finished	297 sq. ft.
Dimensions	34'x28'
Foundation	Basement
	Crawlspace
Bedrooms	2
Full Baths	2
First Ceiling	8'
Max Ridge Height	24'
Roof Framing	Stick
Exterior Walls	2x6

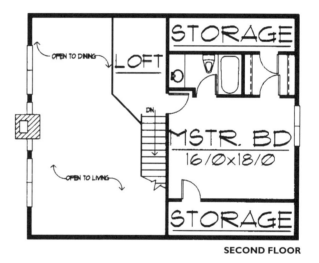

OPEN TO DINING

STORAGE

LOFT

MSTR. BD
16/0x18/0

STORAGE

SECOND FLOOR

OPTIONAL BASEMENT STAIR LOCATION

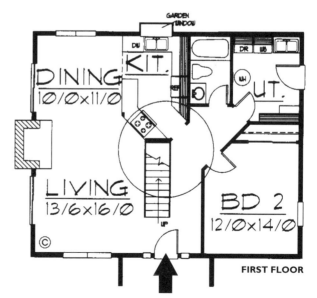

GARDEN WINDOW

DINING
10/0x11/0

KIT.

UT.

LIVING
13/6x16/0

BD 2
12/0x14/0

FIRST FLOOR

Design 93023

Units	Single
Price Code	A
Total Finished	1,249 sq. ft.
Main Finished	1,249 sq. ft.
Porch Unfinished	263 sq. ft.
Dimensions	38'6"x46'
Foundation	Crawlspace
	Slab
Bedrooms	3
Full Baths	2
Max Ridge Height	22'
Roof Framing	Stick
Exterior Walls	2x4

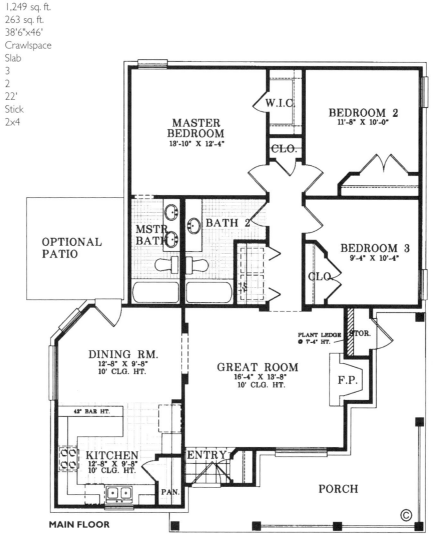

MAIN FLOOR

Units	Single
Price Code	A
Total Finished	1,250 sq. ft.
First Finished	842 sq. ft.
Second Finished	408 sq. ft.
Dimensions	24'x62'
Foundation	Crawlspace
Bedrooms	3
Full Baths	2
Max Ridge Height	24'½"
Roof Framing	Truss
Exterior Walls	2x6

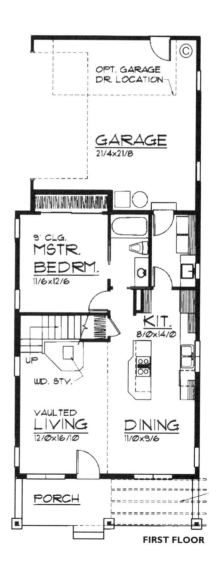

OPT. GARAGE DR LOCATION

GARAGE
21/4x21/8

9' CLG.
MSTR.
BEDRM.
11/6x12/6

KIT.
8/0x14/0

UP

WD. STV.

VAULTED
LIVING
12/0x16/10

DINING
11/0x9/6

PORCH

FIRST FLOOR

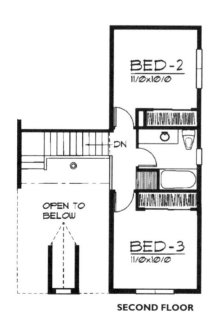

BED-2
11/0x10/0

DN

OPEN TO BELOW

BED-3
11/0x10/0

SECOND FLOOR

Design 59001

1,001-1,500 sq. ft. HOME PLANS

Units	Single
Price Code	B
Total Finished	1,251 sq. ft.
Main Finished	1,251 sq. ft.
Porch Unfinished	191 sq. ft.
Dimensions	40'8"×38'6"
Foundation	Crawlspace
	Slab
Bedrooms	3
Full Baths	2
Main Ceiling	9'
Vaulted Ceiling	14'
Max Ridge Height	22'10"
Roof Framing	Stick
Exterior Walls	2×6

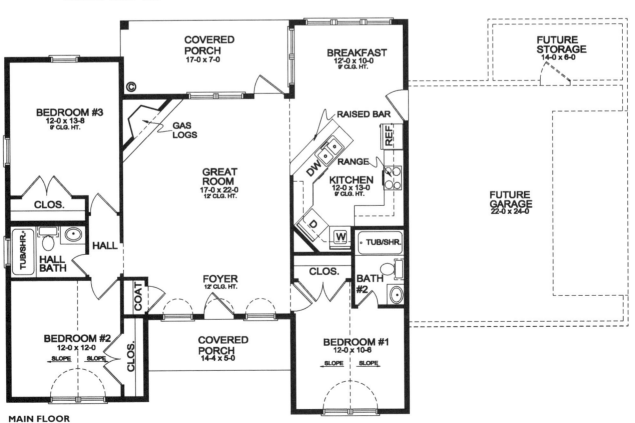

MAIN FLOOR

Units	Single
Price Code	A
Total Finished	1,257 sq. ft.
First Finished	753 sq. ft.
Second Finished	504 sq. ft.
Garage Unfinished	384 sq. ft.
Dimensions	54'x35'8"
Foundation	Basement
Bedrooms	2
Full Baths	1
Half Baths	1
Roof Framing	Stick
Exterior Walls	2x6

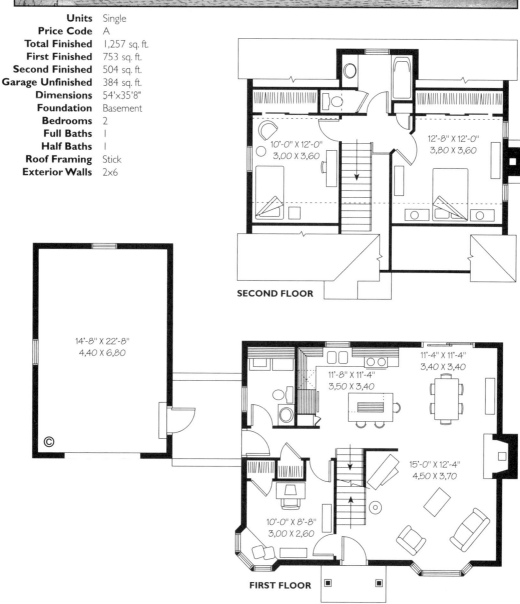

SECOND FLOOR

10'-0" X 12'-0"
3,00 X 3,60

12'-8" X 12'-0"
3,80 X 3,60

14'-8" X 22'-8"
4,40 X 6,80

11'-8" X 11'-4"
3,50 X 3,40

11'-4" X 11'-4"
3,40 X 3,40

15'-0" X 12'-4"
4,50 X 3,70

10'-0" X 8'-8"
3,00 X 2,60

FIRST FLOOR

Design 90822

Units	Single
Price Code	A
Total Finished	1,263 sq. ft.
First Finished	925 sq. ft.
Second Finished	338 sq. ft.
Basement Unfinished	864 sq. ft.
Dimensions	33'x47'
Foundation	Basement
Bedrooms	3
Full Baths	1
Half Baths	1
Roof Framing	Stick
Exterior Walls	2x6

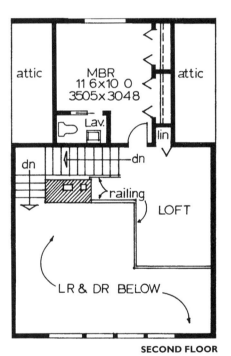

SECOND FLOOR

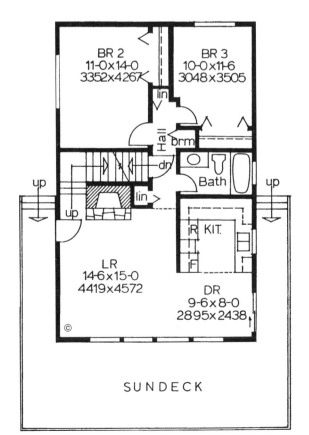

FIRST FLOOR

PHOTOGRAPHY: COURTESY OF THE DESIGNER

Units	Single
Price Code	A
Total Finished	1,272 sq. ft.
First Finished	860 sq. ft.
Second Finished	412 sq. ft.
Dimensions	32'x36'
Foundation	Combo Crawlspace/Slab
Bedrooms	2
Full Baths	2
First Ceiling	8'
Second Ceiling	8'
Vaulted Ceiling	18'-22'
Max Ridge Height	25'
Roof Framing	Stick
Exterior Walls	2x4

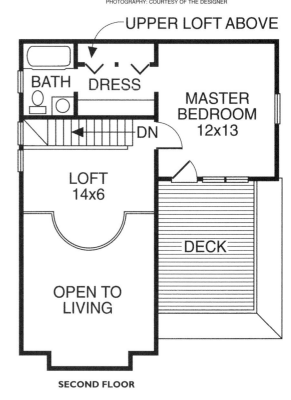

SECOND FLOOR

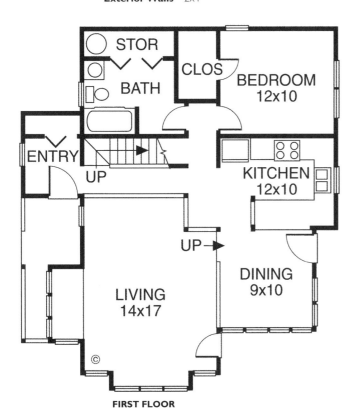

FIRST FLOOR

Please note: The photographed home may have been modified to suit homeowner preferences. If you order plans, have a builder or design professional check them against the photograph to confirm actual construction details.

Design 90048

Units	Single
Price Code	A
Total Finished	1,274 sq. ft.
First Finished	974 sq. ft.
Second Finished	300 sq. ft.
Basement Unfinished	974 sq. ft.
Dimensions	23'8"x55'10"
Foundation	Basement
Bedrooms	3
Full Baths	2
Max Ridge Height	23'
Roof Framing	Stick
Exterior Walls	2x4

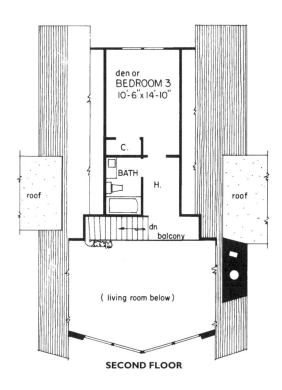

SECOND FLOOR

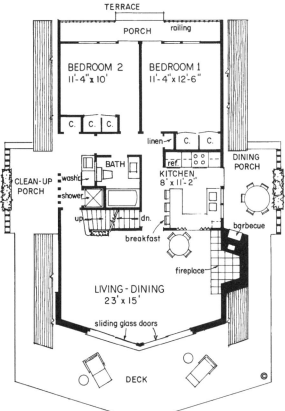

FIRST FLOOR

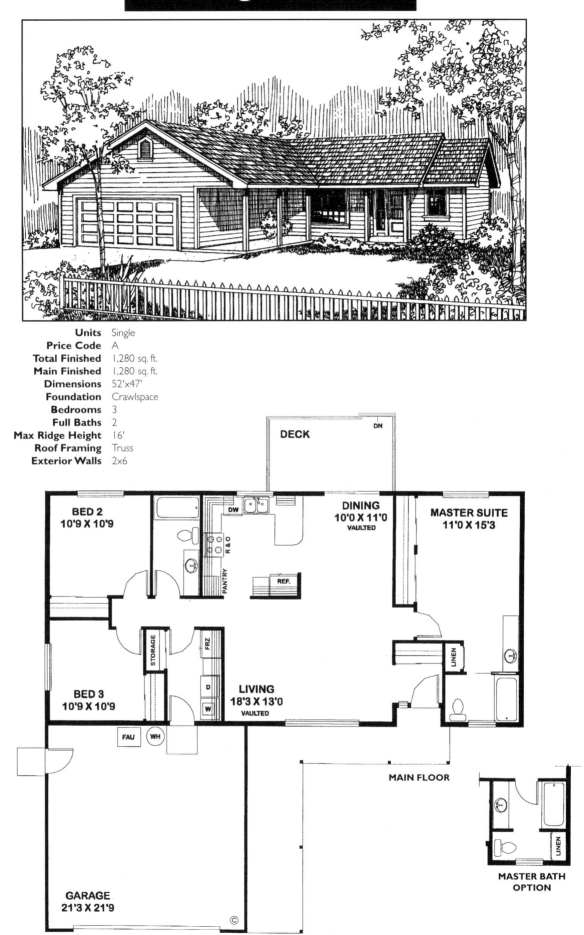

Units	Single
Price Code	A
Total Finished	1,280 sq. ft.
Main Finished	1,280 sq. ft.
Dimensions	52'x47'
Foundation	Crawlspace
Bedrooms	3
Full Baths	2
Max Ridge Height	16'
Roof Framing	Truss
Exterior Walls	2x6

DECK
DN

BED 2
10'9 X 10'9

DINING
10'0 X 11'0
VAULTED

MASTER SUITE
11'0 X 15'3

DW

R & O

PANTRY

REF.

LINEN

STORAGE

FRZ

BED 3
10'9 X 10'9

LIVING
18'3 X 13'0
VAULTED

D

W

FAU WH

MAIN FLOOR

MASTER BATH
OPTION

LINEN

GARAGE
21'3 X 21'9

Design 99238

Units	Single
Price Code	A
Total Finished	1,288 sq. ft.
First Finished	784 sq. ft.
Second Finished	504 sq. ft.
Dimensions	28'x28'
Foundation	Basement
Bedrooms	3
Full Baths	2
Roof Framing	Stick
Exterior Walls	2x4

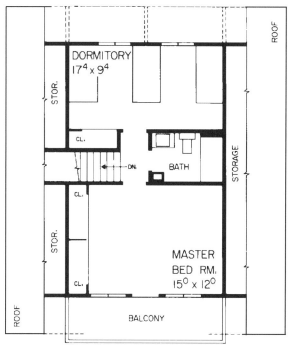

SECOND FLOOR

FIRST FLOOR

Design 91832

Units	Single
Price Code	A
Total Finished	1,288 sq. ft.
Main Finished	1,288 sq. ft.
Basement Unfinished	1,288 sq. ft.
Garage Unfinished	478 sq. ft.
Dimensions	56'x40'
Foundation	Basement
	Crawlspace
	Slab
Bedrooms	2
Full Baths	1
3/4 Baths	1
Main Ceiling	9'
Max Ridge Height	18'8"
Roof Framing	Truss
Exterior Walls	2x6

PATIO

DINING
11/0 x 11/0

GREAT RM
18/2 x 15/4

MASTER
12/8 x 12/10

KIT.
10/8 x 11/8

PANTRY

WASH DRY

DOWN

COVERED
PORCH

LINEN

SH

GARAGE
21/4 x 20/2

BDRM-2
12/8 x 10/0

MAIN FLOOR

Design 92523

Units	Single
Price Code	A
Total Finished	1,293 sq. ft.
Main Finished	1,293 sq. ft.
Garage Unfinished	433 sq. ft.
Porch Unfinished	76 sq. ft.
Dimensions	51'10"x40'4"
Foundation	Slab
Bedrooms	3
Full Baths	2
Max Ridge Height	22'
Roof Framing	Stick
Exterior Walls	2x4

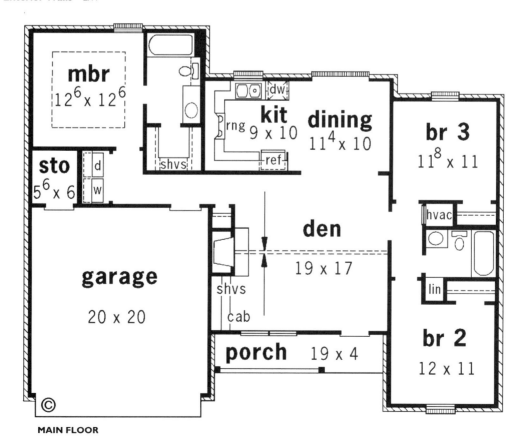

MAIN FLOOR

Units	Single
Price Code	A
Total Finished	1,296 sq. ft.
Main Finished	1,296 sq. ft.
Basement Unfinished	1,336 sq. ft.
Garage Unfinished	380 sq. ft.
Dimensions	46'x42'
Foundation	Basement
	Crawlspace
	Slab
Bedrooms	3
Full Baths	2
Main Ceiling	8'
Vaulted Ceiling	12'
Max Ridge Height	17'6"
Roof Framing	Truss
Exterior Walls	2x4

OPTIONAL MASTER BATH

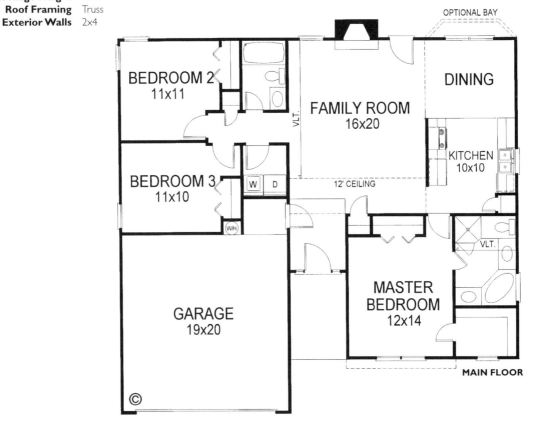

MAIN FLOOR

Units	Single
Price Code	A
Total Finished	1,304 sq. ft.
First Finished	681 sq. ft.
Second Finished	623 sq. ft.
Garage Unfinished	260 sq. ft.
Dimensions	28'x40'
Foundation	Basement
Bedrooms	2
Full Baths	1
Half Baths	1
First Ceiling	8'
Second Ceiling	8'
Roof Framing	Truss
Exterior Walls	2x6

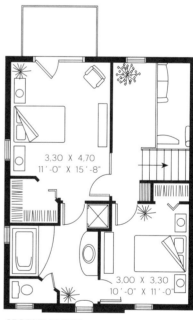

SECOND FLOOR

3,30 X 4,70
11'-0" X 15'-8"

3,00 X 3,30
10'-0" X 11'-0"

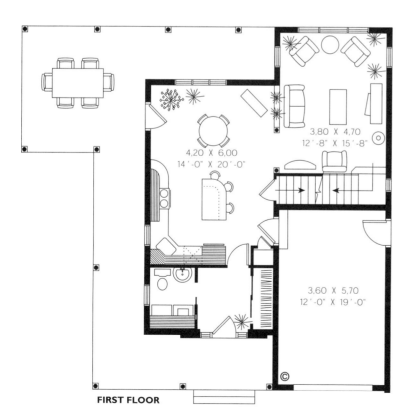

4,20 X 6,00
14'-0" X 20'-0"

3,80 X 4,70
12'-8" X 15'-8"

3,60 X 5,70
12'-0" X 19'-0"

FIRST FLOOR

Units	Single
Price Code	A
Total Finished	1,304 sq. ft.
Main Finished	1,304 sq. ft.
Basement Unfinished	1,326 sq. ft.
Garage Unfinished	458 sq. ft.
Dimensions	50'x41'
Foundation	Basement
	Crawlspace
Bedrooms	3
Full Baths	2
Main Ceiling	8'
Max Ridge Height	23'6"
Roof Framing	Stick
Exterior Walls	2x4

CAD **FILES AVAILABLE**
For more information call
800-235-5700

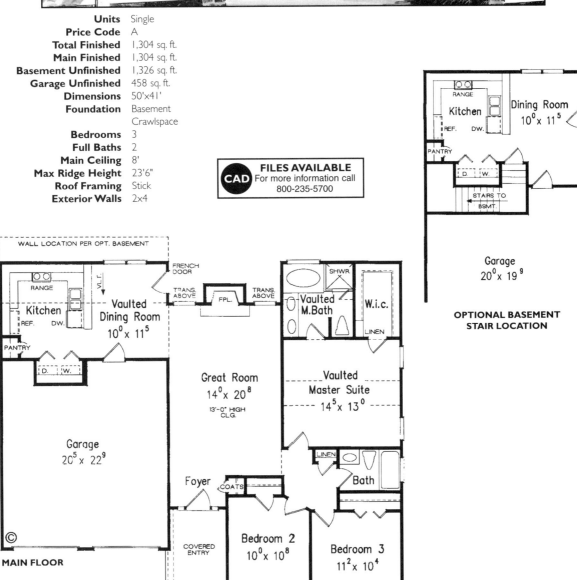

**OPTIONAL BASEMENT
STAIR LOCATION**

MAIN FLOOR

Units	Single
Price Code	A
Total Finished	1,306 sq. ft.
First Finished	1,047 sq. ft.
Second Finished	259 sq. ft.
Dimensions	32'x40'
Foundation	Crawlspace
Bedrooms	2
Full Baths	1
3/4 Baths	1
First Ceiling	8'
Second Ceiling	8'
Vaulted Ceiling	17'
Max Ridge Height	23'8"
Roof Framing	Truss
Exterior Walls	2x6

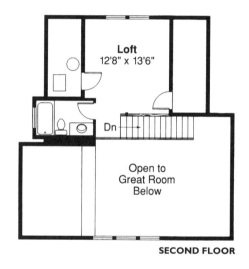

SECOND FLOOR

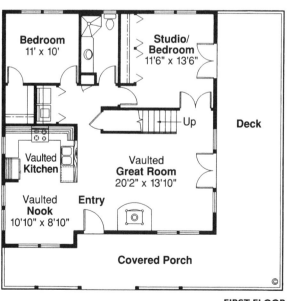

FIRST FLOOR

Merillat®

Visit us at www.merillat.com

Units	Single
Price Code	A
Total Finished	1,312 sq. ft.
Main Finished	1,312 sq. ft.
Basement Unfinished	1,293 sq. ft.
Garage Unfinished	459 sq. ft.
Deck Unfinished	185 sq. ft.
Porch Unfinished	84 sq. ft.
Dimensions	50'x40'
Foundation	Basement
	Crawlspace
	Slab
Bedrooms	3
Full Baths	2
Main Ceiling	8'
Max Ridge Height	20'
Roof Framing	Stick
Exterior Walls	2x6

**OPTIONAL
CRAWLSPACE/SLAB
FOUNDATION**

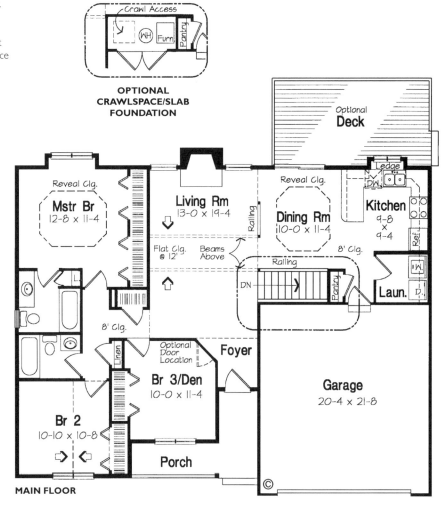

MAIN FLOOR

Design 34004

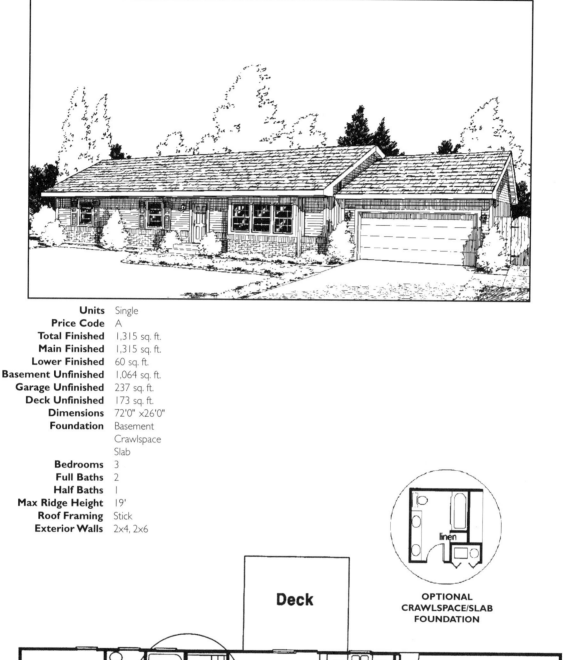

Units	Single
Price Code	A
Total Finished	1,315 sq. ft.
Main Finished	1,315 sq. ft.
Lower Finished	60 sq. ft.
Basement Unfinished	1,064 sq. ft.
Garage Unfinished	237 sq. ft.
Deck Unfinished	173 sq. ft.
Dimensions	72'0" ×26'0"
Foundation	Basement
	Crawlspace
	Slab
Bedrooms	3
Full Baths	2
Half Baths	1
Max Ridge Height	19'
Roof Framing	Stick
Exterior Walls	2x4, 2x6

OPTIONAL
CRAWLSPACE/SLAB
FOUNDATION

Deck

MBr 1
11 x 13-6

Family Rm
13-6 x 15

Kit
9 x 13-6

Garage
22 x 22

W D

DN

linen

Br 2
11 x 9-2

Br 3
11-4 x 9-2

Living Rm
11
x
11-6

Dining
10-8
x
10-6

MAIN FLOOR

Units	Single
Price Code	A
Total Finished	1,317 sq. ft.
First Finished	681 sq. ft.
Second Finished	636 sq. ft.
Garage Unfinished	286 sq. ft.
Dimensions	34'x34'
Foundation	Basement
Bedrooms	3
Full Baths	1
Half Baths	1

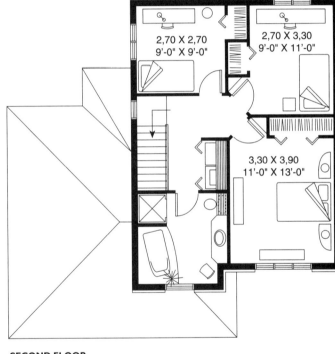

SECOND FLOOR

FIRST FLOOR

Design 34600

PHOTOGRAPHY: MICHELE EVANS CHRISTY

Units	Single
Price Code	A
Total Finished	1,328 sq. ft.
First Finished	1,013 sq. ft.
Second Finished	315 sq. ft.
Basement Unfinished	1,013 sq. ft.
Dimensions	36'x36'
Foundation	Basement
	Crawlspace
	Slab
Bedrooms	3
Full Baths	2
First Ceiling	8'
Second Ceiling	7'6"
Max Ridge Height	23'6"
Roof Framing	Stick
Exterior Walls	2x4, 2x6

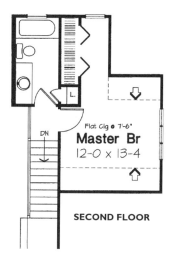

OPTIONAL CRAWLSPACE/SLAB FOUNDATION

SECOND FLOOR

Flat Clg @ 7'-6"
Master Br
12-0 x 13-4

FIRST FLOOR

Please note: The photographed home may have been modified to suit homeowner preferences. If you order plans, have a builder or design professional check them against the photograph to confirm actual construction details.

Units	Single
Price Code	A
Total Finished	1,342 sq. ft.
First Finished	927 sq. ft.
Second Finished	415 sq. ft.
Basement Unfinished	927 sq. ft.
Garage Unfinished	440 sq. ft.
Dimensions	42'x44'
Foundation	Basement
Bedrooms	3
Full Baths	1
3/4 Baths	1
Half Baths	1
First Ceiling	8'
Second Ceiling	8'
Max Ridge Height	25'6"
Roof Framing	Truss
Exterior Walls	2x6

SECOND FLOOR

FIRST FLOOR

Design 98912

Units	Single
Price Code	A
Total Finished	1,345 sq. ft.
Main Finished	1,325 sq. ft.
Lower Finished	20 sq. ft.
Basement Unfinished	556 sq. ft.
Garage Unfinished	724 sq. ft.
Deck Unfinished	157 sq. ft.
Porch Unfinished	216 sq. ft.
Dimensions	52'x42'
Foundation	Basement
Bedrooms	3
Full Baths	2
Main Ceiling	8'
Max Ridge Height	19'
Roof Framing	Stick
Exterior Walls	2x4

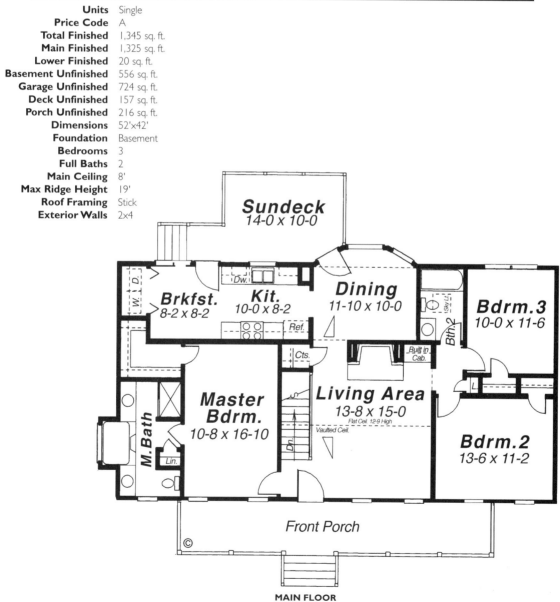

Sundeck 14-0 x 10-0

Brkfst. 8-2 x 8-2

Kit. 10-0 x 8-2

Dining 11-10 x 10-0

Bdrm.3 10-0 x 11-6

Master Bdrm. 10-8 x 16-10

Living Area 13-8 x 15-0
Flat Ceil. 12-9 High
Vaulted Ceil.

Bdrm.2 13-6 x 11-2

M.Bath

Bth.2

Built in Cab.

Dw.

Ref.

Cts.

Lin.

Dn.

W. D.

Sky L.

Front Porch

MAIN FLOOR

Units	Single
Price Code	A
Total Finished	1,346 sq. ft.
Main Finished	1,346 sq. ft.
Dimensions	54'x44'6"
Foundation	Crawlspace
	Slab
Bedrooms	3
Full Baths	2
Main Ceiling	8'
Max Ridge Height	25'
Roof Framing	Stick
Exterior Walls	2x4

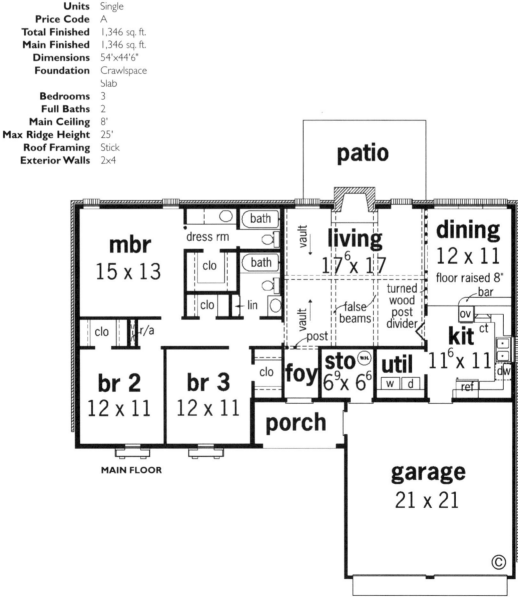

Design 98434

Units	Single
Price Code	A
Total Finished	1,346 sq. ft.
Main Finished	1,346 sq. ft.
Basement Unfinished	1,358 sq. ft.
Garage Unfinished	395 sq. ft.
Dimensions	39'x51'
Foundation	Basement
	Crawlspace
	Slab
Bedrooms	3
Full Baths	2
Max Ridge Height	21'6"
Roof Framing	Stick
Exterior Walls	2x4

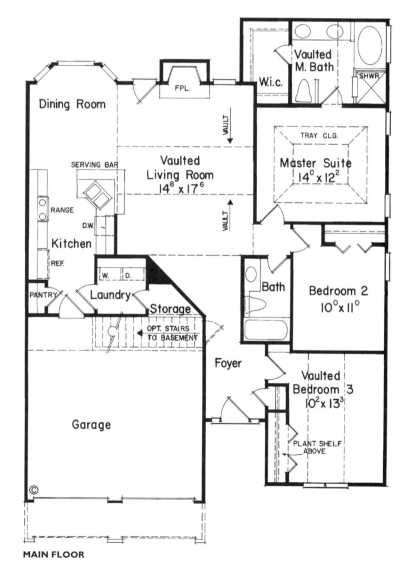

MAIN FLOOR

Design 92432

Units	Single
Price Code	A
Total Finished	1,349 sq. ft.
First Finished	645 sq. ft.
Second Finished	704 sq. ft.
Dimensions	44'×28'
Foundation	Basement
Bedrooms	3
Full Baths	2
Half Baths	1
First Ceiling	8'
Second Ceiling	8'
Max Ridge Height	25'6"
Roof Framing	Truss
Exterior Walls	2x4

Design 90356

Units	Single
Price Code	A
Total Finished	1,351 sq. ft.
First Finished	674 sq. ft.
Second Finished	677 sq. ft.
Basement Unfinished	674 sq. ft.
Dimensions	48'x30'2"
Foundation	Basement
Bedrooms	3
Full Baths	1
3/4 Baths	1
Half Baths	1
Max Ridge Height	25'
Roof Framing	Stick/Truss
Exterior Walls	2x4

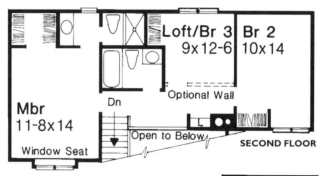

Loft/Br 3
9x12-6

Br 2
10x14

Optional Wall

Mbr
11-8x14

Dn

Window Seat

Open to Below

SECOND FLOOR

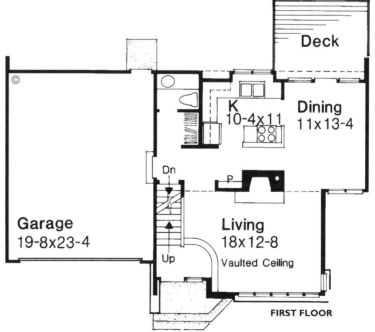

Deck

K
10-4x11

Dining
11x13-4

Dn

P

Garage
19-8x23-4

Up

Living
18x12-8

Vaulted Ceiling

FIRST FLOOR

Units	Single
Price Code	A
Total Finished	1,354 sq. ft.
First Finished	988 sq. ft.
Second Finished	366 sq. ft.
Basement Unfinished	742 sq. ft.
Garage Unfinished	283 sq. ft.
Dimensions	26'x48'
Foundation	Basement
Bedrooms	3
Full Baths	1
3/4 Baths	1
First Ceiling	8'
Vaulted Ceiling	13'6"
Max Ridge Height	32'
Roof Framing	Stick
Exterior Walls	2x6

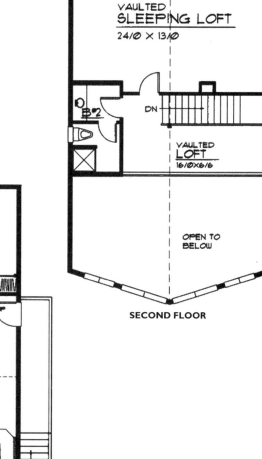

SECOND FLOOR

FIRST FLOOR

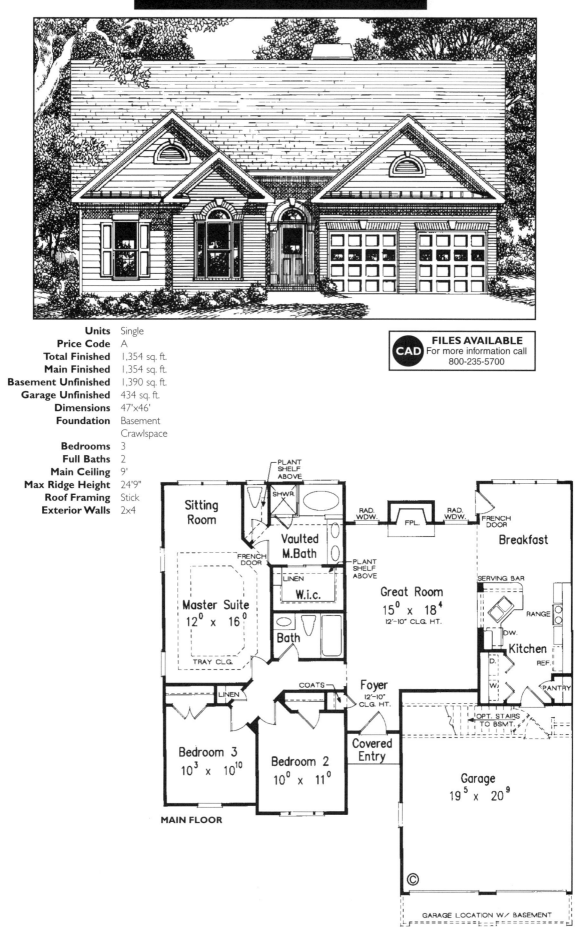

Units	Single
Price Code	A
Total Finished	1,354 sq. ft.
Main Finished	1,354 sq. ft.
Basement Unfinished	1,390 sq. ft.
Garage Unfinished	434 sq. ft.
Dimensions	47'x46'
Foundation	Basement
	Crawlspace
Bedrooms	3
Full Baths	2
Main Ceiling	9'
Max Ridge Height	24'9"
Roof Framing	Stick
Exterior Walls	2x4

CAD FILES AVAILABLE
For more information call
800-235-5700

Sitting Room

PLANT SHELF ABOVE

SHWR.

Vaulted M.Bath

RAD. WDW.   FPL.   RAD. WDW.

FRENCH DOOR

Breakfast

FRENCH DOOR

LINEN

W.i.c.

PLANT SHELF ABOVE

Master Suite
12⁰ x 16⁰

Great Room
15⁰ x 18⁴
12'-10" CLG. HT.

SERVING BAR

RANGE

Bath

DW.

Kitchen

D.

REF.

TRAY CLG.

W.

PANTRY

LINEN

COATS

Foyer
12'-10" CLG. HT.

OPT. STAIRS TO BSMT.

Bedroom 3
10³ x 10¹⁰

Bedroom 2
10⁰ x 11⁰

Covered Entry

Garage
19⁵ x 20⁹

MAIN FLOOR

GARAGE LOCATION W/ BASEMENT

Design 20156

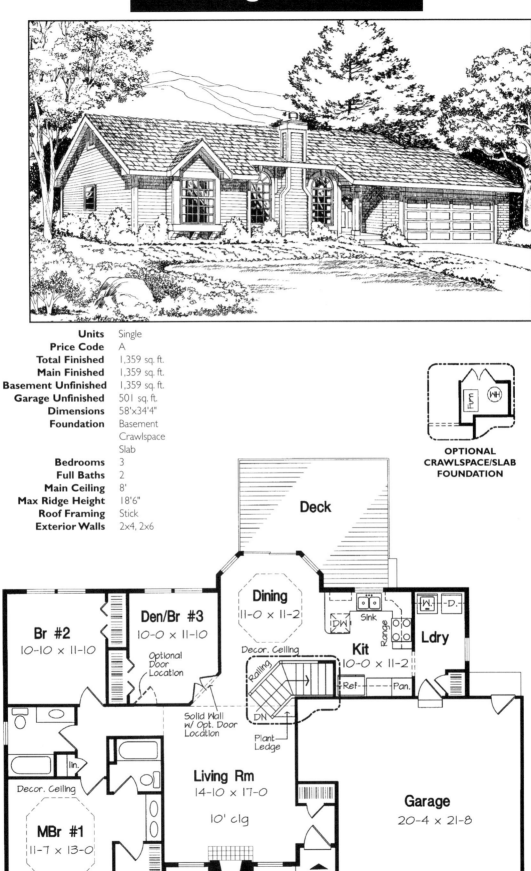

Units	Single
Price Code	A
Total Finished	1,359 sq. ft.
Main Finished	1,359 sq. ft.
Basement Unfinished	1,359 sq. ft.
Garage Unfinished	501 sq. ft.
Dimensions	58'x34'4"
Foundation	Basement
	Crawlspace
	Slab
Bedrooms	3
Full Baths	2
Main Ceiling	8'
Max Ridge Height	18'6"
Roof Framing	Stick
Exterior Walls	2x4, 2x6

OPTIONAL CRAWLSPACE/SLAB FOUNDATION

Deck

Dining 11-0 × 11-2

Decor. Ceiling

Kit 10-0 × 11-2

Sink

Range

DW

Ref

Pan.

Ldry

W.

D.

Br #2 10-10 × 11-10

Den/Br #3 10-0 × 11-10

Optional Door Location

Railing

DN

Plant Ledge

Solid Wall w/ Opt. Door Location

lin.

Decor. Ceiling

MBr #1 11-7 × 13-0

Living Rm 14-10 × 17-0

10' clg

Garage 20-4 × 21-8

Seat

MAIN FLOOR

Units	Single
Price Code	A
Total Finished	1,360 sq. ft.
First Finished	858 sq. ft.
Second Finished	502 sq. ft.
Basement Unfinished	858 sq. ft.
Dimensions	35'×29'8"
Foundation	Basement
Bedrooms	3
Full Baths	2
First Ceiling	8'
Second Ceiling	8'
Max Ridge Height	26'6"
Roof Framing	Truss
Exterior Walls	2×6

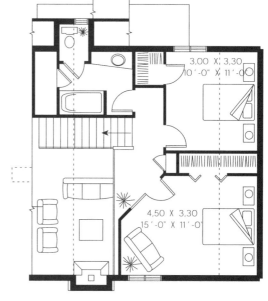

3,00 X 3,30
10'-0" X 11'-0"

4,50 X 3,30
15'-0" X 11'-0"

SECOND FLOOR

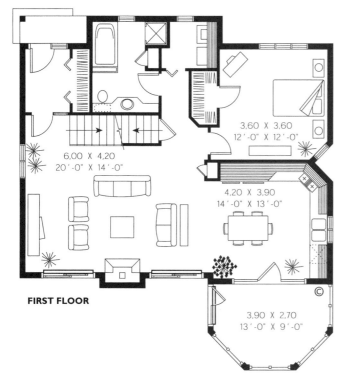

6,00 X 4,20
20'-0" X 14'-0"

3,60 X 3,60
12'-0" X 12'-0"

4,20 X 3,90
14'-0" X 13'-0"

FIRST FLOOR

3,90 X 2,70
13'-0" X 9'-0"

Units	Single
Price Code	A
Total Finished	1,362 sq. ft.
First Finished	864 sq. ft.
Second Finished	498 sq. ft.
Basement Unfinished	864 sq. ft.
Deck Unfinished	340 sq. ft.
Dimensions	35'x40'
Foundation	Basement
	Crawlspace
Bedrooms	2
Full Baths	2
First Ceiling	8'
Max Ridge Height	24'
Roof Framing	Stick
Exterior Walls	2x6

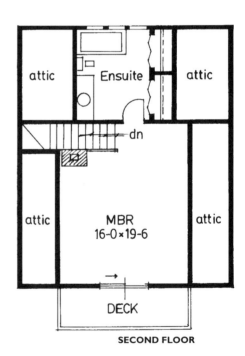

SECOND FLOOR

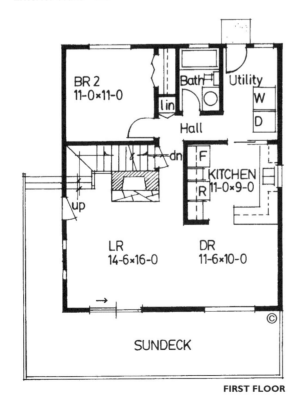

FIRST FLOOR

Design 65186

Units	Single
Price Code	A
Total Finished	1,362 sq. ft.
First Finished	681 sq. ft.
Second Finished	681 sq. ft.
Dimensions	22'8"x32'
Foundation	Basement
Bedrooms	3
Full Baths	1
Half Baths	1

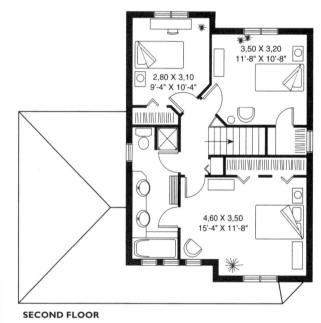

SECOND FLOOR

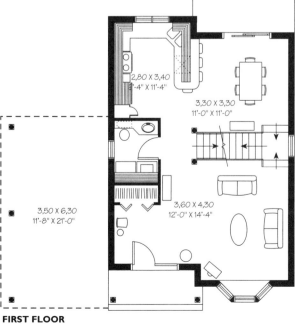

FIRST FLOOR

Units	Single
Price Code	A
Total Finished	1,363 sq. ft.
Main Finished	1,363 sq. ft.
Porch Unfinished	276 sq. ft.
Dimensions	30'x60'
Foundation	Slab
Bedrooms	3
Full Baths	2
Main Ceiling	9'
Max Ridge Height	25'9"
Roof Framing	Stick
Exterior Walls	2x4

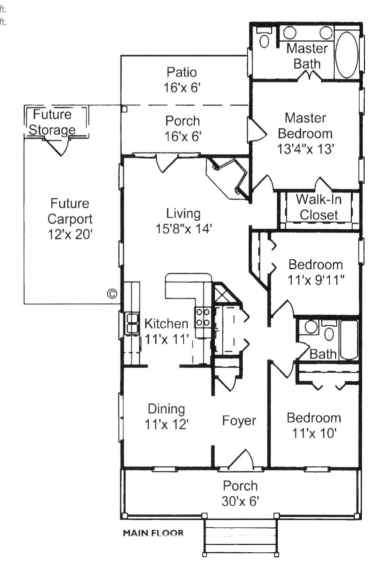

Master Bath

Patio
16'x 6'

Porch
16'x 6'

Master Bedroom
13'4"x 13'

Future Storage

Future Carport
12'x 20'

Living
15'8"x 14'

Walk-In Closet

Bedroom
11'x 9'11"

Kitchen
11'x 11'

Bath

Dining
11'x 12'

Foyer

Bedroom
11'x 10'

Porch
30'x 6'

MAIN FLOOR

Design 98985

Units	Single
Price Code	A
Total Finished	1,365 sq. ft.
Main Finished	1,365 sq. ft.
Garage Unfinished	407 sq. ft.
Dimensions	37'x53'
Foundation	Basement
	Slab
Bedrooms	3
Full Baths	2
Main Ceiling	8'
Max Ridge Height	19'10"
Roof Framing	Stick
Exterior Walls	2x4

OPTIONAL SCREEN PORCH

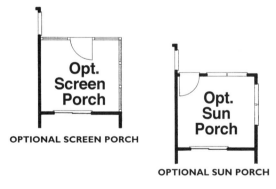

OPTIONAL SUN PORCH

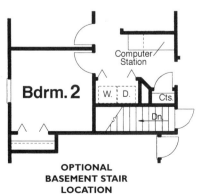

OPTIONAL BASEMENT STAIR LOCATION

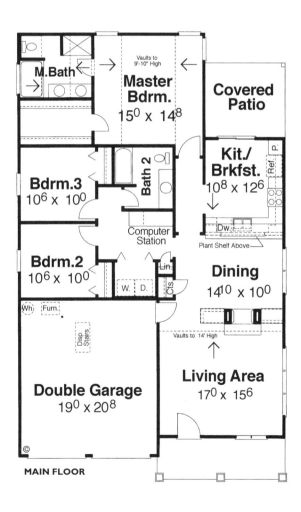

MAIN FLOOR

Design 60013

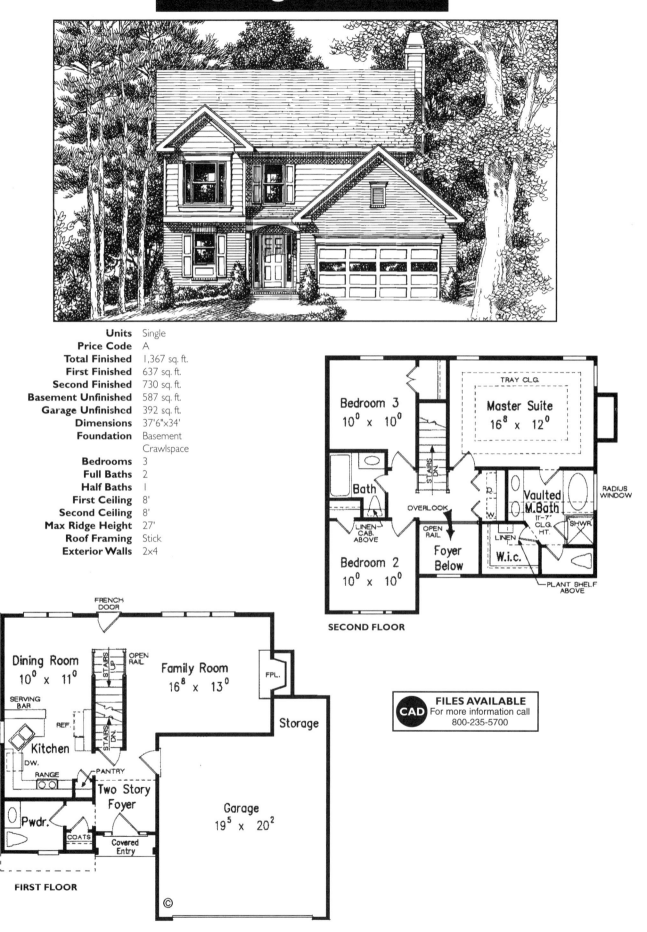

Units	Single
Price Code	A
Total Finished	1,367 sq. ft.
First Finished	637 sq. ft.
Second Finished	730 sq. ft.
Basement Unfinished	587 sq. ft.
Garage Unfinished	392 sq. ft.
Dimensions	37'6"x34'
Foundation	Basement
	Crawlspace
Bedrooms	3
Full Baths	2
Half Baths	I
First Ceiling	8'
Second Ceiling	8'
Max Ridge Height	27'
Roof Framing	Stick
Exterior Walls	2x4

SECOND FLOOR

Bedroom 3 10⁰ x 10⁰

TRAY CLG.

Master Suite 16⁸ x 12⁰

Bath

STAIRS DN.

Vaulted M.Bath 11'-7" CLG. HT.

RADIUS WINDOW

OVERLOOK

LINEN CAB. ABOVE

OPEN RAIL

Foyer Below

W.i.c.

LINEN

SHWR.

Bedroom 2 10⁰ x 10⁰

PLANT SHELF ABOVE

FIRST FLOOR

FRENCH DOOR

Dining Room 10⁰ x 11⁰

STAIRS UP

OPEN RAIL

Family Room 16⁸ x 13⁰

FPL.

SERVING BAR

REF.

STAIRS DN.

Storage

Kitchen

DW.

RANGE

PANTRY

Two Story Foyer

Pwdr.

COATS

Covered Entry

Garage 19⁵ x 20²

CAD FILES AVAILABLE
For more information call
800-235-5700

Design 99639

Units	Single
Price Code	A
Total Finished	1,367 sq. ft.
Main Finished	1,367 sq. ft.
Basement Unfinished	1,267 sq. ft.
Garage Unfinished	431 sq. ft.
Dimensions	71'4"x33'10"
Foundation	Basement
	Slab
Bedrooms	3
Full Baths	2
Main Ceiling	8'
Vaulted Ceiling	11'
Max Ridge Height	20'
Roof Framing	Stick
Exterior Walls	2x6

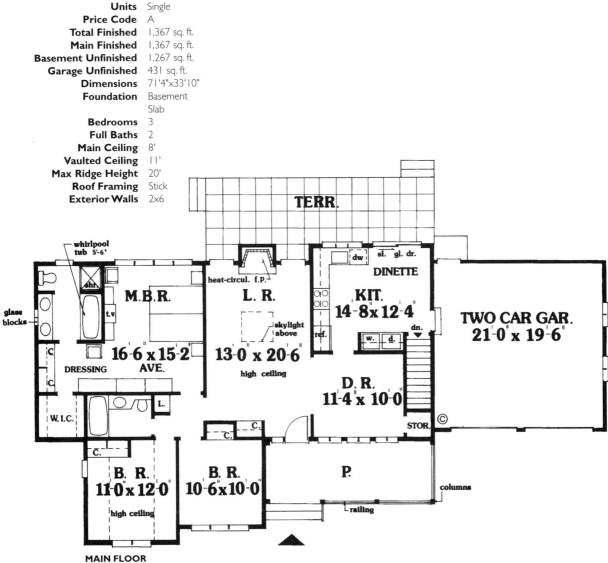

MAIN FLOOR

PHOTOGRAPHY: COURTESY OF THE DESIGNER

Units	Single
Price Code	A
Total Finished	1,375 sq. ft.
Main Finished	1,375 sq. ft.
Basement Unfinished	1,375 sq. ft.
Garage Unfinished	448 sq. ft.
Porch Unfinished	151 sq. ft.
Dimensions	40'x55'8"
Foundation	Basement
Bedrooms	2
Full Baths	2
Main Ceiling	9'
Max Ridge Height	27'
Roof Framing	Stick
Exterior Walls	2x4, 2x6

* Alternate foundation options available at an additional charge. Please call 1-800-235-5700 for more information.

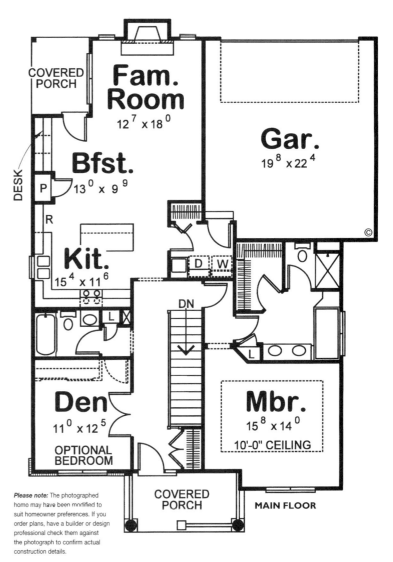

Please note: The photographed home may have been modified to suit homeowner preferences. If you order plans, have a builder or design professional check them against the photograph to confirm actual construction details.

Design 82003

1,001-1,500 sq. ft. HOME PLANS

Units	Single
Price Code	A
Total Finished	1,379 sq. ft.
Main Finished	1,379 sq. ft.
Garage Unfinished	493 sq. ft.
Porch Unfinished	142 sq. ft.
Dimensions	38'4"x68'6"
Foundation	Crawlspace
	Slab
Bedrooms	3
Full Baths	2
Main Ceiling	9'
Roof Framing	Stick
Exterior Walls	2x4

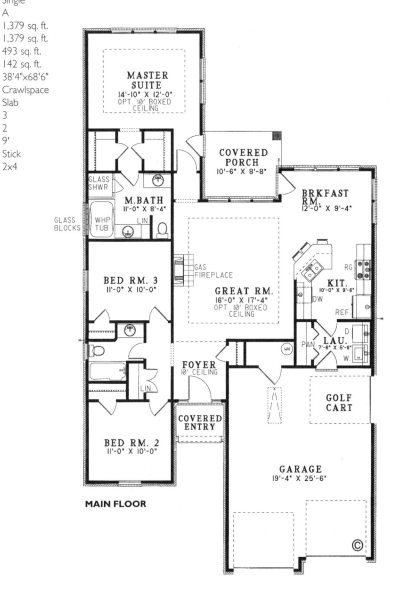

MASTER SUITE
14'-10" X 12'-0"
OPT 10' BOXED CEILING

COVERED PORCH
10'-6" X 8'-8"

BRKFAST RM.
12'-0" X 9'-4"

GLASS SHWR

M. BATH
11'-0" X 8'-4"

GLASS BLOCKS

WHP TUB

LIN

KIT.
10'-0" X 9'-6"

RG

GAS FIREPLACE

DW

REF

BED RM. 3
11'-0" X 10'-0"

GREAT RM.
16'-0" X 17'-4"
OPT 10' BOXED CEILING

LAU.
7'-6" X 5'-6"

PAN

D

W

WH

FOYER
10' CEILING

GOLF CART

LIN

COVERED ENTRY

BED RM. 2
11'-0" X 10'-0"

GARAGE
19'-4" X 25'-6"

MAIN FLOOR

PHOTOGRAPHY: COURTESY OF THE DESIGNER

Units	Single
Price Code	A
Total Finished	1,383 sq. ft.
Main Finished	1,383 sq. ft.
Basement Unfinished	1,460 sq. ft.
Garage Unfinished	416 sq. ft.
Deck Unfinished	120 sq. ft.
Porch Unfinished	29 sq. ft.
Dimensions	50'x40'
Foundation	Basement
	Crawlspace
	Slab
Bedrooms	3
Full Baths	2
Main Ceiling	9'
Max Ridge Height	20'6"
Roof Framing	Truss
Exterior Walls	2x4

Please note: The photographed home may have been modified to suit homeowner preferences. If you order plans, have a builder or design professional check them against the photograph to confirm actual construction details.

DECK/PATIO

DINING ROOM
11'-6" x 9'-4"

GREAT ROOM
16'-0" x 19'-0"

MASTER SUITE
15'-0" x 12'-0"

W.I.C.

KITCHEN
11'-6" x 11'-0"

PANT.

LAUN

MASTER BATH

BATH

FOYER

SUITE 3
10'-0" x 10'-0"

GARAGE
20'-0" x 20'-0"

SUITE 2
11'-6" x 11'-4"

MAIN FLOOR

Design 65165

Units	Single
Price Code	A
Total Finished	1,387 sq. ft.
Main Finished	1,387 sq. ft.
Porch Unfinished	126 sq. ft.
Dimensions	44'8"x34'
Foundation	Basement
Bedrooms	2
Full Baths	1
Main Ceiling	8'
Max Ridge Height	44'8"
Roof Framing	Truss
Exterior Walls	2x6

3,60 X 4,40
12'-0" X 14'-8"

4,80 X 4,20
16'-0" X 14'-0"

3,30 X 4,20
11'-0" X 14'-0"

3,70 X 3,80
12'-4" X 12'-8"

3,60 X 3,90
12'-0" X 13'-0"

MAIN FLOOR

Design 93279

Units	Single
Price Code	A
Total Finished	1,388 sq. ft.
Main Finished	1,388 sq. ft.
Garage Unfinished	400 sq. ft.
Dimensions	48'x46'
Foundation	Crawlspace
	Slab
Bedrooms	3
Full Baths	2
Main Ceiling	8'
Max Ridge Height	18'
Roof Framing	Truss
Exterior Walls	2x4

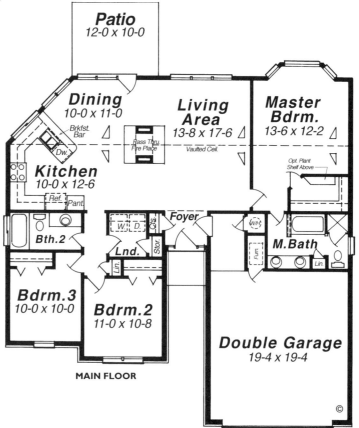

Patio
12-0 x 10-0

Dining
10-0 x 11-0

Brkfst. Bar

Dw.

Living Area
13-8 x 17-6

Pass Thru Fire Place

Vaulted Ceil.

Master Bdrm.
13-6 x 12-2

Opt. Plant Shelf Above

Kitchen
10-0 x 12-6

Ref. Pant.

Bth.2

W. D.

Foyer

W.H.

Furn.

M. Bath

Lin

Lnd.

Lin

Stor.

Bdrm.3
10-0 x 10-0

Bdrm.2
11-0 x 10-8

Double Garage
19-4 x 19-4

MAIN FLOOR

Design 92557

Units	Single
Price Code	A
Total Finished	1,390 sq. ft.
Main Finished	1,390 sq. ft.
Garage Unfinished	590 sq. ft.
Porch Unfinished	66 sq. ft.
Dimensions	67'4"x32'10"
Foundation	Crawlspace
	Slab
Bedrooms	3
Full Baths	2
Main Ceiling	9'
Max Ridge Height	22'6"
Roof Framing	Stick
Exterior Walls	2x4

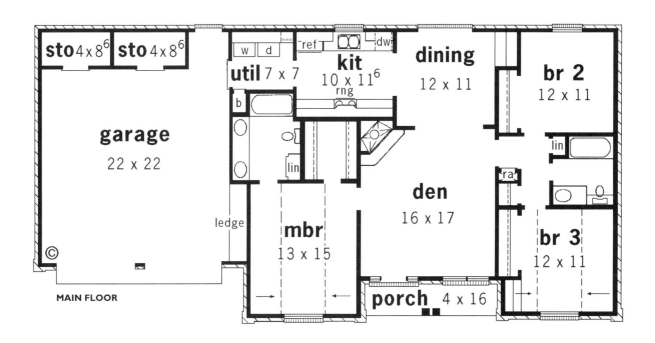

MAIN FLOOR

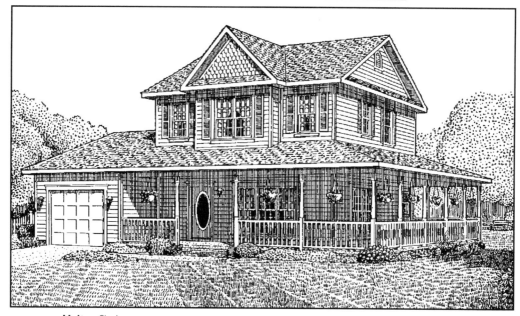

Units	Single
Price Code	A
Total Finished	1,399 sq. ft.
First Finished	732 sq. ft.
Second Finished	667 sq. ft.
Basement Unfinished	732 sq. ft.
Garage Unfinished	406 sq. ft.
Dimensions	46'9"x43'6"
Foundation	Basement
	Crawlspace
	Slab
Bedrooms	3
Full Baths	1
Half Baths	1
First Ceiling	9'
Second Ceiling	8'2"
Max Ridge Height	25'9"
Roof Framing	Truss
Exterior Walls	2x4

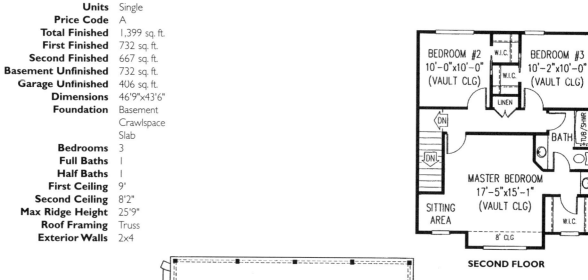

SECOND FLOOR

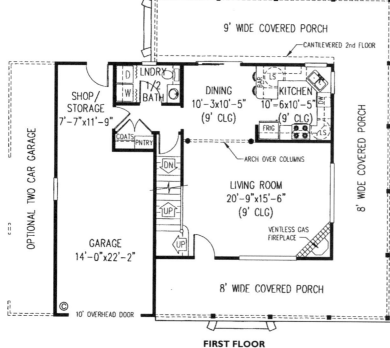

FIRST FLOOR

Design 34054

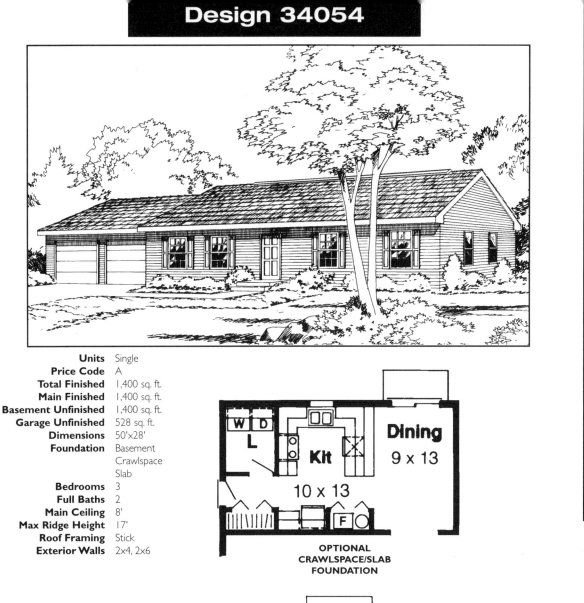

Units	Single
Price Code	A
Total Finished	1,400 sq. ft.
Main Finished	1,400 sq. ft.
Basement Unfinished	1,400 sq. ft.
Garage Unfinished	528 sq. ft.
Dimensions	50'x28'
Foundation	Basement
	Crawlspace
	Slab
Bedrooms	3
Full Baths	2
Main Ceiling	8'
Max Ridge Height	17'
Roof Framing	Stick
Exterior Walls	2x4, 2x6

OPTIONAL CRAWLSPACE/SLAB FOUNDATION

W D
L
Kit
10 x 13
Dining
9 x 13
F

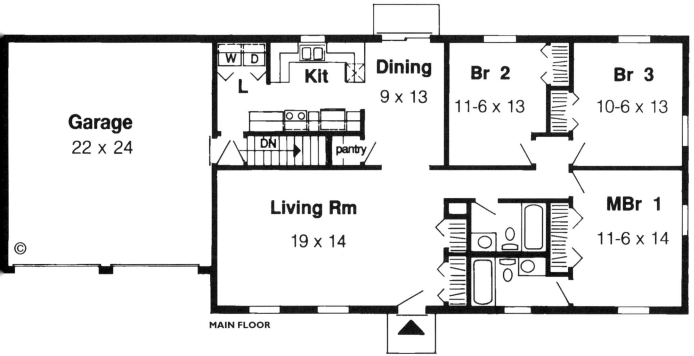

Garage
22 x 24

W D
L
Kit
Dining
9 x 13
DN
pantry

Br 2
11-6 x 13

Br 3
10-6 x 13

Living Rm
19 x 14

MBr 1
11-6 x 14

MAIN FLOOR

Design 99255

Units	Single
Price Code	A
Total Finished	1,400 sq. ft.
First Finished	700 sq. ft.
Second Finished	700 sq. ft.
Garage Unfinished	510 sq. ft.
Dimensions	46'x26'
Foundation	Basement
Bedrooms	3
Full Baths	2
3/4 Baths	1
Half Baths	1
Max Ridge Height	30'
Roof Framing	Stick
Exterior Walls	2x4

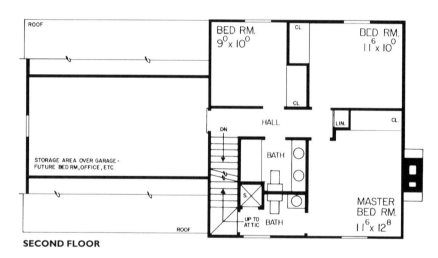

SECOND FLOOR

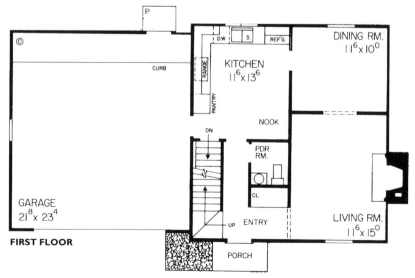

FIRST FLOOR

Design 94690

1,001-1,500 sq.ft. HOME PLANS

Units	Single
Price Code	A
Total Finished	1,401 sq. ft.
Main Finished	1,401 sq. ft.
Porch Unfinished	137 sq. ft.
Dimensions	30'x59'10"
Foundation	Slab
Bedrooms	3
Full Baths	2
Main Ceiling	9'
Max Ridge Height	20'6"
Roof Framing	Stick
Exterior Walls	2x4

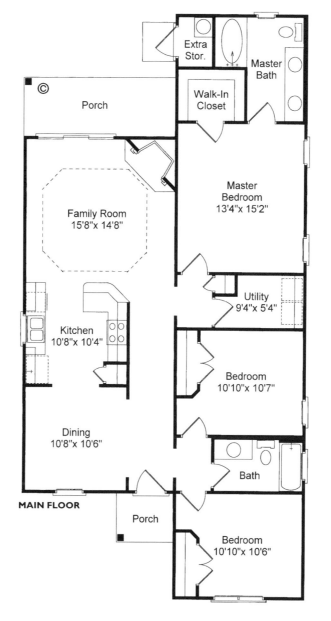

MAIN FLOOR

Units	Single
Price Code	A
Total Finished	1,405 sq. ft.
Main Finished	1,405 sq. ft.
Dimensions	42'x51'
Foundation	Slab
Bedrooms	3
Full Baths	2
Main Ceiling	8'
Max Ridge Height	19'4"
Roof Framing	Stick
Exterior Walls	2x4

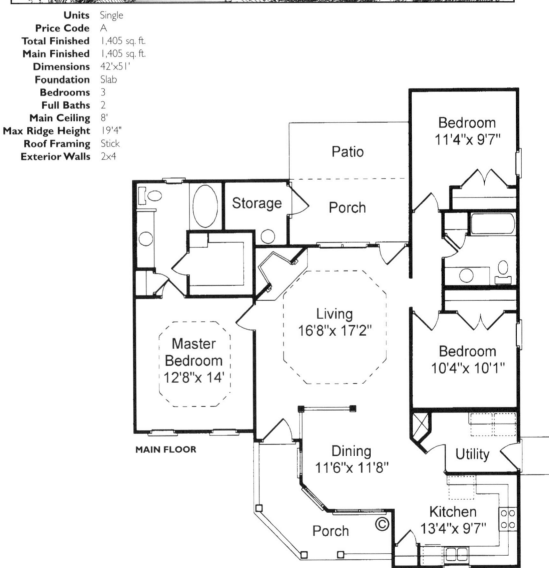

MAIN FLOOR

Design 34601

Units	Single
Price Code	A
Total Finished	1,415 sq. ft.
First Finished	1,007 sq. ft.
Second Finished	408 sq. ft.
Basement Unfinished	1,007 sq. ft.
Porch Unfinished	300 sq. ft.
Dimensions	38'4"x36'
Foundation	Basement
	Crawlspace
	Slab
Bedrooms	3
Full Baths	2
First Ceiling	8'
Second Ceiling	8'
Max Ridge Height	24'6"
Roof Framing	Stick
Exterior Walls	2x4, 2x6

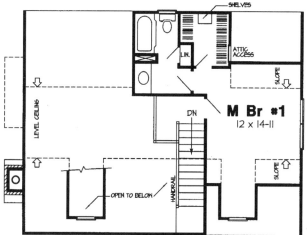

SECOND FLOOR

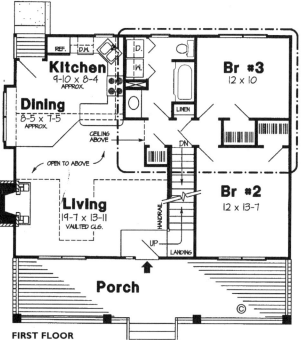

FIRST FLOOR

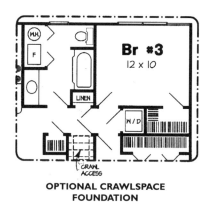

OPTIONAL CRAWLSPACE FOUNDATION

Units	Single
Price Code	A
Total Finished	1,416 sq. ft.
Main Finished	1,416 sq. ft.
Garage Unfinished	480 sq. ft.
Deck Unfinished	160 sq. ft.
Porch Unfinished	48 sq. ft.
Dimensions	49'x49'10"
Foundation	Crawlspace
	Slab
Bedrooms	3
Full Baths	2
Max Ridge Height	22'
Exterior Walls	2x4

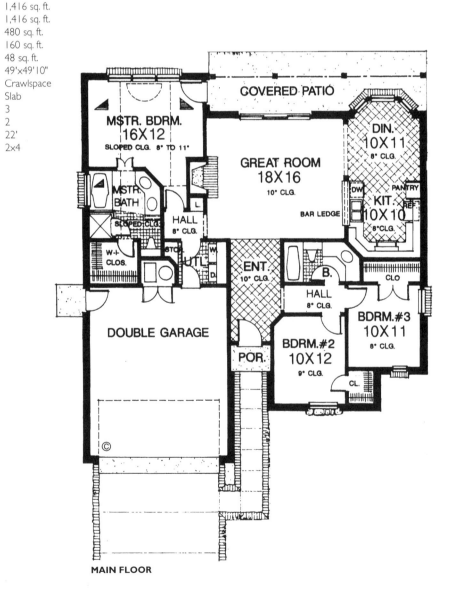

MAIN FLOOR

Design 97113

Units	Single
Price Code	A
Total Finished	1,416 sq. ft.
Main Finished	1,416 sq. ft.
Basement Unfinished	1,416 sq. ft.
Dimensions	48'x55'4"
Foundation	Basement
Bedrooms	3
Full Baths	2
Max Ridge Height	21'8"
Roof Framing	Truss
Exterior Walls	2x6

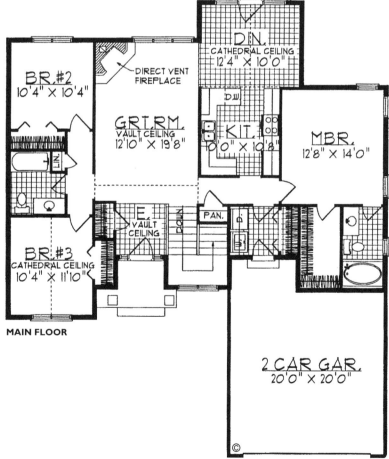

MAIN FLOOR

Units	Single
Price Code	A
Total Finished	1,418 sq. ft.
Main Finished	1,418 sq. ft.
Dimensions	61'x44'
Foundation	Crawlspace
	Slab
Bedrooms	3
Full Baths	2
Max Ridge Height	25'
Roof Framing	Stick
Exterior Walls	2x4

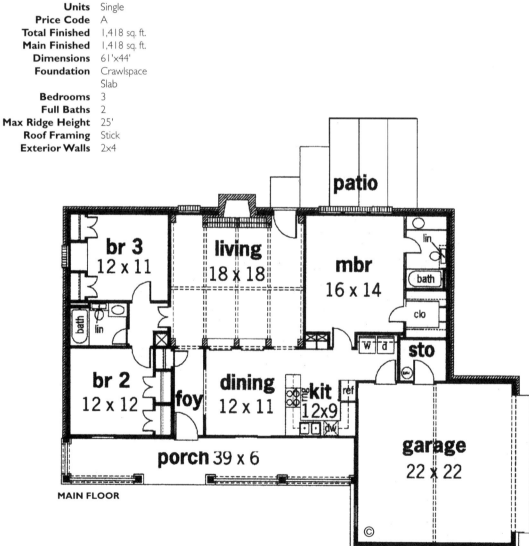

MAIN FLOOR

Design 65636

Units	Single
Price Code	A
Total Finished	1,420 sq. ft.
Main Finished	1,420 sq. ft.
Dimensions	52'x56'
Foundation	Crawlspace
	Slab
Bedrooms	3
Full Baths	2
Max Ridge Height	28'
Roof Framing	Stick
Exterior Walls	2x6

high wood privacy fence

bath
vanity
shvs
lin

mbr
15 x 14

br 2
13 x 12

porch
10 x 10

dining
12 x 10

lin
bath

living
18 x 16

kit
12 x 10
dw
rng
ref

stol 2x6
d
w

br 3
13 x 12
slope   slope

por 12x6

ht/ a/c

garage
22 x 21

MAIN FLOOR

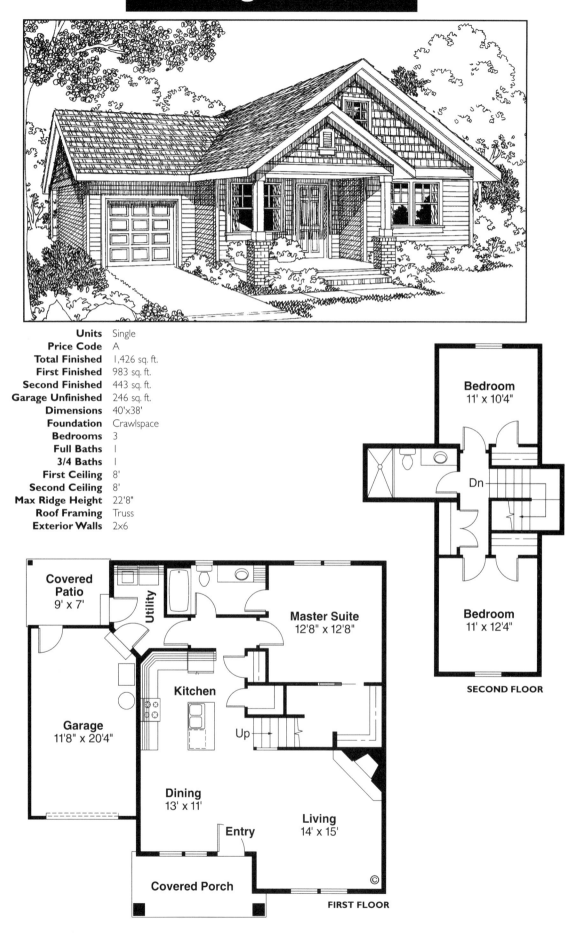

Units	Single
Price Code	A
Total Finished	1,426 sq. ft.
First Finished	983 sq. ft.
Second Finished	443 sq. ft.
Garage Unfinished	246 sq. ft.
Dimensions	40'x38'
Foundation	Crawlspace
Bedrooms	3
Full Baths	1
3/4 Baths	1
First Ceiling	8'
Second Ceiling	8'
Max Ridge Height	22'8"
Roof Framing	Truss
Exterior Walls	2x6

Bedroom
11' x 10'4"

Dn

Bedroom
11' x 12'4"

SECOND FLOOR

Covered Patio
9' x 7'

Utility

Master Suite
12'8" x 12'8"

Kitchen

Garage
11'8" x 20'4"

Up

Dining
13' x 11'

Living
14' x 15'

Entry

Covered Porch

FIRST FLOOR

Design 24711

Units	Single
Price Code	A
Total Finished	1,434 sq. ft.
First Finished	1,018 sq. ft.
Second Finished	416 sq. ft.
Basement Unfinished	1,008 sq. ft.
Garage Unfinished	624 sq. ft.
Porch Unfinished	288 sq. ft.
Dimensions	73'x36'
Foundation	Basement
	Crawlspace
	Slab
Bedrooms	3
Full Baths	2
Max Ridge Height	24'6"
Roof Framing	Stick
Exterior Walls	2x4

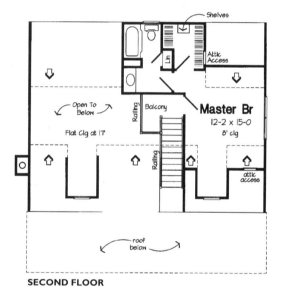

SECOND FLOOR

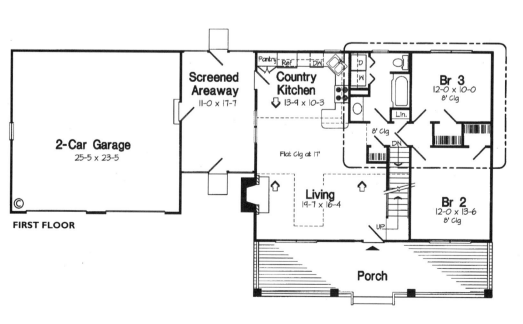

FIRST FLOOR

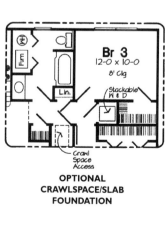

OPTIONAL CRAWLSPACE/SLAB FOUNDATION

Units	Single
Price Code	A
Total Finished	1,438 sq. ft.
Main Finished	1,438 sq. ft.
Garage Unfinished	486 sq. ft.
Deck Unfinished	282 sq. ft.
Porch Unfinished	126 sq. ft.
Dimensions	54'x57'
Foundation	Crawlspace
	Slab
Bedrooms	3
Full Baths	2
Max Ridge Height	19'
Roof Framing	Stick
Exterior Walls	2x4

MAIN FLOOR

Design 65179

Units	Single
Price Code	A
Total Finished	1,450 sq. ft.
First Finished	918 sq. ft.
Second Finished	532 sq. ft.
Basement Finished	918 sq. ft.
Dimensions	26'4"x37'
Foundation	Basement
Bedrooms	3
Full Baths	1
3/4 Baths	1
First Ceiling	8'
Second Ceiling	8'
Max Ridge Height	27'4"
Roof Framing	Truss
Exterior Walls	2x6

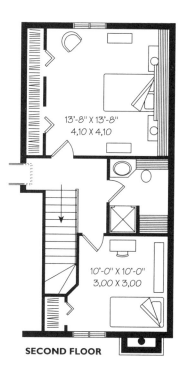

SECOND FLOOR

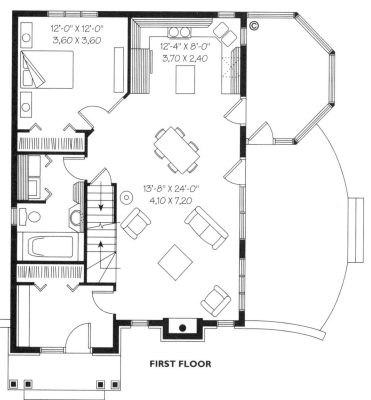

FIRST FLOOR

Design 90412

Units	Single
Price Code	A
Total Finished	1,454 sq. ft.
Main Finished	1,454 sq. ft.
Dimensions	67'x34'10"
Foundation	Basement
	Crawlspace
	Slab
Bedrooms	3
Full Baths	2
Max Ridge Height	16'2"
Roof Framing	Stick
Exterior Walls	2x4

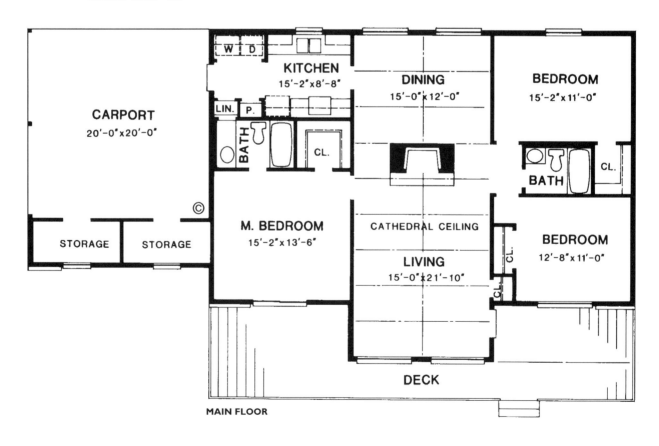

MAIN FLOOR

Design 97137

Units	Single
Price Code	A
Total Finished	1,461 sq. ft.
Main Finished	1,461 sq. ft.
Garage Unfinished	458 sq. ft.
Deck Unfinished	200 sq. ft.
Dimensions	56'x42'
Foundation	Basement
Bedrooms	3
Full Baths	2
Main Ceiling	8'
Max Ridge Height	21'5"
Roof Framing	Truss
Exterior Walls	2x6

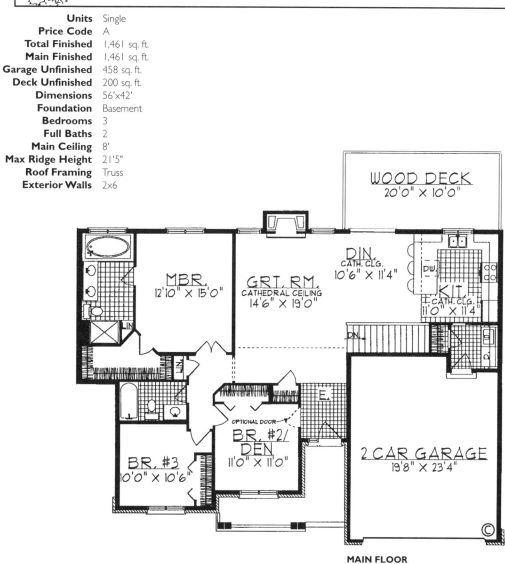

WOOD DECK
20'0" X 10'0"

MBR.
12'10" X 15'0"

GRT. RM.
CATHEDRAL CEILING
14'6" X 19'0"

DIN.
CATH. CLG.
10'6" X 11'4"

KIT.
CATH. CLG.
11'0" X 11'4"

DN.

OPTIONAL DOOR

BR. #2/
DEN
11'0" X 11'0"

BR. #3
10'0" X 10'6"

2 CAR GARAGE
19'8" X 23'4"

MAIN FLOOR

Design 24706

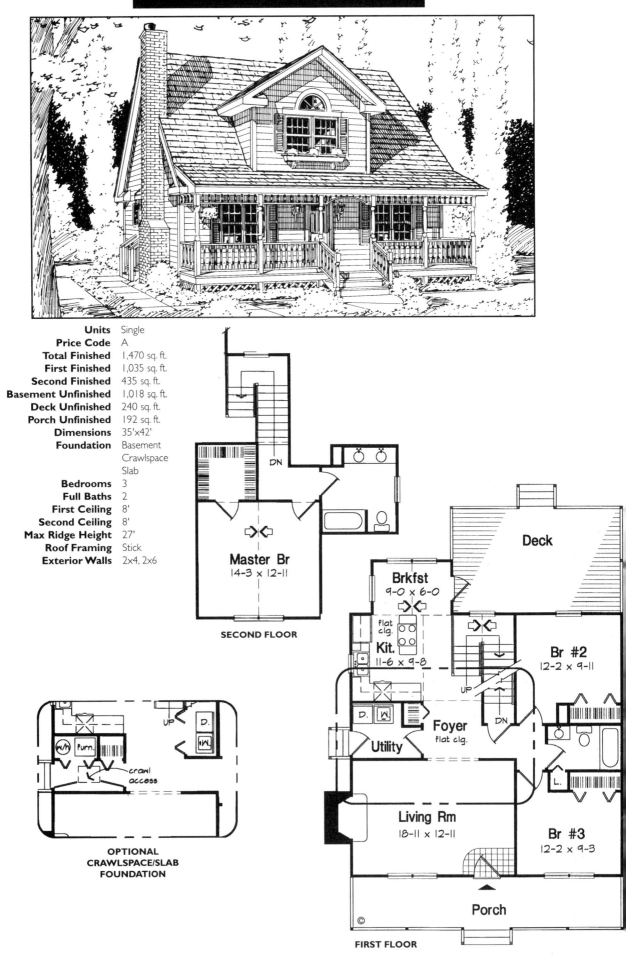

Units	Single
Price Code	A
Total Finished	1,470 sq. ft.
First Finished	1,035 sq. ft.
Second Finished	435 sq. ft.
Basement Unfinished	1,018 sq. ft.
Deck Unfinished	240 sq. ft.
Porch Unfinished	192 sq. ft.
Dimensions	35'x42'
Foundation	Basement
	Crawlspace
	Slab
Bedrooms	3
Full Baths	2
First Ceiling	8'
Second Ceiling	8'
Max Ridge Height	27'
Roof Framing	Stick
Exterior Walls	2x4, 2x6

Master Br
14-3 x 12-11

SECOND FLOOR

**OPTIONAL
CRAWLSPACE/SLAB
FOUNDATION**

crawl access

Deck

Brkfst
9-0 x 6-0

Kit.
11-6 x 9-8

Br #2
12-2 x 9-11

Foyer
flat clg.

Utility

Living Rm
18-11 x 12-11

Br #3
12-2 x 9-3

Porch

FIRST FLOOR

Design 65000

Units	Single
Price Code	A
Total Finished	1,471 sq. ft.
First Finished	895 sq. ft.
Second Finished	576 sq. ft.
Basement Unfinished	895 sq. ft.
Dimensions	26'x36'
Foundation	Basement
Bedrooms	3
Full Baths	2
First Ceiling	8'2"
Second Ceiling	8'2"
Max Ridge Height	23'8"
Roof Framing	Truss
Exterior Walls	2x6

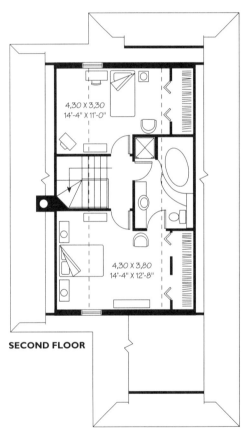

SECOND FLOOR

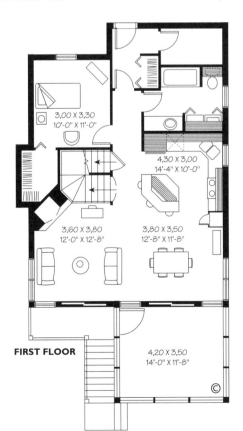

FIRST FLOOR

Units	Single
Price Code	A
Total Finished	1,472 sq. ft.
Main Finished	1,472 sq. ft.
Basement Unfinished	1,472 sq. ft.
Garage Unfinished	424 sq. ft.
Dimensions	48'x56'4"
Foundation	Basement
Bedrooms	3
Full Baths	2
Max Ridge Height	19'8"
Roof Framing	Stick
Exterior Walls	2x6

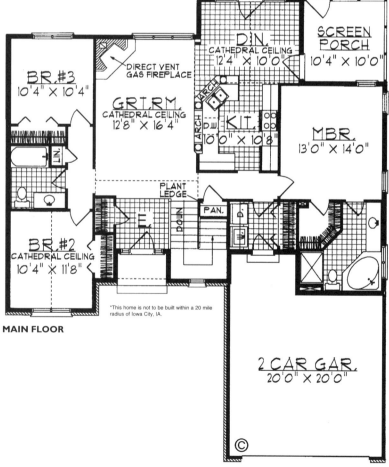

MAIN FLOOR

*This home is not to be built within a 20 mile radius of Iowa City, IA.

Units	Single
Price Code	A
Total Finished	1,475 sq. ft.
Main Finished	1,475 sq. ft.
Garage Unfinished	455 sq. ft.
Porch Unfinished	234 sq. ft.
Dimensions	43'x43'
Foundation	Crawlspace
	Slab
Bedrooms	3
Full Baths	2
Max Ridge Height	24'
Roof Framing	Stick
Exterior Walls	2x4

MASTER BATH OPTION

Garage
20x21

Deck

Walk

Dining
10X11

Bath

Master
16X13

VAULTED CEILING

W
D

Kitchen
14X10

Bath

Br 3
10X11

Family Room
21X15

10' CEILING

Br 2
12-6X11

Porch

MAIN FLOOR

Units	Single
Price Code	A
Total Finished	1,476 sq. ft.
Main Finished	1,476 sq. ft.
Garage Unfinished	528 sq. ft.
Dimensions	69'6"x33'
Foundation	Crawlspace
	Slab
Bedrooms	3
Full Baths	2
Main Ceiling	9'
Roof Framing	Stick
Exterior Walls	2x4

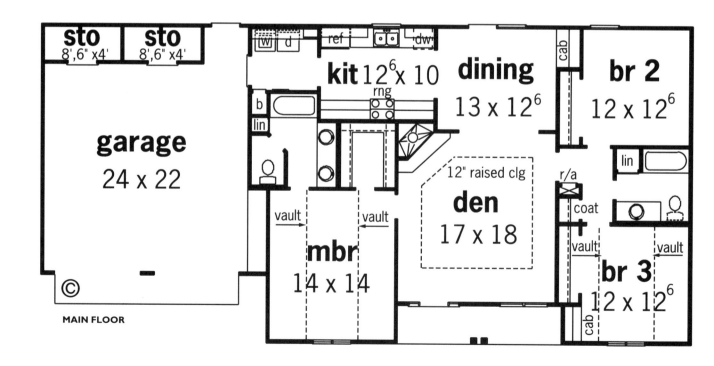

MAIN FLOOR

Design 65001

Units	Single
Price Code	A
Total Finished	1,480 sq. ft.
First Finished	1,024 sq. ft.
Second Finished	456 sq. ft.
Basement Unfinished	1,024 sq. ft.
Dimensions	32'x40'
Foundation	Basement
Bedrooms	2
Full Baths	2
First Ceiling	8'
Second Ceiling	8'
Max Ridge Height	23'8"
Roof Framing	Truss
Exterior Walls	2x6

SECOND FLOOR

2,70 X 3,60
9'-0" X 12'-0"

3,00 X 3,90
10'-0" X 13'-0"

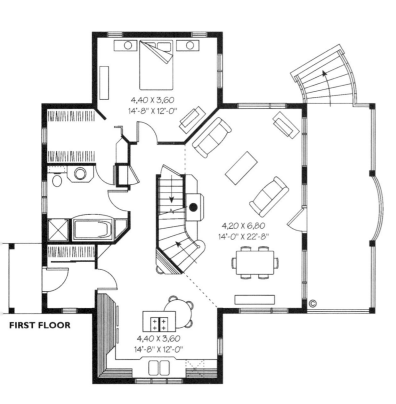

FIRST FLOOR

4,40 3,60
14'-8" X 12'-0"

4,20 X 6,80
14'-0" X 22'-8"

4,40 X 3,60
14'-8" X 12'-0"

Units	Single
Price Code	G
Total Finished	1,485 sq. ft.
First Finished	924 sq. ft.
Second Finished	561 sq. ft.
Porch Unfinished	504 sq. ft.
Dimensions	42'x34'
Foundation	Basement
	Crawlspace
	Slab
Bedrooms	3
Full Baths	2
First Ceiling	8'
Second Ceiling	8'
Max Ridge Height	30'
Exterior Walls	2x6

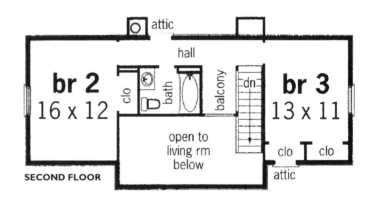

SECOND FLOOR

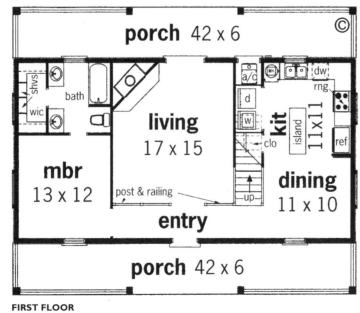

FIRST FLOOR

Design 61033

Units Single
Price Code A
Total Finished 1,485 sq. ft.
Main Finished 1,485 sq. ft.
Dimensions 51'6"x49'10"
Foundation Crawlspace
Slab
Bedrooms 3
Full Baths 2

MAIN FLOOR

Units	Single
Price Code	A
Total Finished	1,485 sq. ft.
Main Finished	1,485 sq. ft.
Garage Unfinished	415 sq. ft.
Porch Unfinished	180 sq. ft.
Dimensions	51'6"x49'10"
Foundation	Crawlspace
	Slab
Bedrooms	3
Full Baths	2
Main Ceiling	9'
Roof Framing	Stick
Exterior Walls	2x4

MAIN FLOOR

Design 91797

1,001-1,500 sq.ft. HOME PLANS

Units	Single
Price Code	A
Total Finished	1,485 sq. ft.
Main Finished	1,485 sq. ft.
Garage Unfinished	701 sq. ft.
Dimensions	51'6"x63'
Foundation	Crawlspace
Bedrooms	3
Full Baths	2
Max Ridge Height	22'
Roof Framing	Stick/Truss
Exterior Walls	2x6

DECK

FAMILY ROOM
14⁶ x 18⁶

MASTER SUITE
13² x 14¹⁰

BEDROOM 2
11⁴ x 10²

WALK-IN CLOSET

SPA

EATING BAR
R & O

PANTRY

ENTRY

DN

LIVING ROOM
13⁶ x 11⁶

BEDROOM 3
12⁶ x 10²

SINK UTILITY
WSH DRY

KITCHEN

REF.

FAU WH

SHOP / STORAGE
14² x 10⁰

DN

NOOK
9⁰ x 9⁶

DN

PORCH

MAIN FLOOR

GARAGE
23¹⁰ x 21⁸

©

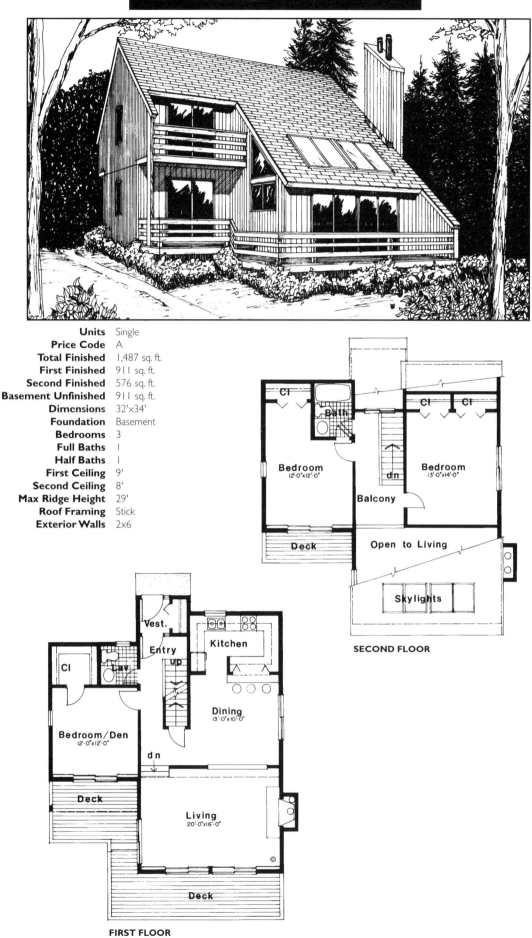

Units	Single
Price Code	A
Total Finished	1,487 sq. ft.
First Finished	911 sq. ft.
Second Finished	576 sq. ft.
Basement Unfinished	911 sq. ft.
Dimensions	32'x34'
Foundation	Basement
Bedrooms	3
Full Baths	1
Half Baths	1
First Ceiling	9'
Second Ceiling	8'
Max Ridge Height	29'
Roof Framing	Stick
Exterior Walls	2x6

SECOND FLOOR

FIRST FLOOR

Design 64181

Units	Single
Price Code	F
Total Finished	1,487 sq. ft.
Main Finished	1,487 sq. ft.
Garage Unfinished	567 sq. ft.
Porch Unfinished	104 sq. ft.
Dimensions	52'x65'6"
Foundation	Crawlspace
Bedrooms	3
Full Baths	2
Max Ridge Height	22'2"
Roof Framing	Stick/Truss
Exterior Walls	2x6

* Alternate foundation options available at an additional charge.
Please call 1-800-235-5700 for more information.

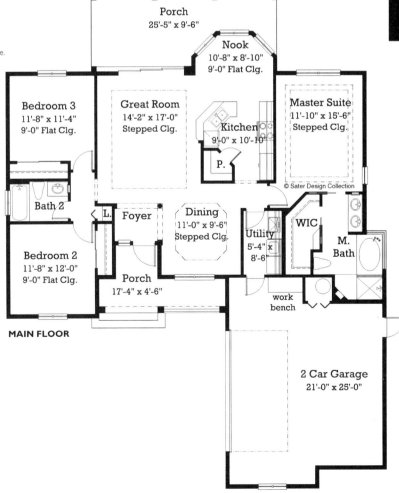

MAIN FLOOR

Porch
25'-5" x 9'-6"

Nook
10'-8" x 8'-10"
9'-0" Flat Clg.

Bedroom 3
11'-8" x 11'-4"
9'-0" Flat Clg.

Great Room
14'-2" x 17'-0"
Stepped Clg.

Kitchen
9'-0" x 10'-10"

Master Suite
11'-10" x 15'-6"
Stepped Clg.

P.

Bath 2

© Sater Design Collection

L.

Foyer

Dining
11'-0" x 9'-6"
Stepped Clg.

Utility
5'-4" x 8'-6"

WIC

M. Bath

Bedroom 2
11'-8" x 12'-0"
9'-0" Flat Clg.

Porch
17'-4" x 4'-6"

work bench

2 Car Garage
21'-0" x 25'-0"

PHOTOGRAPHY: JOHN EHRENCLOU

Units	Single
Price Code	A
Total Finished	1,492 sq. ft.
Main Finished	1,492 sq. ft.
Basement Unfinished	1,486 sq. ft.
Garage Unfinished	462 sq. ft.
Dimensions	56'x48'
Foundation	Basement
	Crawlspace
	Slab
Bedrooms	3
Full Baths	2
Main Ceiling	8'
Vaulted Ceiling	13'
Max Ridge Height	19'
Roof Framing	Stick
Exterior Walls	2x4, 2x6

Please note: The photographed home may have been modified to suit homeowner preferences. If you order plans, have a builder or design professional check them against the photograph to confirm actual construction details.

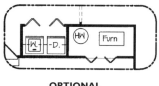

**OPTIONAL
CRAWLSPACE/SLAB
FOUNDATION**

MAIN FLOOR

Design 99106

Units	Single
Price Code	A
Total Finished	1,495 sq. ft.
Main Finished	1,495 sq. ft.
Basement Unfinished	1,495 sq. ft.
Dimensions	48'x58'8"
Foundation	Basement
Bedrooms	3
Full Baths	2
Max Ridge Height	20'6"
Roof Framing	Truss
Exterior Walls	2x4

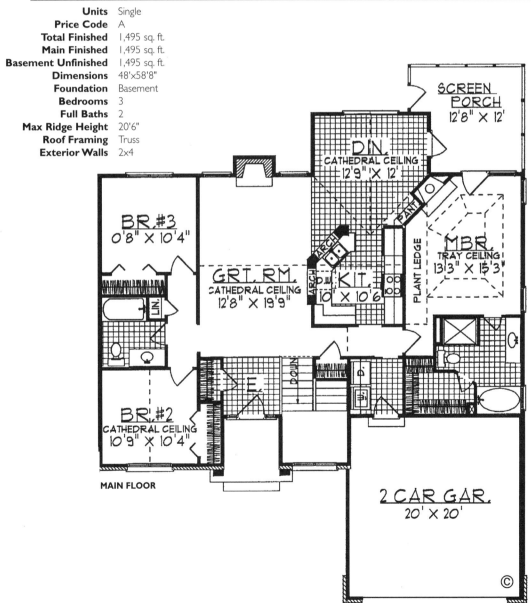

SCREEN PORCH
12'8" X 12'

DIN.
CATHEDRAL CEILING
12'9" X 12'

BR #3
0'8" X 10'4"

MBR
TRAY CEILING
13'3" X 15'3"

GRT. RM.
CATHEDRAL CEILING
12'8" X 19'9"

KIT.
10' X 10'6"

BR. #2
CATHEDRAL CEILING
10'9" X 10'4"

MAIN FLOOR

2 CAR GAR.
20' X 20'

Units	Single
Price Code	A
Total Finished	1,500 sq. ft.
Main Finished	1,500 sq. ft.
Garage Unfinished	417 sq. ft.
Porch Unfinished	57 sq. ft.
Dimensions	48'6"x48'4"
Foundation	Crawlspace
	Slab
Bedrooms	3
Full Baths	2
Main Ceiling	8'
Roof Framing	Stick
Exterior Walls	2x4

MAIN FLOOR

Design 98441

Units	Single
Price Code	B
Total Finished	1,502 sq. ft.
Main Finished	1,502 sq. ft.
Basement Unfinished	1,555 sq. ft.
Garage Unfinished	448 sq. ft.
Dimensions	51'x50'6"
Foundation	Basement Crawlspace
Bedrooms	3
Full Baths	2
Max Ridge Height	24'9"
Roof Framing	Stick
Exterior Walls	2x4

CAD FILES AVAILABLE For more information call 800-235-5700

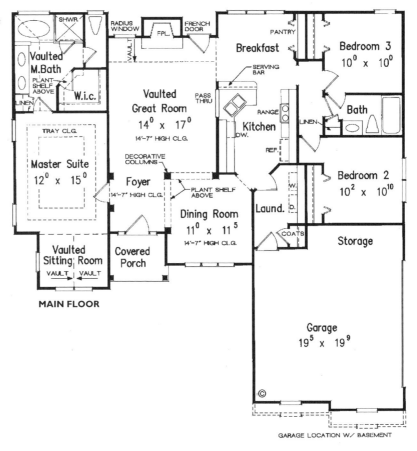

MAIN FLOOR

GARAGE LOCATION W/ BASEMENT

Visit us at www.merillat.com

Merillat®

Units	Single
Price Code	B
Total Finished	1,505 sq. ft.
First Finished	692 sq. ft.
Second Finished	813 sq. ft.
Basement Unfinished	699 sq. ft.
Garage Unfinished	484 sq. ft.
Dimensions	42'x34'4"
Foundation	Basement
	Crawlspace
	Slab
Bedrooms	4
Full Baths	1
3/4 Baths	1
Half Baths	1
First Ceiling	8'
Second Ceiling	8'
Max Ridge Height	26'
Roof Framing	Stick
Exterior Walls	2x6

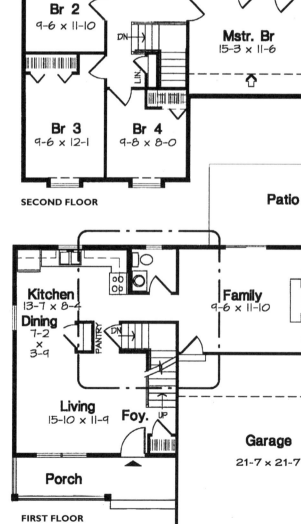

SECOND FLOOR

Br 2
9-6 x 11-10

Mstr. Br
15-3 x 11-6

Br 3
9-6 x 12-1

Br 4
9-8 x 8-0

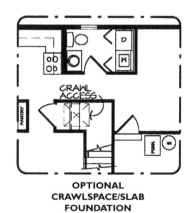

**OPTIONAL
CRAWLSPACE/SLAB
FOUNDATION**

FIRST FLOOR

Kitchen
13-7 x 8-4

Dining
7-2 x 3-9

Family
9-6 x 11-10

Patio

Living
15-10 x 11-9

Foy.

Porch

Garage
21-7 x 21-7

Design 92649

Units	Single
Price Code	B
Total Finished	1,508 sq. ft.
Main Finished	1,508 sq. ft.
Basement Unfinished	1,439 sq. ft.
Garage Unfinished	440 sq. ft.
Dimensions	60'x47'
Foundation	Basement
Bedrooms	3
Full Baths	2
Main Ceiling	8'
Max Ridge Height	21'9"
Roof Framing	Truss
Exterior Walls	2x4

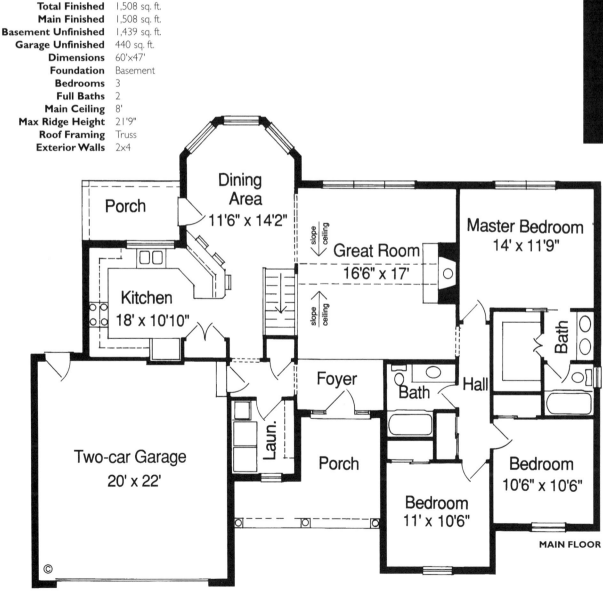

Porch

Dining Area
11'6" x 14'2"

Kitchen
18' x 10'10"

slope ceiling

Great Room
16'6" x 17'

slope ceiling

Master Bedroom
14' x 11'9"

Bath

Foyer

Bath

Hall

Laun.

Two-car Garage
20' x 22'

Porch

Bedroom
11' x 10'6"

Bedroom
10'6" x 10'6"

MAIN FLOOR

Units	Single
Price Code	B
Total Finished	1,510 sq. ft.
Main Finished	1,510 sq. ft.
Porch Unfinished	132 sq. ft.
Dimensions	38'x58'6"
Foundation	Slab
Bedrooms	3
Full Baths	2
Main Ceiling	9'
Max Ridge Height	21'4"
Roof Framing	Stick
Exterior Walls	2x4

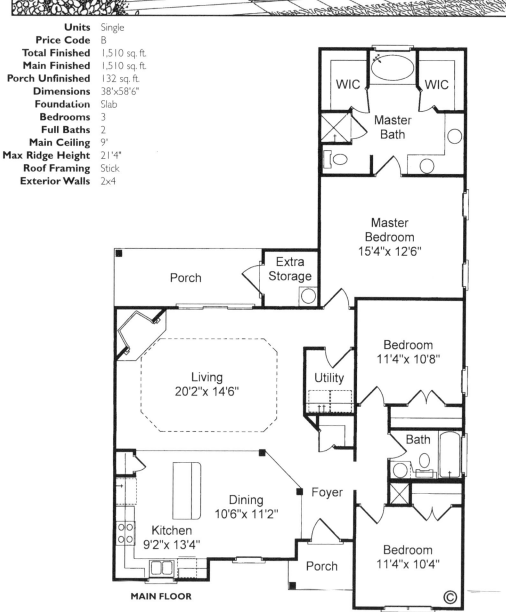

MAIN FLOOR

Design 65198

Units	Single
Price Code	B
Total Finished	1,519 sq. ft.
First Finished	788 sq. ft.
Second Finished	731 sq. ft.
Garage Unfinished	266 sq. ft.
Foundation	Basement
Bedrooms	3
Full Baths	1
3/4 Baths	1

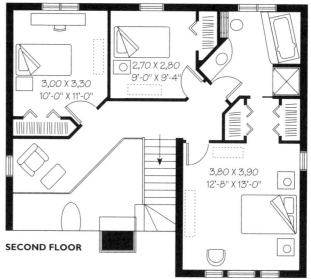

3,00 X 3,30
10'-0" X 11'-0"

2,70 X 2,80
9'-0" X 9'-4"

3,80 X 3,90
12'-8" X 13'-0"

SECOND FLOOR

3,30 X 3,90
11'-0" X 13'-0"

3,1 X 2,70
10'-4" X 9'-0"

2,70 X 2,00
9'-0" X 6'-8"

4,20 X 5,10
14'-0" X 17'-0"

3,80 X 6,20
12'-8" X 20'-8"

FIRST FLOOR

Visit us at www.merillat.com

Merillat.

Design 34055

Units	Single
Price Code	B
Total Finished	1,527 sq. ft.
Main Finished	1,527 sq. ft.
Basement Unfinished	1,344 sq. ft.
Garage Unfinished	425 sq. ft.
Dimensions	70'x28'
Foundation	Basement
	Crawlspace
	Slab
Bedrooms	4
Full Baths	2
Max Ridge Height	18'
Roof Framing	Stick
Exterior Walls	2x4, 2x6

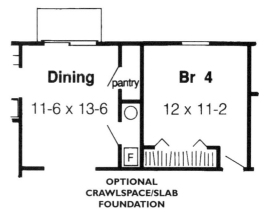

OPTIONAL CRAWLSPACE/SLAB FOUNDATION

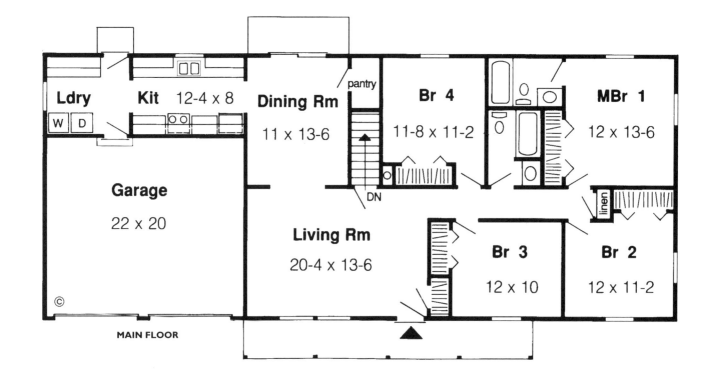

MAIN FLOOR

Design 62036

Units	Single
Price Code	B
Total Finished	1,538 sq. ft.
Main Finished	1,538 sq. ft.
Dimensions	50'x56'
Foundation	Basement
	Crawlspace
	Slab
Bedrooms	3
Full Baths	2

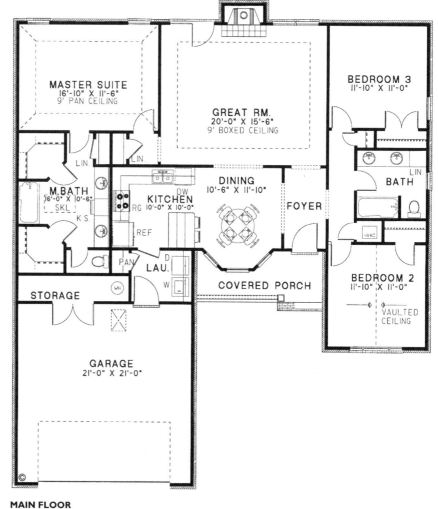

MAIN FLOOR

Units	Single
Price Code	B
Total Finished	1,539 sq. ft.
Main Finished	1,539 sq. ft.
Basement Unfinished	1,530 sq. ft.
Garage Unfinished	460 sq. ft.
Deck Unfinished	160 sq. ft.
Porch Unfinished	182 sq. ft.
Dimensions	50'x45'4"
Foundation	Basement
	Crawlspace
	Slab
Bedrooms	3
Full Baths	2
Main Ceiling	8'
Max Ridge Height	21'
Roof Framing	Stick
Exterior Walls	2x6

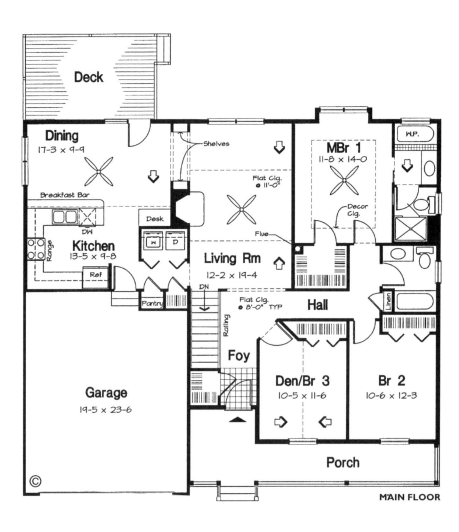

MAIN FLOOR

Design 93161

Units	Single
Price Code	B
Total Finished	1,540 sq. ft.
Main Finished	1,540 sq. ft.
Basement Unfinished	1,540 sq. ft.
Dimensions	60'4"x46'
Foundation	Basement
Bedrooms	3
Full Baths	2
Main Ceiling	8'
Vaulted Ceiling	12'6"
Max Ridge Height	21'4"
Roof Framing	Stick
Exterior Walls	2x6

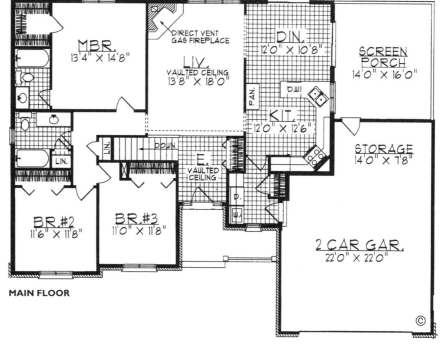

MAIN FLOOR

Visit us at www.merillat.com

Units	Single
Price Code	B
Total Finished	1,544 sq. ft.
First Finished	984 sq. ft.
Second Finished	560 sq. ft.
Deck Unfinished	468 sq. ft.
Dimensions	34'x28'
Foundation	Basement
Bedrooms	3
Full Baths	1
3/4 Baths	1
First Ceiling	8'
Second Ceiling	8'
Max Ridge Height	25'2"
Roof Framing	Truss
Exterior Walls	2x6

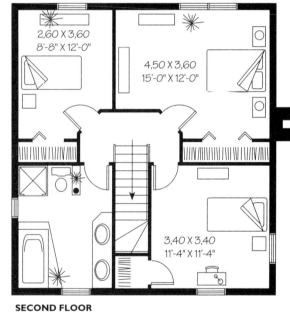

SECOND FLOOR

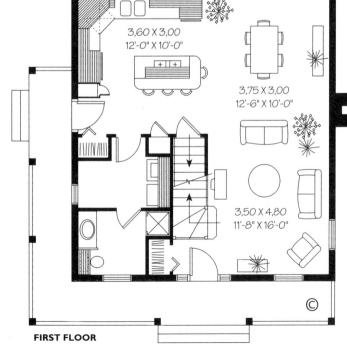

FIRST FLOOR

Units	Single
Price Code	B
Total Finished	1,544 sq. ft.
Main Finished	1,544 sq. ft.
Bonus Unfinished	284 sq. ft.
Basement Unfinished	1,544 sq. ft.
Garage Unfinished	440 sq. ft.
Dimensions	54'x47'6"
Foundation	Basement
	Crawlspace
Bedrooms	3
Full Baths	2
Main Ceiling	9'2"
Second Ceiling	8'2"
Max Ridge Height	26'6"
Roof Framing	Stick
Exterior Walls	2x4

CAD FILES AVAILABLE
For more information call
800-235-5700

OPTIONAL BASEMENT STAIR LOCATION

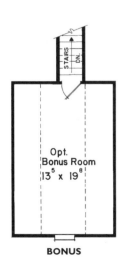

BONUS

Opt. Bonus Room 13⁵ x 19⁸

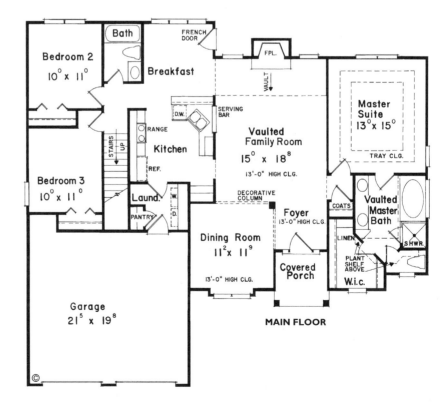

MAIN FLOOR

Units	Single
Price Code	B
Total Finished	1,546 sq. ft.
Main Finished	1,546 sq. ft.
Basement Unfinished	1,530 sq. ft.
Garage Unfinished	440 sq. ft.
Dimensions	60'x13'
Foundation	Basement
Bedrooms	3
Full Baths	1
3/4 Baths	1
Main Ceiling	9'2"
Max Ridge Height	23'
Roof Framing	Truss
Exterior Walls	2x4

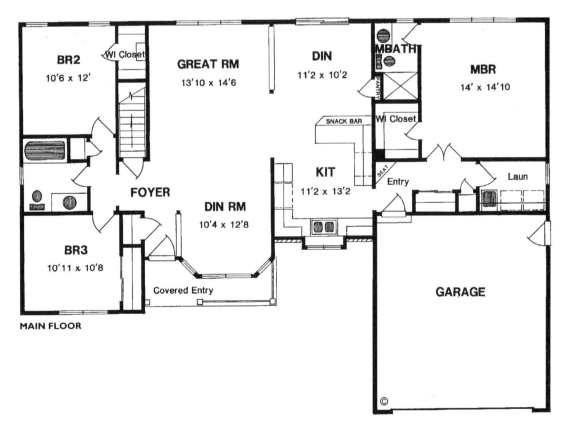

MAIN FLOOR

Design 93455

Units	Single
Price Code	B
Total Finished	1,550 sq. ft.
Main Finished	1,550 sq. ft.
Garage Unfinished	548 sq. ft.
Dimensions	68'3"x73'8"
Foundation	Crawlspace
	Slab
Bedrooms	3
Full Baths	2
Max Ridge Height	19'9"
Roof Framing	Stick
Exterior Walls	2x4

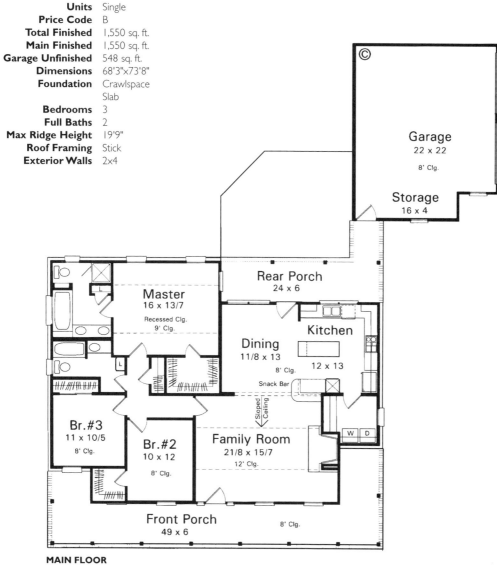

MAIN FLOOR

Design 24654

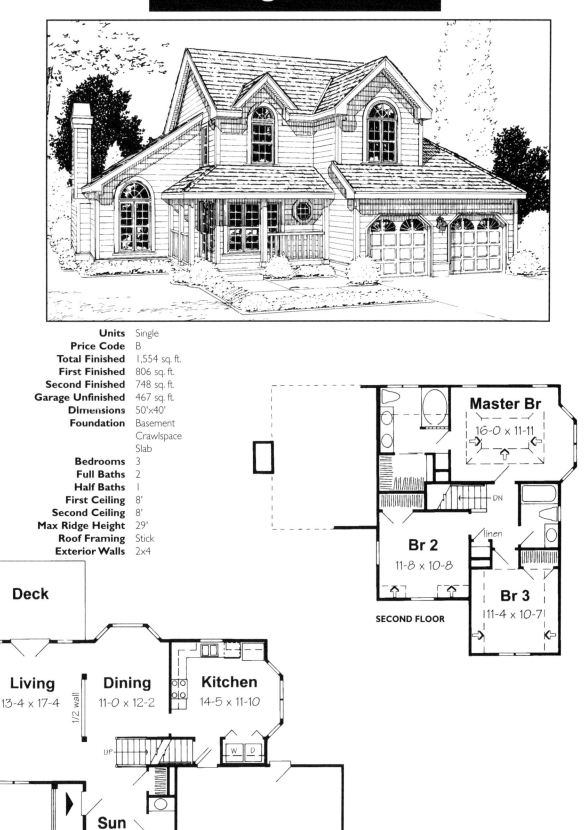

Units	Single
Price Code	B
Total Finished	1,554 sq. ft.
First Finished	806 sq. ft.
Second Finished	748 sq. ft.
Garage Unfinished	467 sq. ft.
Dimensions	50'x40'
Foundation	Basement
	Crawlspace
	Slab
Bedrooms	3
Full Baths	2
Half Baths	1
First Ceiling	8'
Second Ceiling	8'
Max Ridge Height	29'
Roof Framing	Stick
Exterior Walls	2x4

Master Br
16-0 x 11-11

Br 2
11-8 x 10-8

Br 3
11-4 x 10-7

linen

DN

SECOND FLOOR

Deck

Living
13-4 x 17-4

1/2 wall

Dining
11-0 x 12-2

Kitchen
14-5 x 11-10

UP

W | D

Sun Rm

Garage
21-4 x 21-8

FIRST FLOOR

Design 99152

Units	Single
Price Code	B
Total Finished	1,557 sq. ft.
Main Finished	1,557 sq. ft.
Basement Unfinished	1,557 sq. ft.
Garage Unfinished	440 sq. ft.
Dimensions	53'x49'
Foundation	Basement
Bedrooms	3
Full Baths	2
Max Ridge Height	21'
Roof Framing	Truss
Exterior Walls	2x4

DIN.
13'0" X 10'0"

GREAT RM.
CATHEDRAL CEILING
14'8" X 21'0"

MBR.
TRAY CEILING
15'4" X 15'0"

KIT.
12'8" X 10'10"

BR. #3
11'10" X 10'0"

BR. #2
12'0" X 10'4"

2 CAR GAR.
21'4" X 20'8"

MAIN FLOOR

Units	Single
Price Code	B
Total Finished	1,557 sq. ft.
Main Finished	1,557 sq. ft.
Garage Unfinished	434 sq. ft.
Porch Unfinished	137 sq. ft.
Dimensions	50'x50'
Foundation	Basement
	Crawlspace
	Slab
Bedrooms	3
Full Baths	2
Main Ceiling	9'
Max Ridge Height	24'
Roof Framing	Truss
Exterior Walls	2x6

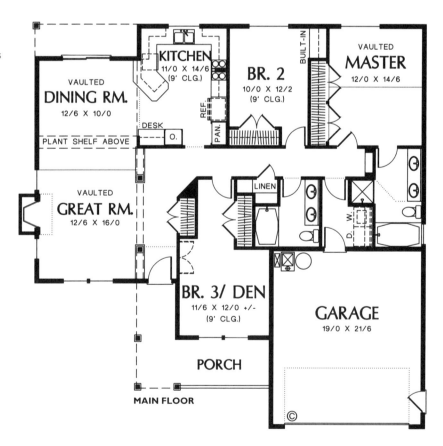

MAIN FLOOR

Units	Single
Price Code	B
Total Finished	1,559 sq. ft.
First Finished	945 sq. ft.
Second Finished	614 sq. ft.
Dimensions	34'x31'
Foundation	Basement
Bedrooms	3
Full Baths	I
3/4 Baths	I

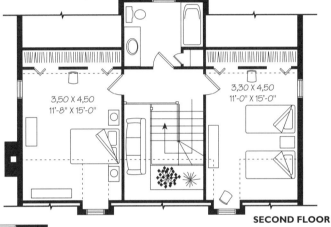

3,50 X 4,50
11'-8" X 15'-0"

3,30 X 4,50
11'-0" X 15'-0"

SECOND FLOOR

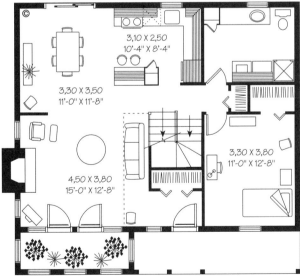

3,10 X 2,50
10'-4" X 8'-4"

3,30 X 3,50
11'-0" X 11'-8"

3,30 X 3,80
11'-0" X 12'-8"

4,50 X 3,80
15'-0" X 12'-8"

FIRST FLOOR

Merillat.

Visit us at www.merillat.com

Units	Single
Price Code	B
Total Finished	1,560 sq. ft.
First Finished	1,061 sq. ft.
Second Finished	499 sq. ft.
Basement Unfinished	1,061 sq. ft.
Porch Unfinished	339 sq. ft.
Dimensions	44'x34'
Foundation	Basement
	Crawlspace
	Slab
Bedrooms	3
Full Baths	2
Half Baths	1
First Ceiling	8'
Second Ceiling	8'
Max Ridge Height	26'
Roof Framing	Stick
Exterior Walls	2x4, 2x6

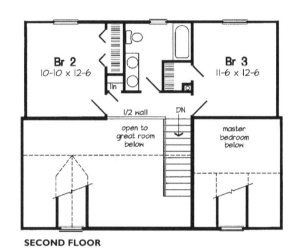

SECOND FLOOR

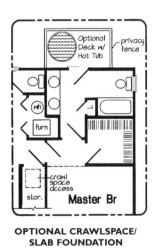

**OPTIONAL CRAWLSPACE/
SLAB FOUNDATION**

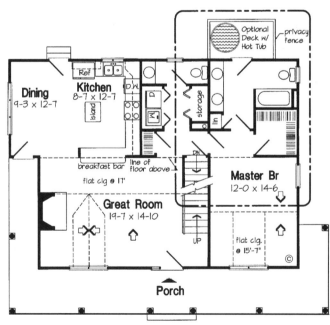

FIRST FLOOR

Design 24705

Units	Single
Price Code	B
Total Finished	1,562 sq. ft.
First Finished	1,062 sq. ft.
Second Finished	500 sq. ft.
Lower Unfinished	678 sq. ft.
Basement Unfinished	384 sq. ft.
Deck Unfinished	298 sq. ft.
Porch Unfinished	19 sq. ft.
Dimensions	45'5"x27'
Foundation	Basement
Bedrooms	3
Full Baths	2
First Ceiling	8'
Second Ceiling	8'
Max Ridge Height	32'
Roof Framing	Stick
Exterior Walls	2x4

SECOND FLOOR

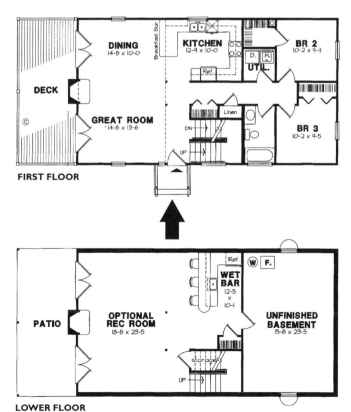

FIRST FLOOR

LOWER FLOOR

Units	Single
Price Code	B
Total Finished	1,567 sq. ft.
Main Finished	1,567 sq. ft.
Bonus Unfinished	462 sq. ft.
Basement Unfinished	1,567 sq. ft.
Garage Unfinished	504 sq. ft.
Porch Unfinished	152 sq. ft.
Dimensions	67'6"x46'8"
Foundation	Basement
	Slab
Bedrooms	3
Full Baths	2
Main Ceiling	9'
Max Ridge Height	25'
Roof Framing	Stick
Exterior Walls	2x6

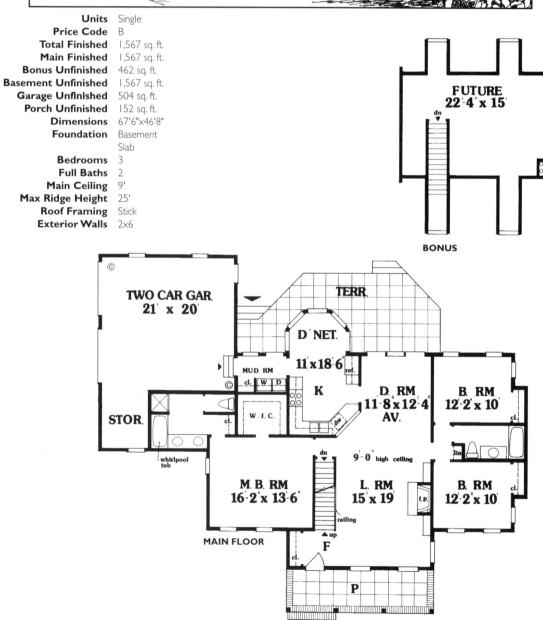

Design 66044

Units	Single
Price Code	B
Total Finished	1,573 sq. ft.
Main Finished	1,573 sq. ft.
Dimensions	48'x51'
Foundation	Slab
Bedrooms	3
Full Baths	2
Main Ceiling	8'-10'
Max Ridge Height	24'
Roof Framing	Stick
Exterior Walls	2x4

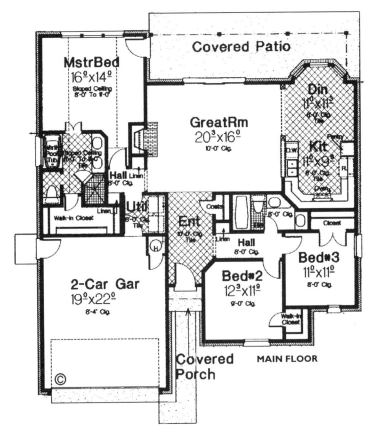

Units	Single
Price Code	B
Total Finished	1,575 sq. ft.
Main Finished	1,575 sq. ft.
Basement Unfinished	1,575 sq. ft.
Garage Unfinished	475 sq. ft.
Dimensions	60'x40'4"
Foundation	Basement
	Crawlspace
	Slab
Bedrooms	3
Full Baths	2
Main Ceiling	8'-10'
Max Ridge Height	19'6"
Roof Framing	Stick
Exterior Walls	2x4, 2x6

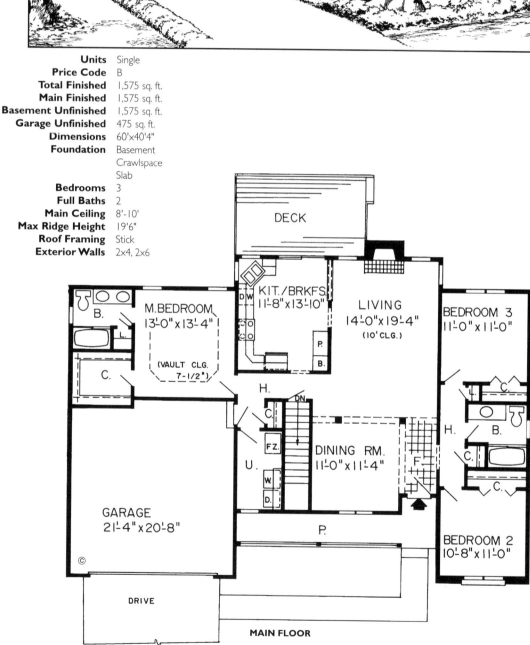

Design 24708

1,501-2,000 sq.ft. HOME PLANS

Units	Single
Price Code	B
Total Finished	1,576 sq. ft.
Main Finished	1,576 sq. ft.
Basement Unfinished	1,454 sq. ft.
Garage Unfinished	576 sq. ft.
Porch Unfinished	391 sq. ft.
Dimensions	93'x36'
Foundation	Basement
	Crawlspace
	Slab
Bedrooms	3
Full Baths	2
Main Ceiling	8'
Max Ridge Height	19'
Roof Framing	Stick
Exterior Walls	2x4

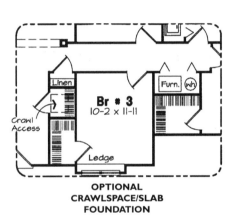

**OPTIONAL
CRAWLSPACE/SLAB
FOUNDATION**

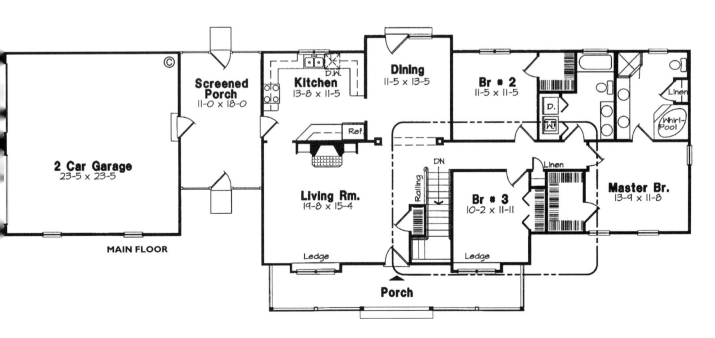

MAIN FLOOR

PHOTOGRAPHY: JOHN EHRENCLOU

Units	Single
Price Code	B
Total Finished	1,583 sq. ft.
Main Finished	1,583 sq. ft.
Basement Unfinished	1,573 sq. ft.
Garage Unfinished	484 sq. ft.
Dimensions	70'x46'
Foundation	Basement
	Crawlspace
	Slab
Bedrooms	3
Full Baths	2
Main Ceiling	8'
Max Ridge Height	20'
Roof Framing	Stick
Exterior Walls	2x4, 2x6

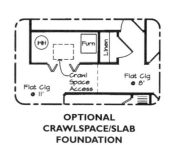

**OPTIONAL
CRAWLSPACE/SLAB
FOUNDATION**

Please note: The photographed home may have been modified to suit homeowner preferences. If you order plans, have a builder or design professional check them against the photograph to confirm actual construction details.

Deck
(Optional)

Living Rm
15-8 x 17-2
Approx.

Dining
12-0 x 11-5
Approx.

MBr 1
14-1 x 15-7

Opt. Decor Ceiling

Plant Shelf

Skylt

Shelves

W. D.

Ldry

DN

Linen

Flat Clg
● 11'

Flat Clg
● 8'

Range
Pantry
Ref

Kitchen
13-5 x 9-8

Foy

Den/Br 3
10-5 x 11-11

Br 2
10-5 x 11-11

Garage
21-8 x 21-5

DW

Brkfst
10-5 x 9-0

MAIN FLOOR

Design 91840

Units	Single
Price Code	B
Total Finished	1,588 sq. ft.
Main Finished	1,588 sq. ft.
Basement Unfinished	1,576 sq. ft.
Garage Unfinished	528 sq. ft.
Porch Unfinished	80 sq. ft.
Dimensions	66'x50'
Foundation	Basement
Bedrooms	3
Full Baths	2
Main Ceiling	8'
Max Ridge Height	20'
Roof Framing	Truss
Exterior Walls	2x6

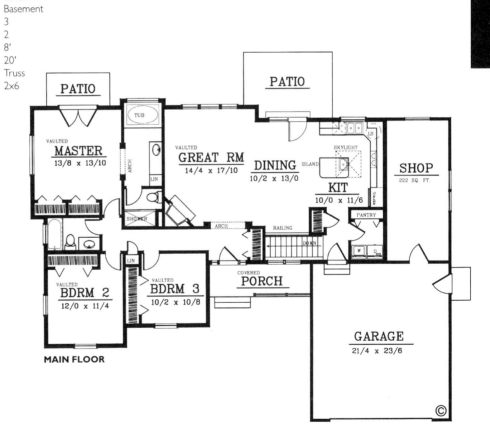

MAIN FLOOR

Merillat®

Visit us at www.merillat.com

Units	Single
Price Code	B
Total Finished	1,593 sq. ft.
Main Finished	1,593 sq. ft.
Basement Unfinished	1,664 sq. ft.
Dimensions	50'x55'
Foundation	Basement
	Crawlspace
	Slab
Bedrooms	3
Full Baths	2
Max Ridge Height	20'6"
Roof Framing	Stick
Exterior Walls	2x4

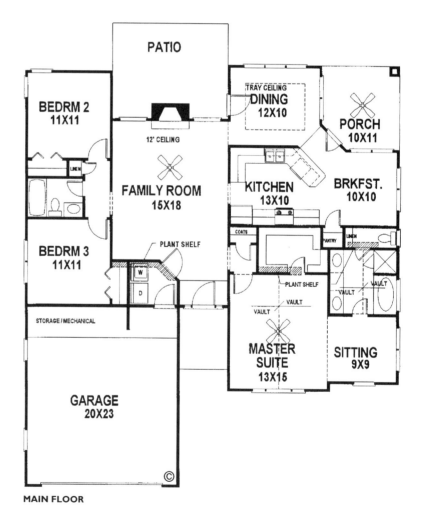

MAIN FLOOR

Design 96542

Units	Single
Price Code	B
Total Finished	1,594 sq. ft.
Main Finished	1,594 sq. ft.
Garage Unfinished	525 sq. ft.
Porch Unfinished	284 sq. ft.
Dimensions	79'x45'
Foundation	Crawlspace
	Slab
Bedrooms	3
Full Baths	2
Main Ceiling	9'
Max Ridge Height	26'6"
Roof Framing	Stick
Exterior Walls	2x4

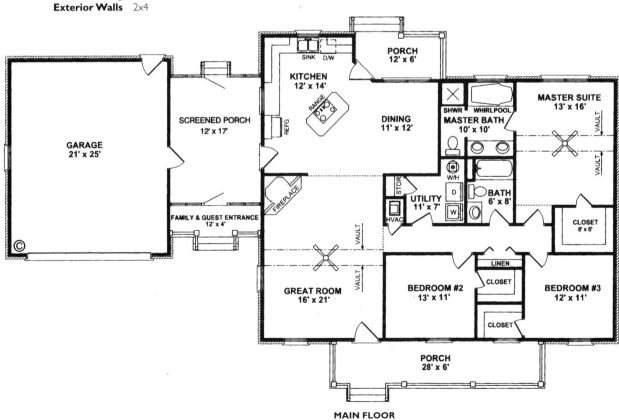

MAIN FLOOR

Design 97762

Units	Single
Price Code	B
Total Finished	1,594 sq. ft.
Main Finished	1,594 sq. ft.
Basement Unfinished	1,594 sq. ft.
Garage Unfinished	512 sq. ft.
Deck Unfinished	328 sq. ft.
Porch Unfinished	125 sq. ft.
Dimensions	52'8"x55'5"
Foundation	Basement
Bedrooms	3
Full Baths	2
Main Ceiling	8'
Vaulted Ceiling	10'
Max Ridge Height	23'6"
Roof Framing	Truss
Exterior Walls	2×4

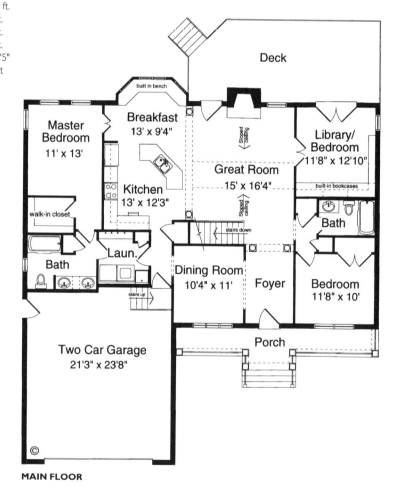

MAIN FLOOR

To order blueprints, call **800-235-5700** or visit us on the web, **familyhomeplans.com**

Design 94827

Units	Single
Price Code	B
Total Finished	1,595 sq. ft.
Main Finished	1,595 sq. ft.
Basement Unfinished	1,595 sq. ft.
Garage Unfinished	491 sq. ft.
Dimensions	63'x50'6"
Foundation	Basement
	Crawlspace
	Slab
Bedrooms	3
Full Baths	2
Max Ridge Height	22'
Roof Framing	Stick
Exterior Walls	2x4

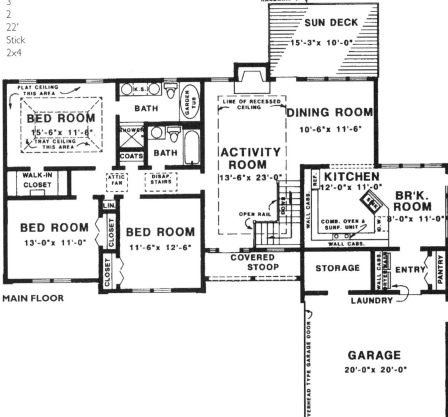

MAIN FLOOR

Design 98560

Units	Single
Price Code	B
Total Finished	1,596 sq. ft.
First Finished	1,192 sq. ft.
Second Finished	404 sq. ft.
Garage Unfinished	410 sq. ft.
Dimensions	50'x39'11"
Foundation	Basement
	Crawlspace
	Slab
Bedrooms	3
Full Baths	2
Half Baths	1
Max Ridge Height	23'6"
Roof Framing	Stick
Exterior Walls	2x6

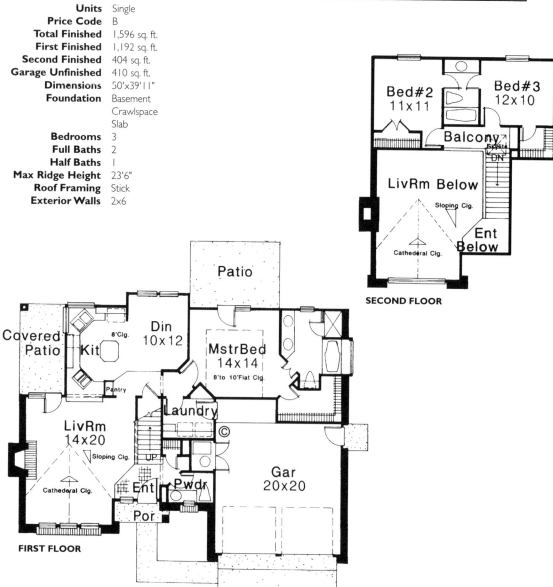

SECOND FLOOR

Bed#2 11x11
Bed#3 12x10
Balcony
LivRm Below
Sloping Clg.
Ent Below
Cathederal Clg.

FIRST FLOOR

Covered Patio
Kit
Din 10x12
Patio
MstrBed 14x14
8'to 10'Flat Clg.
Pantry
Laundry
LivRm 14x20
Sloping Clg.
UP
Cathederal Clg.
Ent
Pwdr
Gar 20x20
Por

Design 90697

1,501-2,000 sq. ft. HOME PLANS

Units	Single
Price Code	B
Total Finished	1,597 sq. ft.
Main Finished	1,597 sq. ft.
Basement Unfinished	1,512 sq. ft.
Garage Unfinished	380 sq. ft.
Dimensions	75'4"x38'8"
Foundation	Basement
	Slab
Bedrooms	3
Full Baths	2

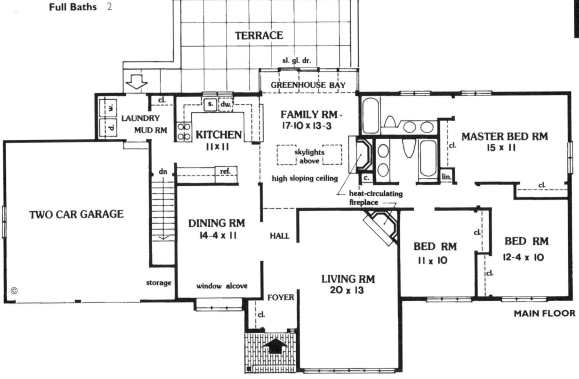

TERRACE

sl. gl. dr.

GREENHOUSE BAY

LAUNDRY MUD RM

cl.

s. dw.

KITCHEN
11 x 11

FAMILY RM
17-10 x 13-3

skylights above

high sloping ceiling

heat-circulating fireplace

MASTER BED RM
15 x 11

cl.

lin.

cl.

ref.

dn

DINING RM
14-4 x 11

HALL

TWO CAR GARAGE

storage

window alcove

LIVING RM
20 x 13

FOYER

cl.

BED RM
11 x 10

cl.

cl.

BED RM
12-4 x 10

MAIN FLOOR

Visit us at www.merillat.com

Merillat

Units	Single
Price Code	B
Total Finished	1,598 sq. ft.
First Finished	812 sq. ft.
Second Finished	786 sq. ft.
Garage Unfinished	560 sq. ft.
Dimensions	52'x28'
Foundation	Crawlspace
	Slab
Bedrooms	3
Full Baths	2
Half Baths	1
First Ceiling	8'
Second Ceiling	8'
Vaulted Ceiling	15'
Max Ridge Height	25'10"
Roof Framing	Truss
Exterior Walls	2x4

SECOND FLOOR

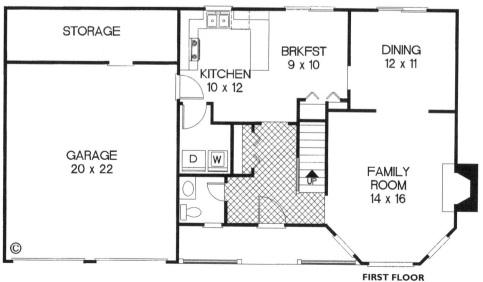

FIRST FLOOR

Design 69118

Units	Single
Price Code	B
Total Finished	1,600 sq. ft.
First Finished	896 sq. ft.
Second Finished	704 sq. ft.
Garage Unfinished	400 sq. ft.
Dimensions	52'x34'
Foundation	Slab
Bedrooms	3
Full Baths	1
3/4 Baths	1
Half Baths	1
First Ceiling	9'
Second Ceiling	8'
Max Ridge Height	28'
Roof Framing	Truss
Exterior Walls	2x6

Attic Storage

Master Suite 12'2" x 13'4"

Bedroom 10'2" x 13'4"

Dn

Bedroom 10' x 12'

SECOND FLOOR

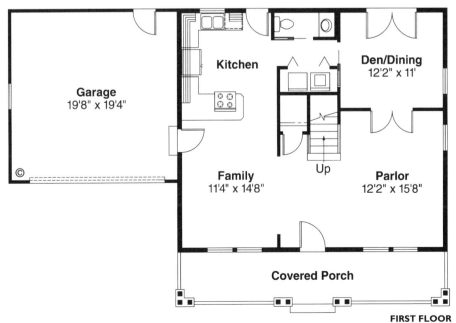

Garage 19'8" x 19'4"

Kitchen

Den/Dining 12'2" x 11'

Family 11'4" x 14'8"

Up

Parlor 12'2" x 15'8"

Covered Porch

FIRST FLOOR

Units	Single
Price Code	B
Total Finished	1,600 sq. ft.
Main Finished	1,600 sq. ft.
Dimensions	48'x40'
Foundation	Crawlspace
	Slab
	Pier/Post
Bedrooms	4
Full Baths	2
Max Ridge Height	16'
Roof Framing	Stick/Truss
Exterior Walls	2x6

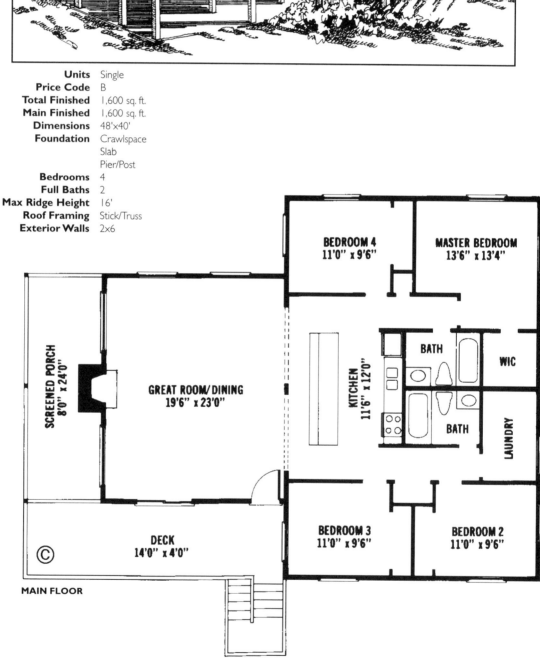

SCREENED PORCH
8'0" x 24'0"

GREAT ROOM/DINING
19'6" x 23'0"

BEDROOM 4
11'0" x 9'6"

MASTER BEDROOM
13'6" x 13'4"

KITCHEN
11'6" x 12'0"

BATH

WIC

BATH

LAUNDRY

DECK
14'0" x 4'0"

BEDROOM 3
11'0" x 9'6"

BEDROOM 2
11'0" x 9'6"

MAIN FLOOR

Design 98406

1,501-2,000 sq.ft. HOME PLANS

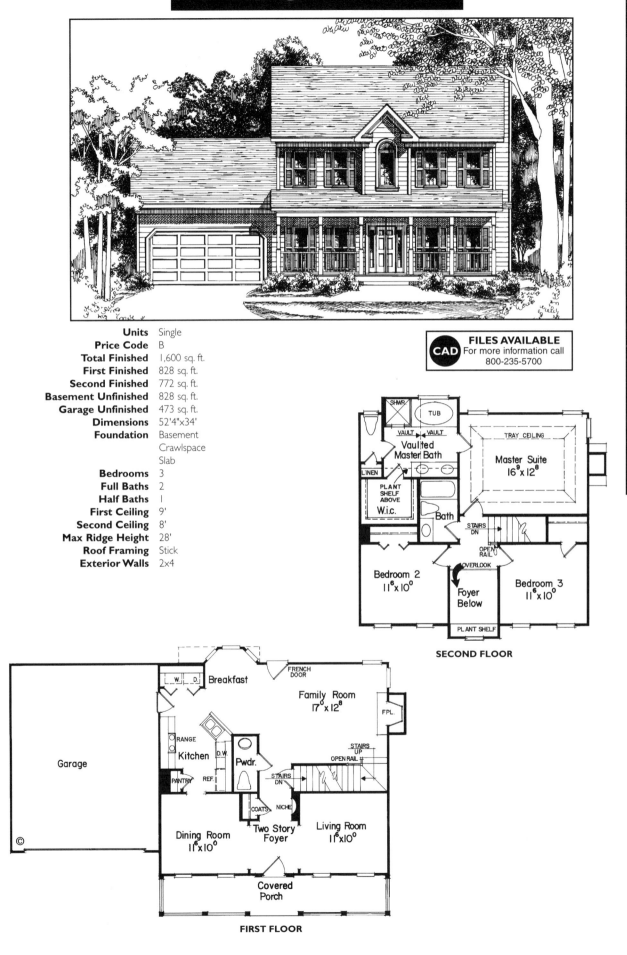

Units	Single
Price Code	B
Total Finished	1,600 sq. ft.
First Finished	828 sq. ft.
Second Finished	772 sq. ft.
Basement Unfinished	828 sq. ft.
Garage Unfinished	473 sq. ft.
Dimensions	52'4"x34'
Foundation	Basement
	Crawlspace
	Slab
Bedrooms	3
Full Baths	2
Half Baths	1
First Ceiling	9'
Second Ceiling	8'
Max Ridge Height	28'
Roof Framing	Stick
Exterior Walls	2x4

CAD FILES AVAILABLE
For more information call
800-235-5700

SECOND FLOOR

SHWR. TUB
VAULT VAULT
Vaulted Master Bath
LINEN
PLANT SHELF ABOVE
W.i.c.
Bath
TRAY CEILING
Master Suite
16⁹ x 12⁸
STAIRS DN
OPEN RAIL
OVERLOOK
Bedroom 2
11⁶ x 10⁰
Foyer Below
Bedroom 3
11⁶ x 10⁰
PLANT SHELF

FIRST FLOOR

W. D. Breakfast
FRENCH DOOR
Family Room
17⁰ x 12⁸
FPL.
RANGE
Kitchen
D.W.
Pwdr.
Garage
PANTRY REF.
STAIRS UP
OPEN RAIL
STAIRS DN
COATS NICHE
Dining Room
11⁶ x 10⁰
Two Story Foyer
Living Room
11⁶ x 10⁰
Covered Porch

Design 62058

Units	Single
Price Code	C
Total Finished	1,601 sq. ft.
Main Finished	1,601 sq. ft.
Garage Unfinished	771 sq. ft.
Porch Unfinished	279 sq. ft.
Dimensions	39'x77'2"
Foundation	Crawlspace
	Slab
Bedrooms	3
Full Baths	2
Main Ceiling	9'
Max Ridge Height	22'
Roof Framing	Stick
Exterior Walls	2x4

MAIN FLOOR

To order blueprints, call **800-235-5700** or visit us on the web, **family**homeplans.com

Units	Single
Price Code	B
Total Finished	1,604 sq. ft.
Main Finished	1,604 sq. ft.
Bonus Unfinished	316 sq. ft.
Garage Unfinished	529 sq. ft.
Deck Unfinished	718 sq. ft.
Dimensions	57'x59'
Foundation	Crawlspace
	Slab
Bedrooms	3
Full Baths	2
Main Ceiling	9'
Max Ridge Height	28'
Exterior Walls	2x4

* Alternate foundation options available at an additional charge.
Please call 1-800-235-5700 for more information.

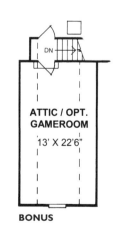

ATTIC / OPT. GAMEROOM
13' X 22'6"

BONUS

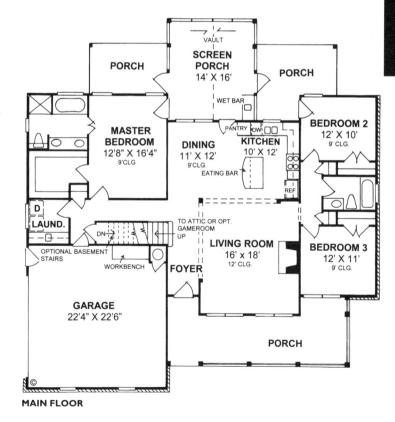

MAIN FLOOR

Units	Single
Price Code	B
Total Finished	1,606 sq. ft.
Main Finished	1,606 sq. ft.
Basement Unfinished	1,575 sq. ft.
Garage Unfinished	545 sq. ft.
Dimensions	60'x46'
Foundation	Basement
Bedrooms	3
Full Baths	2
Main Ceiling	8'
Max Ridge Height	20'
Roof Framing	Stick
Exterior Walls	2x6

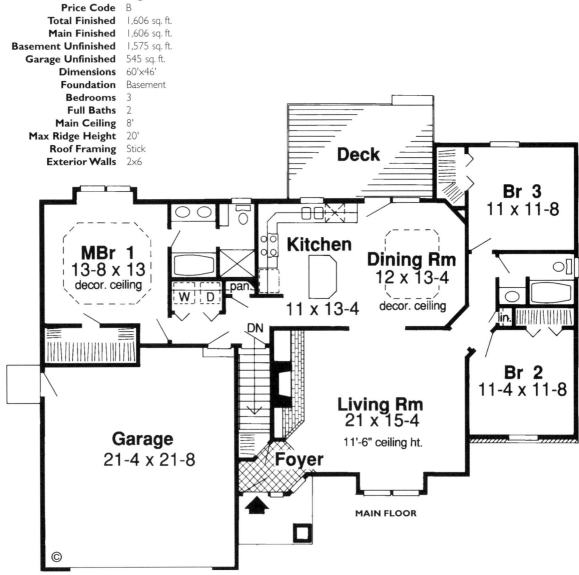

Deck

Br 3
11 x 11-8

MBr 1
13-8 x 13
decor. ceiling

Kitchen
11 x 13-4

Dining Rm
12 x 13-4
decor. ceiling

W D pan.

lin.

DN

Br 2
11-4 x 11-8

Garage
21-4 x 21-8

Living Rm
21 x 15-4
11'-6" ceiling ht.

Foyer

MAIN FLOOR

Design 65191

1,501-2,000 sq. ft. HOME PLANS

Units	Single
Price Code	B
Total Finished	1,606 sq. ft.
First Finished	902 sq. ft.
Second Finished	704 sq. ft.
Dimensions	34'8"x37'4"
Foundation	Basement
Bedrooms	3
Full Baths	1
Half Baths	1

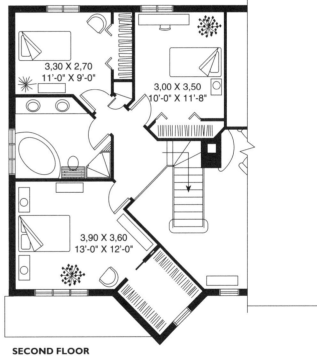

SECOND FLOOR

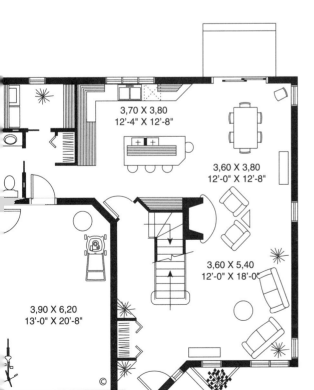

FIRST FLOOR

Units	Single
Price Code	B
Total Finished	1,611 sq. ft.
Main Finished	1,611 sq. ft.
Garage Unfinished	430 sq. ft.
Deck Unfinished	228 sq. ft.
Porch Unfinished	163 sq. ft.
Dimensions	66'4"x43'10"
Foundation	Basement
Bedrooms	3
Full Baths	2
Main Ceiling	8'
Vaulted Ceiling	10'
Tray Ceiling	10'
Max Ridge Height	22'6"
Roof Framing	Truss
Exterior Walls	2x4

MAIN FLOOR

Design 64196

Units	Single
Price Code	G
Total Finished	1,616 sq. ft.
Main Finished	1,616 sq. ft.
Bonus Unfinished	362 sq. ft.
Garage Unfinished	534 sq. ft.
Dimensions	64'x54'6"
Foundation	Crawlspace
Bedrooms	3
Full Baths	2
Max Ridge Height	23'2"
Roof Framing	Stick/Truss
Exterior Walls	2x6

* Alternate foundation options available at an additional charge.
Please call 1-800-235-5700 for more information.

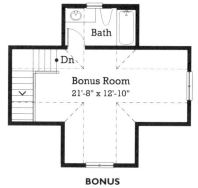

BONUS

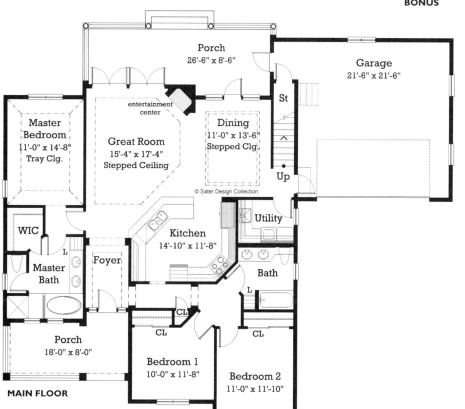

MAIN FLOOR

Bath

Bonus Room
21'-8" x 12'-10"

Porch
26'-6" x 8'-6"

Garage
21'-6" x 21'-6"

entertainment center

Master Bedroom
11'-0" x 14'-8"
Tray Clg.

Great Room
15'-4" x 17'-4"
Stepped Ceiling

Dining
11'-0" x 13'-6"
Stepped Clg.

© Sater Design Collection

Up

WIC

Utility

Master Bath

Foyer

Kitchen
14'-10" x 11'-8"

Bath

Porch
18'-0" x 8'-0"

Bedroom 1
10'-0" x 11'-8"

Bedroom 2
11'-0" x 11'-10"

1,501-2,000 sq.ft. HOME PLANS

Design 98416

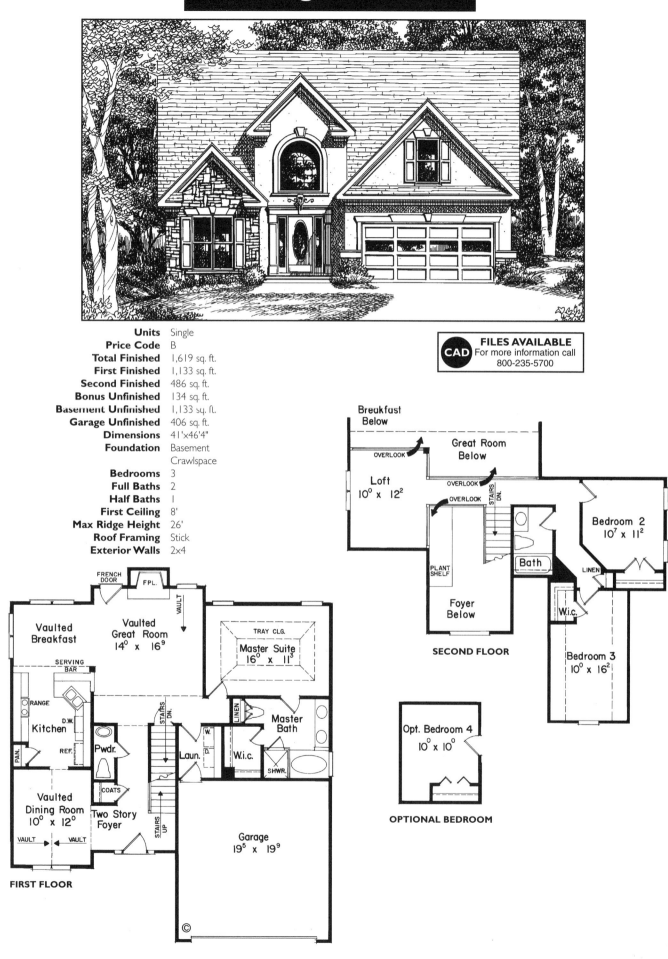

Units	Single
Price Code	B
Total Finished	1,619 sq. ft.
First Finished	1,133 sq. ft.
Second Finished	486 sq. ft.
Bonus Unfinished	134 sq. ft.
Basement Unfinished	1,133 sq. ft.
Garage Unfinished	406 sq. ft.
Dimensions	41'x46'4"
Foundation	Basement
	Crawlspace
Bedrooms	3
Full Baths	2
Half Baths	1
First Ceiling	8'
Max Ridge Height	26'
Roof Framing	Stick
Exterior Walls	2x4

CAD FILES AVAILABLE For more information call 800-235-5700

SECOND FLOOR

Breakfast Below

Great Room Below

OVERLOOK

Loft 10⁰ x 12²

OVERLOOK

STAIRS DN.

Bath

Bedroom 2 10⁷ x 11²

LINEN

PLANT SHELF

Foyer Below

W.i.c.

Bedroom 3 10⁰ x 16²

Opt. Bedroom 4 10⁰ x 10⁰

OPTIONAL BEDROOM

FRENCH DOOR FPL.

Vaulted Breakfast

Vaulted Great Room 14⁰ x 16⁹

VAULT

TRAY CLG.

Master Suite 16⁰ x 11³

SERVING BAR

RANGE

DW.

Kitchen

PAN.

REF.

Pwdr.

COATS

Vaulted Dining Room 10⁰ x 12⁰

VAULT VAULT

Two Story Foyer

STAIRS DN.

STAIRS UP

Laun.

W. D.

LINEN

W.i.c.

Master Bath

SHWR.

Garage 19⁵ x 19⁹

FIRST FLOOR

Design 64017

1,501-2,000 sq.ft. HOME PLANS

Units	Single
Price Code	B
Total Finished	1,624 sq. ft.
Main Finished	1,624 sq. ft.
Bonus Unfinished	142 sq. ft.
Garage Unfinished	462 sq. ft.
Dimensions	60'x48'
Foundation	Crawlspace
	Slab
Bedrooms	3
Full Baths	2
Main Ceiling	8'
Roof Framing	Stick
Exterior Walls	2x4

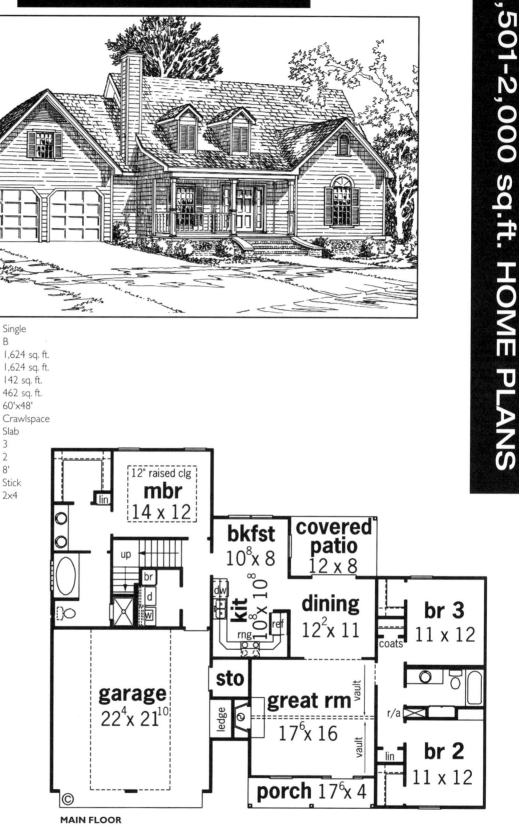

MAIN FLOOR

Merillat®

Visit us at www.merillat.com

To order blueprints, call **800-235-5700** or visit us on the web, **familyhomeplans.com**   **191**

Units	Single
Price Code	B
Total Finished	1,625 sq. ft.
Main Finished	1,625 sq. ft.
Basement Unfinished	1,625 sq. ft.
Garage Unfinished	455 sq. ft.
Dimensions	54'x48'4"
Foundation	Basement
	Crawlspace
	Slab
Bedrooms	3
Full Baths	2
Main Ceiling	8'-9'
Max Ridge Height	22'
Roof Framing	Stick
Exterior Walls	2x4, 2x6

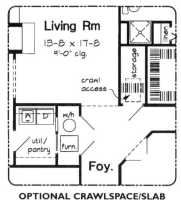

OPTIONAL CRAWLSPACE/SLAB FOUNDATION

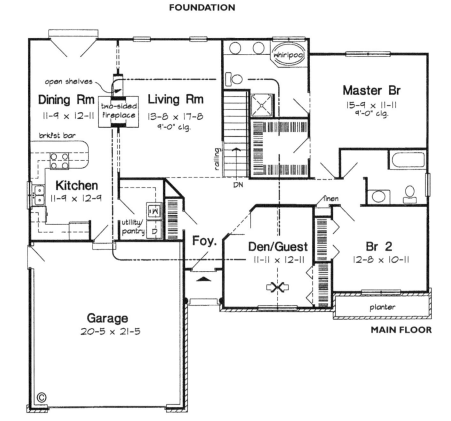

MAIN FLOOR

Design 65194

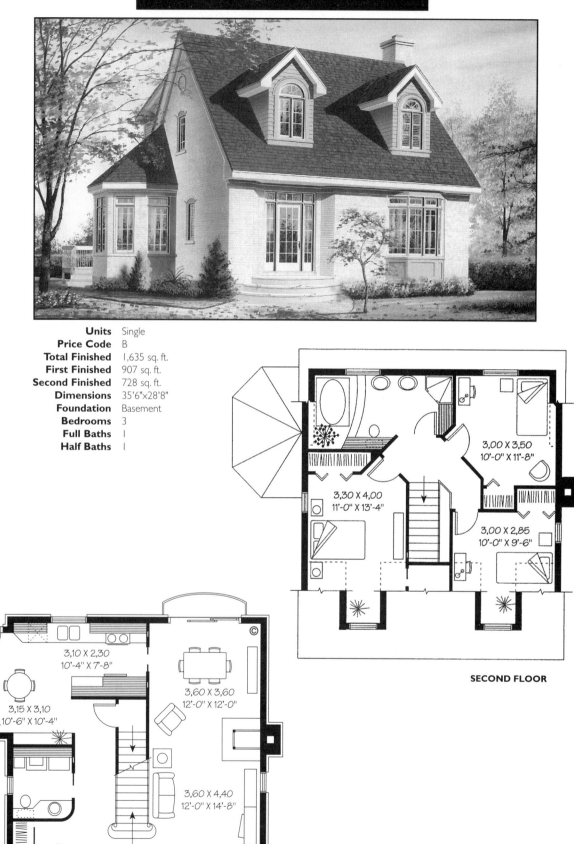

Units	Single
Price Code	B
Total Finished	1,635 sq. ft.
First Finished	907 sq. ft.
Second Finished	728 sq. ft.
Dimensions	35'6"x28'8"
Foundation	Basement
Bedrooms	3
Full Baths	1
Half Baths	1

SECOND FLOOR

3,30 X 4,00
11'-0" X 13'-4"

3,00 X 3,50
10'-0" X 11'-8"

3,00 X 2,85
10'-0" X 9'-6"

3,10 X 2,30
10'-4" X 7'-8"

3,15 X 3,10
10'-6" X 10'-4"

3,60 X 3,60
12'-0" X 12'-0"

3,60 X 4,40
12'-0" X 14'-8"

FIRST FLOOR

Units	Single
Price Code	B
Total Finished	1,640 sq. ft.
Main Finished	1,640 sq. ft.
Garage Unfinished	408 sq. ft.
Deck Unfinished	72 sq. ft.
Porch Unfinished	60 sq. ft.
Dimensions	50'x56'4"
Foundation	Slab
Bedrooms	3
Full Baths	2
Max Ridge Height	24'2"
Roof Framing	Stick
Exterior Walls	2x4

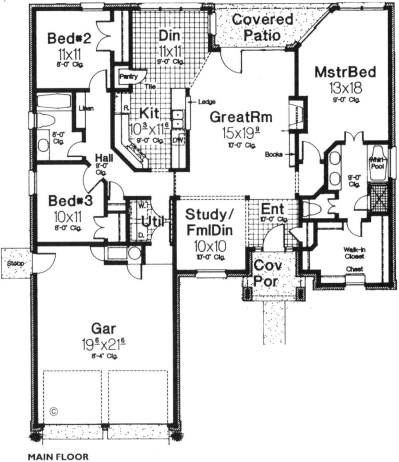

MAIN FLOOR

Design 24717

Units	Single
Price Code	B
Total Finished	1,642 sq. ft.
Main Finished	1,642 sq. ft.
Basement Unfinished	1,642 sq. ft.
Garage Unfinished	430 sq. ft.
Porch Unfinished	156 sq. ft.
Dimensions	59'x44'
Foundation	Basement
	Crawlspace
	Slab
Bedrooms	3
Full Baths	2
Main Ceiling	9'
Vaulted Ceiling	13'6"
Max Ridge Height	24'
Roof Framing	Stick
Exterior Walls	2x4

DN 14R

**OPTIONAL BASEMENT
STAIR LOCATION**

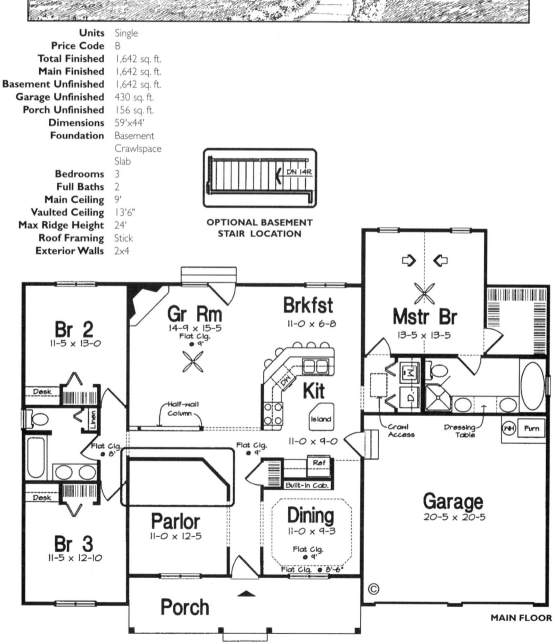

MAIN FLOOR

Units	Single
Price Code	B
Total Finished	1,642 sq. ft.
Main Finished	1,642 sq. ft.
Basement Unfinished	1,642 sq. ft.
Porch Unfinished	192 sq. ft.
Dimensions	59'x66'
Foundation	Basement
Bedrooms	3
Full Baths	1
3/4 Baths	1
Half Baths	1
Max Ridge Height	22'
Roof Framing	Stick
Exterior Walls	2x6

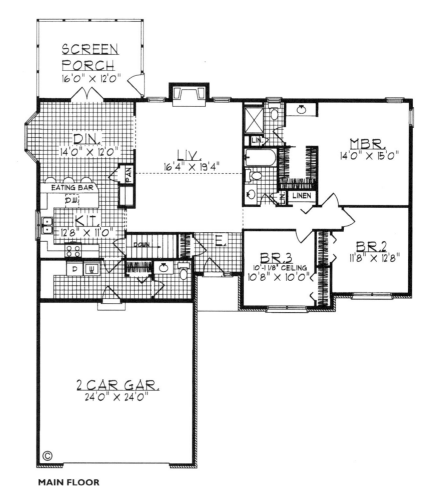

MAIN FLOOR

Units	Single
Price Code	B
Total Finished	1,643 sq. ft.
First Finished	1,064 sq. ft.
Second Finished	579 sq. ft.
Dimensions	38'x34'
Foundation	Basement
Bedrooms	3
Full Baths	2
Half Baths	1
First Ceiling	8'
Second Ceiling	8'
Vaulted Ceiling	14'
Max Ridge Height	21'6"
Exterior Walls	2x4

STORAGE

BEDROOM 3
15X12

DN

OPEN TO BELOW

BEDROOM 2
15X12

SECOND FLOOR

SKYLIGHT

DINING
12x12

KITCHEN
10x12

VAULT

DN

VAULT

D

W

COATS

UP

MASTER BEDRM
15x13

FAMILY ROOM
18x15

FIRST FLOOR

Visit us at www.merillat.com

Merillat.

Design 92422

Units	Single
Price Code	B
Total Finished	1,647 sq. ft.
First Finished	1,288 sq. ft.
Second Finished	359 sq. ft.
Dimensions	28'x46'
Foundation	Slab
Bedrooms	2
Full Baths	1
First Ceiling	8'
Second Ceiling	11'
Vaulted Ceiling	20'
Max Ridge Height	25'3"
Roof Framing	Stick
Exterior Walls	2x4

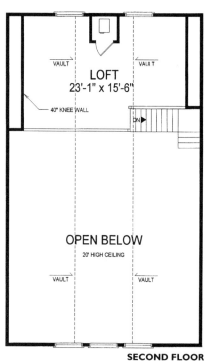

SECOND FLOOR

LOFT
23'-1" x 15'-6"

40" KNEE WALL

OPEN BELOW
20' HIGH CEILING

VAULT   VAULT

DN

BEDROOM 1
11'-10" x 10'-0"

BEDROOM 2
11'-4" x 10'-0"

COATS

W/D

LINEN

PANTRY

UP

GREAT ROOM
27'-4" x 29'-5"
20' HIGH CEILING

VAULT   VAULT

DECK/PATIO
11'-6" x 18'-8"

DECK
7'-6" x 36'-0"

PORCH
24'-4" x 7'-6"

FIRST FLOOR

Design 96513

Units	Single
Price Code	B
Total Finished	1,648 sq. ft.
Main Finished	1,648 sq. ft.
Garage Unfinished	479 sq. ft.
Dimensions	68'x50'
Foundation	Crawlspace
	Slab
Bedrooms	3
Full Baths	2
Half Baths	1
Main Ceiling	9'
Max Ridge Height	20'
Roof Framing	Stick
Exterior Walls	2x4

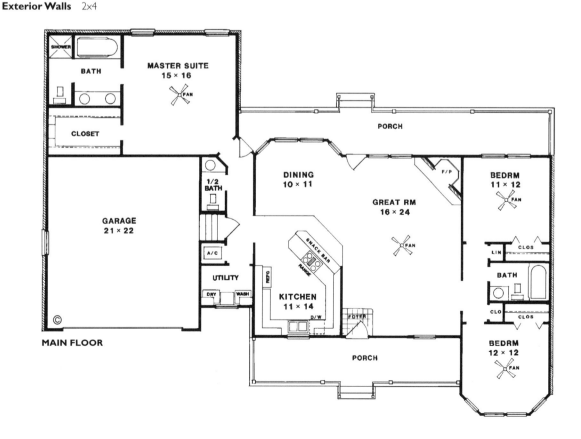

MAIN FLOOR

Units	Single
Price Code	B
Total Finished	1,654 sq. ft.
Main Finished	1,654 sq. ft.
Garage Unfinished	480 sq. ft.
Porch Unfinished	401 sq. ft.
Dimensions	68'x46'
Foundation	Crawlspace
	Slab
Bedrooms	3
Full Baths	2
Half Baths	1
Main Ceiling	9'
Max Ridge Height	21'
Roof Framing	Stick
Exterior Walls	2x4

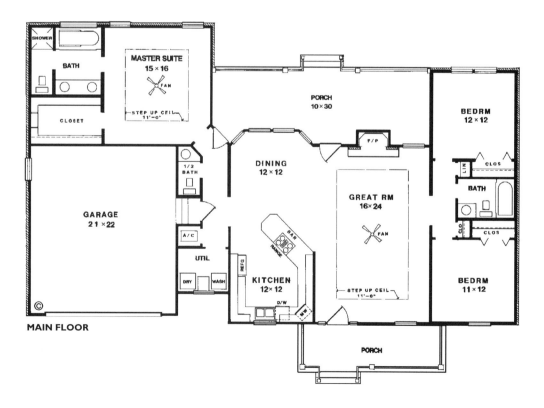

MAIN FLOOR

Design 65635

PHOTOGRAPHY: COURTESY OF THE DESIGNER

Units	Single
Price Code	B
Total Finished	1,655 sq. ft.
Main Finished	1,655 sq. ft.
Dimensions	52'x66'
Foundation	Crawlspace
	Slab
Bedrooms	3
Full Baths	2
Max Ridge Height	26'
Roof Framing	Stick
Exterior Walls	2x6

Please note: The photographed home may have been modified to suit homeowner preferences. If you order plans, have a builder or design professional check them against the photograph to confirm actual construction details.

lin · bath · shv · clo · shr

mbr 16 x 14

por 10x6 slope clg

ref · kit 14x12 · dw · ov · pan · ct · bar · skylight

sto 10x6 · w.h. · w · d · util · sto · clo · HEAT B A/C

dining 14 x 14

porch 14 x 10 skylight · slope clg

br 2 12 x 12 · clo · clo

living 18 x 18 · lin · van · bath · clo

porch 18 x 6

br 3 12 x 12 · slope clg

garage 22 x 22

©

MAIN FLOOR

To order blueprints, call **800-235-5700** or visit us on the web, **familyhomeplans.com**

Units	Single
Price Code	B
Total Finished	1,660 sq. ft.
Main Finished	1,660 sq. ft.
Garage Unfinished	484 sq. ft.
Porch Unfinished	447 sq. ft.
Dimensions	66'10"x46'5"
Foundation	Crawlspace
	Slab
Bedrooms	3
Full Baths	2
Main Ceiling	9'
Max Ridge Height	20'6"
Roof Framing	Stick
Exterior Walls	2x4

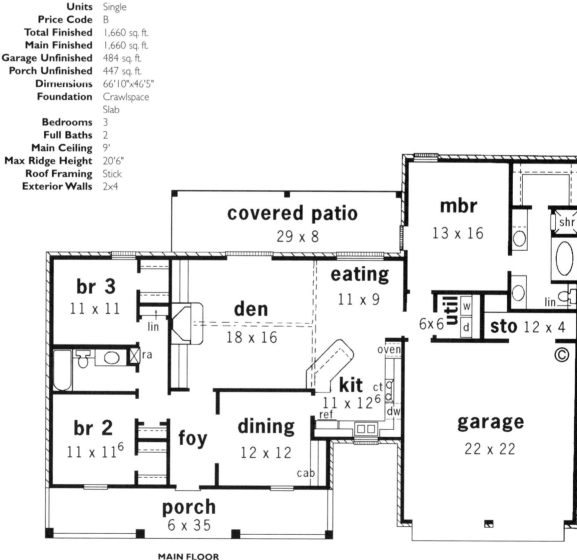

MAIN FLOOR

Units	Single
Price Code	B
Total Finished	1,661 sq. ft.
Main Finished	1,661 sq. ft.
Basement Unfinished	1,642 sq. ft.
Garage Unfinished	546 sq. ft.
Deck Unfinished	194 sq. ft.
Porch Unfinished	40 sq. ft.
Dimensions	56'x46'
Foundation	Basement
	Crawlspace
	Slab
Bedrooms	3
Full Baths	2
Main Ceiling	8'
Tray Ceiling	10'
Max Ridge Height	23'
Roof Framing	Stick
Exterior Walls	2x4

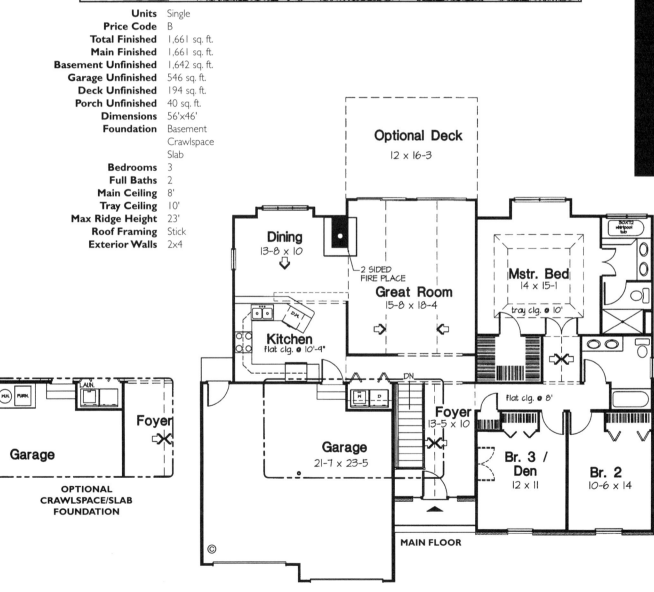

Optional Deck 12 x 16-3

Dining 13-8 x 10

2 SIDED FIRE PLACE

Great Room 15-8 x 18-4

Mstr. Bed 14 x 15-1
tray clg. @ 10'

30x12 whirlpool tub

Kitchen flat clg. @ 10'-9"

DN

flat clg. @ 8'

Foyer 13-5 x 10

Garage 21-7 x 23-5

Br. 3 / Den 12 x 11

Br. 2 10-6 x 14

MAIN FLOOR

M.H. FURN. LAUN.

Foyer

Garage

OPTIONAL CRAWLSPACE/SLAB FOUNDATION

Units	Single
Price Code	B
Total Finished	1,664 sq. ft.
Main Finished	1,664 sq. ft.
Basement Unfinished	1,600 sq. ft.
Garage Unfinished	440 sq. ft.
Dimensions	48'x63'
Foundation	Basement
	Crawlspace
	Slab
Bedrooms	3
Full Baths	2
Max Ridge Height	22'6"
Roof Framing	Stick
Exterior Walls	2x4

Patio

MstrBed
13x17

Master

Bar

LivRm
18x20
10'Ceiling

Bed#3
11x13

Kit
8x10

Pant

B#2

Ent

Din
10'Ceiling

Util

Por

Bed#2
11x13

Gar
20x22

MAIN FLOOR

Design 94923

PHOTOGRAPHY: COURTESY OF THE DESIGNER

Units	Single
Price Code	B
Total Finished	1,666 sq. ft.
Main Finished	1,666 sq. ft.
Basement Unfinished	1,666 sq. ft.
Garage Unfinished	496 sq. ft.
Dimensions	55'4"x48'
Foundation	Basement
Bedrooms	3
Full Baths	2
Max Ridge Height	22'9"
Roof Framing	Stick
Exterior Walls	2x4

* Alternate foundation options available at an additional charge.
Please call 1-800-235-5700 for more information.

Please note: The photographed home may have been modified to suit homeowner preferences. If you order plans, have a builder or design professional check them against the photograph to confirm actual construction details.

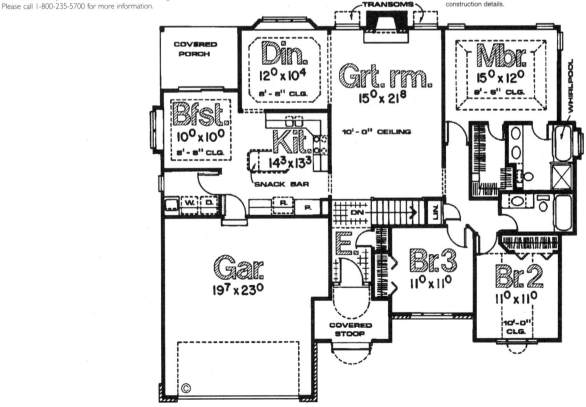

MAIN FLOOR

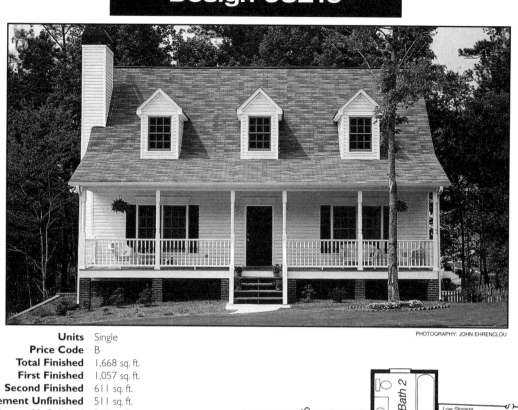

PHOTOGRAPHY: JOHN EHRENCLOU

Units	Single
Price Code	B
Total Finished	1,668 sq. ft.
First Finished	1,057 sq. ft.
Second Finished	611 sq. ft.
Basement Unfinished	511 sq. ft.
Garage Unfinished	546 sq. ft.
Dimensions	40'4"x38'
Foundation	Basement
Bedrooms	3
Full Baths	2
Half Baths	1
First Ceiling	8'
Second Ceiling	8'
Max Ridge Height	23'
Roof Framing	Stick
Exterior Walls	2x4

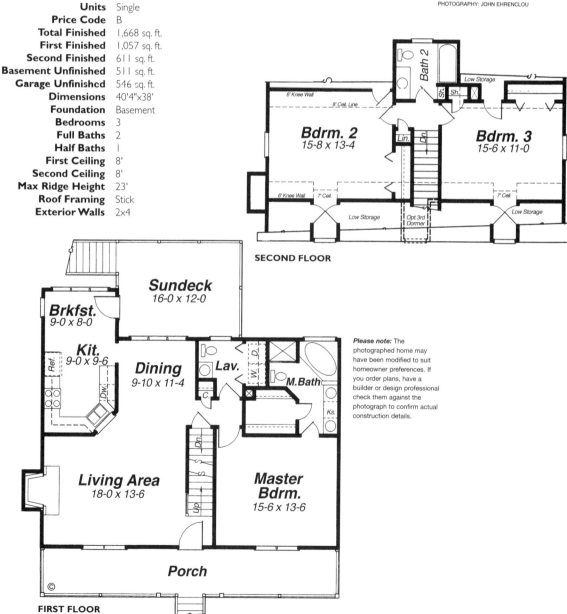

SECOND FLOOR

FIRST FLOOR

Please note: The photographed home may have been modified to suit homeowner preferences. If you order plans, have a builder or design professional check them against the photograph to confirm actual construction details.

Design 67007

Units	Single
Price Code	B
Total Finished	1,670 sq. ft.
Main Finished	1,670 sq. ft.
Bonus Unfinished	350 sq. ft.
Garage Unfinished	474 sq. ft.
Porch Unfinished	10 sq. ft.
Dimensions	53'x55'9"
Foundation	Slab
Bedrooms	3
Full Baths	2
Main Ceiling	8'
Vaulted Ceiling	11'
Tray Ceiling	13'
Max Ridge Height	24'9"
Roof Framing	Truss

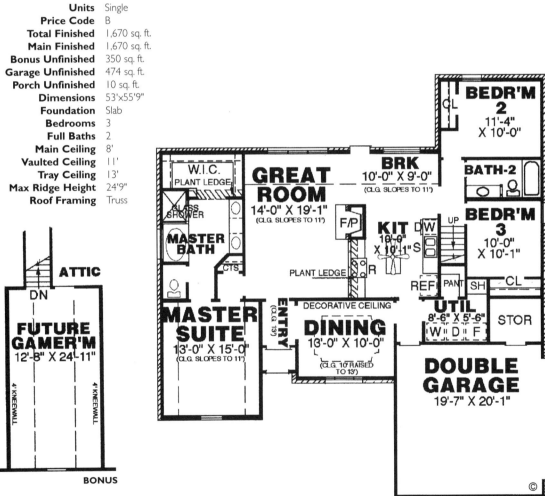

ATTIC

DN

FUTURE GAMER'M
12'-8" X 24'-11"

4' KNEEWALL

BONUS

MAIN FLOOR

Units	Single
Price Code	B
Total Finished	1,671 sq. ft.
Main Finished	1,671 sq. ft.
Basement Unfinished	1,685 sq. ft.
Garage Unfinished	400 sq. ft.
Dimensions	50'x51'
Foundation	Basement
	Crawlspace
	Slab
Bedrooms	3
Full Baths	2
Main Ceiling	9'
Max Ridge Height	22'6"
Roof Framing	Stick
Exterior Walls	2x4

CAD FILES AVAILABLE
For more information call
800-235-5700

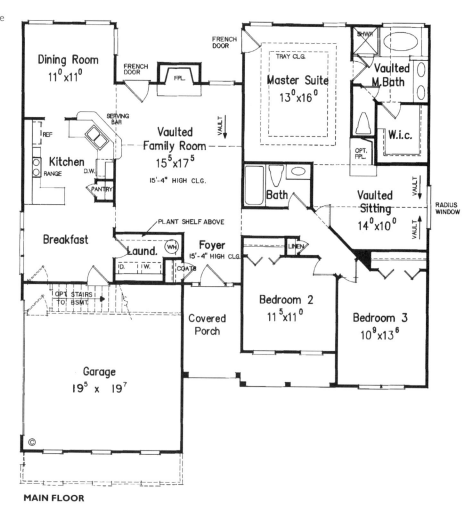

MAIN FLOOR

Design 98476

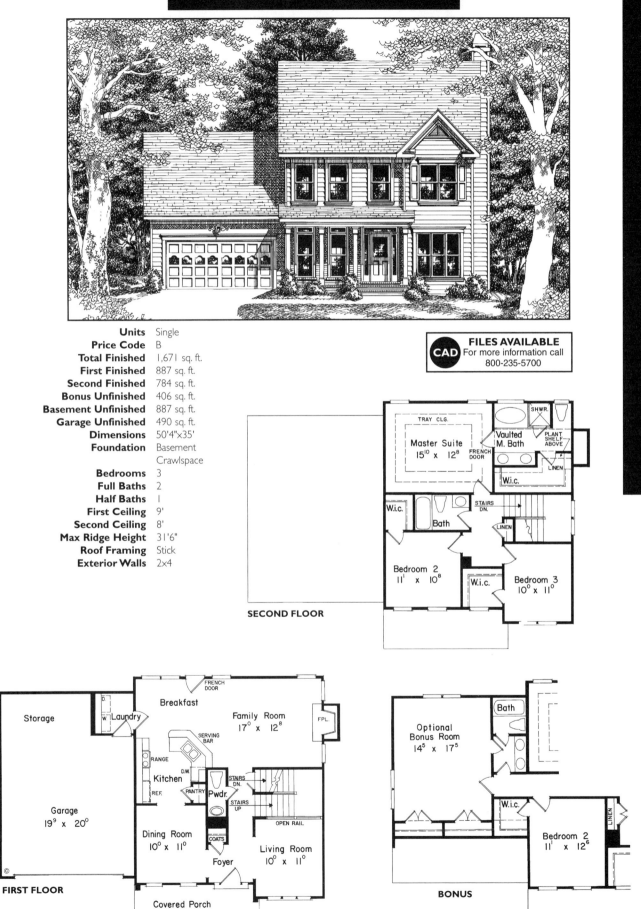

Units	Single
Price Code	B
Total Finished	1,671 sq. ft.
First Finished	887 sq. ft.
Second Finished	784 sq. ft.
Bonus Unfinished	406 sq. ft.
Basement Unfinished	887 sq. ft.
Garage Unfinished	490 sq. ft.
Dimensions	50'4"x35'
Foundation	Basement
	Crawlspace
Bedrooms	3
Full Baths	2
Half Baths	1
First Ceiling	9'
Second Ceiling	8'
Max Ridge Height	31'6"
Roof Framing	Stick
Exterior Walls	2x4

CAD FILES AVAILABLE
For more information call
800-235-5700

SECOND FLOOR

TRAY CLG.

Master Suite 15¹⁰ x 12⁸

Vaulted M. Bath

SHWR.

PLANT SHELF ABOVE

FRENCH DOOR

LINEN

W.i.c.

W.i.c.

Bath

STAIRS DN.

LINEN

Bedroom 2 11' x 10⁸

W.i.c.

Bedroom 3 10⁰ x 11⁰

FIRST FLOOR

Storage

Laundry

Breakfast

FRENCH DOOR

Family Room 17⁰ x 12⁸

FPL.

SERVING BAR

D.W.

RANGE

Kitchen

REF.

PANTRY

STAIRS DN.

Pwdr.

STAIRS UP

OPEN RAIL

COATS

Garage 19⁹ x 20⁰

Dining Room 10⁰ x 11⁰

Foyer

Living Room 10⁰ x 11⁰

Covered Porch

BONUS

Bath

Optional Bonus Room 14⁵ x 17⁵

W.i.c.

LINEN

Bedroom 2 11' x 12⁶

Units	Single
Price Code	B
Total Finished	1,672 sq. ft.
Main Finished	1,672 sq. ft.
Garage Unfinished	566 sq. ft.
Dimensions	80'x32'
Foundation	Basement
	Crawlspace
	Slab
Bedrooms	3
Full Baths	2
Max Ridge Height	19'
Roof Framing	Stick
Exterior Walls	2x4, 2x6

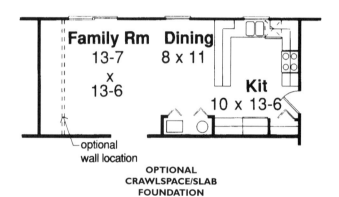

Family Rm 13-7 x 13-6   **Dining** 8 x 11   **Kit** 10 x 13-6

optional wall location

OPTIONAL CRAWLSPACE/SLAB FOUNDATION

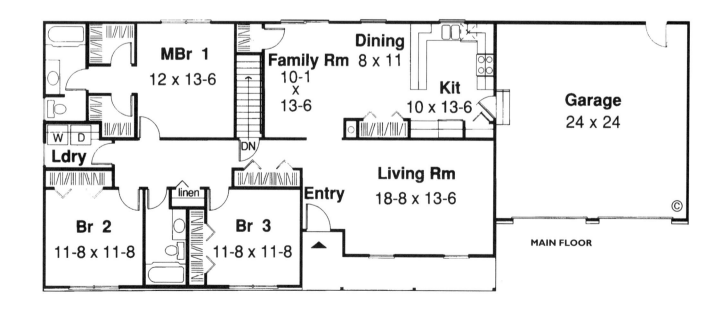

MBr 1 12 x 13-6
Family Rm 10-1 x 13-6
Dining 8 x 11
Kit 10 x 13-6
Garage 24 x 24
Living Rm 18-8 x 13-6
Ldry
W   D
Br 2 11-8 x 11-8
linen
Br 3 11-8 x 11-8
Entry
DN
MAIN FLOOR

Design 98431

Units	Single
Price Code	B
Total Finished	1,675 sq. ft.
First Finished	882 sq. ft.
Second Finished	793 sq. ft.
Bonus Unfinished	416 sq. ft.
Basement Unfinished	882 sq. ft.
Garage Unfinished	510 sq. ft.
Dimensions	49'6"x35'4"
Foundation	Basement Crawlspace Slab
Bedrooms	3
Full Baths	2
Half Baths	1
First Ceiling	8'
Second Ceiling	8'
Max Ridge Height	29'6"
Roof Framing	Stick
Exterior Walls	2x4

CAD FILES AVAILABLE For more information call 800-235-5700

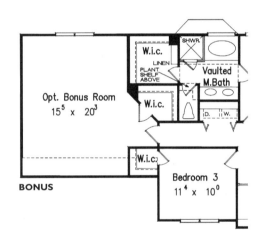

BONUS

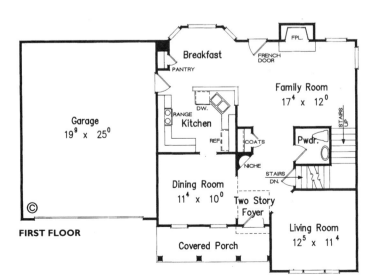

FIRST FLOOR

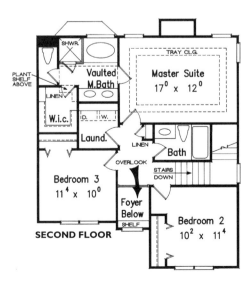

SECOND FLOOR

Units	Single
Price Code	B
Total Finished	1,677 sq. ft.
First Finished	1,064 sq. ft.
Second Finished	613 sq. ft.
Basement Unfinished	1,604 sq. ft.
Deck Unfinished	474 sq. ft.
Porch Unfinished	32 sq. ft.
Dimensions	28'x40'
Foundation	Basement
	Crawlspace
Bedrooms	2
Full Baths	2
First Ceiling	8'
Second Ceiling	8'
Max Ridge Height	26'6"
Roof Framing	Stick
Exterior Walls	2x6

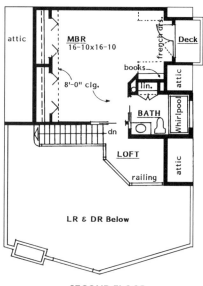

SECOND FLOOR

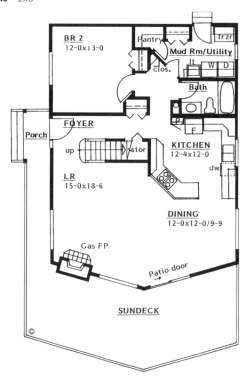

FIRST FLOOR

Win free blueprints!

2 Easy Ways to Enter

1. Log on to www.garlinghouse.com and fill out our questionnaire on-line
   —OR—
2. Fill out the questionnaire below and mail to:
   Free Home Plans Contest
   Garlinghouse, LLC
   174 Oakwood Drive
   Glastonbury, CT 06033

. To Enter
Jo purchase necessary. Limit one entry per person per calendar month.
. Contest Period
May 15, 2004 to May 15, 2005.
. Selection of Winners
Dne drawing will be held on or near the last day of each month during the drawing period. One winner will be selected each month by a random drawing from all entries received during the previous month. Odds of winning depend on the number of entries received.
. Prize
four-copy set (our "Minimum 4-Set Construction Package") of he home plan of the winner's choice will be awarded to one

winner per month during the contest period. Home plans not offered for sale by the Garlinghouse Company are not eligible.
5. Eligibility
This drawing is open to U.S. residents who are 18 years of age or older at the time of entry. Employees and consultants of Garlinghouse and its parent, affiliates, subsidiaries, advertising and promotion agencies and members of the immediate families of any Garlinghouse employee or consultant are not eligible to enter. Void where prohibited by law.
6. Terms & Conditions
The Garlinghouse Company is not responsible for taxes or shipping charges. *For complete rules, terms and conditions, additional fine print, and information regarding notification of winners, log on to* www.garlinghouse.com.

---

the Garlinghouse company

Name: _____

Address: _____

City: _____ State: _____ Zip: _____

Daytime telephone number: (____) _____ Email: _____

Where did you buy this publication?
-] Newsstand
-] Grocery store
-] Pharmacy/Conv. store
-] Lumberyard/Home Center
-] Bookstore
-] Other _____

Please specify store: _____

Why did you buy this publication?
-] Value
-] Number of plans
-] Appealing cover photo
-] Impulse
-] Other _____

What style are you most interested in?
-] Farmhouse or Country
-] Colonial
-] Rustic Cottage or Cabin
-] Victorian
-] European
-] Traditional
-] Other _____

When are you planning to build?
-] Within 6 months
-] 6-12 months
-] 1-2 years
-] More than 2 years
-] Undecided

What is the approximate size of the home?
- ☐ Under 1,000 square feet
- ☐ 1,000 to 2,000
- ☐ 2,000 to 3,000
- ☐ 3,000 to 4,000
- ☐ Over 4,000

What type of home?
- ☐ One level
- ☐ Two story with all bedrooms on second floor
- ☐ Two story with one or two bedrooms on first floor
- ☐ Other _____

Have you bought land? ☐ Yes ☐ No

Please provide any other comments.
Let us know if you have special requirements (e.g. you want a great-room but no living room) or specific property features (e.g. you have a sloped or narrow lot).

_____
_____
_____

Design 96543

Units	Single
Price Code	B
Total Finished	1,680 sq. ft.
Main Finished	1,680 sq. ft.
Garage Unfinished	592 sq. ft.
Porch Unfinished	259 sq. ft.
Dimensions	54'x61'
Foundation	Crawlspace
	Slab
Bedrooms	3
Full Baths	2
Main Ceiling	9'
Vaulted Ceiling	14'
Tray Ceiling	12'
Max Ridge Height	23'
Roof Framing	Stick
Exterior Walls	2x4

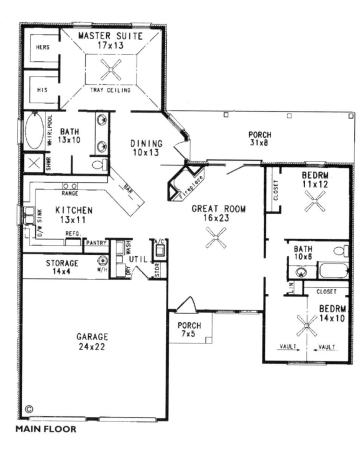

MAIN FLOOR

Design 67021

Units	Single
Price Code	B
Total Finished	1,680 sq. ft.
Main Finished	1,680 sq. ft.
Dimensions	50'x45'
Foundation	Slab
Bedrooms	4
Full Baths	2
Roof Framing	Stick
Exterior Walls	2x4

MAIN FLOOR

Units	Single
Price Code	B
Total Finished	1,681 sq. ft.
Main Finished	1,681 sq. ft.
Garage Unfinished	427 sq. ft.
Dimensions	55'8"x53'2"
Foundation	Slab
Bedrooms	3
Full Baths	2
Main Ceiling	9'
Vaulted Ceiling	11'
Tray Ceiling	11'
Max Ridge Height	21'8"
Roof Framing	Stick

MAIN FLOOR

Design 97207

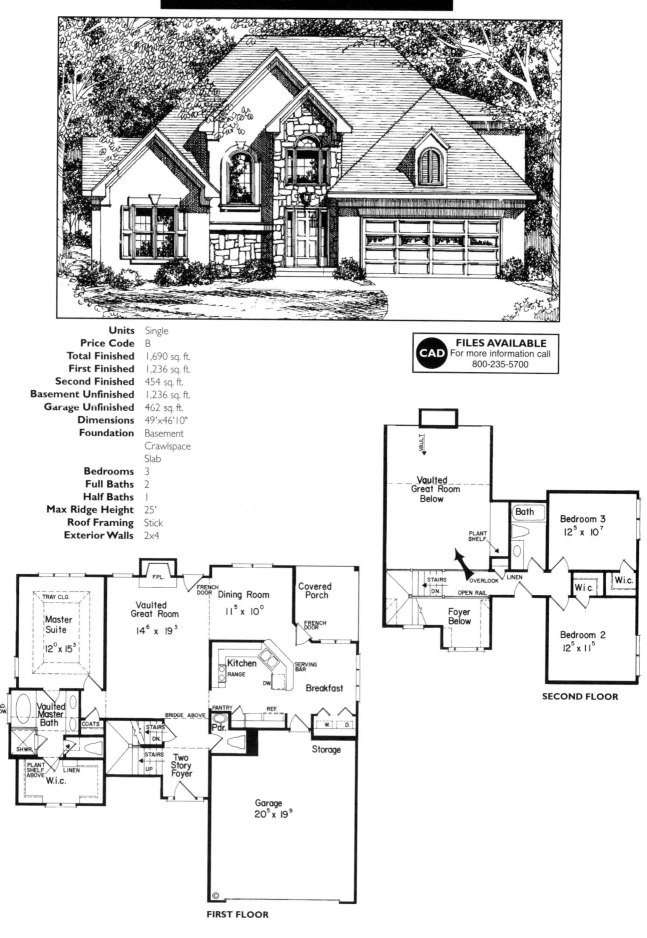

Units	Single
Price Code	B
Total Finished	1,690 sq. ft.
First Finished	1,236 sq. ft.
Second Finished	454 sq. ft.
Basement Unfinished	1,236 sq. ft.
Garage Unfinished	462 sq. ft.
Dimensions	49'x46'10"
Foundation	Basement
	Crawlspace
	Slab
Bedrooms	3
Full Baths	2
Half Baths	1
Max Ridge Height	25'
Roof Framing	Stick
Exterior Walls	2x4

CAD FILES AVAILABLE
For more information call
800-235-5700

SECOND FLOOR

VAULT

Vaulted
Great Room
Below

Bath

Bedroom 3
12⁵ x 10⁷

PLANT
SHELF

STAIRS
DN.

OVERLOOK

LINEN

W.i.c.

W.i.c.

OPEN RAIL

Foyer
Below

Bedroom 2
12⁵ x 11⁵

FIRST FLOOR

FPL.

TRAY CLG.

Master
Suite
12⁰ x 15³

Vaulted
Great Room
14⁶ x 19³

FRENCH
DOOR

Dining Room
11⁵ x 10⁰

Covered
Porch

FRENCH
DOOR

RAD.
WDW.

Vaulted
Master
Bath

COATS

SHWR.

PLANT
SHELF
ABOVE

LINEN

W.i.c.

BRIDGE ABOVE

STAIRS
DN.

STAIRS
UP

Two
Story
Foyer

Kitchen

RANGE

DW.

SERVING
BAR

Breakfast

PANTRY

Pdr.

REF.

W.   D.

Storage

Garage
20⁵ x 19⁹

Units	Single
Price Code	B
Total Finished	1,692 sq. ft.
Main Finished	1,692 sq. ft.
Bonus Unfinished	358 sq. ft.
Basement Unfinished	1,705 sq. ft.
Garage Unfinished	472 sq. ft.
Dimensions	54'x56'6"
Foundation	Basement
	Crawlspace
Bedrooms	3
Full Baths	2
Max Ridge Height	27'
Roof Framing	Stick
Exterior Walls	2x4

FILES AVAILABLE
For more information call
800-235-5700

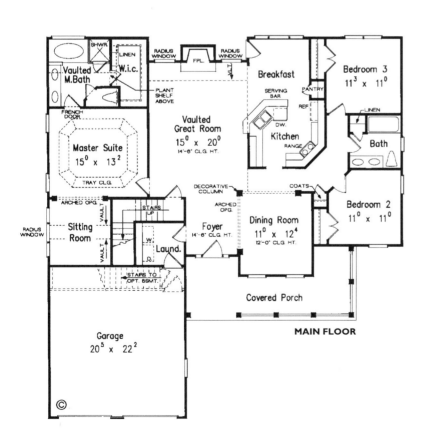

MAIN FLOOR

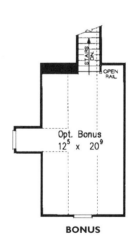

BONUS

Design 50013

Units	Single
Price Code	B
Total Finished	1,697 sq. ft.
First Finished	1,263 sq. ft.
Second Finished	434 sq. ft.
Basement Unfinished	1,263 sq. ft.
Garage Unfinished	393 sq. ft.
Porch Unfinished	111 sq. ft.
Dimensions	55'2"x57'3"
Foundation	Basement
Bedrooms	3
Full Baths	2
Half Baths	1
First Ceiling	8'
Second Ceiling	8'
Max Ridge Height	24'6"
Roof Framing	Truss
Exterior Walls	2x4

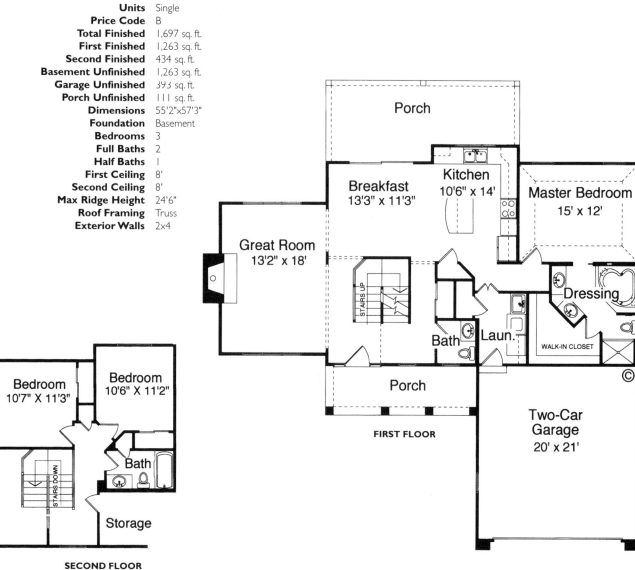

Porch

Kitchen
10'6" x 14'

Master Bedroom
15' x 12'

Breakfast
13'3" x 11'3"

Great Room
13'2" x 18'

STAIRS UP

Dressing

Bath

Laun.

WALK-IN CLOSET

Porch

FIRST FLOOR

Two-Car Garage
20' x 21'

Bedroom
10'7" X 11'3"

Bedroom
10'6" X 11'2"

Bath

STAIRS DOWN

Storage

SECOND FLOOR

Design 81011

Units	Single
Price Code	B
Total Finished	1,698 sq. ft.
First Finished	951 sq. ft.
Second Finished	747 sq. ft.
Bonus Unfinished	254 sq. ft.
Garage Unfinished	703 sq. ft.
Dimensions	50'x44'6"
Foundation	Crawlspace
Bedrooms	3
Full Baths	2
3/4 Baths	1
First Ceiling	9'
Second Ceiling	8'
Max Ridge Height	28'
Exterior Walls	2x6

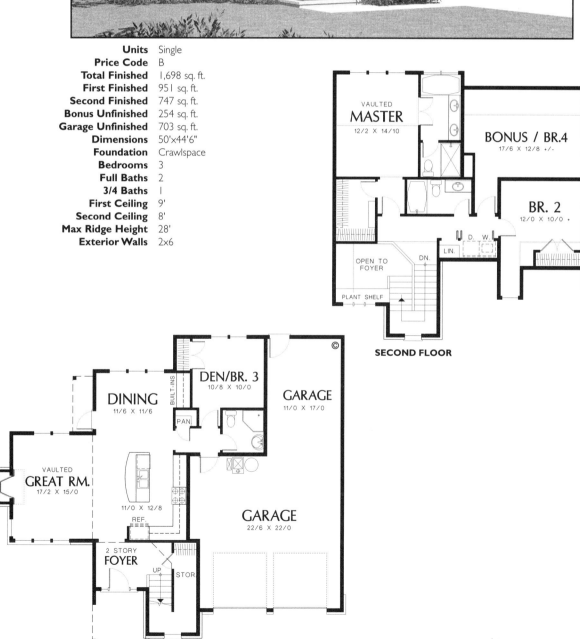

SECOND FLOOR

FIRST FLOOR

Units	Single
Price Code	B
Total Finished	1,699 sq. ft.
Main Finished	1,699 sq. ft.
Dimensions	50'x51'
Foundation	Crawlspace
Bedrooms	3
Full Baths	2
Main Ceiling	9'
Max Ridge Height	23'
Roof Framing	Truss
Exterior Walls	2x6

VAULTED
MASTER
11/0 X 15/0 +

PORCH

NOOK
8/0 X 10/0 +/-
(9' CLG.)

FAMILY
11/0 X 13/4
(9' CLG.)

10/2 x 10/4 +/-

REF.

O.

W. D.

BR. 2
11/0 X 10/0
(9' CLG.)

GARAGE
20/0 X 23/6 +/-

DINING
13/0 X 10/0
(9' CLG.)

L.

LIVING
13/0 X 12/0 +/-
(9' CLG.)

BR. 3
11/0 X 10/0
(9' CLG.)

MAIN FLOOR

Design 64504

Units	Single
Price Code	D
Total Finished	1,700 sq. ft.
Main Finished	1,700 sq. ft.
Dimensions	50'x42'
Foundation	Crawlspace
Bedrooms	3
Full Baths	2
Main Ceiling	9'
Max Ridge Height	24'
Roof Framing	Truss
Exterior Walls	2x4

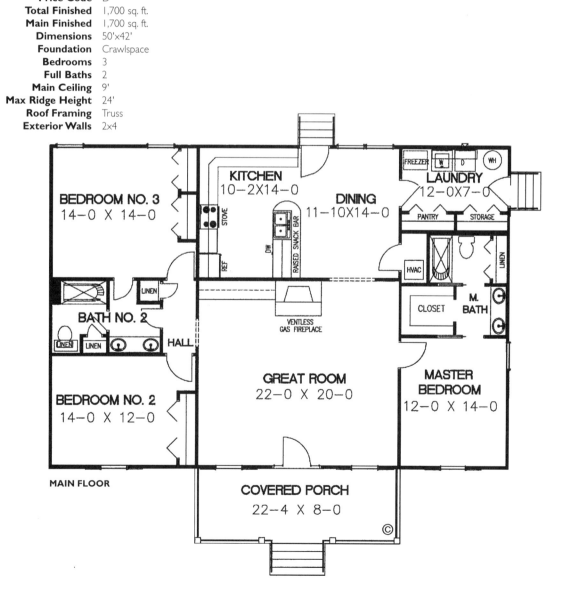

MAIN FLOOR

Design 90930

Units	Single
Price Code	B
Total Finished	1,702 sq. ft.
First Finished	1,238 sq. ft.
Second Finished	464 sq. ft.
Basement Unfinished	1,175 sq. ft.
Garage Unfinished	484 sq. ft.
Deck Unfinished	509 sq. ft.
Dimensions	34'x56'
Foundation	Basement
Bedrooms	3
Full Baths	1
3/4 Baths	1
First Ceiling	8'
Max Ridge Height	26'6"
Roof Framing	Stick
Exterior Walls	2x6

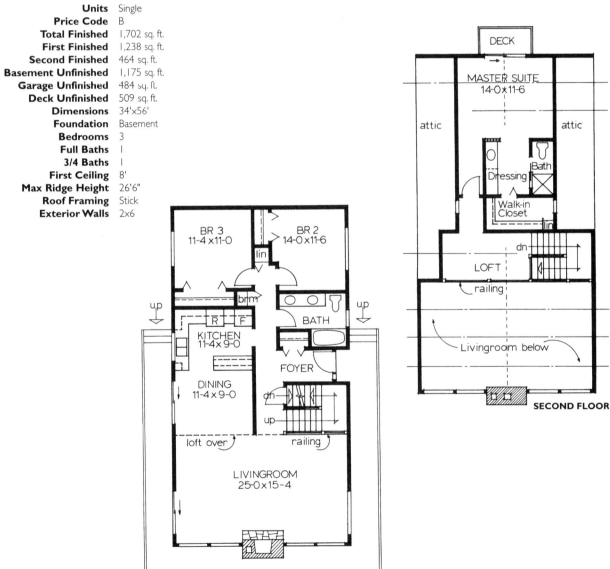

Design 94250

Units	Single
Price Code	F
Total Finished	1,706 sq. ft.
First Finished	906 sq. ft.
Second Finished	714 sq. ft.
Lower Finished	86 sq. ft.
Basement Unfinished	155 sq. ft.
Garage Unfinished	950 sq. ft.
Deck Unfinished	116 sq. ft.
Porch Unfinished	471 sq. ft.
Dimensions	40'x37'
Foundation	Pier/Post
Bedrooms	2
Full Baths	2
Half Baths	1
First Ceiling	8'
Second Ceiling	8'
Max Ridge Height	47'6"
Roof Framing	Stick/Truss
Exterior Walls	2x6

* Alternate foundation options available at an additional charge.
Please call 1-800-235-5700 for more information.

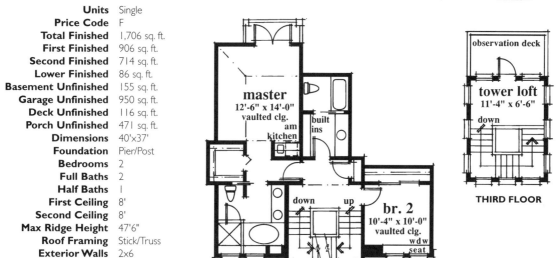

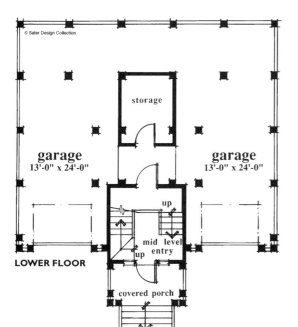

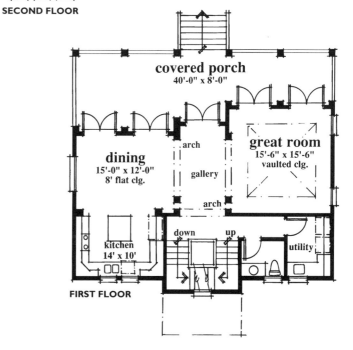

Design 24319

Units	Single
Price Code	B
Total Finished	1,710 sq. ft.
First Finished	728 sq. ft.
Second Finished	573 sq. ft.
Lower Finished	409 sq. ft.
Garage Unfinished	244 sq. ft.
Dimensions	28'x32'
Foundation	Basement
Bedrooms	3
Full Baths	2
First Ceiling	8'
Second Ceiling	8'
Max Ridge Height	33'
Roof Framing	Stick
Exterior Walls	2x4, 2x6

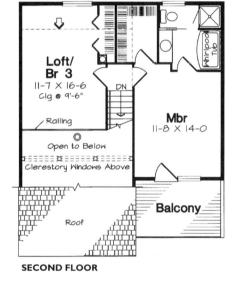

SECOND FLOOR

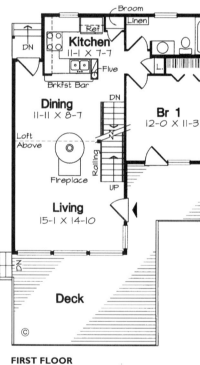

FIRST FLOOR

LOWER FLOOR

Design 98456

1,501-2,000 sq.ft. HOME PLANS

Units	Single
Price Code	B
Total Finished	1,715 sq. ft.
Main Finished	1,715 sq. ft.
Basement Unfinished	1,715 sq. ft.
Garage Unfinished	450 sq. ft.
Dimensions	55'x51'6"
Foundation	Basement
	Crawlspace
	Slab
Bedrooms	3
Full Baths	2
Main Ceiling	9'1"
Max Ridge Height	25'
Roof Framing	Stick
Exterior Walls	2x4

CAD **FILES AVAILABLE**
For more information call
800-235-5700

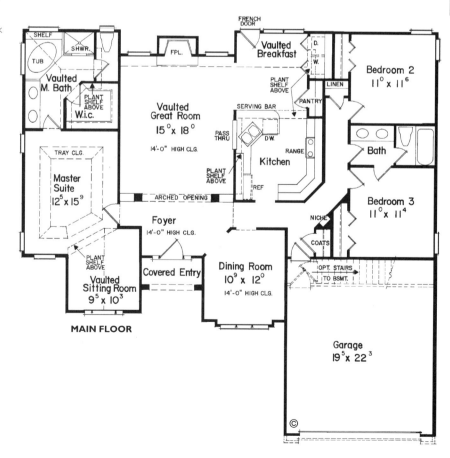

MAIN FLOOR

Units	Single
Price Code	B
Total Finished	1,716 sq. ft.
Main Finished	1,716 sq. ft.
Dimensions	56'x55'
Foundation	Crawlspace
	Slab
Bedrooms	4
Full Baths	2
Main Ceiling	8'
Max Ridge Height	20'
Roof Framing	Stick
Exterior Walls	2x4

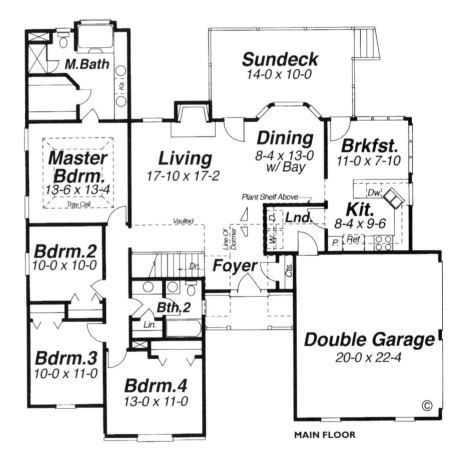

MAIN FLOOR

Design 82072

Units	Single
Price Code	C
Total Finished	1,722 sq. ft.
Main Finished	1,722 sq. ft.
Garage Unfinished	462 sq. ft.
Porch Unfinished	198 sq. ft.
Dimensions	58'x53'6"
Foundation	Basement
	Crawlspace
	Slab
Bedrooms	3
Full Baths	2
Exterior Walls	2x4

MAIN FLOOR

Merillat®

Visit us at www.merillat.com

PHOTOGRAPHY: JOHN EHRENCLOU

Units	Single
Price Code	B
Total Finished	1,737 sq. ft.
Main Finished	1,737 sq. ft.
Basement Unfinished	1,727 sq. ft.
Garage Unfinished	484 sq. ft.
Dimensions	72'1"x13'
Foundation	Basement
	Crawlspace
	Slab
Bedrooms	3
Full Baths	2
Main Ceiling	8'
Max Ridge Height	21'
Roof Framing	Stick
Exterior Walls	2x6

Please note: The photographed home may have been modified to suit homeowner preferences. If you order plans, have a builder or design professional check them against the photograph to confirm actual construction details.

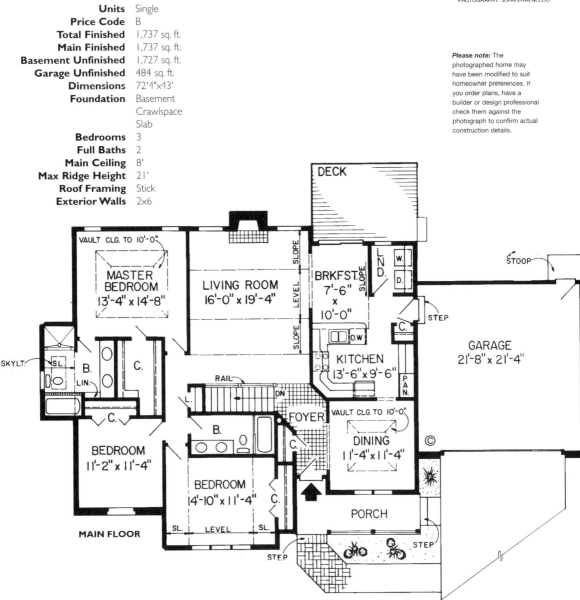

MAIN FLOOR

Design 90406

Units	Single
Price Code	B
Total Finished	1,737 sq. ft.
First Finished	954 sq. ft.
Second Finished	783 sq. ft.
Dimensions	30'x37'6"
Foundation	Basement
	Crawlspace
	Slab
Bedrooms	4
Full Baths	3
First Ceiling	8'
Second Ceiling	8'
Vaulted Ceiling	13'6"
Max Ridge Height	26'
Roof Framing	Stick
Exterior Walls	2x4

SECOND FLOOR

FIRST FLOOR

Units	Single
Price Code	B
Total Finished	1,739 sq. ft.
Main Finished	1,739 sq. ft.
Basement Unfinished	1,739 sq. ft.
Dimensions	54'x48'
Foundation	Basement
Bedrooms	3
Full Baths	2
Half Baths	1
Max Ridge Height	22'6"
Roof Framing	Stick
Exterior Walls	2x6

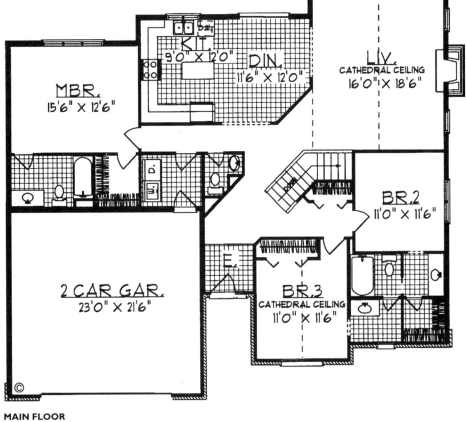

KIT.
9'0" X 12'0"

DIN.
11'6" X 12'0"

LIV.
CATHEDRAL CEILING
16'0" X 18'6"

MBR.
15'6" X 12'6"

BR.2
11'0" X 11'6"

2 CAR GAR.
23'0" X 21'6"

BR.3
CATHEDRAL CEILING
11'0" X 11'6"

MAIN FLOOR

Design 67006

Units	Single
Price Code	B
Total Finished	1,744 sq. ft.
Main Finished	1,744 sq. ft.
Bonus Unfinished	264 sq. ft.
Garage Unfinished	487 sq. ft.
Porch Unfinished	24 sq. ft.
Dimensions	51'x63'
Foundation	Slab
Bedrooms	3
Full Baths	2
Main Ceiling	8'
Vaulted Ceiling	13'6"
Max Ridge Height	23'
Roof Framing	Stick
Exterior Walls	2x4

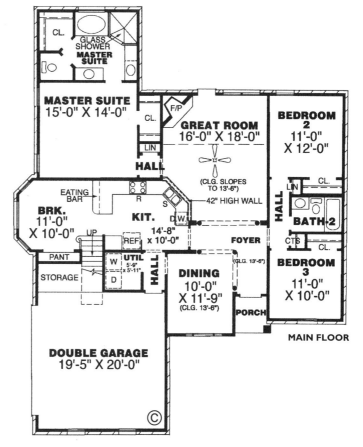

MASTER SUITE
15'-0" X 14'-0"

GREAT ROOM
16'-0" X 18'-0"

(CLG. SLOPES TO 13'-6")

42" HIGH WALL

BEDROOM 2
11'-0" X 12'-0"

BATH-2

BEDROOM 3
11'-0" X 10'-0"

EATING BAR

BRK.
11'-0" X 10'-0"

KIT.
14'-8" x 10'-0"

FOYER
(CLG. 13'-6")

PANT

UTIL
5'-9" x 5'-11"

STORAGE

DINING
10'-0" X 11'-9"
(CLG. 13'-6")

PORCH

DOUBLE GARAGE
19'-5" X 20'-0"

MAIN FLOOR

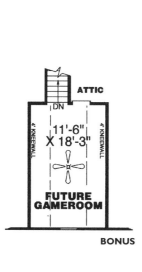

ATTIC

DN

11'-6" X 18'-3"

4' KNEEWALL

FUTURE GAMEROOM

BONUS

PHOTOGRAPHY: JOHN EHRENCLOU

Units	Single
Price Code	B
Total Finished	1,750 sq. ft.
Main Finished	1,750 sq. ft.
Basement Unfinished	1,083 sq. ft.
Garage Unfinished	796 sq. ft.
Porch Unfinished	100 sq. ft.
Dimensions	66'x50'
Foundation	Basement
	Crawlspace
	Slab
Bedrooms	2
Full Baths	2
Main Ceiling	8'
Max Ridge Height	24'6"
Roof Framing	Stick
Exterior Walls	2x4, 2x6

Please note: The photographed home may have been modified to suit homeowner preferences. If you order plans, have a builder or design professional check them against the photograph to confirm actual construction details.

OPTIONAL CRAWLSPACE/SLAB FOUNDATION

Optional Deck

Master Br
11-6 x 16-0

Great Rm
22-5 x 15-0

Screened Porch
9-9 x 9-9

Brkfst Bar

Kitchen
11-4 x 9-0

Dining Rm
15-0 x 9-6

Foyer

Cabinets

Railing

Br
9-0 x 11-0

Pantry

Air-Lock

Breakfast
11-0 x 8-0

Desk

Porch

Garage
32-0 x 28-0

Den
15-0 x 10-0
8'-6" Clg.

MAIN FLOOR

Design 97757

Units	Single
Price Code	B
Total Finished	1,755 sq. ft.
Main Finished	1,755 sq. ft.
Basement Unfinished	1,725 sq. ft.
Garage Unfinished	796 sq. ft.
Deck Unfinished	44 sq. ft.
Porch Unfinished	138 sq. ft.
Dimensions	78'6"x47'7"
Foundation	Basement
Bedrooms	3
Full Baths	2
Main Ceiling	8'
Max Ridge Height	22'
Roof Framing	Truss
Exterior Walls	2x4

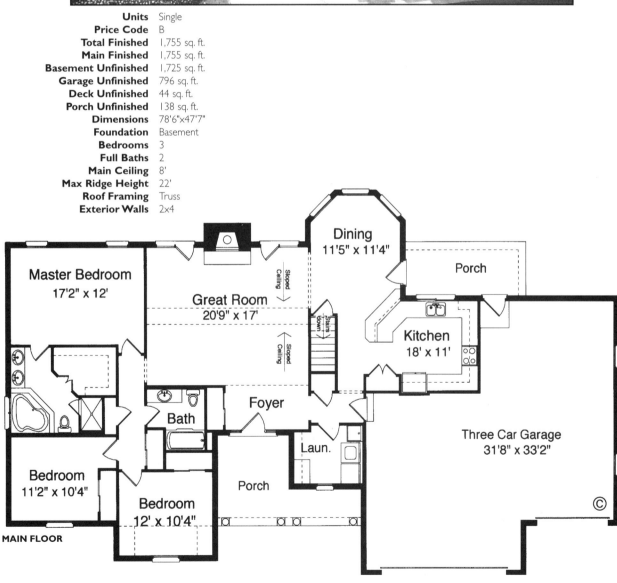

MAIN FLOOR

Master Bedroom 17'2" x 12'

Great Room 20'9" x 17'

Dining 11'5" x 11'4"

Porch

Kitchen 18' x 11'

Sloped Ceiling

Stairs Down

Foyer

Bath

Laun.

Three Car Garage 31'8" x 33'2"

Bedroom 11'2" x 10'4"

Bedroom 12' x 10'4"

Porch

Units	Single
Price Code	C
Total Finished	1,756 sq. ft.
Main Finished	1,756 sq. ft.
Basement Unfinished	1,756 sq. ft.
Dimensions	59'x58'
Foundation	Basement
Bedrooms	3
Full Baths	2
Max Ridge Height	21'10"
Roof Framing	Truss
Exterior Walls	2x6

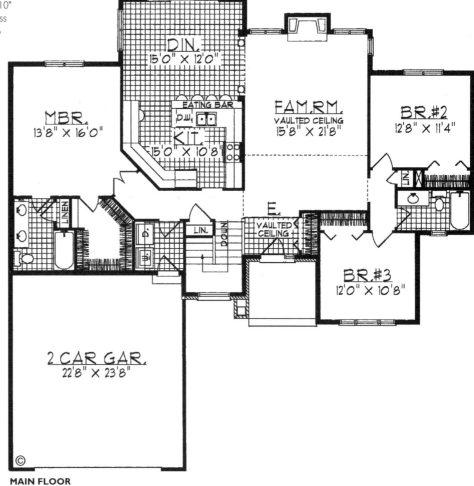

MAIN FLOOR

Design 34077

1,501-2,000 sq. ft. HOME PLANS

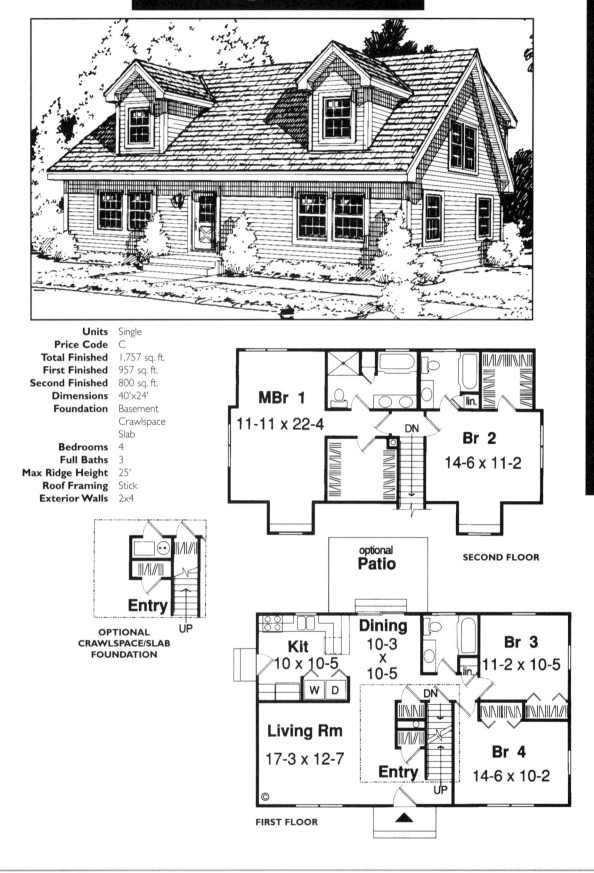

Units	Single
Price Code	C
Total Finished	1,757 sq. ft.
First Finished	957 sq. ft.
Second Finished	800 sq. ft.
Dimensions	40'x24'
Foundation	Basement
	Crawlspace
	Slab
Bedrooms	4
Full Baths	3
Max Ridge Height	25'
Roof Framing	Stick
Exterior Walls	2x4

MBr 1
11-11 x 22-4

DN

Br 2
14-6 x 11-2

lin.

SECOND FLOOR

Entry

UP

OPTIONAL CRAWLSPACE/SLAB FOUNDATION

optional
Patio

Kit
10 x 10-5

W | D

Dining
10-3
x
10-5

lin.

Br 3
11-2 x 10-5

Living Rm
17-3 x 12-7

DN

Entry

UP

Br 4
14-6 x 10-2

FIRST FLOOR

Visit us at www.merillat.com

Merillat.

Units	Single
Price Code	C
Total Finished	1,757 sq. ft.
First Finished	1,080 sq. ft.
Second Finished	677 sq. ft.
Basement Unfinished	1,080 sq. ft.
Garage Unfinished	576 sq. ft.
Porch Unfinished	192 sq. ft.
Dimensions	60'x36'
Foundation	Crawlspace
Bedrooms	3
Full Baths	2
Half Baths	1
First Ceiling	8'
Second Ceiling	8'
Max Ridge Height	22'6"
Roof Framing	Stick
Exterior Walls	2x6

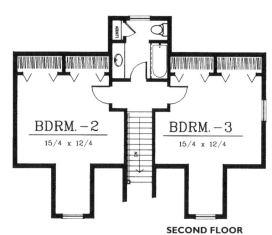

BDRM.−2
15/4 x 12/4

BDRM.−3
15/4 x 12/4

SECOND FLOOR

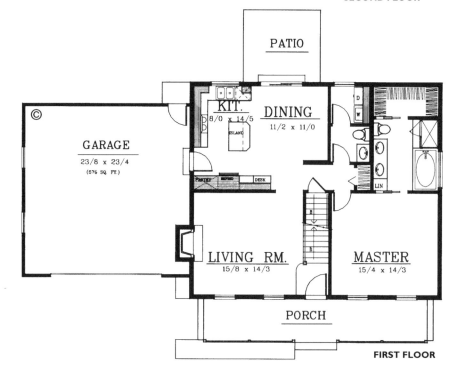

PATIO

GARAGE
23/8 x 23/4
(576 SQ. FT.)

KIT.
8/0 x 14/5

DINING
11/2 x 11/0

LIVING RM.
15/8 x 14/3

MASTER
15/4 x 14/3

PORCH

FIRST FLOOR

Design 65254

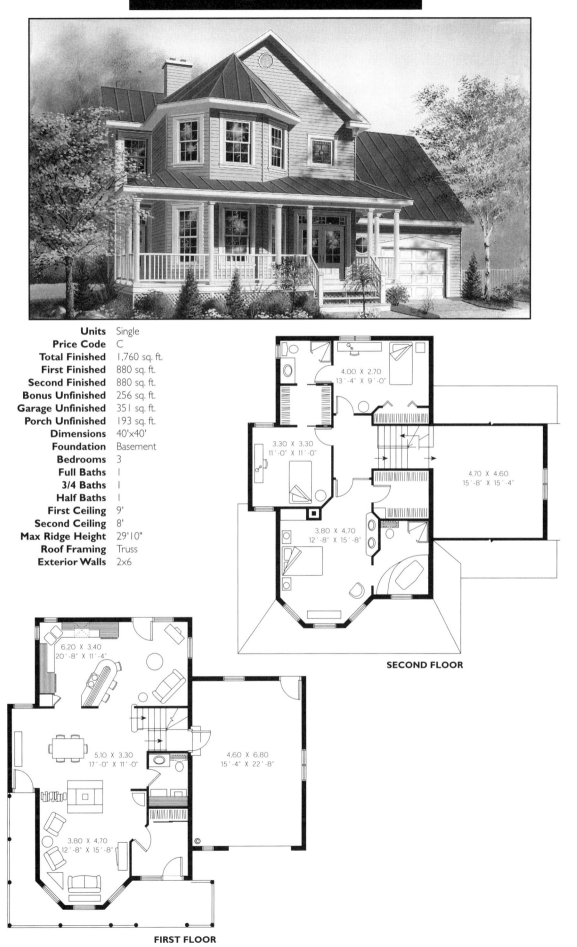

Units	Single
Price Code	C
Total Finished	1,760 sq. ft.
First Finished	880 sq. ft.
Second Finished	880 sq. ft.
Bonus Unfinished	256 sq. ft.
Garage Unfinished	351 sq. ft.
Porch Unfinished	193 sq. ft.
Dimensions	40'x40'
Foundation	Basement
Bedrooms	3
Full Baths	1
3/4 Baths	1
Half Baths	1
First Ceiling	9'
Second Ceiling	8'
Max Ridge Height	29'10"
Roof Framing	Truss
Exterior Walls	2x6

SECOND FLOOR

FIRST FLOOR

Design 34901

PHOTOGRAPHY: LAURIE SOLOMON

Units	Single
Price Code	C
Total Finished	1,763 sq. ft.
First Finished	909 sq. ft.
Second Finished	854 sq. ft.
Basement Unfinished	899 sq. ft.
Garage Unfinished	491 sq. ft.
Dimensions	48'x44'
Foundation	Basement
	Crawlspace
	Slab
Bedrooms	3
Full Baths	1
3/4 Baths	1
Half Baths	1
First Ceiling	8'
Second Ceiling	8'
Tray Ceiling	9'
Max Ridge Height	29'
Roof Framing	Stick
Exterior Walls	2x4, 2x6

SECOND FLOOR

Master Br
14-3 x 17-5

Br 3
12-2 x 10-1

Br 2
13-11 x 11-9

Railing

**OPTIONAL
CRAWLSPACE/SLAB
FOUNDATION**

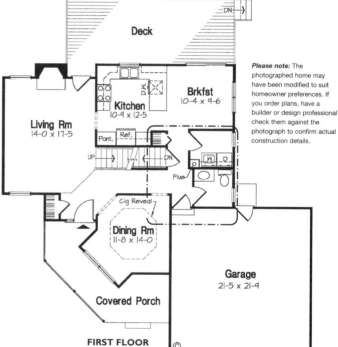

Deck

Living Rm
14-0 x 17-5

Kitchen
10-9 x 12-5

Brkfst
10-4 x 9-6

Dining Rm
11-8 x 14-0

Clg Reveal

Garage
21-5 x 21-4

Covered Porch

Please note: The photographed home may have been modified to suit homeowner preferences. If you order plans, have a builder or design professional check them against the photograph to confirm actual construction details.

FIRST FLOOR

Design 93133

Units	Single
Price Code	C
Total Finished	1,763 sq. ft.
Main Finished	1,763 sq. ft.
Basement Unfinished	1,763 sq. ft.
Garage Unfinished	658 sq. ft.
Dimensions	67'8"x42'8"
Foundation	Basement
Bedrooms	3
Full Baths	2
Main Ceiling	8'
Vaulted Ceiling	14'
Max Ridge Height	22'
Roof Framing	Truss
Exterior Walls	2x6

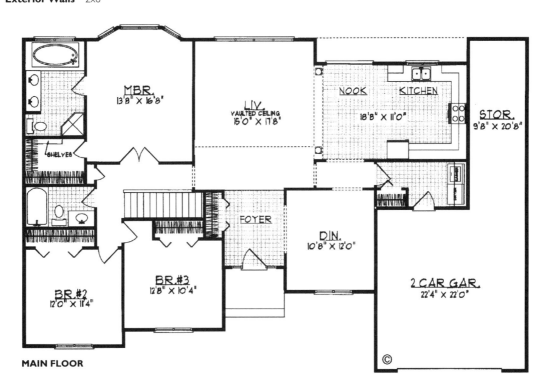

MAIN FLOOR

Units	Single
Price Code	C
Total Finished	1,764 sq. ft.
First Finished	887 sq. ft.
Second Finished	877 sq. ft.
Basement Unfinished	859 sq. ft.
Garage Unfinished	484 sq. ft.
Deck Unfinished	261 sq. ft.
Porch Unfinished	252 sq. ft.
Dimensions	61'x46'
Foundation	Basement
Bedrooms	3
Full Baths	2
Half Baths	1
First Ceiling	8'
Max Ridge Height	26'
Roof Framing	Stick
Exterior Walls	2x4

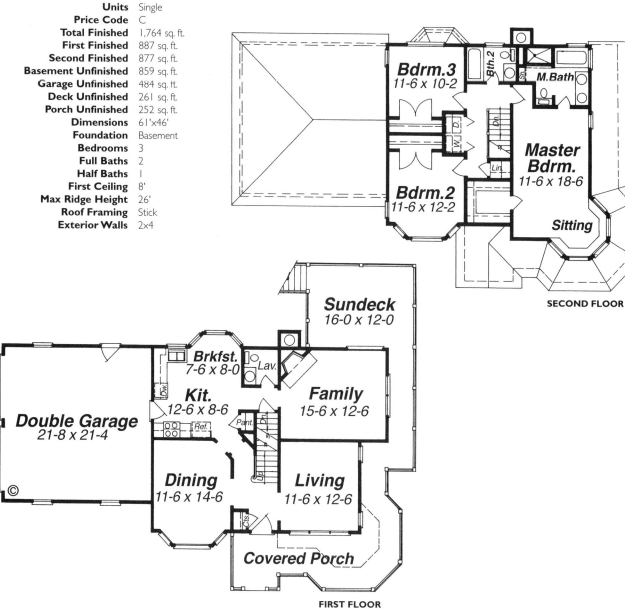

Bdrm.3 11-6 x 10-2

Bth.2

M.Bath

Bdrm.2 11-6 x 12-2

Master Bdrm. 11-6 x 18-6

Sitting

SECOND FLOOR

Sundeck 16-0 x 12-0

Brkfst. 7-6 x 8-0

Lav.

Kit. 12-6 x 8-6

Family 15-6 x 12-6

Double Garage 21-8 x 21-4

Pant.

Dining 11-6 x 14-6

Living 11-6 x 12-6

Covered Porch

FIRST FLOOR

Design 94204

PHOTOGRAPHY: COURTESY OF THE DESIGNER

Units	Single
Price Code	C
Total Finished	1,764 sq. ft.
First Finished	1,189 sq. ft.
Second Finished	575 sq. ft.
Bonus Unfinished	581 sq. ft.
Garage Unfinished	658 sq. ft.
Dimensions	46'x44'6"
Foundation	Pier/Post
Bedrooms	3
Full Baths	2
Half Baths	1
Max Ridge Height	36'
Roof Framing	Stick/Truss
Exterior Walls	2x6

* Alternate foundation options available at an additional charge.
Please call 1-800-235-5700 for more information.

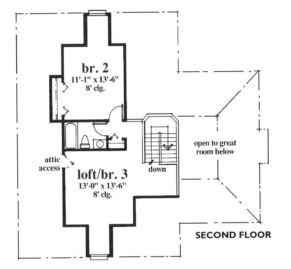

SECOND FLOOR

- br. 2 — 11'-1" x 13'-6" 8' clg.
- loft/br. 3 — 13'-0" x 13'-6" 8' clg.
- open to great room below
- attic access
- down

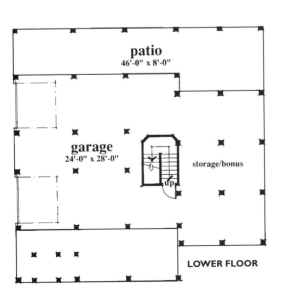

LOWER FLOOR

- patio — 46'-0" x 8'-0"
- garage — 24'-0" x 28'-0"
- storage/bonus
- up

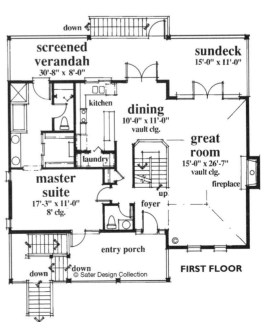

FIRST FLOOR

- screened verandah — 30'-8" x 8'-0"
- sundeck — 15'-0" x 11'-0"
- kitchen
- dining — 10'-0" x 11'-0" vault clg.
- great room — 15'-0" x 26'-7" vault clg.
- laundry
- master suite — 17'-3" x 11'-0" 8' clg.
- foyer
- fireplace
- entry porch
- down
- up
- © Sater Design Collection

Please note: The photographed home may have been modified to suit homeowner preferences. If you order plans, have a builder or design professional check them against the photograph to confirm actual construction details.

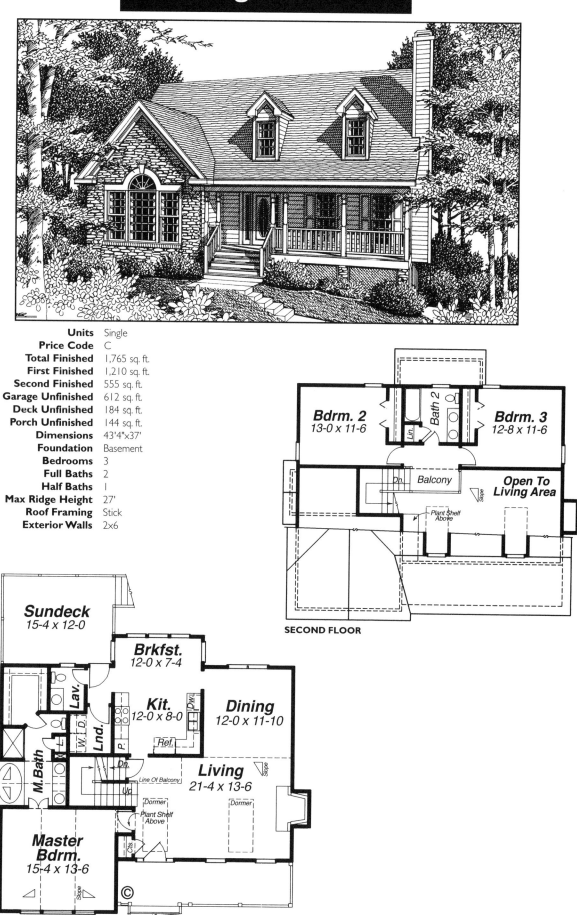

Units	Single
Price Code	C
Total Finished	1,765 sq. ft.
First Finished	1,210 sq. ft.
Second Finished	555 sq. ft.
Garage Unfinished	612 sq. ft.
Deck Unfinished	184 sq. ft.
Porch Unfinished	144 sq. ft.
Dimensions	43'4"x37'
Foundation	Basement
Bedrooms	3
Full Baths	2
Half Baths	1
Max Ridge Height	27'
Roof Framing	Stick
Exterior Walls	2x6

Bdrm. 2
13-0 x 11-6

Bath 2

Lin.

Bdrm. 3
12-8 x 11-6

Dn. **Balcony**

Open To Living Area

Slope

Plant Shelf Above

SECOND FLOOR

Sundeck
15-4 x 12-0

Brkfst.
12-0 x 7-4

Kit.
12-0 x 8-0

DW

Dining
12-0 x 11-10

Lav.

W.D.

Lnd.

P.

Ref.

W.L.

M.Bath

Dn.

Up

Line Of Balcony

Living
21-4 x 13-6

Slope

Dormer

Dormer

Plant Shelf Above

Clts.

Master Bdrm.
15-4 x 13-6

Slope

©

FIRST FLOOR

Design 64018

Units	Single
Price Code	C
Total Finished	1,767 sq. ft.
Main Finished	1,767 sq. ft.
Bonus Unfinished	262 sq. ft.
Garage Unfinished	462 sq. ft.
Dimensions	67'10"x48'5"
Foundation	Crawlspace
	Slab
Bedrooms	3
Full Baths	2
Main Ceiling	9'
Roof Framing	Stick
Exterior Walls	2x4

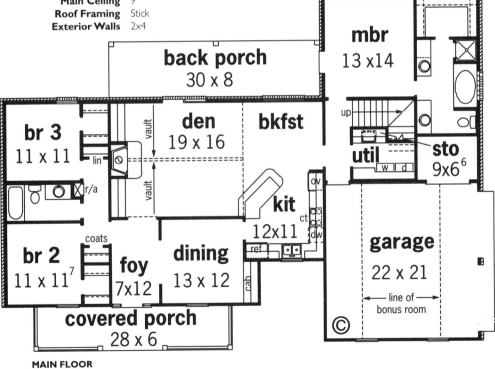

back porch 30 x 8

mbr 13 x14

den 19 x 16

bkfst

br 3 11 x 11

up

util

sto 9x6⁶

kit 12x11

br 2 11 x 11⁷

coats

foy 7x12

dining 13 x 12

garage 22 x 21

line of bonus room

covered porch 28 x 6

MAIN FLOOR

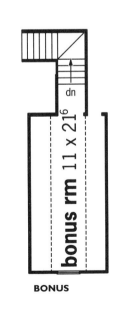

bonus rm 11 x 21⁶

dn

BONUS

Units	Single
Price Code	C
Total Finished	1,767 sq. ft.
First Finished	1,108 sq. ft.
Second Finished	659 sq. ft.
Basement Unfinished	875 sq. ft.
Porch Unfinished	145 sq. ft.
Dimensions	67'x30'
Foundation	Basement
Bedrooms	3
Full Baths	2
Half Baths	1
Max Ridge Height	21'
Roof Framing	Truss
Exterior Walls	2x4

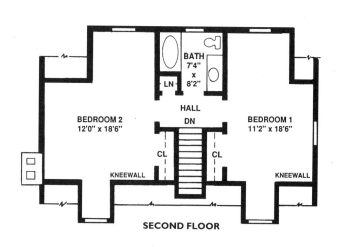

SECOND FLOOR

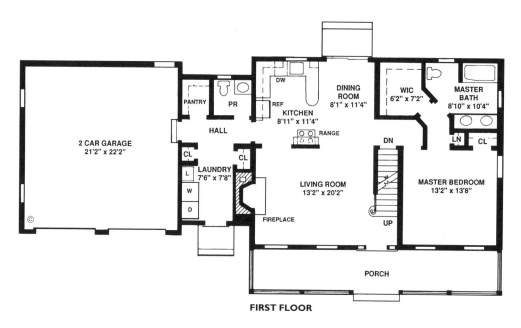

FIRST FLOOR

PHOTOGRAPHY: COURTESY OF THE DESIGNER

Units	Single
Price Code	C
Total Finished	1,768 sq. ft.
First Finished	905 sq. ft.
Second Finished	863 sq. ft.
Basement Unfinished	905 sq. ft.
Garage Unfinished	487 sq. ft.
Dimensions	40'8"x46'
Foundation	Basement
Bedrooms	3
Full Baths	2
Half Baths	1
First Ceiling	8'
Max Ridge Height	30'6"
Roof Framing	Stick
Exterior Walls	2x4

* Alternate foundation options available at an additional charge.
Please call 1-800-235-5700 for more information.

SECOND FLOOR

Please note: The photographed home may have been modified to suit homeowner preferences. If you order plans, have a builder or design professional check them against the photograph to confirm actual construction details.

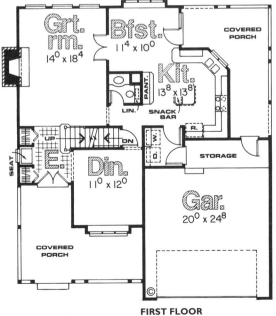

FIRST FLOOR

Units	Single
Price Code	C
Total Finished	1,771 sq. ft.
Main Finished	1,771 sq. ft.
Basement Unfinished	1,194 sq. ft.
Garage Unfinished	517 sq. ft.
Porch Unfinished	106 sq. ft.
Dimensions	54'x50'
Foundation	Slab
	Combo
	Basement/Crawlspace
	Crawlspace
Bedrooms	2
Full Baths	2
Main Ceiling	8'
Vaulted Ceiling	13'6"
Max Ridge Height	23'6"
Roof Framing	Stick
Exterior Walls	2x4

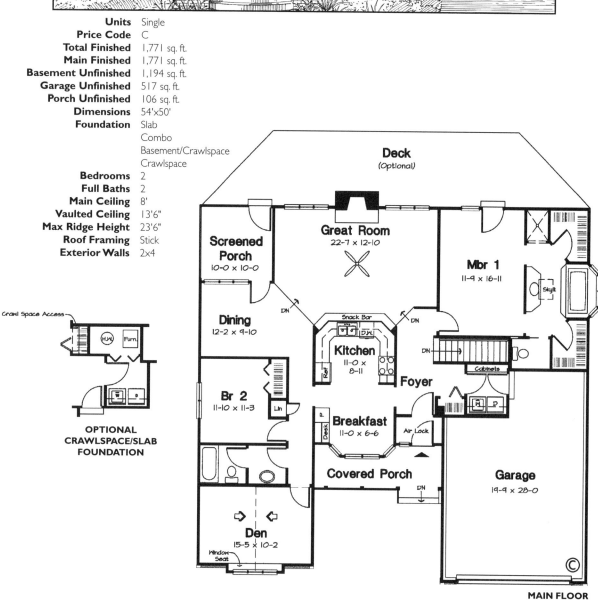

Crawl Space Access

OPTIONAL CRAWLSPACE/SLAB FOUNDATION

Deck (Optional)

Great Room 22-7 x 12-10

Screened Porch 10-0 x 10-0

Mbr 1 11-9 x 16-11

Skylt

Dining 12-2 x 9-10

DN

Snack Bar

Kitchen 11-0 x 8-11

DN

Cabinets

Br 2 11-10 x 11-3

Foyer

Breakfast 11-0 x 6-6

Air Lock

Den 15-5 x 10-2

Window Seat

Covered Porch

DN

Garage 19-9 x 28-0

MAIN FLOOR

Design 93261

Units	Single
Price Code	C
Total Finished	1,778 sq. ft.
Main Finished	1,778 sq. ft.
Basement Unfinished	1,008 sq. ft.
Garage Unfinished	728 sq. ft.
Dimensions	62'x28'
Foundation	Basement
Bedrooms	3
Full Baths	2
Main Ceiling	8'
Vaulted Ceiling	10'4"
Max Ridge Height	26'
Roof Framing	Stick/Truss
Exterior Walls	2x4

Sundeck
16-0 x 14-0

Pant.

Dining
12-6 x 11-6

Kit.
9-0 x 11-4

Dw.

Brkfst.
9-8 x 13-6

M.Bath

Bdrm. 3
13-6 x 11-0

Ref.

Desk

Dn.

Master Bdrm.
13-6 x 17-2

Cts.

Foyer
5-8 x 11-6

Living Area
19-8 x 15-6

W. D.

Dress.

Bth. 2

Ks.

Bdrm. 2
13-6 x 11-8

Porch

MAIN FLOOR

Design 98464

Units	Single
Price Code	C
Total Finished	1,779 sq. ft.
Main Finished	1,779 sq. ft.
Basement Unfinished	1,818 sq. ft.
Garage Unfinished	499 sq. ft.
Dimensions	57'x56'4"
Foundation	Basement
	Crawlspace
Bedrooms	3
Full Baths	2
Main Ceiling	9'
Max Ridge Height	24'6"
Roof Framing	Stick
Exterior Walls	2x4

CAD **FILES AVAILABLE**
For more information call
800-235-5700

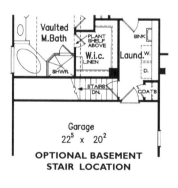

**OPTIONAL BASEMENT
STAIR LOCATION**

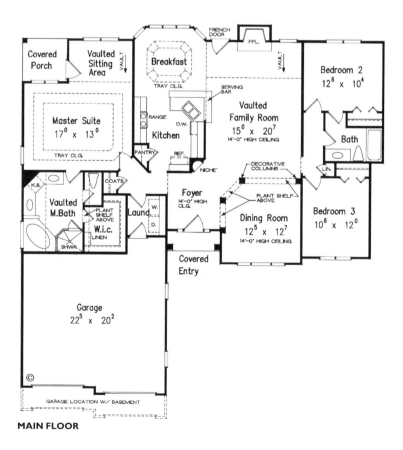

MAIN FLOOR

Design 92630

PHOTOGRAPHY: DONNA & RON KOLB, EXPOSURES UNLIMITED

Units	Single
Price Code	C
Total Finished	1,782 sq. ft.
Main Finished	1,782 sq. ft.
Basement Unfinished	1,735 sq. ft.
Garage Unfinished	407 sq. ft.
Dimensions	67'2"x47'
Foundation	Basement
Bedrooms	3
Full Baths	2
Max Ridge Height	20'
Roof Framing	Truss
Exterior Walls	2x4

Please note: The photographed home may have been modified to suit homeowner preferences. If you order plans, have a builder or design professional check them against the photograph to confirm actual construction details.

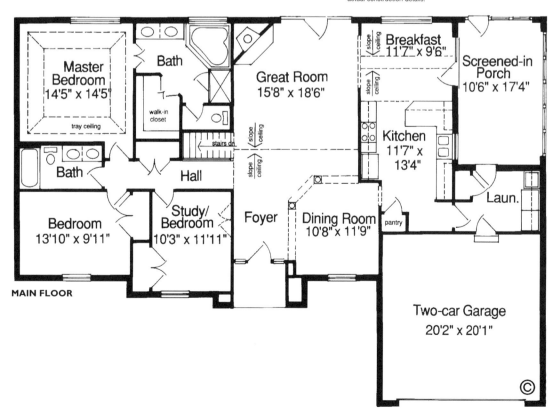

MAIN FLOOR

Units	Single
Price Code	C
Total Finished	1,783 sq. ft.
Main Finished	1,783 sq. ft.
Garage Unfinished	576 sq. ft.
Dimensions	82'10"x58'
Foundation	Slab
Bedrooms	3
Full Baths	1
3/4 Baths	1
Main Ceiling	8'
Max Ridge Height	16'
Roof Framing	Stick
Exterior Walls	2x4

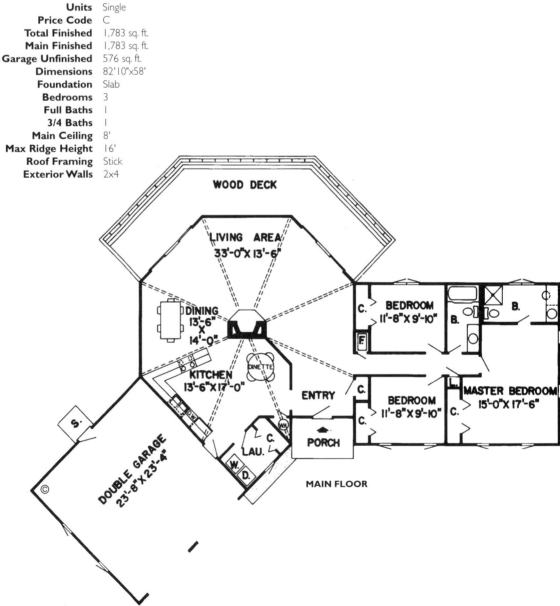

Design 65190

Units	Single
Price Code	C
Total Finished	1,784 sq. ft.
First Finished	824 sq. ft.
Second Finished	960 sq. ft.
Garage Unfinished	314 sq. ft.
Dimensions	38'×35'
Foundation	Basement
Bedrooms	3
Full Baths	I
Half Baths	I

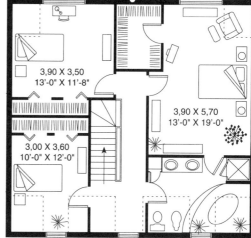

SECOND FLOOR

FIRST FLOOR

Visit us at www.merillat.com

Merillat.

Units	Single
Price Code	C
Total Finished	1,785 sq. ft.
First Finished	891 sq. ft.
Second Finished	894 sq. ft.
Basement Unfinished	891 sq. ft.
Garage Unfinished	534 sq. ft.
Dimensions	46'8"x35'8"
Foundation	Basement
	Crawlspace
	Slab
Bedrooms	3
Full Baths	1
3/4 Baths	1
Half Baths	1
First Ceiling	8'
Second Ceiling	8'
Max Ridge Height	28'
Roof Framing	Stick
Exterior Walls	2x4

Br 2
11-6 x 11-4

Br 3
11 x 11-4

linen

DN

open to below

1/2 wall

railing

Mstr Br
13-4 x 15

SECOND FLOOR

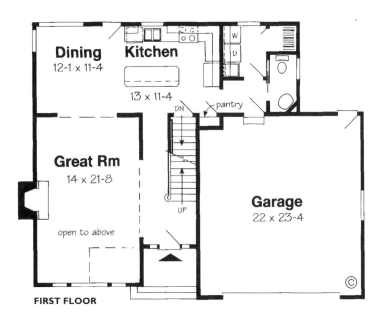

Dining
12-1 x 11-4

Kitchen
13 x 11-4

W D

DN

pantry

Great Rm
14 x 21-8

UP

Garage
22 x 23-4

open to above

FIRST FLOOR

Design 64500

Units	Single
Price Code	C
Total Finished	1,785 sq. ft.
Main Finished	1,785 sq. ft.
Basement Unfinished	1,785 sq. ft.
Garage Unfinished	528 sq. ft.
Porch Unfinished	334 sq. ft.
Dimensions	56'x32'
Foundation	Basement
	Crawlspace
	Slab
Bedrooms	3
Full Baths	2
3/4 Baths	1
Main Ceiling	9'
Max Ridge Height	24'
Roof Framing	Stick
Exterior Walls	2x4

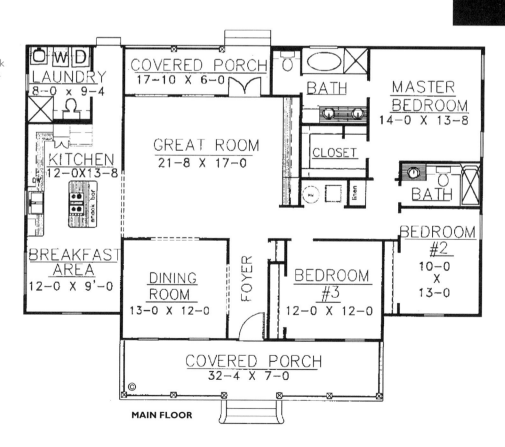

MAIN FLOOR

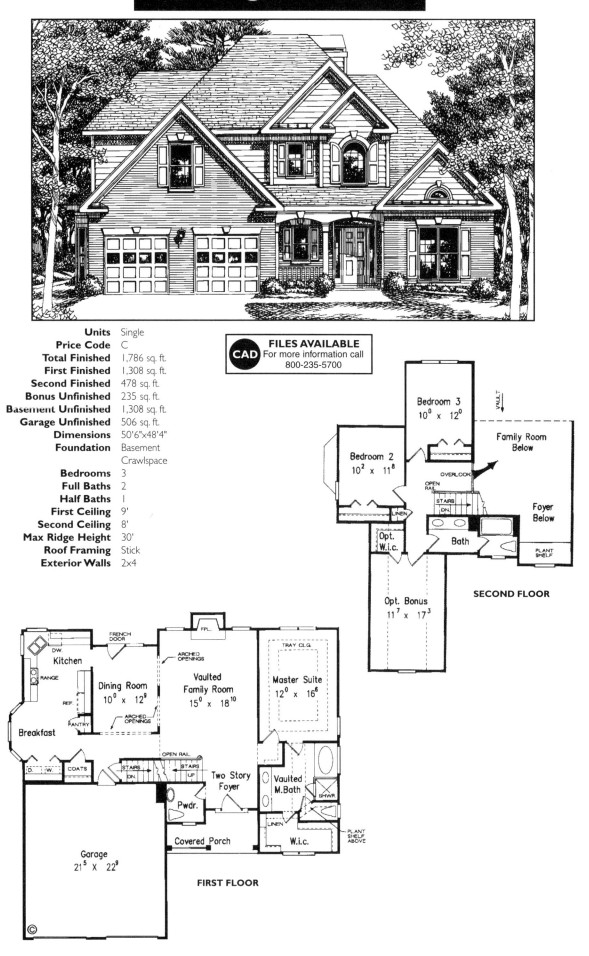

Units	Single
Price Code	C
Total Finished	1,786 sq. ft.
First Finished	1,308 sq. ft.
Second Finished	478 sq. ft.
Bonus Unfinished	235 sq. ft.
Basement Unfinished	1,308 sq. ft.
Garage Unfinished	506 sq. ft.
Dimensions	50'6"x48'4"
Foundation	Basement
	Crawlspace
Bedrooms	3
Full Baths	2
Half Baths	1
First Ceiling	9'
Second Ceiling	8'
Max Ridge Height	30'
Roof Framing	Stick
Exterior Walls	2x4

CAD FILES AVAILABLE For more information call 800-235-5700

SECOND FLOOR

Bedroom 3 10⁰ x 12⁰
Bedroom 2 10² x 11⁸
Family Room Below
Foyer Below
Opt. W.i.c.
Bath
Opt. Bonus 11⁷ x 17³
OVERLOOK
OPEN RAIL
STAIRS DN.
LINEN
VAULT
PLANT SHELF

FIRST FLOOR

Kitchen
Dining Room 10⁰ x 12⁹
Vaulted Family Room 15⁰ x 18¹⁰
Master Suite 12⁰ x 16⁶
Breakfast
PANTRY
REF.
RANGE
DW.
FRENCH DOOR
ARCHED OPENINGS
FPL.
TRAY CLG.
COATS
D. W.
STAIRS DN.
STAIRS UP
OPEN RAIL
Two Story Foyer
Pwdr.
Vaulted M.Bath
SHWR.
LINEN
W.i.c.
PLANT SHELF ABOVE
Covered Porch
Garage 21⁵ x 22⁹

Design 92420

Units	Single
Price Code	B
Total Finished	1,787 sq. ft.
Main Finished	1,787 sq. ft.
Bonus Unfinished	263 sq. ft.
Basement Unfinished	1,787 sq. ft.
Dimensions	55'8"x56'6"
Foundation	Basement
	Crawlspace
Bedrooms	3
Full Baths	2
Main Ceiling	9'
Vaulted Ceiling	11'
Tray Ceiling	11'
Max Ridge Height	21'
Roof Framing	Stick
Exterior Walls	2x4

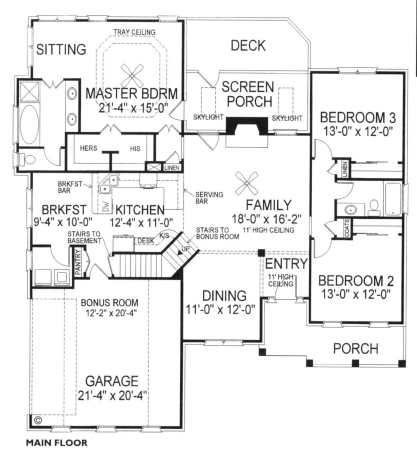

MAIN FLOOR

Units	Single
Price Code	C
Total Finished	1,792 sq. ft.
Main Finished	1,792 sq. ft.
Basement Unfinished	818 sq. ft.
Garage Unfinished	857 sq. ft.
Porch Unfinished	336 sq. ft.
Dimensions	56'x32'
Foundation	Basement
Bedrooms	3
Full Baths	2
Main Ceiling	8'
Max Ridge Height	25'
Roof Framing	Stick
Exterior Walls	2x4, 2x6

MAIN FLOOR

Design 97108

Units	Single
Price Code	C
Total Finished	1,794 sq. ft.
Main Finished	1,794 sq. ft.
Basement Unfinished	1,794 sq. ft.
Dimensions	65'4"x51'4"
Foundation	Basement
Bedrooms	3
Full Baths	2
Max Ridge Height	26'2"
Roof Framing	Truss
Exterior Walls	2x6

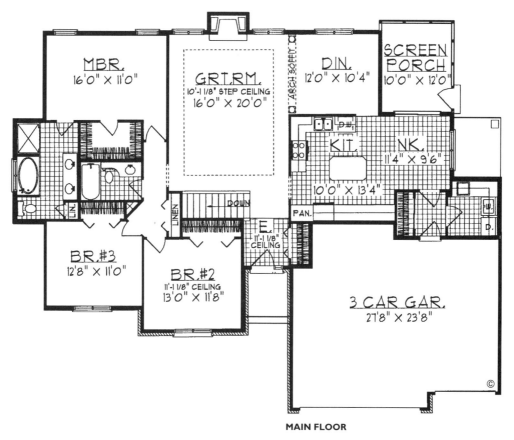

MBR.
16'0" X 11'0"

GRT. RM.
10'-1 1/8" STEP CEILING
16'0" X 20'0"

DIN.
12'0" X 10'4"

SCREEN PORCH
10'0" X 12'0"

KIT.
10'0" X 13'4"

NK.
11'4" X 9'6"

PAN.

DOWN

LINEN

E.
11'-1 1/8" CEILING

BR. #3
12'8" X 11'0"

BR. #2
11'-1 1/8" CEILING
13'0" X 11'8"

3 CAR GAR.
27'8" X 23'8"

MAIN FLOOR

Units	Single
Price Code	C
Total Finished	1,795 sq. ft.
Main Finished	1,795 sq. ft.
Garage Unfinished	482 sq. ft.
Deck Unfinished	240 sq. ft.
Porch Unfinished	42 sq. ft.
Dimensions	53'x61'
Foundation	Slab
Bedrooms	3
Full Baths	2
Main Ceiling	8'-10'
Max Ridge Height	24'6"
Roof Framing	Stick
Exterior Walls	2x4

COVERED PATIO

BRKFST. AREA 11⁶ X 10
10'-0" CEILING

COVERED PATIO

MASTER BEDROOM 14 X 14⁶
VAULTED CEILING 8'-0" TO 10'-0"

KITCHEN

PANTRY

REF.

D.W.

GREAT ROOM 14 X 20
10'-0" CEILING

CLOSET

BEDRM. TWO 11 X 13
8'-0" CEILING

LINEN

BATH TWO

HALL

MSTR BATH

WHIRLPOOL

W.I. CLOSET

HALLWAY

UTILITY

DRY

WASH

H.W.

STUDY 10 X 11⁶
10'-0" CEILING

ENTRY

COAT

LINEN

LINEN

CLOSET

SEAT

BEDRM. THREE 12 X 11
8'-0" CEILING

MAIN FLOOR

COVERED PORCH

DOUBLE GARAGE

©

Design 62052

Units	Single
Price Code	C
Total Finished	1,797 sq. ft.
First Finished	1,356 sq. ft.
Second Finished	441 sq. ft.
Dimensions	48'x43'
Foundation	Basement
	Crawlspace
	Slab
Bedrooms	3
Full Baths	2
Half Baths	1

SECOND FLOOR

FIRST FLOOR

Design 61048

Units	Single
Price Code	C
Total Finished	1,798 sq. ft.
Main Finished	1,798 sq. ft.
Garage Unfinished	417 sq. ft.
Porch Unfinished	196 sq. ft.
Dimensions	54'2"x56'2"
Foundation	Basement
	Crawlspace
	Slab
Bedrooms	3
Full Baths	2
Main Ceiling	8'
Roof Framing	Stick
Exterior Walls	2x4

MAIN FLOOR

Design 65377

Units	Single
Price Code	C
Total Finished	1,801 sq. ft.
First Finished	960 sq. ft.
Second Finished	841 sq. ft.
Dimensions	36'x30'
Foundation	Basement
Bedrooms	3
Full Baths	1
Half Baths	1

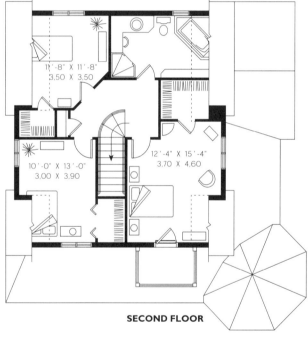

11'-8" X 11'-8"
3,50 X 3,50

12'-4" X 15'-4"
3,70 X 4,60

10'-0" X 13'-0"
3,00 X 3,90

SECOND FLOOR

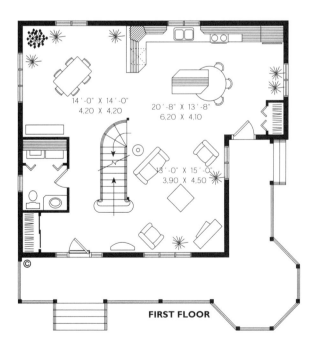

14'-0" X 14'-0"
4,20 X 4,20

20'-8" X 13'-8"
6,20 X 4,10

13'-0" X 15'-0"
3,90 X 4,50

FIRST FLOOR

Merillat.

Visit us at www.merillat.com

Units	Single
Price Code	C
Total Finished	1,804 sq. ft.
Main Finished	1,804 sq. ft.
Basement Unfinished	1,804 sq. ft.
Garage Unfinished	506 sq. ft.
Deck Unfinished	220 sq. ft.
Porch Unfinished	156 sq. ft.
Dimensions	62'x55'8"
Foundation	Basement
	Crawlspace
	Slab
Bedrooms	3
Full Baths	2
Main Ceiling	8'
Max Ridge Height	22'1"
Roof Framing	Stick
Exterior Walls	2x4

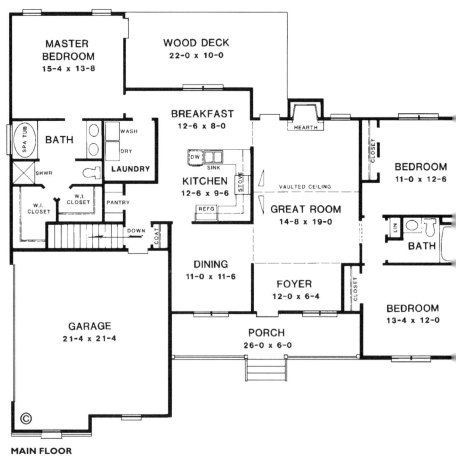

MAIN FLOOR

Design 93413

Units	Single
Price Code	C
Total Finished	1,808 sq. ft.
First Finished	1,271 sq. ft.
Second Finished	537 sq. ft.
Basement Unfinished	1,271 sq. ft.
Garage Unfinished	555 sq. ft.
Dimensions	44'4"x73'2"
Foundation	Basement
Bedrooms	3
Full Baths	2
Half Baths	1
Max Ridge Height	28'
Roof Framing	Stick
Exterior Walls	2x4

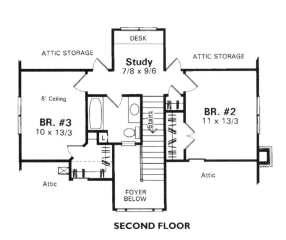

SECOND FLOOR

FIRST FLOOR

Units	Single
Price Code	C
Total Finished	1,811 sq. ft.
Main Finished	1,811 sq. ft.
Basement Unfinished	1,811 sq. ft.
Garage Unfinished	484 sq. ft.
Deck Unfinished	336 sq. ft.
Porch Unfinished	390 sq. ft.
Dimensions	89'6"x44'4"
Foundation	Basement
	Crawlspace
	Slab
Bedrooms	3
Full Baths	2
Main Ceiling	8'
Max Ridge Height	16'4"
Roof Framing	Stick
Exterior Walls	2x4

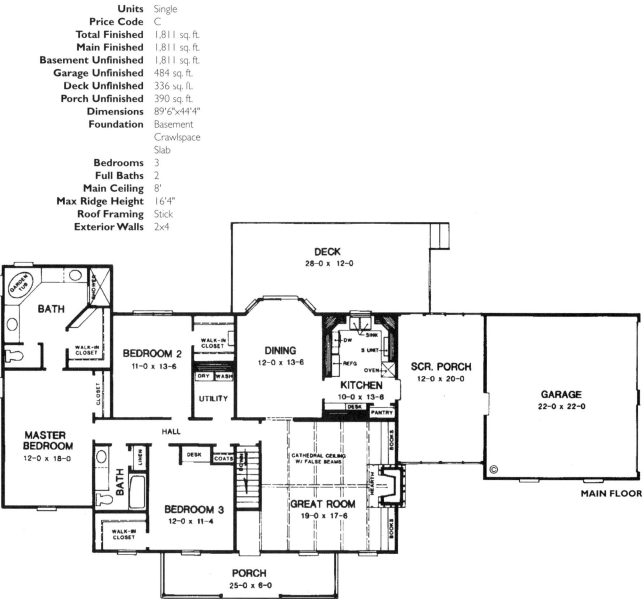

Design 67000

Units	Single
Price Code	C
Total Finished	1,815 sq. ft.
Main Finished	1,815 sq. ft.
Dimensions	58'3"x66'1"
Foundation	Slab
Bedrooms	3
Full Baths	2
Main Ceiling	8'
Max Ridge Height	24'
Roof Framing	Stick
Exterior Walls	2x4

1,501-2,000 sq. ft. HOME PLANS

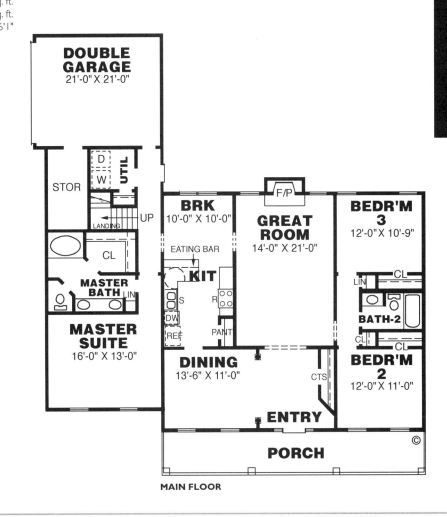

MAIN FLOOR

Visit us at www.merillat.com

Merillat.

Units Single
Price Code G
Total Finished 1,822 sq. ft.
Main Finished 1,822 sq. ft.
Garage Unfinished 537 sq. ft.
Dimensions 58'x67'2"
Foundation Basement
Bedrooms 3
Full Baths 2
Max Ridge Height 26'10"
Roof Framing Stick
Exterior Walls 2x6

* Alternate foundation options available at an additional charge.
Please call 1-800-235-5700 for more information.

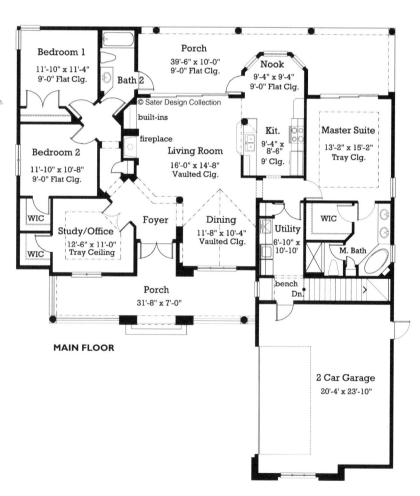

MAIN FLOOR

Design 90457

1,501-2,000 sq. ft. HOME PLANS

Units	Single
Price Code	C
Total Finished	1,830 sq. ft.
First Finished	1,224 sq. ft.
Second Finished	606 sq. ft.
Bonus Unfinished	306 sq. ft.
Basement Unfinished	1,204 sq. ft.
Deck Unfinished	192 sq. ft.
Porch Unfinished	130 sq. ft.
Dimensions	40'x36'4"
Foundation	Basement
	Crawlspace
Bedrooms	3
Full Baths	2
Half Baths	1
First Ceiling	8'
Second Ceiling	8'
Max Ridge Height	25'10"
Roof Framing	Stick
Exterior Walls	2x4

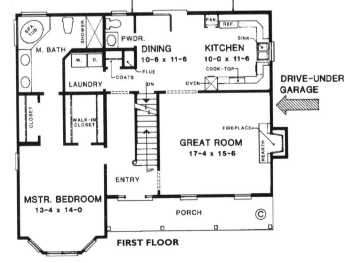

Units	Single
Price Code	C
Total Finished	1,830 sq. ft.
Main Finished	1,830 sq. ft.
Garage Unfinished	759 sq. ft.
Deck Unfinished	315 sq. ft.
Porch Unfinished	390 sq. ft.
Dimensions	75'x52'3"
Foundation	Basement
	Crawlspace
	Slab
Bedrooms	3
Full Baths	2
Max Ridge Height	27'3"
Roof Framing	Stick
Exterior Walls	2x4

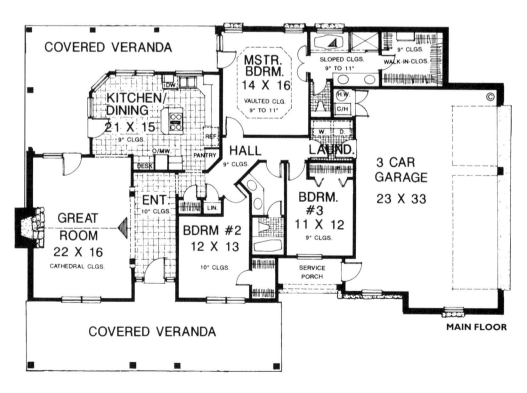

Design 99208

1,501-2,000 sq. ft. HOME PLANS

Units	Single
Price Code	C
Total Finished	1,830 sq. ft.
Main Finished	1,830 sq. ft.
Basement Unfinished	1,830 sq. ft.
Dimensions	75'x43'5"
Foundation	Basement
Bedrooms	3
Full Baths	2
Max Ridge Height	25'
Roof Framing	Truss
Exterior Walls	2x6

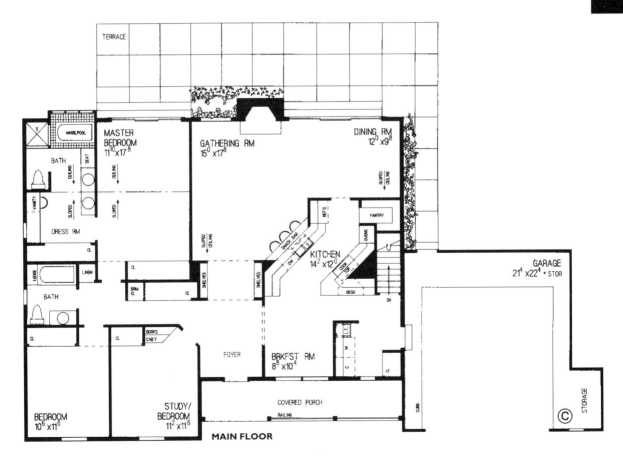

TERRACE

MASTER BEDROOM 11¹⁰x17⁸

GATHERING RM 15⁰x17⁸

DINING RM 12⁰x9⁸

WHIRLPOOL

BATH

SEAT

CEILING

SLOPED CEILING

PANTRY

DRESS RM

SLOPED CEILING

KITCHEN 14²x12⁰

GARAGE 21⁴x22⁴ + STOR

LINEN

SHELVES

DESK

BATH

BOOKS CAB'T

FOYER

BRKFST RM 8⁶x10⁴

STORAGE

BEDROOM 10⁶x11⁶

STUDY/ BEDROOM 11²x11⁶

COVERED PORCH
RAILING

MAIN FLOOR

Design 34031

Units	Single
Price Code	C
Total Finished	1,831 sq. ft.
Main Finished	1,831 sq. ft.
Basement Unfinished	1,831 sq. ft.
Garage Unfinished	484 sq. ft.
Dimensions	60'x52'
Foundation	Basement
	Crawlspace
	Slab
Bedrooms	3
Full Baths	2
Half Baths	1
Main Ceiling	8'
Max Ridge Height	22'
Roof Framing	Stick
Exterior Walls	2x4, 2x6

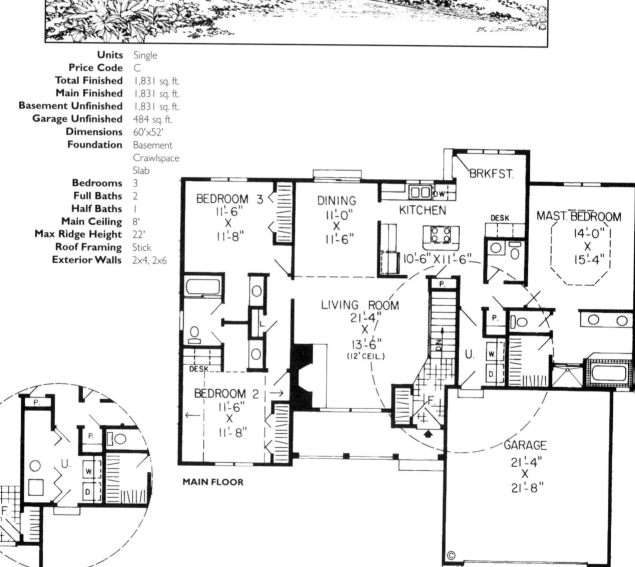

OPTIONAL
CRAWLSPACE/SLAB
FOUNDATION

MAIN FLOOR

To order blueprints, call **800-235-5700** or visit us on the web, **familyhomeplans.com**

Design 98467

Units	Single
Price Code	C
Total Finished	1,832 sq. ft.
Main Finished	1,832 sq. ft.
Bonus Unfinished	68 sq. ft.
Basement Unfinished	1,832 sq. ft.
Garage Unfinished	451 sq. ft.
Dimensions	59'6"x52'6"
Foundation	Basement
	Crawlspace
Bedrooms	3
Full Baths	2
Half Baths	1
Main Ceiling	9'
Max Ridge Height	26'
Roof Framing	Stick
Exterior Walls	2x4

CAD FILES AVAILABLE
For more information call
800-235-5700

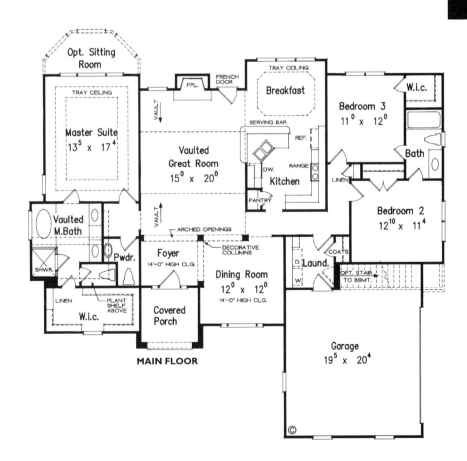

MAIN FLOOR

Units	Single
Price Code	C
Total Finished	1,837 sq. ft.
First Finished	1,448 sq. ft.
Second Finished	389 sq. ft.
Garage Unfinished	312 sq. ft.
Dimensions	54'x44'
Foundation	Crawlspace
Bedrooms	2
Full Baths	1
3/4 Baths	2
Max Ridge Height	28'
Roof Framing	Stick
Exterior Walls	2x6

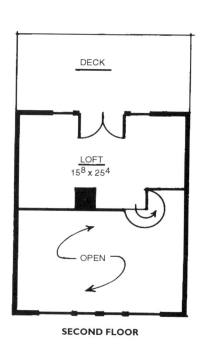

SECOND FLOOR

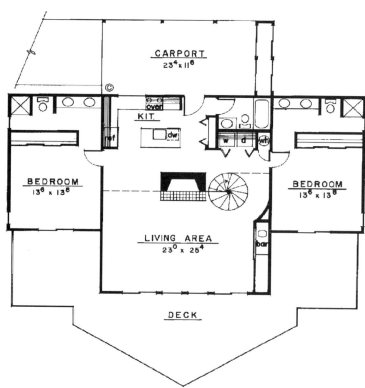

FIRST FLOOR

Design 68169

Units	Single
Price Code	C
Total Finished	1,838 sq. ft.
Main Finished	1,838 sq. ft.
Bonus Unfinished	394 sq. ft.
Garage Unfinished	568 sq. ft.
Deck Unfinished	936 sq. ft.
Dimensions	65'x56'
Foundation	Crawlspace
	Slab
Bedrooms	3
Full Baths	2
Main Ceiling	9'
Max Ridge Height	24'
Exterior Walls	2x4

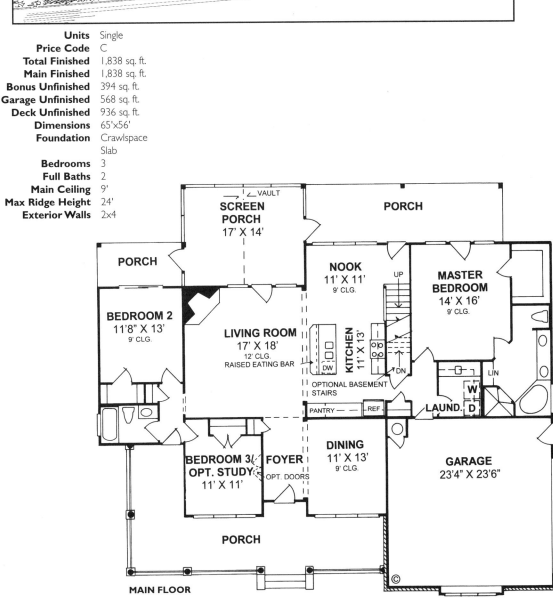

MAIN FLOOR

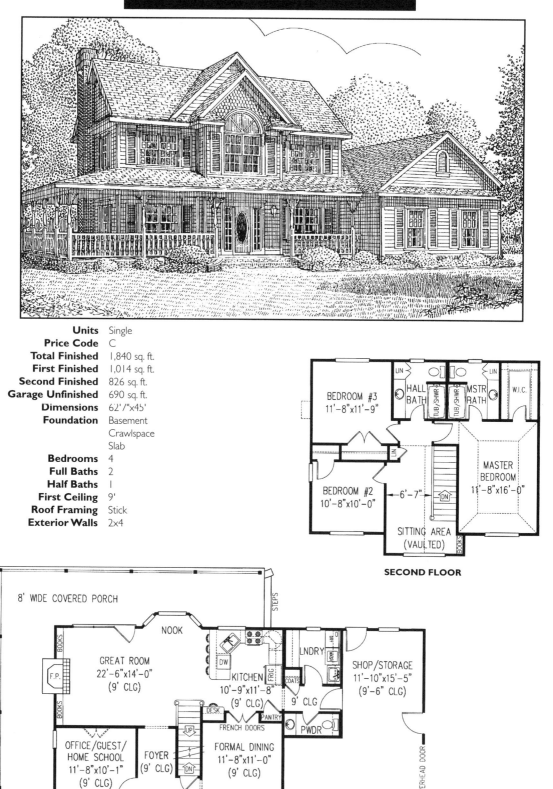

Units	Single
Price Code	C
Total Finished	1,840 sq. ft.
First Finished	1,014 sq. ft.
Second Finished	826 sq. ft.
Garage Unfinished	690 sq. ft.
Dimensions	62'7"x45'
Foundation	Basement
	Crawlspace
	Slab
Bedrooms	4
Full Baths	2
Half Baths	1
First Ceiling	9'
Roof Framing	Stick
Exterior Walls	2x4

SECOND FLOOR

BEDROOM #3
11'-8"x11'-9"

HALL BATH

MSTR BATH

W.I.C.

BEDROOM #2
10'-8"x10'-0"

MASTER BEDROOM
11'-8"x16'-0"

6'-7"

SITTING AREA (VAULTED)

FIRST FLOOR

8' WIDE COVERED PORCH

NOOK

GREAT ROOM
22'-6"x14'-0"
(9' CLG)

KITCHEN
10'-9"x11'-8"
(9' CLG)

DW

LNDRY

SHOP/STORAGE
11'-10"x15'-5"
(9'-6" CLG)

FRIG

COATS

9' CLG

DESK

PANTRY

FRENCH DOORS

PWDR

OFFICE/GUEST/
HOME SCHOOL
11'-8"x10'-1"
(9' CLG)

FOYER
(9' CLG)

UP

DN

FORMAL DINING
11'-8"x11'-0"
(9' CLG)

GARAGE
21'-0"x21'-10"
(9'-6" CLG)

COATS

8' WIDE COVERED PORCH

STEPS

9' OVERHEAD DOOR

9' OVERHEAD DOOR

Design 82073

Units	Single
Price Code	C
Total Finished	1,841 sq. ft.
First Finished	921 sq. ft.
Second Finished	920 sq. ft.
Bonus Unfinished	233 sq. ft.
Garage Unfinished	529 sq. ft.
Porch Unfinished	188 sq. ft.
Dimensions	55'4"×38'2"
Foundation	Basement Crawlspace Slab
Bedrooms	3
Full Baths	2
Half Baths	1
First Ceiling	8'
Exterior Walls	2x4

SECOND FLOOR

FIRST FLOOR

Units	Single
Price Code	B
Total Finished	1,842 sq. ft.
Main Finished	1,842 sq. ft.
Bonus Unfinished	386 sq. ft.
Dimensions	54'x63'
Foundation	Crawlspace
	Slab
Bedrooms	3
Full Baths	2
Main Ceiling	9
Max Ridge Height	30'
Exterior Walls	2x4

* Alternate foundation options available at an additional charge.
Please call 1-800-235-5700 for more information.

OPTIONAL GAMEROOM
20'4" X 16'

BONUS

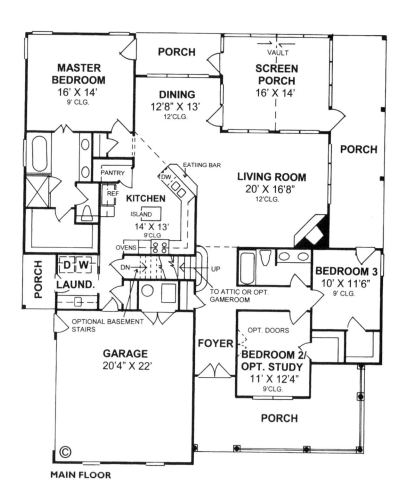

MASTER BEDROOM 16' X 14' 9' CLG.

PORCH

SCREEN PORCH 16' X 14' VAULT

DINING 12'8" X 13' 12'CLG.

PORCH

PANTRY

REF

KITCHEN ISLAND 14' X 13' 9'CLG

EATIING BAR

DW

LIVING ROOM 20' X 16'8" 12'CLG.

OVENS

PORCH

D W **LAUND.**

DN

UP

TO ATTIC OR OPT. GAMEROOM

BEDROOM 3 10' X 11'6" 9' CLG.

OPTIONAL BASEMENT STAIRS

GARAGE 20'4" X 22'

FOYER

OPT. DOORS

BEDROOM 2/ OPT. STUDY 11' X 12'4" 9'CLG.

PORCH

MAIN FLOOR

Design 90466

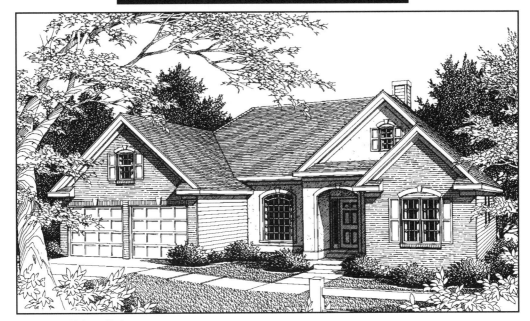

Units	Single
Price Code	C
Total Finished	1,845 sq. ft.
Main Finished	1,845 sq. ft.
Garage Unfinished	512 sq. ft.
Deck Unfinished	216 sq. ft.
Porch Unfinished	38 sq. ft.
Dimensions	57'2"x54'10"
Foundation	Crawlspace
	Slab
Bedrooms	3
Full Baths	2
Half Baths	1
Main Ceiling	8'
Max Ridge Height	23'10"
Roof Framing	Stick
Exterior Walls	2x4

MAIN FLOOR

Design 98425

Units	Single
Price Code	C
Total Finished	1,845 sq. ft.
Main Finished	1,845 sq. ft.
Bonus Unfinished	409 sq. ft.
Basement Unfinished	1,845 sq. ft.
Garage Unfinished	529 sq. ft.
Dimensions	56'x60'
Foundation	Basement
	Crawlspace
Bedrooms	3
Full Baths	2
Half Baths	1
Main Ceiling	9'
Max Ridge Height	26'6"
Roof Framing	Stick
Exterior Walls	2x4

CAD FILES AVAILABLE
For more information call
800-235-5700

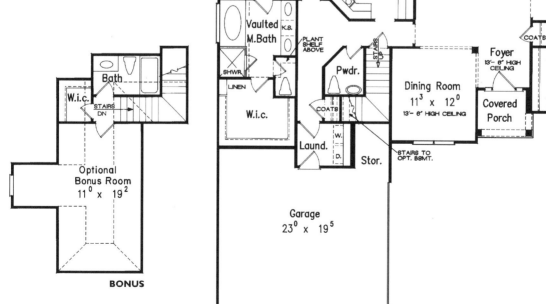

Optional Bonus Room
$11^0 \times 19^2$

BONUS

Master Suite
$14^0 \times 17^0$
TRAY CEILING

Vaulted M.Bath

W.i.c.

Breakfast

Kitchen

Laund.

Stor.

Garage
$23^0 \times 19^5$

Pwdr.

Vaulted Living Room
$15^6 \times 20^2$
13'- 6" HIGH CEILING

Dining Room
$11^3 \times 12^0$
13'- 6" HIGH CEILING

Foyer
13'- 6" HIGH CEILING

Covered Porch

Bedroom 2
$11^2 \times 11^0$

Bath

Bedroom 3
$11^2 \times 11^6$

MAIN FLOOR

Design 99491

PHOTOGRAPHY: COURTESY OF THE DESIGNER

Units	Single
Price Code	C
Total Finished	1,846 sq. ft.
First Finished	919 sq. ft.
Second Finished	927 sq. ft.
Garage Unfinished	414 sq. ft.
Dimensions	44'x40'
Foundation	Basement
	Slab
Bedrooms	4
Full Baths	2
Half Baths	1
Max Ridge Height	26'10"
Roof Framing	Stick
Exterior Walls	2x4

* Alternate foundation options available at an additional charge.
Please call 1-800-235-5700 for more information.

SECOND FLOOR

Mbr
12 x 16
9'-4" CEILING

Br
10 x 11

Br
10 x 11

DN

WHIRLPOOL

L.

Br
10 x 11
10'-0" CEILING

LIN.

OPEN TO BELOW

PLANT SHELF

Please note: The photographed home may have been modified to suit homeowner preferences. If you order plans, have a builder or design professional check them against the photograph to confirm actual construction details.

FIRST FLOOR

Kit
9 x 11

Bfst
10 x 16

Grt rm
18 x 14

R.

W

D

Dn
10 x 13

DN

UP

Gar
20 x 19

WRAPAROUND PORCH

Design 97295

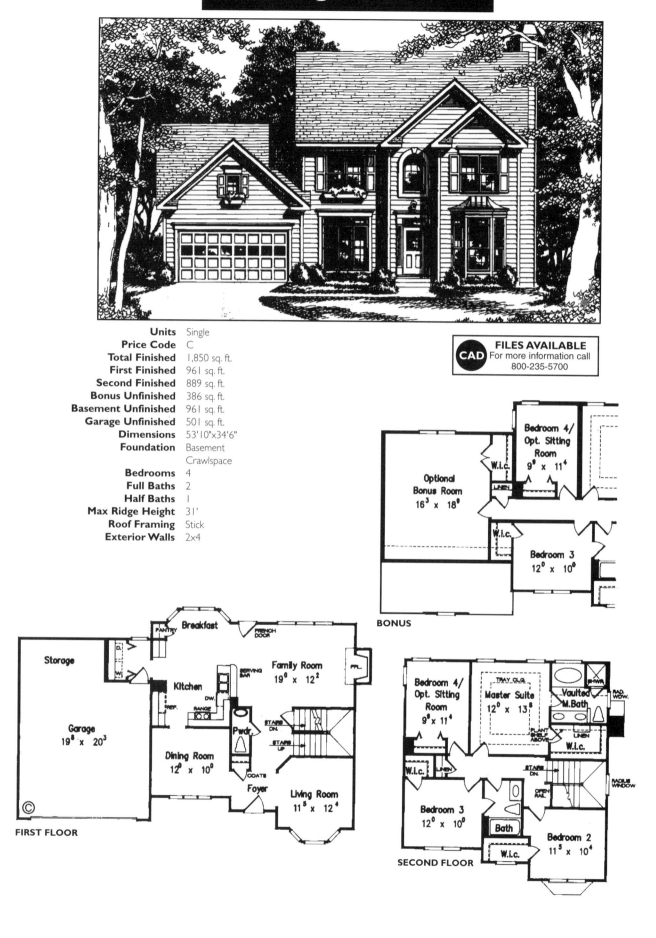

Units	Single
Price Code	C
Total Finished	1,850 sq. ft.
First Finished	961 sq. ft.
Second Finished	889 sq. ft.
Bonus Unfinished	386 sq. ft.
Basement Unfinished	961 sq. ft.
Garage Unfinished	501 sq. ft.
Dimensions	53'10"x34'6"
Foundation	Basement
	Crawlspace
Bedrooms	4
Full Baths	2
Half Baths	1
Max Ridge Height	31'
Roof Framing	Stick
Exterior Walls	2x4

CAD FILES AVAILABLE
For more information call
800-235-5700

BONUS

Optional Bonus Room 16³ x 18⁹

Bedroom 4/ Opt. Sitting Room 9⁹ x 11⁴

W.i.c.
LINEN
W.i.c.

Bedroom 3 12⁰ x 10⁰

FIRST FLOOR

Storage

Garage 19⁸ x 20³

Breakfast
PANTRY
FRENCH DOOR
Kitchen
SERVING BAR
Family Room 19⁰ x 12²
FPL

DW
RANGE
REF
Pwdr
STAIRS DN.
STAIRS UP

Dining Room 12⁰ x 10⁰
COATS
Foyer
Living Room 11⁵ x 12⁴

SECOND FLOOR

Bedroom 4/ Opt. Sitting Room 9⁹ x 11⁴

TRAY CLG.
Master Suite 12⁰ x 13⁸

SHWR
Vaulted M.Bath
RAD. WDW.

PLANT SHELF ABOVE
LINEN
W.I.C.

W.I.C.
LINEN

STAIRS DN.
OPEN RAIL
RADIUS WINDOW

Bedroom 3 12⁰ x 10⁰
Bath
W.I.C.
Bedroom 2 11⁵ x 10⁴

Design 32291

PHOTOGRAPHY: BETH SINGER

Units	Single
Price Code	C
Total Finished	1,852 sq. ft.
First Finished	936 sq. ft.
Second Finished	916 sq. ft.
Garage Unfinished	576 sq. ft.
Deck Unfinished	568 sq. ft.
Porch Unfinished	224 sq. ft.
Dimensions	70'x68'
Foundation	Crawlspace Pier/Post
Bedrooms	3
3/4 Baths	3
First Ceiling	9'
Second Ceiling	8'
Max Ridge Height	30'3"
Roof Framing	Stick
Exterior Walls	2x6

VERANDA

DECK

DINING
15x9

LIVING
18x23

SUNROOM
13x14

KITCHEN
14x9

LDRY

D
W

R

UP

ENTRY

GARAGE
23x23

UP

Please note: The photographed home may have been modified to suit homeowner preferences. If you order plans, have a builder or design professional check them against the photograph to confirm actual construction details.

FIRST FLOOR

MASTER
BEDROOM
12x16

HALL

BEDROOM
14x9

DN.

CLOS

OPEN

BEDROOM
14x9

SECOND FLOOR

Units	Single
Price Code	C
Total Finished	1,852 sq. ft.
Main Finished	1,852 sq. ft.
Garage Unfinished	757 sq. ft.
Dimensions	70'x45'
Foundation	Crawlspace
Bedrooms	3
Full Baths	2

MASTER
16/2 X 14/0
(9' CLG.)

GREAT RM.
17/6 X 20/6
(12'-4" CLG.)

DINING
11/6 X 13/0
(9' CLG.)

SHOP /
3RD CAR
12/6 X 19/6

8/6 X 15/0

BUILT-IN

NICHE

PAN.

DEN
11/0 X 10/0
(9' CLG.)

BR. 2
11/0 X 12/6
(9' CLG.)

BR. 3
11/2 X 12/0
(9' CLG.)

GARAGE
21/0 X 22/6

LIN.

W. D.

REF.

MAIN FLOOR

Units	Single
Price Code	D
Total Finished	1,853 sq. ft.
First Finished	1,342 sq. ft.
Second Finished	511 sq. ft.
Garage Unfinished	1,740 sq. ft.
Dimensions	44'x40'
Foundation	Pier/Post
Bedrooms	3
Full Baths	2
First Ceiling	8'
Second Ceiling	8'
Max Ridge Height	37'
Roof Framing	Stick
Exterior Walls	2x6

* Alternate foundation options available at an additional charge.
Please call 1-800-235-5700 for more information.

SECOND FLOOR

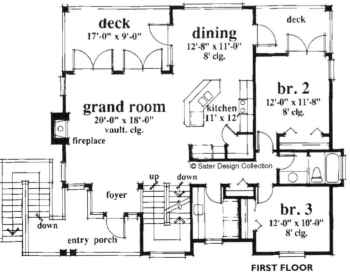

FIRST FLOOR

© Sater Design Collection

Design 24704

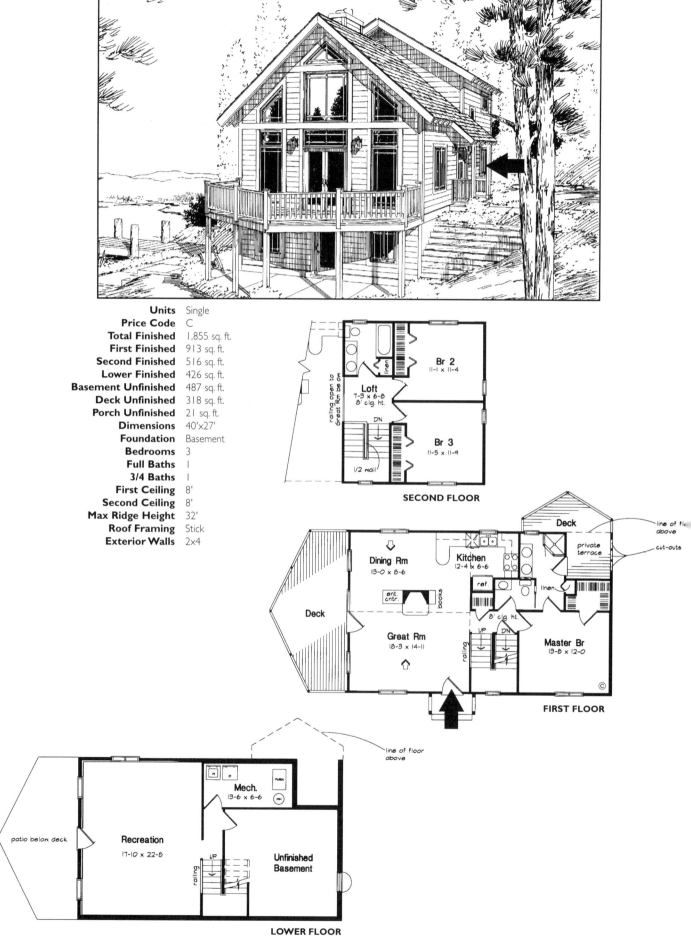

Units	Single
Price Code	C
Total Finished	1,855 sq. ft.
First Finished	913 sq. ft.
Second Finished	516 sq. ft.
Lower Finished	426 sq. ft.
Basement Unfinished	487 sq. ft.
Deck Unfinished	318 sq. ft.
Porch Unfinished	21 sq. ft.
Dimensions	40'x27'
Foundation	Basement
Bedrooms	3
Full Baths	1
3/4 Baths	1
First Ceiling	8'
Second Ceiling	8'
Max Ridge Height	32'
Roof Framing	Stick
Exterior Walls	2x4

SECOND FLOOR

Br 2
11-1 x 11-4

Loft
7-3 x 6-8
8' clg. ht.

DN

1/2 wall

Br 3
11-5 x 11-9

railing open to Great Rm below

linen

FIRST FLOOR

Deck

private terrace

line of floor above

cut-outs

Dining Rm
13-0 x 8-6

Kitchen
12-4 x 6-6

ent. cntr.

books

ref.

linen

8' clg. ht.

Deck

Great Rm
18-3 x 14-11

railing

UP

DN

Master Br
13-8 x 12-0

LOWER FLOOR

line of floor above

patio below deck

Mech.
13-6 x 6-6

Recreation
17-10 x 22-8

UP

railing

Unfinished Basement

Design 98408

Units	Single
Price Code	C
Total Finished	1,856 sq. ft.
Main Finished	1,856 sq. ft.
Basement Unfinished	1,856 sq. ft.
Garage Unfinished	429 sq. ft.
Dimensions	59'x54'6"
Foundation	Basement
	Crawlspace
	Slab
Bedrooms	3
Full Baths	2
Main Ceiling	9'
Max Ridge Height	25'6"
Roof Framing	Stick
Exterior Walls	2x4

CAD FILES AVAILABLE For more information call 800-235-5700

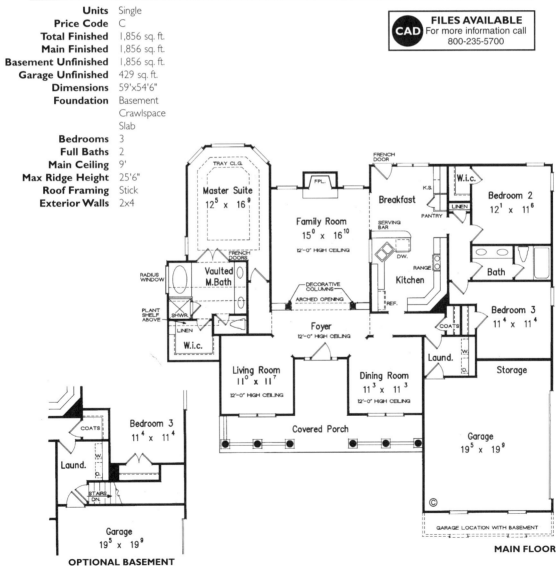

OPTIONAL BASEMENT STAIR LOCATION

MAIN FLOOR

Units	Single
Price Code	C
Total Finished	1,859 sq. ft.
Main Finished	1,859 sq. ft.
Basement Unfinished	1,859 sq. ft.
Garage Unfinished	750 sq. ft.
Dimensions	69'8"x43'
Foundation	Basement
Bedrooms	3
Full Baths	2
Half Baths	1
Main Ceiling	8'2"
Max Ridge Height	23'7"
Roof Framing	Truss
Exterior Walls	2x6

MAIN FLOOR

Design 65645

1,501-2,000 sq.ft. HOME PLANS

PHOTOGRAPHY: COURTESY OF THE DESIGNER

Units	Single
Price Code	C
Total Finished	1,865 sq. ft.
Main Finished	1,865 sq. ft.
Dimensions	62'x64'
Foundation	Crawlspace Slab
Bedrooms	3
Full Baths	2
Main Ceiling	8'
Max Ridge Height	27'
Roof Framing	Stick
Exterior Walls	2x6

sto 11 x 6
sto 11 x 6

garage 22 x 22

patio

slope

w d
frz
util

sto
lin
van
bath
skylight
seat shr
clo
slope

br 3 13 x 12
skylight

living 20 x 16

ref
pan
kit 12 x 12

ov
rng

mbr 18 x 14
slope
slope

lin
bath
hall

dining 12 x 12

foy

dw

Please note: The photographed home may have been modified to suit homeowner preferences. If you order plans, have a builder or design professional check them against the photograph to confirm actual construction details.

br 2 13 x 12
slope slope

porch 20 x 4

eating 12 x 10
slope slope

MAIN FLOOR

Units	Single
Price Code	C
Total Finished	1,868 sq. ft.
Main Finished	1,868 sq. ft.
Garage Unfinished	400 sq. ft.
Dimensions	45'x66'
Foundation	Slab
Bedrooms	4
Full Baths	2
Max Ridge Height	19'10"
Roof Framing	Truss

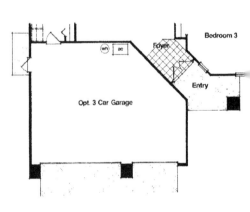

3-CAR GARAGE OPTION

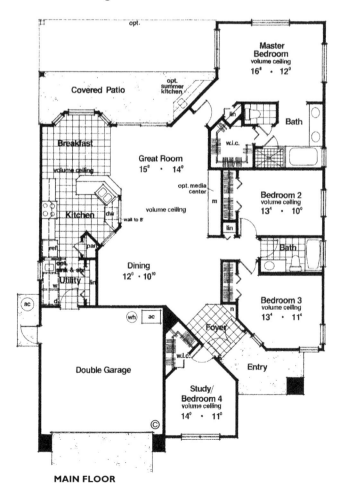

MAIN FLOOR

Design 94989

PHOTOGRAPHY: COURTESY OF THE DESIGNER

Units	Single
Price Code	C
Total Finished	1,869 sq. ft.
First Finished	1,421 sq. ft.
Second Finished	448 sq. ft.
Basement Unfinished	1,421 sq. ft.
Garage Unfinished	480 sq. ft.
Dimensions	52'x47'4"
Foundation	Basement
Bedrooms	3
Full Baths	1
3/4 Baths	1
Half Baths	1
Max Ridge Height	25'
Roof Framing	Stick
Exterior Walls	2x4

* Alternate foundation options available at an additional charge.
Please call 1-800-235-5700 for more information.

Please note: The photographed home may have been modified to suit homeowner preferences. If you order plans, have a builder or design professional check them against the photograph to confirm actual construction details.

FIRST FLOOR

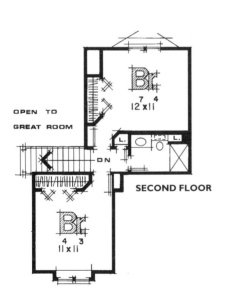

SECOND FLOOR

OPEN TO GREAT ROOM

Units	Single
Price Code	C
Total Finished	1,872 sq. ft.
First Finished	891 sq. ft.
Second Finished	981 sq. ft.
Basement Unfinished	891 sq. ft.
Dimensions	48'×28'
Foundation	Basement
Bedrooms	3
Full Baths	1
3/4 Baths	1
First Ceiling	8'
Second Ceiling	8'
Max Ridge Height	32'6"
Roof Framing	Truss
Exterior Walls	2×6

SECOND FLOOR

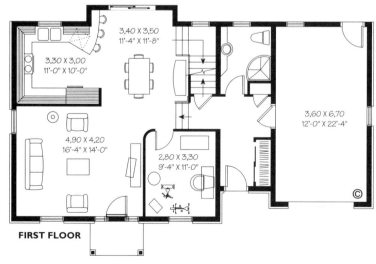

FIRST FLOOR

Design 98454

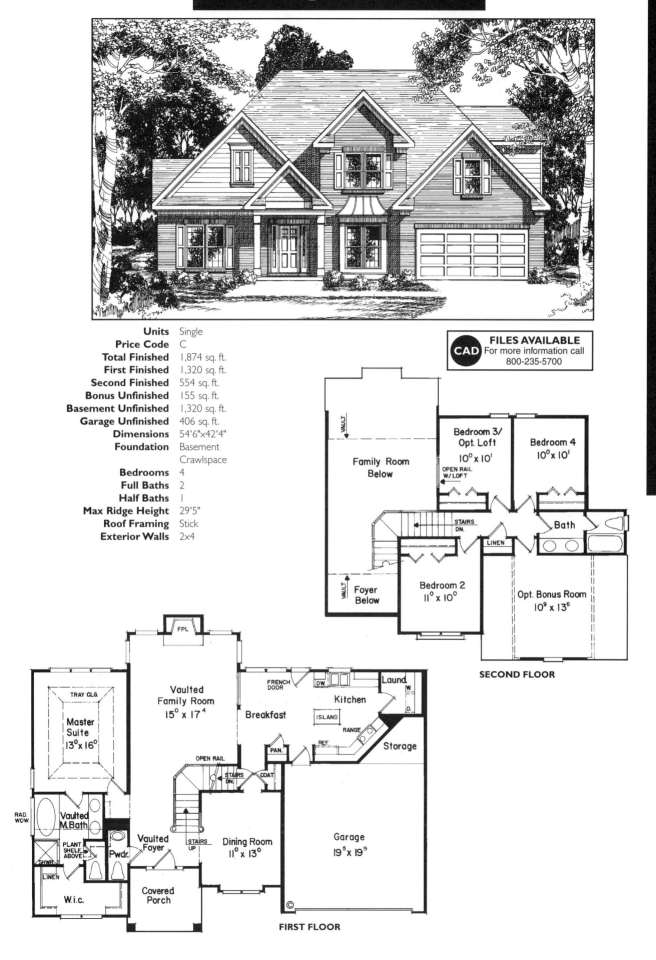

Units	Single
Price Code	C
Total Finished	1,874 sq. ft.
First Finished	1,320 sq. ft.
Second Finished	554 sq. ft.
Bonus Unfinished	155 sq. ft.
Basement Unfinished	1,320 sq. ft.
Garage Unfinished	406 sq. ft.
Dimensions	54'6"x42'4"
Foundation	Basement Crawlspace
Bedrooms	4
Full Baths	2
Half Baths	I
Max Ridge Height	29'5"
Roof Framing	Stick
Exterior Walls	2x4

CAD FILES AVAILABLE For more information call 800-235-5700

SECOND FLOOR

Family Room Below

VAULT

Bedroom 3/ Opt. Loft 10⁰ x 10¹

OPEN RAIL W/ LOFT

Bedroom 4 10⁰ x 10¹

STAIRS DN.

LINEN

Bath

Foyer Below

VAULT

Bedroom 2 II⁰ x 10⁰

Opt. Bonus Room 10⁹ x 13⁶

FIRST FLOOR

FPL

TRAY CLG.

Master Suite 13⁰x 16⁰

Vaulted Family Room 15⁰ x 17⁴

FRENCH DOOR

DW

Laund.

Kitchen

ISLAND

RANGE

Breakfast

RAD. WDW.

Vaulted M.Bath

PLANT SHELF ABOVE

Pwdr.

Vaulted Foyer

OPEN RAIL

STAIRS DN.

COAT

PAN.

REF.

Storage

SHWR.

LINEN

W.I.C.

STAIRS UP

Covered Porch

Dining Room II⁰ x 13⁰

Garage 19⁵ x 19⁹

Units	Single
Price Code	C
Total Finished	1,880 sq. ft.
Main Finished	1,880 sq. ft.
Dimensions	57'x61'4"
Foundation	Crawlspace
Bedrooms	4
Full Baths	2

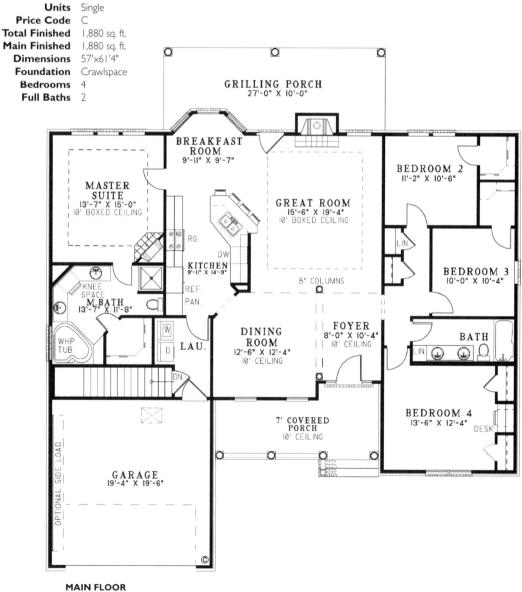

GRILLING PORCH
27'-0" X 10'-0"

BREAKFAST ROOM
9'-11" X 9'-7"

MASTER SUITE
13'-7" X 15'-0"
10' BOXED CEILING

GREAT ROOM
15'-6" X 19'-4"
10' BOXED CEILING

BEDROOM 2
11'-2" X 10'-6"

RG.

DW

KITCHEN
9'-11" X 14'-9"

REF.
PAN.

LIN

8" COLUMNS

BEDROOM 3
10'-0" X 10'-4"

KNEE SPACE

M.BATH
13'-7" X 11'-8"

WHP TUB

W

D

LAU.

DINING ROOM
12'-6" X 12'-4"
10' CEILING

FOYER
8'-0" X 10'-4"
10' CEILING

LIN

BATH

DN

7' COVERED PORCH
10' CEILING

BEDROOM 4
13'-6" X 12'-4"

DESK

OPTIONAL SIDE LOAD

GARAGE
19'-4" X 19'-6"

MAIN FLOOR

Design 98430

Units	Single
Price Code	C
Total Finished	1,884 sq. ft.
Main Finished	1,884 sq. ft.
Basement Unfinished	1,908 sq. ft.
Garage Unfinished	495 sq. ft.
Dimensions	50'x55'4"
Foundation	Basement Crawlspace Slab
Bedrooms	3
Full Baths	2
Half Baths	1
Main Ceiling	9'
Max Ridge Height	25'
Roof Framing	Stick
Exterior Walls	2x4

CAD FILES AVAILABLE
For more information call
800-235-5700

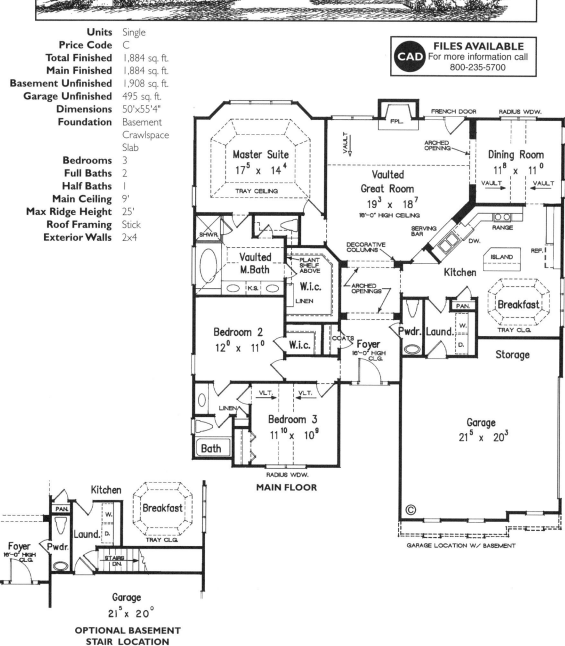

MAIN FLOOR

Master Suite 17⁵ x 14⁴ · TRAY CEILING
Vaulted Great Room 19³ x 18⁷ · 18'-0" HIGH CEILING
Dining Room 11⁸ x 11⁰
Vaulted M.Bath
W.i.c. · LINEN
Kitchen
Breakfast · TRAY CLG.
Bedroom 2 12⁰ x 11⁰
Foyer 16'-0" HIGH CLG.
Pwdr. Laund.
Storage
Bedroom 3 11¹⁰ x 10⁹
Bath
Garage 21⁵ x 20³
RADIUS WDW.
GARAGE LOCATION W/ BASEMENT

OPTIONAL BASEMENT STAIR LOCATION
Kitchen · Breakfast · TRAY CLG.
Laund. · Foyer 16'-0" HIGH CLG. · Pwdr.
STAIRS DN.
Garage 21⁵ x 20⁰

Units	Single
Price Code	C
Total Finished	1,890 sq. ft.
Main Finished	1,890 sq. ft.
Garage Unfinished	565 sq. ft.
Porch Unfinished	241 sq. ft.
Dimensions	65'10"x53'5"
Foundation	Crawlspace
	Slab
Bedrooms	3
Full Baths	2
Main Ceiling	10'
Max Ridge Height	21'6"
Roof Framing	Stick
Exterior Walls	2x4

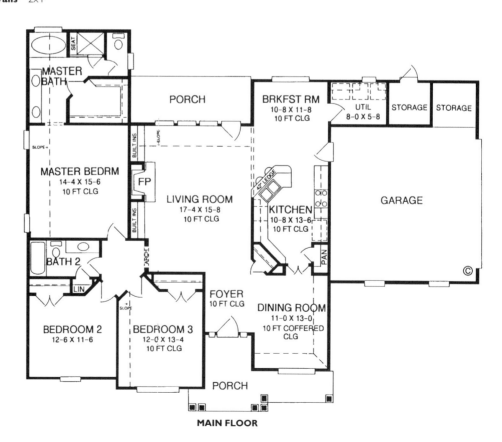

MAIN FLOOR

Design 69503

1,501-2,000 sq. ft. HOME PLANS

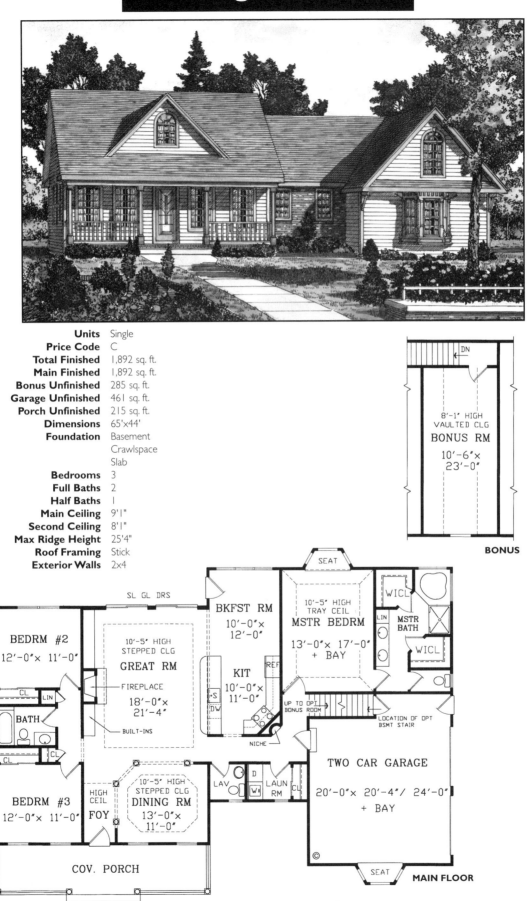

Units	Single
Price Code	C
Total Finished	1,892 sq. ft.
Main Finished	1,892 sq. ft.
Bonus Unfinished	285 sq. ft.
Garage Unfinished	461 sq. ft.
Porch Unfinished	215 sq. ft.
Dimensions	65'x44'
Foundation	Basement
	Crawlspace
	Slab
Bedrooms	3
Full Baths	2
Half Baths	1
Main Ceiling	9'1"
Second Ceiling	8'1"
Max Ridge Height	25'4"
Roof Framing	Stick
Exterior Walls	2x4

8'-1" HIGH VAULTED CLG
BONUS RM
10'-6" x 23'-0"

BONUS

SL GL DRS

BKFST RM
10'-0" x 12'-0"

SEAT

10'-5" HIGH TRAY CEIL
MSTR BEDRM
13'-0" x 17'-0" + BAY

WICL

MSTR BATH

WICL

LIN

10'-5" HIGH STEPPED CLG
GREAT RM
FIREPLACE
18'-0" x 21'-4"
BUILT-INS

KIT
10'-0" x 11'-0"

REF

NICHE

UP TO OPT BONUS ROOM

LOCATION OF OPT BSMT STAIR

BEDRM #2
12'-0" x 11'-0"

CL   LIN

BATH

CL

BEDRM #3
12'-0" x 11'-0"

HIGH CEIL
FOY

10'-5" HIGH STEPPED CLG
DINING RM
13'-0" x 11'-0"

LAV

D W

LAUN RM

CL

TWO CAR GARAGE
20'-0" x 20'-4" / 24'-0" + BAY

COV. PORCH

SEAT   **MAIN FLOOR**

Units	Single
Price Code	C
Total Finished	1,892 sq. ft.
Main Finished	1,892 sq. ft.
Garage Unfinished	374 sq. ft.
Porch Unfinished	198 sq. ft.
Dimensions	42'x66'10"
Foundation	Basement
	Crawlspace
	Slab
Bedrooms	3
Full Baths	2
Main Ceiling	9'
Roof Framing	Stick
Exterior Walls	2x4

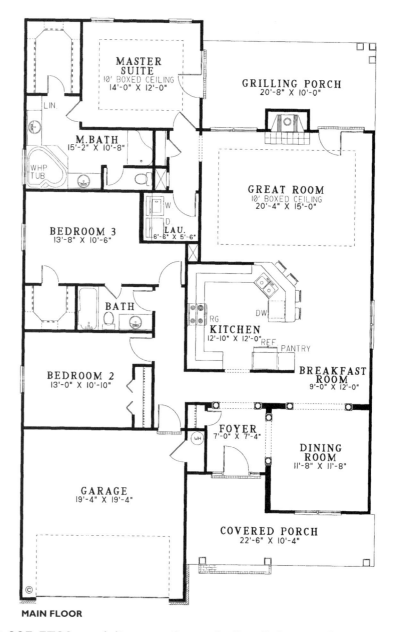

MASTER SUITE
10' BOXED CEILING
14'-0" X 12'-0"

GRILLING PORCH
20'-8" X 10'-0"

LIN.

M. BATH
15'-2" X 10'-8"

WHP TUB

GREAT ROOM
10' BOXED CEILING
20'-4" X 15'-0"

W
D
LAU.
6'-6" X 5'-6"

BEDROOM 3
13'-8" X 10'-6"

BATH

KITCHEN
12'-10" X 12'-0"

RG.
DW
REF.
PANTRY

BREAKFAST ROOM
9'-0" X 12'-0"

BEDROOM 2
13'-0" X 10'-10"

FOYER
7'-0" X 7'-4"

WH

DINING ROOM
11'-8" X 11'-8"

GARAGE
19'-4" X 19'-4"

COVERED PORCH
22'-6" X 10'-4"

MAIN FLOOR

Units	Single
Price Code	C
Total Finished	1,898 sq. ft.
First Finished	915 sq. ft.
Second Finished	983 sq. ft.
Basement Unfinished	915 sq. ft.
Garage Unfinished	271 sq. ft.
Dimensions	38'x38'
Foundation	Basement
Bedrooms	3
Full Baths	2
Half Baths	1
Max Ridge Height	26'11"
Roof Framing	Truss
Exterior Walls	2x6

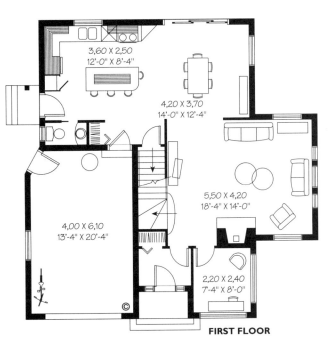

FIRST FLOOR

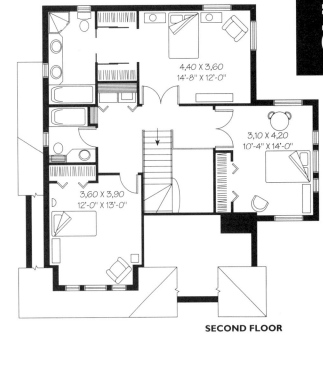

SECOND FLOOR

Units	Single
Price Code	C
Total Finished	1,906 sq. ft.
Main Finished	1,224 sq. ft.
Lower Finished	682 sq. ft.
Basement Unfinished	520 sq. ft.
Dimensions	42'x32'
Foundation	Basement
Bedrooms	4
Full Baths	3
Max Ridge Height	21'4"
Roof Framing	Truss
Exterior Walls	2x6

MAIN FLOOR

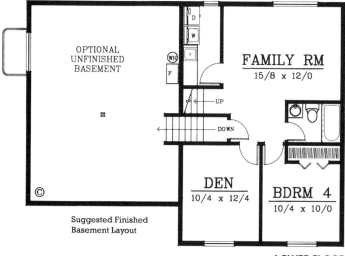

LOWER FLOOR

Design 99113

Units	Single
Price Code	C
Total Finished	1,906 sq. ft.
Main Finished	1,906 sq. ft.
Basement Unfinished	1,906 sq. ft.
Dimensions	72'x44'8"
Foundation	Basement
Bedrooms	3
Full Baths	2
Half Baths	1
Max Ridge Height	12'4"
Roof Framing	Truss
Exterior Walls	2x6

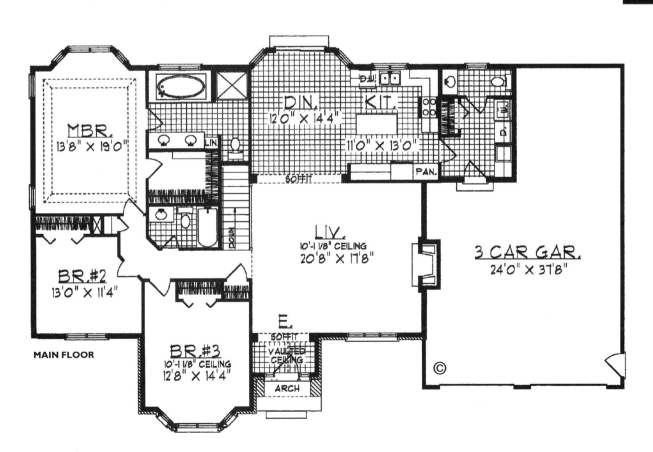

MAIN FLOOR

MBR. 13'8" X 19'0"

DIN. 12'0" X 14'4"

KIT. 11'0" X 13'0"

PAN.

LIV. 10'-1 1/8" CEILING 20'8" X 17'8"

3 CAR GAR. 24'0" X 37'8"

BR. #2 13'0" X 11'4"

BR. #3 10'-1 1/8" CEILING 12'8" X 14'4"

SOFFIT VAULTED CEILING

ARCH

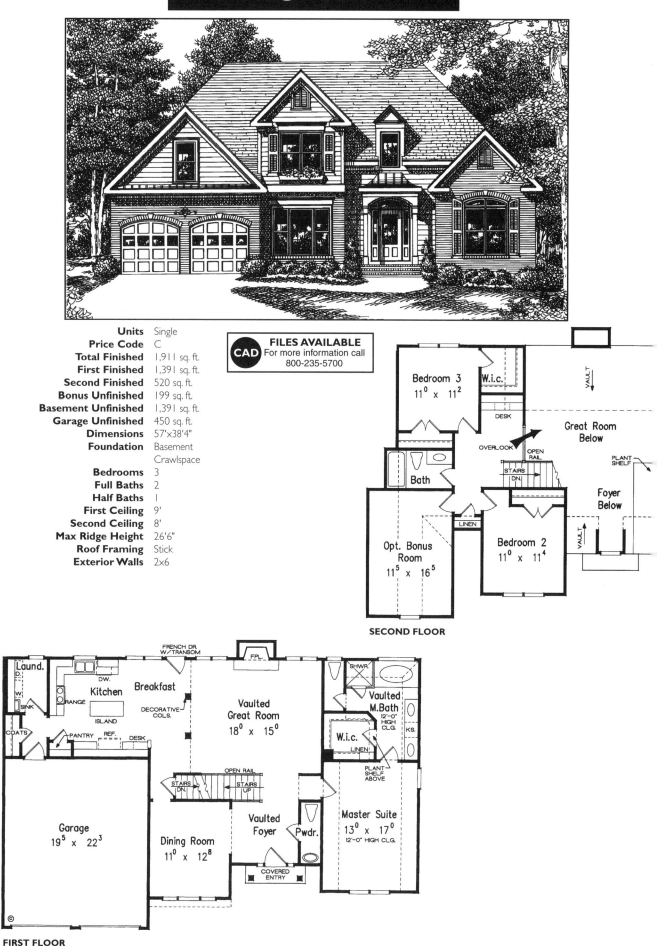

Units	Single
Price Code	C
Total Finished	1,911 sq. ft.
First Finished	1,391 sq. ft.
Second Finished	520 sq. ft.
Bonus Unfinished	199 sq. ft.
Basement Unfinished	1,391 sq. ft.
Garage Unfinished	450 sq. ft.
Dimensions	57'x38'4"
Foundation	Basement Crawlspace
Bedrooms	3
Full Baths	2
Half Baths	1
First Ceiling	9'
Second Ceiling	8'
Max Ridge Height	26'6"
Roof Framing	Stick
Exterior Walls	2x6

CAD FILES AVAILABLE For more information call 800-235-5700

SECOND FLOOR

Bedroom 3
11⁰ x 11²

W.i.c.

VAULT

DESK

Great Room Below

OVERLOOK

OPEN RAIL

PLANT SHELF

Bath

STAIRS DN.

Foyer Below

LINEN

VAULT

Opt. Bonus Room
11⁵ x 16⁵

Bedroom 2
11⁰ x 11⁴

FIRST FLOOR

Laund.
D.

W.

SINK

COATS

Kitchen

DW.

RANGE

ISLAND

PANTRY

REF.

DESK

Breakfast

DECORATIVE COLS.

FRENCH DR. W/TRANSOM

FPL.

Vaulted Great Room
18⁰ x 15⁰

SHWR.

Vaulted M.Bath
12'-0" HIGH CLG.

KS.

W.i.c.

LINEN

PLANT SHELF ABOVE

STAIRS DN.

OPEN RAIL

STAIRS UP

Garage
19⁵ x 22³

Dining Room
11⁰ x 12⁸

Vaulted Foyer

Pwdr.

Master Suite
13⁰ x 17⁰
12'-0" HIGH CLG.

COVERED ENTRY

Design 94966

Units	Single
Price Code	C
Total Finished	1,911 sq. ft.
Main Finished	1,911 sq. ft.
Garage Unfinished	481 sq. ft.
Dimensions	56'x58'
Foundation	Basement
Bedrooms	3
Full Baths	2
Max Ridge Height	22'7"
Roof Framing	Stick
Exterior Walls	2x4

* Alternate foundation options available at an additional charge.
Please call 1-800-235-5700 for more information.

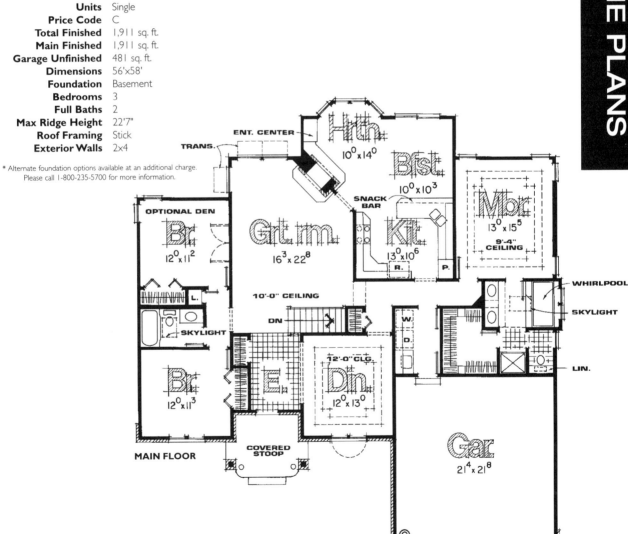

Units	Single
Price Code	B
Total Finished	1,912 sq. ft.
Main Finished	1,912 sq. ft.
Garage Unfinished	502 sq. ft.
Deck Unfinished	212 sq. ft.
Porch Unfinished	62 sq. ft.
Dimensions	57'x61'
Foundation	Slab
Bedrooms	3
Full Baths	2
Main Ceiling	8'-10'
Max Ridge Height	26'
Roof Framing	Stick
Exterior Walls	2x4

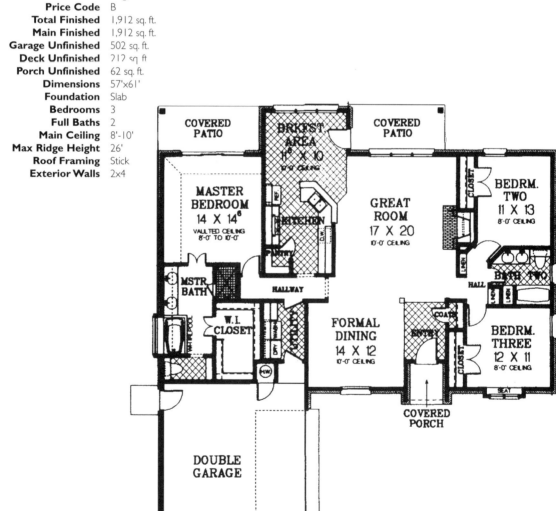

MAIN FLOOR

Design 91579

Units	Single
Price Code	C
Total Finished	1,913 sq. ft.
First Finished	1,111 sq. ft.
Second Finished	802 sq. ft.
Garage Unfinished	440 sq. ft.
Porch Unfinished	180 sq. ft.
Dimensions	50'x47'
Foundation	Crawlspace
Bedrooms	3
Full Baths	1
3/4 Baths	1
Half Baths	1
First Ceiling	9'
Second Ceiling	8'
Max Ridge Height	33'
Roof Framing	Truss
Exterior Walls	2x6

MASTER
12/0 X 14/4

GREAT RM
BELOW

DN

BR. 3
11/2 X 10/0

BR. 2
12/2 X 10/0

SECOND FLOOR

NOOK
12/0 X 10/0
(9' CLG)

TWO STORY
GREAT RM.
17/0 X 13/0

12/0 X 12/6

GARAGE
19/8 X 21/4

UP

DEN
11/2 X 10/0

DINING RM.
12/6 X 11/0

PORCH

FIRST FLOOR

Design 68175

Units	Single
Price Code	C
Total Finished	1,915 sq. ft.
Main Finished	1,915 sq. ft.
Bonus Unfinished	308 sq. ft.
Garage Unfinished	530 sq. ft.
Deck Unfinished	680 sq. ft.
Dimensions	57'x58'
Foundation	Crawlspace
	Slab
Bedrooms	3
Full Baths	2
Main Ceiling	9'
Max Ridge Height	26'
Exterior Walls	2x4

* Alternate foundation options available at an additional charge.
Please call 1-800-235-5700 for more information.

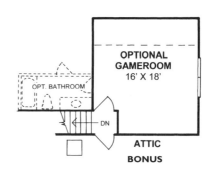

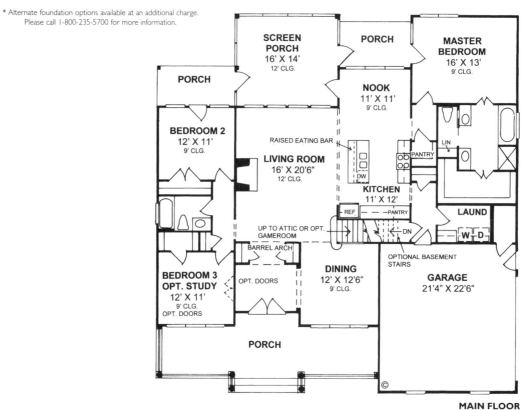

MAIN FLOOR

Design 93216

Units	Single
Price Code	C
Total Finished	1,918 sq. ft.
First Finished	986 sq. ft.
Second Finished	932 sq. ft.
Bonus Unfinished	274 sq. ft.
Basement Unfinished	882 sq. ft.
Garage Unfinished	532 sq. ft.
Dimensions	54'x34'
Foundation	Basement
	Crawlspace
	Slab
Bedrooms	3
Full Baths	2
Half Baths	1
Max Ridge Height	29'
Roof Framing	Stick
Exterior Walls	2x4

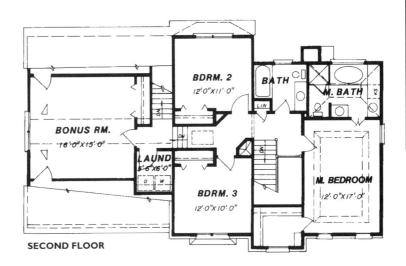

SECOND FLOOR

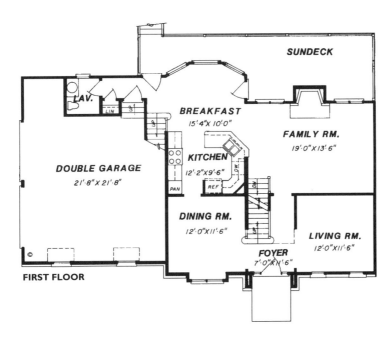

FIRST FLOOR

Design 90480

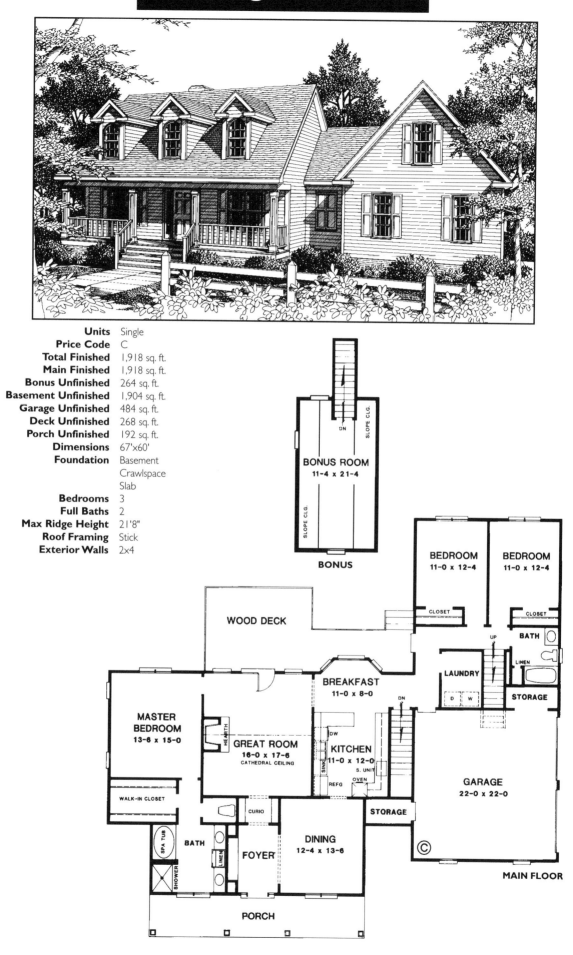

Units	Single
Price Code	C
Total Finished	1,918 sq. ft.
Main Finished	1,918 sq. ft.
Bonus Unfinished	264 sq. ft.
Basement Unfinished	1,904 sq. ft.
Garage Unfinished	484 sq. ft.
Deck Unfinished	268 sq. ft.
Porch Unfinished	192 sq. ft.
Dimensions	67'x60'
Foundation	Basement
	Crawlspace
	Slab
Bedrooms	3
Full Baths	2
Max Ridge Height	21'8"
Roof Framing	Stick
Exterior Walls	2x4

BONUS ROOM
11-4 x 21-4

BONUS

BEDROOM
11-0 x 12-4

BEDROOM
11-0 x 12-4

CLOSET

CLOSET

BATH

LAUNDRY

LINEN

STORAGE

WOOD DECK

BREAKFAST
11-0 x 8-0

MASTER
BEDROOM
13-6 x 15-0

GREAT ROOM
16-0 x 17-6
CATHEDRAL CEILING

KITCHEN
11-0 x 12-0

GARAGE
22-0 x 22-0

WALK-IN CLOSET

CURIO

STORAGE

SPA TUB

BATH

LINEN

FOYER

DINING
12-4 x 13-6

SHOWER

PORCH

MAIN FLOOR

Design 99117

Units	Single
Price Code	C
Total Finished	1,919 sq. ft.
Main Finished	1,919 sq. ft.
Basement Unfinished	1,919 sq. ft.
Dimensions	60'x58'
Foundation	Basement
Bedrooms	3
Full Baths	2
Max Ridge Height	20'10"
Roof Framing	Truss
Exterior Walls	2x6

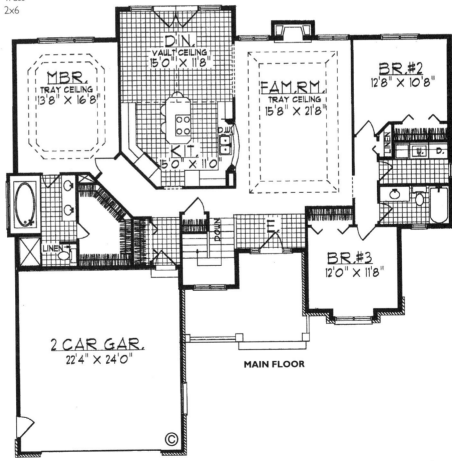

MBR.
TRAY CEILING
13'8" X 16'8"

D.N.
VAULT CEILING
15'0" X 11'8"

FAM.RM.
TRAY CEILING
15'8" X 21'8"

BR. #2
12'8" X 10'8"

KIT.
15'0" X 11'0"

LINEN

LINEN

DOWN

BR. #3
12'0" X 11'8"

2 CAR GAR.
22'4" X 24'0"

MAIN FLOOR

Units	Single
Price Code	C
Total Finished	1,921 sq. ft.
Main Finished	1,099 sq. ft.
Lower Finished	822 sq. ft.
Bonus Unfinished	310 sq. ft.
Garage Unfinished	447 sq. ft.
Porch Unfinished	1,032 sq. ft.
Dimensions	60'x41'
Foundation	Basement
Bedrooms	3
Full Baths	1
3/4 Baths	3
Main Ceiling	9'
Max Ridge Height	30'10"
Roof Framing	Truss
Exterior Walls	2x6

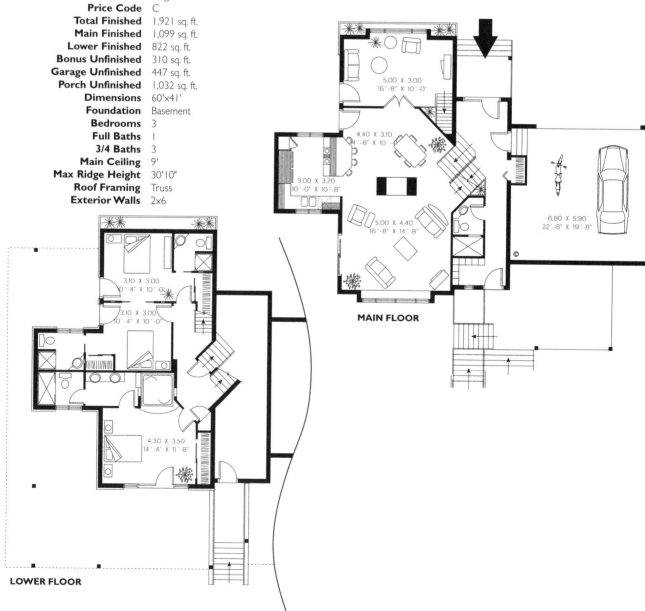

MAIN FLOOR

LOWER FLOOR

Design 82051

Units	Single
Price Code	C
Total Finished	1,921 sq. ft.
Main Finished	1,921 sq. ft.
Bonus Unfinished	812 sq. ft.
Garage Unfinished	505 sq. ft.
Porch Unfinished	959 sq. ft.
Dimensions	84'x55'6"
Foundation	Basement
	Crawlspace
	Slab
Bedrooms	3
Full Baths	2
Main Ceiling	8'
Roof Framing	Stick
Exterior Walls	2x4

GAME ROOM
37'-4" X 18'-8"

ATTIC STORAGE

BATH

BONUS

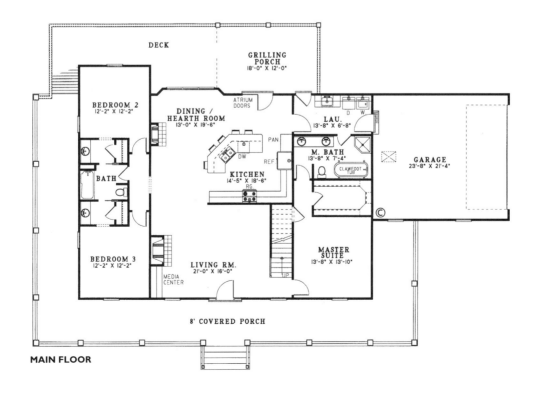

DECK

GRILLING PORCH
18'-0" X 12'-0"

BEDROOM 2
12'-2" X 12'-2"

DINING / HEARTH ROOM
13'-0" X 19'-6"

ATRIUM DOORS

LAU.
13'-8" X 6'-8"

GARAGE
23'-8" X 21'-4"

BATH

KITCHEN
14'-5" X 18'-6"

PAN

M. BATH
13'-8" X 7'-4"

CLAWFOOT TUB

BEDROOM 3
12'-2" X 12'-2"

MEDIA CENTER

LIVING RM.
21'-0" X 16'-0"

MASTER SUITE
13'-8" X 13'-10"

8' COVERED PORCH

MAIN FLOOR

Units	Single
Price Code	C
Total Finished	1,921 sq. ft.
First Finished	1,064 sq. ft.
Second Finished	857 sq. ft.
Basement Unfinished	1,064 sq. ft.
Dimensions	62'x34'
Foundation	Basement
	Crawlspace
	Slab
Bedrooms	3
Full Baths	2
Half Baths	1
First Ceiling	8'
Second Ceiling	8'
Max Ridge Height	26'4"
Roof Framing	Stick
Exterior Walls	2x6

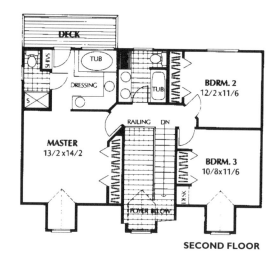

SECOND FLOOR

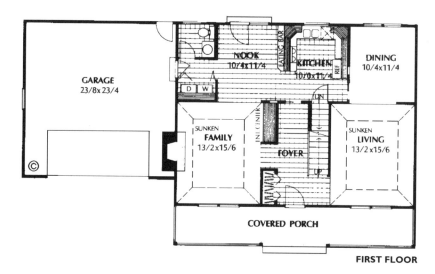

FIRST FLOOR

Design 96544

Units	Single
Price Code	C
Total Finished	1,925 sq. ft.
First Finished	1,329 sq. ft.
Second Finished	596 sq. ft.
Garage Unfinished	316 sq. ft.
Porch Unfinished	533 sq. ft.
Dimensions	64'x46'
Foundation	Crawlspace
	Slab
Bedrooms	3
Full Baths	2
Half Baths	1
First Ceiling	9'
Tray Ceiling	12'
Max Ridge Height	27'
Roof Framing	Stick
Exterior Walls	2x4

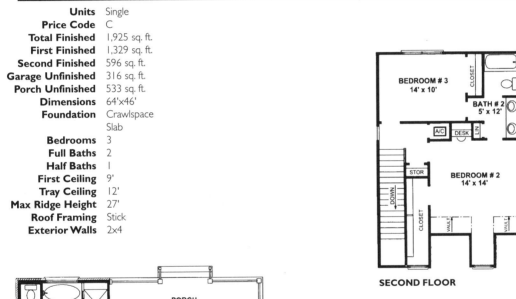

SECOND FLOOR

FIRST FLOOR

Design 52011

Units	Single
Price Code	C
Total Finished	1,927 sq. ft.
Main Finished	1,927 sq. ft.
Basement Unfinished	1,941 sq. ft.
Garage Unfinished	440 sq. ft.
Dimensions	54'x55'
Foundation	Basement
	Crawlspace
Bedrooms	3
Full Baths	2
Main Ceiling	9'
Max Ridge Height	24'
Roof Framing	Stick
Exterior Walls	2x4

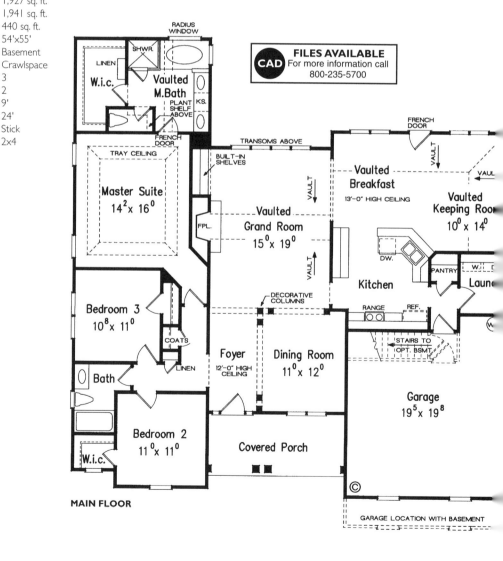

CAD FILES AVAILABLE
For more information call
800-235-5700

MAIN FLOOR

Design 34851

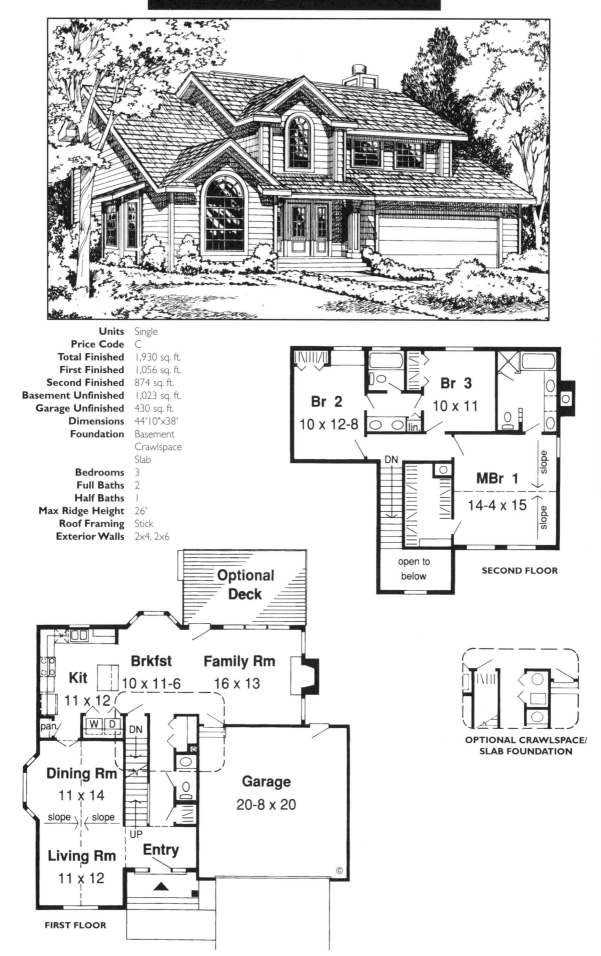

Units	Single
Price Code	C
Total Finished	1,930 sq. ft.
First Finished	1,056 sq. ft.
Second Finished	874 sq. ft.
Basement Unfinished	1,023 sq. ft.
Garage Unfinished	430 sq. ft.
Dimensions	44'10"x38'
Foundation	Basement
	Crawlspace
	Slab
Bedrooms	3
Full Baths	2
Half Baths	1
Max Ridge Height	26'
Roof Framing	Stick
Exterior Walls	2x4, 2x6

SECOND FLOOR

Br 2
10 x 12-8

Br 3
10 x 11

MBr 1
14-4 x 15

DN

open to below

slope

OPTIONAL CRAWLSPACE/ SLAB FOUNDATION

FIRST FLOOR

Optional Deck

Kit
11 x 12

Brkfst
10 x 11-6

Family Rm
16 x 13

pan.

W D

DN

Dining Rm
11 x 14

Garage
20-8 x 20

slope slope

Living Rm
11 x 12

UP

Entry

Design 94902

PHOTOGRAPHY: COURTESY OF THE DESIGNER

Units	Single
Price Code	C
Total Finished	1,931 sq. ft.
First Finished	944 sq. ft.
Second Finished	987 sq. ft.
Basement Unfinished	944 sq. ft.
Garage Unfinished	557 sq. ft.
Dimensions	54'x42'
Foundation	Basement
Bedrooms	4
Full Baths	2
Half Baths	1
First Ceiling	8'
Max Ridge Height	29'
Roof Framing	Stick
Exterior Walls	2x4

* Alternate foundation options available at an additional charge.
Please call 1-800-235-5700 for more information.

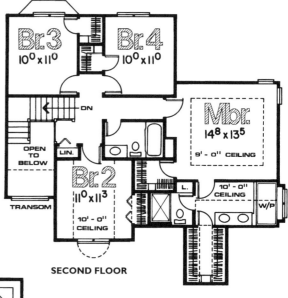

SECOND FLOOR

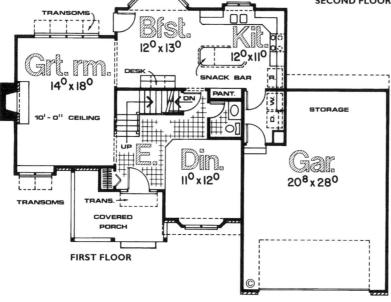

FIRST FLOOR

Please note: The photographed home may have been modified to suit homeowner preferences. If you order plans, have a builder or design professional check them against the photograph to confirm actual construction details.

Design 65647

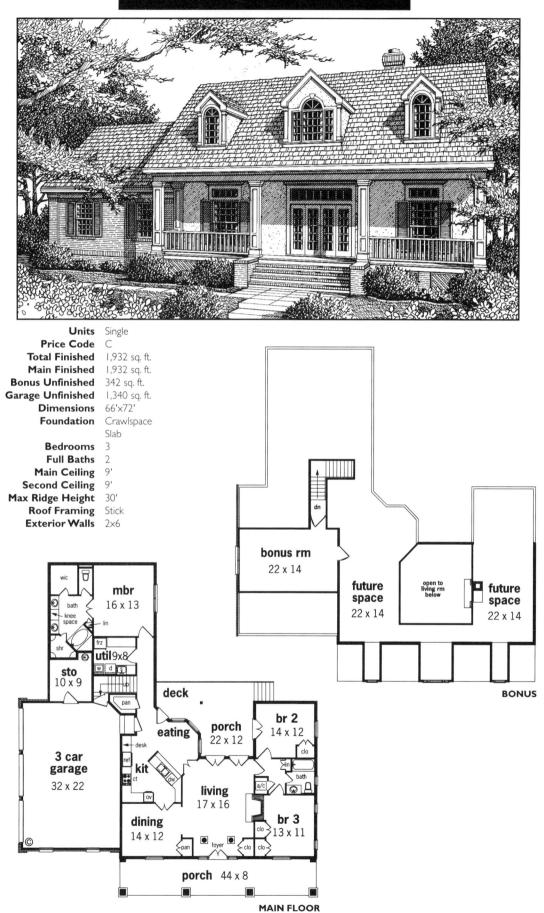

Units	Single
Price Code	C
Total Finished	1,932 sq. ft.
Main Finished	1,932 sq. ft.
Bonus Unfinished	342 sq. ft.
Garage Unfinished	1,340 sq. ft.
Dimensions	66'x72'
Foundation	Crawlspace
	Slab
Bedrooms	3
Full Baths	2
Main Ceiling	9'
Second Ceiling	9'
Max Ridge Height	30'
Roof Framing	Stick
Exterior Walls	2x6

BONUS

bonus rm 22 x 14

future space 22 x 14

open to living rm below

future space 22 x 14

dn

MAIN FLOOR

wic

mbr 16 x 13

bath

knee space

lin

frz

util 9x8

w d s

shr

sto 10 x 9

pan

up

deck

eating

porch 22 x 12

br 2 14 x 12

clo

desk

ref

kit

ct

dw

ov

3 car garage 32 x 22

living 17 x 16

a/c

lin

bath

clo

br 3 13 x 11

dining 14 x 12

pan

foyer

clo

clo

porch 44 x 8

Units	Single
Price Code	C
Total Finished	1,932 sq. ft.
Main Finished	1,932 sq. ft.
Garage Unfinished	552 sq. ft.
Deck Unfinished	225 sq. ft.
Dimensions	65'10"x53'5"
Foundation	Crawlspace
	Slab
Bedrooms	3
Full Baths	2
Max Ridge Height	22'4"
Roof Framing	Stick
Exterior Walls	2x4

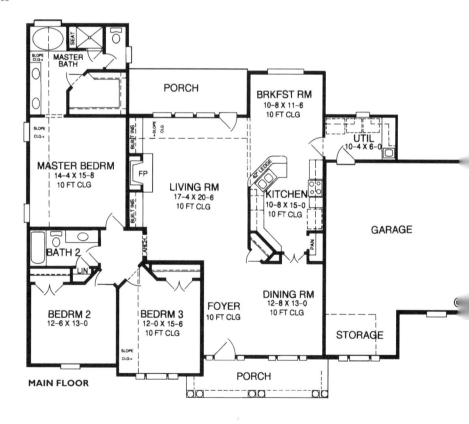

MAIN FLOOR

Design 82034

Units	Single
Price Code	C
Total Finished	1,940 sq. ft.
Main Finished	1,940 sq. ft.
Garage Unfinished	417 sq. ft.
Porch Unfinished	188 sq. ft.
Dimensions	58'x54'10"
Foundation	Crawlspace
	Slab
Bedrooms	4
Full Baths	2
Main Ceiling	8'
Roof Framing	Stick
Exterior Walls	2x4

COVERED PORCH 18'-5" X 4'-0"

BREAKFAST ROOM 9'-4" X 10'-11"

BEDROOM 4 13'-6" X 14'-6"

MASTER SUITE 15'-0" X 15'-0" 9' PAN CEILING

GREAT ROOM 9' BOX CEILING 15'-0" X 19'-6"

BUILT-INS

KITCHEN 9'-11" X 12'-7" REF. RG. DW PAN.

BATH

KNEE SPACE

M.BATH 15'-0" X 11'-8"

DINING ROOM 11'-6" X 9'-8"

FOYER 7'-0" X 7'-0"

LIN

BEDROOM 3 10'-0" X 10'-4"

WHP TUB

LAU. W D

STORAGE WH H-VAC

10" RND. COL W/ BASE

4' PORCH

BEDROOM 2 12'-4" X 10'-6"

GARAGE 20'-10" X 20'-0"

MAIN FLOOR

Units	Single
Price Code	C
Total Finished	1,941 sq. ft.
Main Finished	1,941 sq. ft.
Bonus Unfinished	200 sq. ft.
Basement Unfinished	1,592 sq. ft.
Garage Unfinished	720 sq. ft.
Deck Unfinished	204 sq. ft.
Porch Unfinished	54 sq. ft.
Dimensions	60'x62'
Foundation	Basement Slab
Bedrooms	3
Full Baths	2
Half Baths	1
Main Ceiling	9'
Second Ceiling	7'8"
Vaulted Ceiling	17'
Max Ridge Height	23'
Roof Framing	Stick/Truss
Exterior Walls	2x6

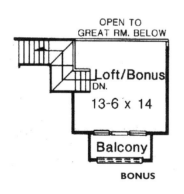

OPEN TO GREAT RM. BELOW

Loft/Bonus
DN.
13-6 x 14

Balcony

BONUS

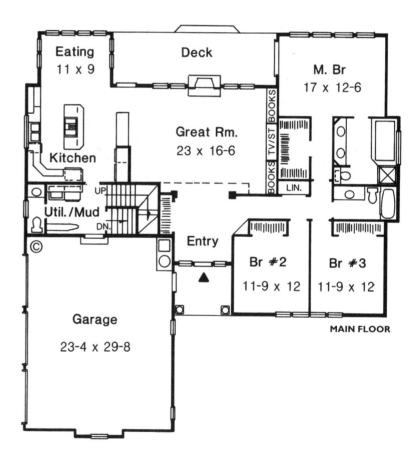

Eating 11 x 9

Deck

M. Br 17 x 12-6

Great Rm. 23 x 16-6

BOOKS TV/ST BOOKS

LIN.

Kitchen

UP

Util./Mud

DN.

Entry

Br #2 11-9 x 12

Br #3 11-9 x 12

Garage 23-4 x 29-8

MAIN FLOOR

Design 98435

Units	Single
Price Code	C
Total Finished	1,945 sq. ft.
Main Finished	1,945 sq. ft.
Dimensions	56'6"x52'6"
Foundation	Basement
	Crawlspace
Bedrooms	4
Full Baths	2
Main Ceiling	9'
Max Ridge Height	26'4"
Roof Framing	Stick
Exterior Walls	2x4

CAD **FILES AVAILABLE**
For more information call
800-235-5700

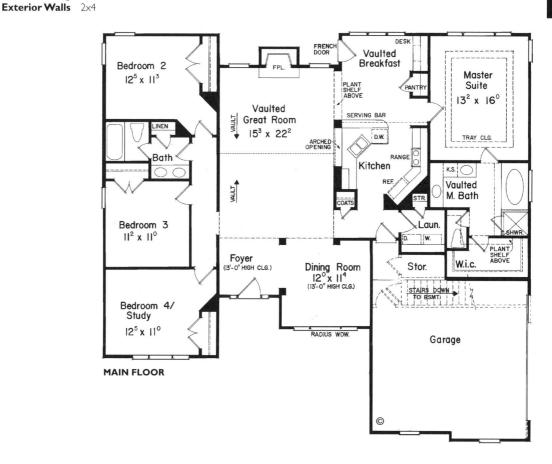

MAIN FLOOR

Units	Single
Price Code	C
Total Finished	1,947 sq. ft.
Main Finished	1,947 sq. ft.
Basement Unfinished	1,947 sq. ft.
Dimensions	69'8"x46'
Foundation	Basement
Bedrooms	3
Full Baths	2
Half Baths	1
Main Ceiling	8'
Max Ridge Height	22'4"
Roof Framing	Truss
Exterior Walls	2x6

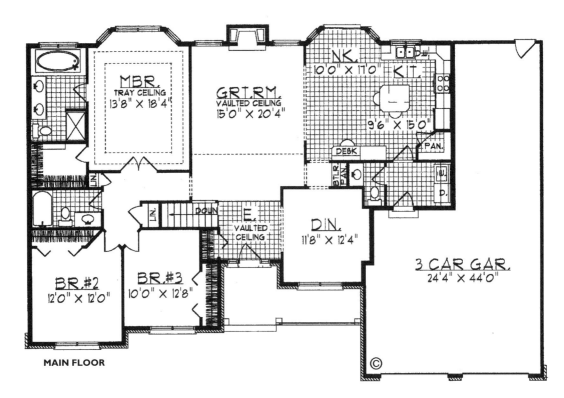

MAIN FLOOR

Design 82078

Units	Single
Price Code	C
Total Finished	1,957 sq. ft.
Main Finished	1,957 sq. ft.
Bonus Unfinished	479 sq. ft.
Garage Unfinished	417 sq. ft.
Porch Unfinished	203 sq. ft.
Dimensions	66'x55'
Foundation	Basement Crawlspace Slab
Bedrooms	3
Full Baths	2
Exterior Walls	2x4

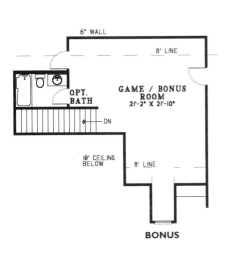

BONUS

MAIN FLOOR

Visit us at www.merillat.com

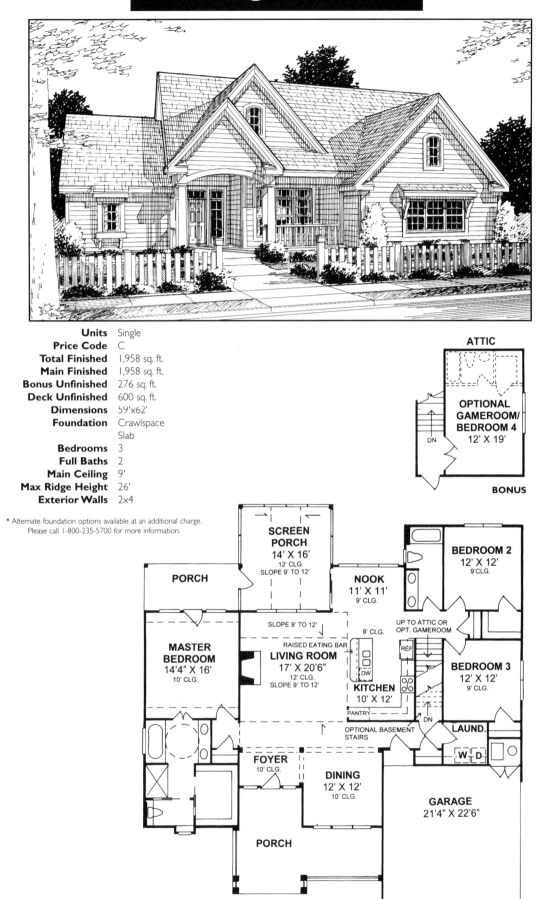

Units	Single
Price Code	C
Total Finished	1,958 sq. ft.
Main Finished	1,958 sq. ft.
Bonus Unfinished	276 sq. ft.
Deck Unfinished	600 sq. ft.
Dimensions	59'x62'
Foundation	Crawlspace
	Slab
Bedrooms	3
Full Baths	2
Main Ceiling	9'
Max Ridge Height	26'
Exterior Walls	2x4

* Alternate foundation options available at an additional charge.
Please call 1-800-235-5700 for more information.

ATTIC

OPTIONAL GAMEROOM/ BEDROOM 4
12' X 19'

DN

BONUS

SCREEN PORCH
14' X 16'
12' CLG.
SLOPE 9' TO 12'

PORCH

NOOK
11' X 11'
9' CLG.

BEDROOM 2
12' X 12'
9' CLG.

SLOPE 9' TO 12'

UP TO ATTIC OR OPT. GAMEROOM

RAISED EATING BAR

MASTER BEDROOM
14'4" X 16'
10' CLG.

LIVING ROOM
17' X 20'6"
12' CLG,
SLOPE 9' TO 12'

DW

BEDROOM 3
12' X 12'
9' CLG.

REF

KITCHEN
10' X 12'

PANTRY

DN

LAUND.

OPTIONAL BASEMENT STAIRS

W D

FOYER
10' CLG.

DINING
12' X 12'
10' CLG.

GARAGE
21'4" X 22'6"

PORCH

MAIN FLOOR

Design 97227

Units	Single
Price Code	C
Total Finished	1,960 sq. ft.
Main Finished	1,960 sq. ft.
Basement Unfinished	1,993 sq. ft.
Garage Unfinished	476 sq. ft.
Dimensions	59'x62'
Foundation	Basement
	Crawlspace
Bedrooms	4
Full Baths	3
Main Ceiling	9'1⅛"
Max Ridge Height	24'
Roof Framing	Stick
Exterior Walls	2x4

CAD FILES AVAILABLE
For more information call
800-235-5700

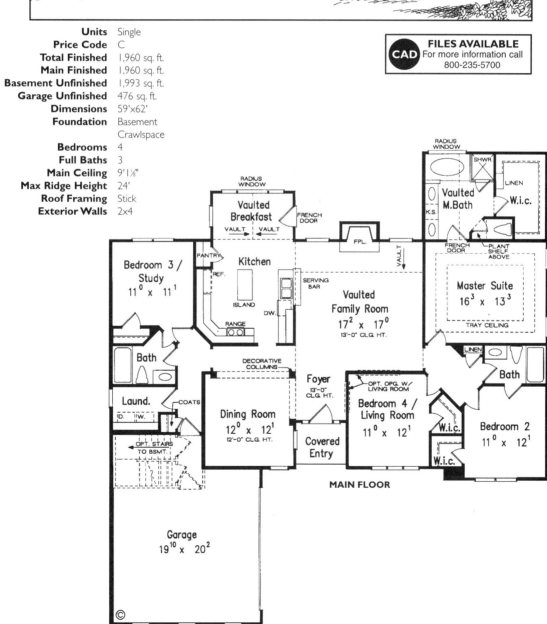

MAIN FLOOR

Design 92668

PHOTOGRAPHY: DONNA & RON KOLB, EXPOSURES UNLIMITED

Units	Single
Price Code	C
Total Finished	1,970 sq. ft.
First Finished	1,497 sq. ft.
Second Finished	473 sq. ft.
Bonus Unfinished	401 sq. ft.
Basement Unfinished	1,420 sq. ft.
Garage Unfinished	468 sq. ft.
Porch Unfinished	91 sq. ft.
Dimensions	55'x63'6"
Foundation	Basement
Bedrooms	3
Full Baths	2
Half Baths	1
First Ceiling	8'
Second Ceiling	8'
Vaulted Ceiling	18'
Tray Ceiling	9'
Max Ridge Height	27'2"
Roof Framing	Truss
Exterior Walls	2x4

SECOND FLOOR

Great Room Below

Bedroom 12'3" x 12'

Foyer Below

Bedroom 11'5" x 11'5"

Hall

Bath

wood rail

plant shelf

Bonus Loft 10'5" x 12'6"

Bonus Room 10'5" x 17'2"

FIRST FLOOR

Bath

9' ceiling height

Bedroom 13' x 14'

Foyer

Great Room 19'10" x 15'2"

Dining Room 11'5" x 13'4"

Breakfast 11'11" x 12'

Kitchen 11'11" x 11'8"

Bath

Laun.

Two-car Garage 21' x 23'10"

Please note: The photographed home may have been modified to suit homeowner preferences. If you order plans, have a builder or design professional check them against the photograph to confirm actual construction details.

Design 65219

Units	Single
Price Code	C
Total Finished	1,973 sq. ft.
First Finished	1,304 sq. ft.
Second Finished	669 sq. ft.
Dimensions	40'x62'
Foundation	Basement
Bedrooms	3
Full Baths	2

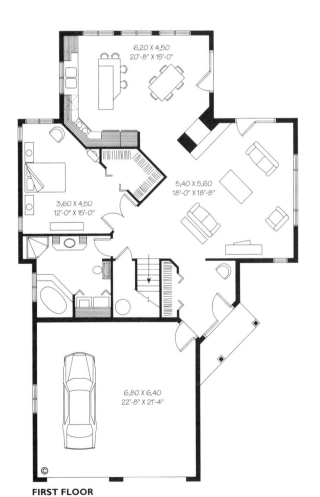

FIRST FLOOR

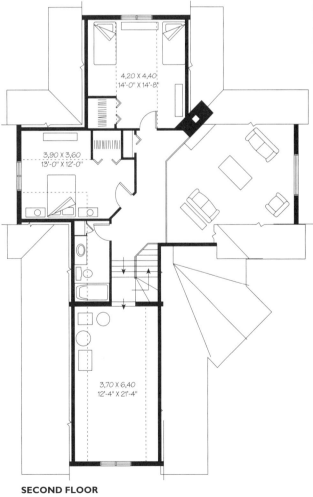

SECOND FLOOR

Design 65210

Units	Single
Price Code	C
Total Finished	1,976 sq. ft.
First Finished	924 sq. ft.
Second Finished	1,052 sq. ft.
Basement Unfinished	1,067 sq. ft.
Garage Unfinished	388 sq. ft.
Porch Unfinished	596 sq. ft.
Dimensions	44'8"x36'
Foundation	Basement
Bedrooms	4
Full Baths	2
Half Baths	1
First Ceiling	9'
Second Ceiling	8'
Max Ridge Height	33'5"
Roof Framing	Truss
Exterior Walls	2x6

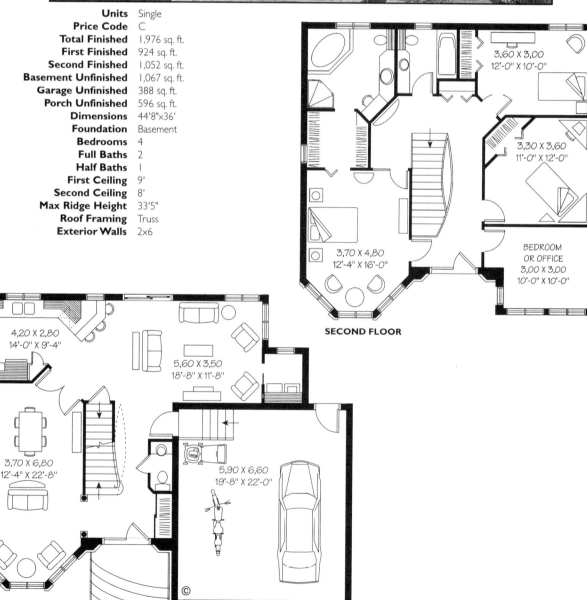

SECOND FLOOR

3,60 X 3,00
12'-0" X 10'-0"

3,30 X 3,60
11'-0" X 12'-0"

BEDROOM
OR OFFICE
3,00 X 3,00
10'-0" X 10'-0"

3,70 X 4,80
12'-4" X 16'-0"

4,20 X 2,80
14'-0" X 9'-4"

5,60 X 3,50
18'-8" X 11'-8"

3,70 X 6,80
12'-4" X 22'-8"

5,90 X 6,60
19'-8" X 22'-0"

FIRST FLOOR

Design 24400

PHOTOGRAPHY: VICTORIA PALAGI

Units	Single
Price Code	C
Total Finished	1,978 sq. ft.
First Finished	1,034 sq. ft.
Second Finished	944 sq. ft.
Basement Unfinished	984 sq. ft.
Garage Unfinished	675 sq. ft.
Dimensions	67'6"x39'6"
Foundation	Basement Crawlspace Slab
Bedrooms	4
Full Baths	2
Half Baths	1
First Ceiling	9'
Second Ceiling	8'
Max Ridge Height	29'
Roof Framing	Stick
Exterior Walls	2x4, 2x6

OPTIONAL MASTER BATH

OPTIONAL CRAWLSPACE/SLAB FOUNDATION

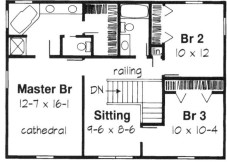

SECOND FLOOR

Please note: The photographed home may have been modified to suit homeowner preferences. If you order plans, have a builder or design professional check them against the photograph to confirm actual construction details.

FIRST FLOOR

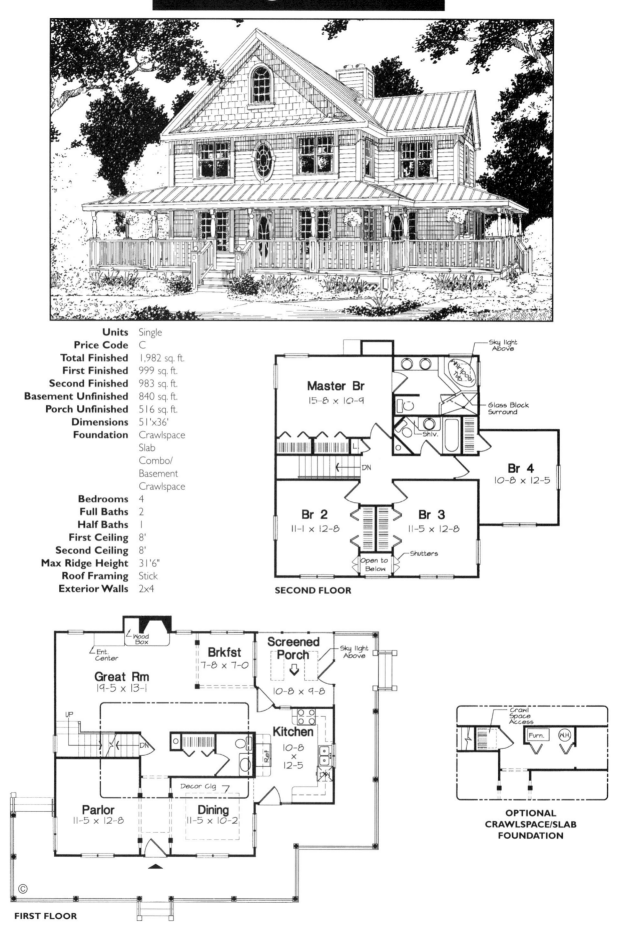

Units	Single
Price Code	C
Total Finished	1,982 sq. ft.
First Finished	999 sq. ft.
Second Finished	983 sq. ft.
Basement Unfinished	840 sq. ft.
Porch Unfinished	516 sq. ft.
Dimensions	51'x36'
Foundation	Crawlspace
	Slab
	Combo/
	Basement
	Crawlspace
Bedrooms	4
Full Baths	2
Half Baths	1
First Ceiling	8'
Second Ceiling	8'
Max Ridge Height	31'6"
Roof Framing	Stick
Exterior Walls	2x4

SECOND FLOOR

Master Br
15-8 x 10-9

Br 4
10-8 x 12-5

Br 2
11-1 x 12-8

Br 3
11-5 x 12-8

Sky light Above

Glass Block Surround

Shlr.

Open to Below

Shutters

DN

FIRST FLOOR

Wood Box

Ent. Center

Brkfst
7-8 x 7-0

Screened Porch
10-8 x 9-8

Sky light Above

Great Rm
19-5 x 13-1

Kitchen
10-8 x 12-5

Decor Clg

Parlor
11-5 x 12-8

Dining
11-5 x 10-2

UP

DN

Ref.

OPTIONAL CRAWLSPACE/SLAB FOUNDATION

Crawl Space Access

Furn.

W.H.

Design 92427

Units	Single
Price Code	C
Total Finished	1,982 sq. ft.
Main Finished	1,982 sq. ft.
Bonus Unfinished	386 sq. ft.
Basement Unfinished	1,982 sq. ft.
Dimensions	63'x58'
Foundation	Basement
	Crawlspace
Bedrooms	3
Full Baths	2
Half Baths	1
Main Ceiling	9'
Vaulted Ceiling	14'4"
Tray Ceiling	12'4"
Max Ridge Height	21'10"
Roof Framing	Stick
Exterior Walls	2x4

MAIN FLOOR

Units	Single
Price Code	C
Total Finished	1,985 sq. ft.
Main Finished	1,985 sq. ft.
Bonus Unfinished	191 sq. ft.
Dimensions	54'x54'
Foundation	Slab
Bedrooms	3
Full Baths	2
Main Ceiling	9'
Max Ridge Height	24'
Roof Framing	Stick/Truss
Exterior Walls	2x4

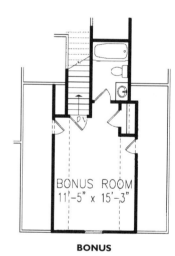

BONUS ROOM
11'-5" x 15'-3"

BONUS

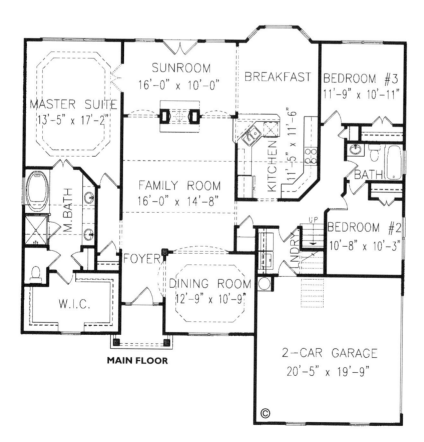

MASTER SUITE
13'-5" x 17'-2"

SUNROOM
16'-0" x 10'-0"

BREAKFAST

BEDROOM #3
11'-9" x 10'-11"

M. BATH

FAMILY ROOM
16'-0" x 14'-8"

KITCHEN
11'-5" x 11'-6"

BATH

FOYER

W.I.C.

DINING ROOM
12'-9" x 10'-9"

LNDRY

UP

BEDROOM #2
10'-8" x 10'-3"

2-CAR GARAGE
20'-5" x 19'-9"

MAIN FLOOR

Design 92544

Units	Single
Price Code	C
Total Finished	1,987 sq. ft.
Main Finished	1,987 sq. ft.
Garage Unfinished	515 sq. ft.
Porch Unfinished	274 sq. ft.
Dimensions	67'x49'
Foundation	Crawlspace
	Slab
Bedrooms	4
Full Baths	2
Half Baths	1
Main Ceiling	9'
Max Ridge Height	22'
Roof Framing	Truss
Exterior Walls	2x4

Units	Single
Price Code	C
Total Finished	1,987 sq. ft.
First Finished	949 sq. ft.
Second Finished	1,038 sq. ft.
Bonus Unfinished	232 sq. ft.
Basement Unfinished	949 sq. ft.
Garage Unfinished	484 sq. ft.
Deck Unfinished	192 sq. ft.
Dimensions	47'4"x36'5"
Foundation	Basement
	Crawlspace
	Slab
Bedrooms	3
Full Baths	2
Half Baths	1
Max Ridge Height	29'
Roof Framing	Stick
Exterior Walls	2x4

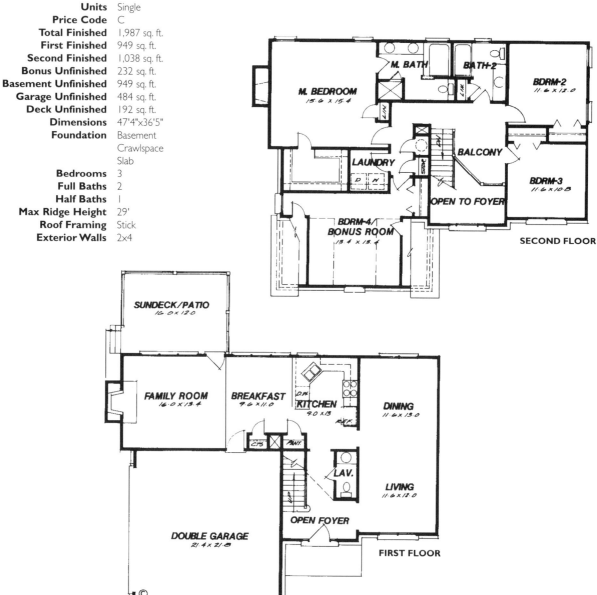

Design 92421

Units	Single
Price Code	C
Total Finished	1,992 sq. ft.
Main Finished	1,992 sq. ft.
Dimensions	63'x57'2"
Foundation	Basement
	Crawlspace
	Slab
Bedrooms	3
Full Baths	2
Half Baths	1
Main Ceiling	9'
Vaulted Ceiling	13'10"
Tray Ceiling	12'
Max Ridge Height	20'

SCREENED PORCH 15'4" x 13'10"

DECK 11'0" x 7'6"

MASTER SUITE 21'4" x 15'0"

SITTING

BRKFST 11'0" x 10'10"

BEDROOM 3 13'0" x 11'0"

8' HIGH OPENING

FAMILY ROOM 16'0" x 24'1"

KITCHEN 13'8" x 9'6"

PANTRY

LINEN COATS

10' CEILING

9' CEILING

DINING 11'0" x 12'0"

TRAY CEILING

OPTIONAL STAIRS TO BASEMENT

BEDROOM 2 13'0" x 11'0"

LIVING 11'0" x 12'0"

PORCH 15'4" x 5'4"

3 CAR GARAGE 21'4" x 29'10"

2 CAR GARAGE OPTION

MAIN FLOOR

PHOTOGRAPHY: MARK ENGLUND

Units	Single
Price Code	C
Total Finished	1,993 sq. ft.
Main Finished	1,993 sq. ft.
Basement Unfinished	1,993 sq. ft.
Garage Unfinished	521 sq. ft.
Deck Unfinished	180 sq. ft.
Dimensions	60'x48'4"
Foundation	Basement
Bedrooms	3
Full Baths	2
Main Ceiling	8'
Max Ridge Height	23'3"
Roof Framing	Truss
Exterior Walls	2x4

Please note: The photographed home may have been modified to suit homeowner preferences. If you order plans, have a builder or design professional check them against the photograph to confirm actual construction details.

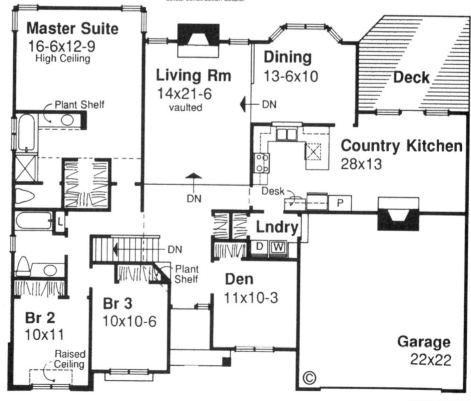

MAIN FLOOR

Design 34679

Units	Single
Price Code	C
Total Finished	1,994 sq. ft.
Main Finished	1,331 sq. ft.
Lower Finished	663 sq. ft.
Garage Unfinished	584 sq. ft.
Dimensions	48'x28'
Foundation	Basement
Bedrooms	3
Full Baths	2
Half Baths	1
Main Ceiling	8'
Max Ridge Height	22'
Roof Framing	Stick
Exterior Walls	2x4, 2x6

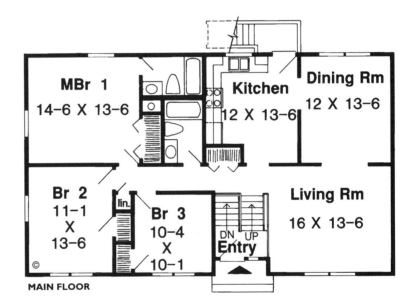

MBr 1 14-6 X 13-6

Kitchen 12 X 13-6

Dining Rm 12 X 13-6

Br 2 11-1 X 13-6

lin.

Br 3 10-4 X 10-1

Entry DN UP

Living Rm 16 X 13-6

MAIN FLOOR

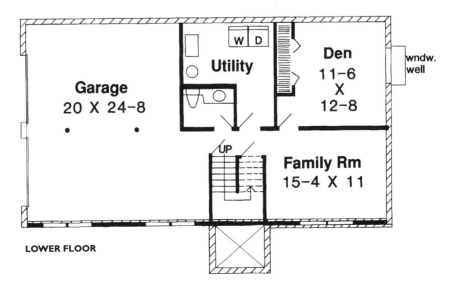

Garage 20 X 24-8

W D

Utility

Den 11-6 X 12-8

wndw. well

UP

Family Rm 15-4 X 11

LOWER FLOOR

Units	Single
Price Code	C
Total Finished	1,995 sq. ft.
First Finished	1,365 sq. ft.
Second Finished	630 sq. ft.
Basement Unfinished	1,419 sq. ft.
Garage Unfinished	426 sq. ft.
Porch Unfinished	89 sq. ft.
Dimensions	44'x54'
Foundation	Basement
	Crawlspace
	Slab
Bedrooms	4
Full Baths	2
Half Baths	1
First Ceiling	9'
Second Ceiling	8'
Max Ridge Height	25'6"
Roof Framing	Truss
Exterior Walls	2x4

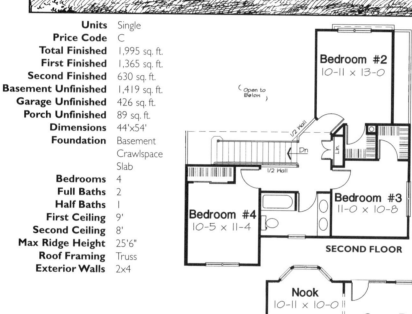

SECOND FLOOR

Bedroom #2 10-11 × 13-0

Open to Below

Bedroom #4 10-5 × 11-4

Bedroom #3 11-0 × 10-8

OPTIONAL CRAWLSPACE/ SLAB FOUNDATION

FIRST FLOOR

Nook 10-11 × 10-0

Great Room 18-6 × 15-6 (Open to Above)

Master Bedroom 13-5 × 13-0

Kitchen 10-11 × 15-11

M. Bath

Dining Room 10-11 × 12-0

Covered Porch

Garage 19 5 × 21-11

Design 63049

Units	Single
Price Code	C
Total Finished	1,997 sq. ft.
Main Finished	1,997 sq. ft.
Bonus Unfinished	310 sq. ft.
Garage Unfinished	502 sq. ft.
Dimensions	64'x57'
Foundation	Basement
Bedrooms	2
Full Baths	2
Half Baths	1
Main Ceiling	10'
Max Ridge Height	23'
Roof Framing	Truss
Exterior Walls	2x4

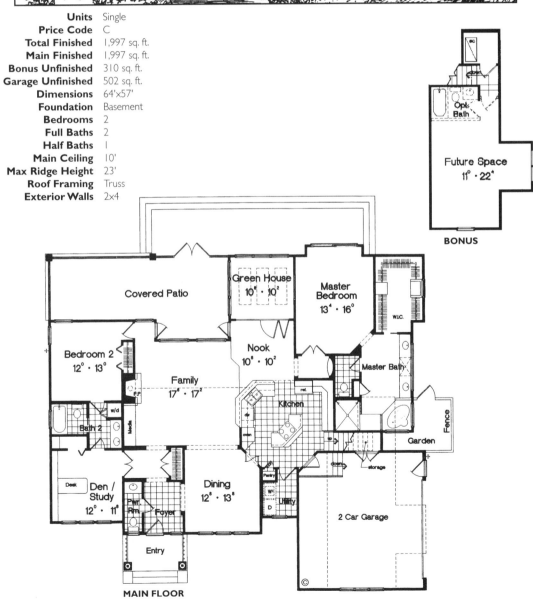

BONUS

MAIN FLOOR

PHOTOGRAPHY: COURTESY OF THE DESIGNER

Units	Single
Price Code	C
Total Finished	1,998 sq. ft.
First Finished	1,093 sq. ft.
Second Finished	905 sq. ft.
Basement Unfinished	1,093 sq. ft.
Garage Unfinished	527 sq. ft.
Dimensions	55'4"×37'8"
Foundation	Basement
Bedrooms	3
Full Baths	2
Half Baths	1
First Ceiling	8'
Second Ceiling	8'
Max Ridge Height	29'
Roof Framing	Stick
Exterior Walls	2×4

* Alternate foundation options available at an additional charge.
Please call 1-800-235-5700 for more information.

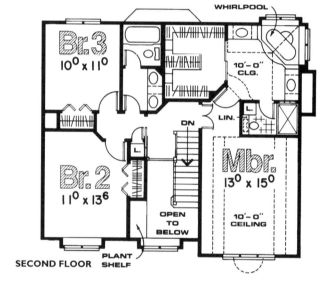

SECOND FLOOR

Please note: The photographed home may have been modified to suit homeowner preferences. If you order plans, have a builder or design professional check them against the photograph to confirm actual construction details.

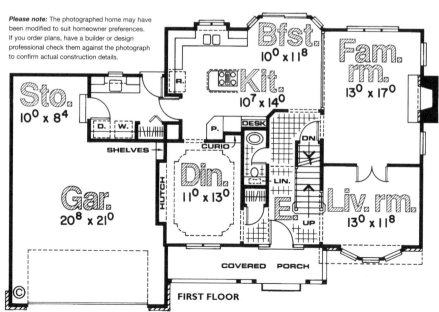

FIRST FLOOR

Design 94900

Units	Single
Price Code	C
Total Finished	1,999 sq. ft.
First Finished	1,421 sq. ft.
Second Finished	578 sq. ft.
Basement Unfinished	1,421 sq. ft.
Garage Unfinished	480 sq. ft.
Dimensions	52'x47'4"
Foundation	Basement
Bedrooms	4
Full Baths	2
Half Baths	1
First Ceiling	8'
Max Ridge Height	28'3"
Roof Framing	Stick
Exterior Walls	2x4

* Alternate foundation options available at an additional charge.
Please call 1-800-235-5700 for more information.

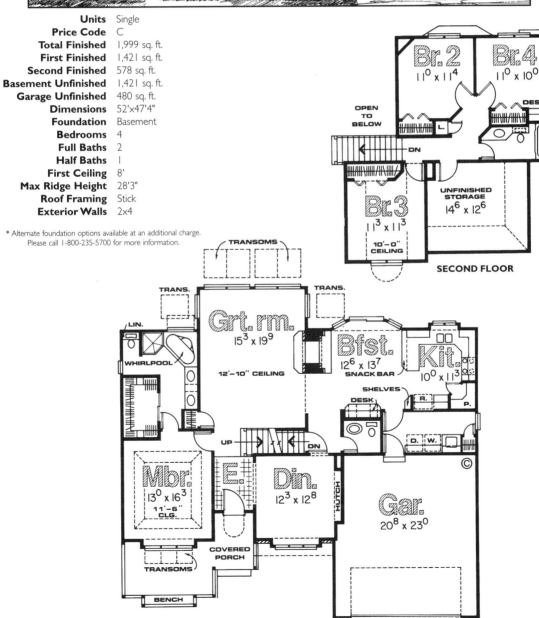

Units	Single
Price Code	D
Total Finished	2,001 sq. ft.
Main Finished	2,001 sq. ft.
Basement Unfinished	979 sq. ft.
Garage Unfinished	455 sq. ft.
Deck Unfinished	220 sq. ft.
Porch Unfinished	21 sq. ft.
Dimensions	39'6"x84'10"
Bedrooms	3
Full Baths	2
Main Ceiling	8'
Max Ridge Height	27'7"
Roof Framing	Stick
Exterior Walls	2x4

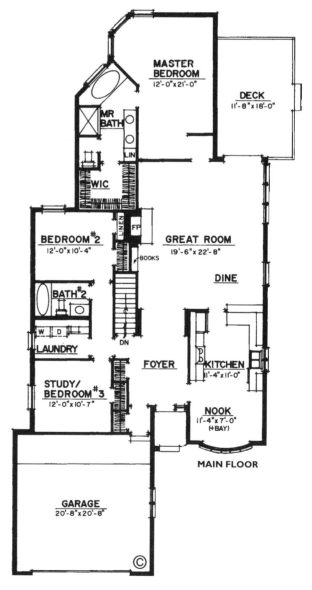

MASTER BEDROOM 12'-0"x21'-0"

DECK 11'-8"x18'-0"

MR BATH

LIN

WIC

BEDROOM #2 12'-0"x10'-4"

LINEN

FP

BOOKS

GREAT ROOM 19'-6"x22'-8"

DINE

BATH #2

W D

DN

LAUNDRY

FOYER

KITCHEN 11'-4"x11'-0"

STUDY/ BEDROOM #3 12'-0"x10'-7"

NOOK 11'-4"x7'-0" (+BAY)

MAIN FLOOR

GARAGE 20'-8"x20'-8"

Design 65228

Units	Single
Price Code	D
Total Finished	2,005 sq. ft.
First Finished	880 sq. ft.
Second Finished	1,125 sq. ft.
Basement Unfinished	880 sq. ft.
Deck Unfinished	237 sq. ft.
Dimensions	30'x54'
Foundation	Basement
Bedrooms	3
Full Baths	2
Half Baths	1
First Ceiling	8'
Second Ceiling	8'
Max Ridge Height	29'3"

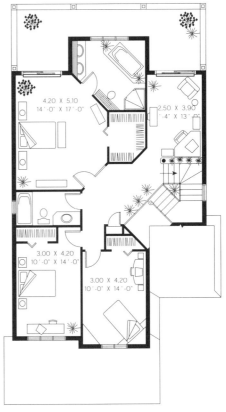

SECOND FLOOR

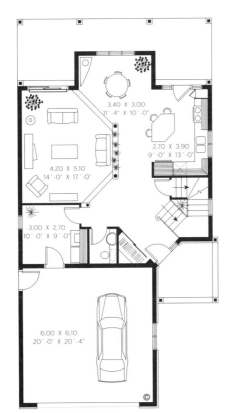

FIRST FLOOR

Design 68160

Units	Single
Price Code	D
Total Finished	2,005 sq. ft.
First Finished	1,486 sq. ft.
Second Finished	519 sq. ft.
Bonus Unfinished	264 sq. ft.
Deck Unfinished	858 sq. ft.
Dimensions	50'x60'
Foundation	Crawlspace Slab
Bedrooms	3
Full Baths	2
Half Baths	1
First Ceiling	9'
Max Ridge Height	27'
Exterior Walls	2x4

* Alternate foundation options available at an additional charge.
Please call 1-800-235-5700 for more information.

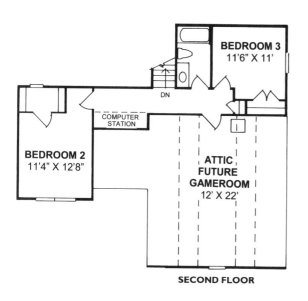

SECOND FLOOR

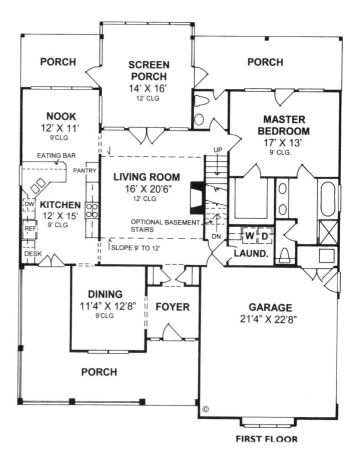

FIRST FLOOR

Design 98594

Units	Single
Price Code	D
Total Finished	2,006 sq. ft.
Main Finished	2,006 sq. ft.
Garage Unfinished	651 sq. ft.
Deck Unfinished	220 sq. ft.
Dimensions	72'x41'4"
Foundation	Crawlspace
	Slab
Bedrooms	3
Full Baths	2
Half Baths	I
Max Ridge Height	26'6"
Roof Framing	Stick
Exterior Walls	2x4

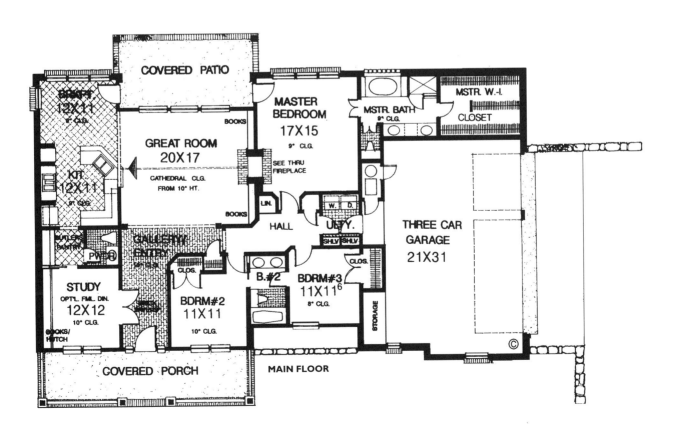

Design 97151

Units	Single
Price Code	D
Total Finished	2,007 sq. ft.
Main Finished	2,007 sq. ft.
Deck Unfinished	144 sq. ft.
Dimensions	67'x53'
Foundation	Basement
Bedrooms	3
Full Baths	2
Max Ridge Height	24'
Roof Framing	Truss
Exterior Walls	2x6

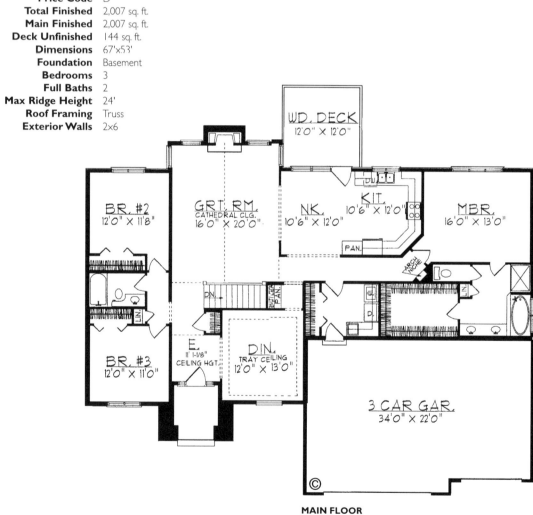

MAIN FLOOR

Design 65125

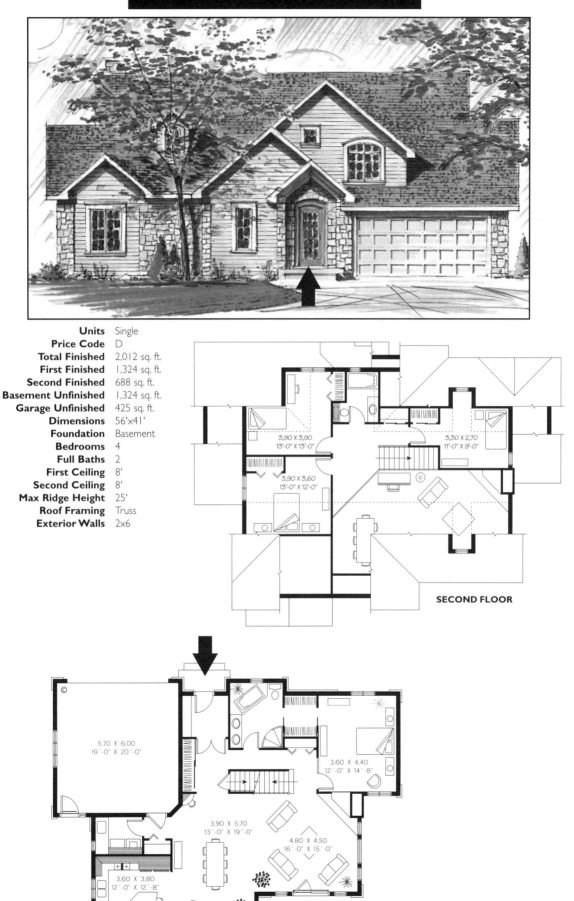

Units	Single
Price Code	D
Total Finished	2,012 sq. ft.
First Finished	1,324 sq. ft.
Second Finished	688 sq. ft.
Basement Unfinished	1,324 sq. ft.
Garage Unfinished	425 sq. ft.
Dimensions	56'x41'
Foundation	Basement
Bedrooms	4
Full Baths	2
First Ceiling	8'
Second Ceiling	8'
Max Ridge Height	25'
Roof Framing	Truss
Exterior Walls	2x6

SECOND FLOOR

FIRST FLOOR

Units	Single
Price Code	D
Total Finished	2,015 sq. ft.
First Finished	1,280 sq. ft.
Second Finished	735 sq. ft.
Porch Unfinished	80 sq. ft.
Dimensions	32'x40'
Foundation	Crawlspace
Bedrooms	3
Full Baths	2
Half Baths	1
First Ceiling	8'
Second Ceiling	8'
Max Ridge Height	32'
Roof Framing	Stick
Exterior Walls	2x6

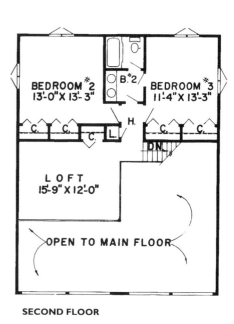

SECOND FLOOR

FIRST FLOOR

Design 97619

Units	Single
Price Code	D
Total Finished	2,032 sq. ft.
Main Finished	2,032 sq. ft.
Basement Unfinished	1,471 sq. ft.
Garage Unfinished	561 sq. ft.
Dimensions	58'6"x43'1"
Foundation	Basement
Bedrooms	4
Full Baths	2
Main Ceiling	9'
Max Ridge Height	24'
Roof Framing	Stick
Exterior Walls	2x4

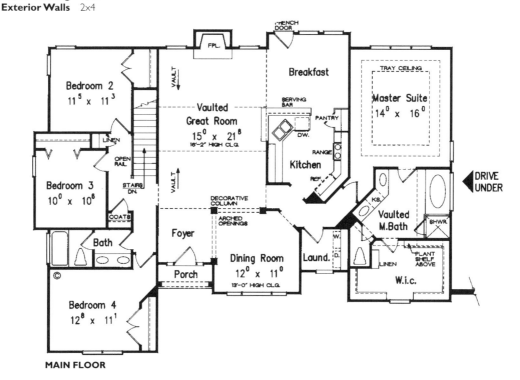

MAIN FLOOR

Design 32109

PHOTOGRAPHY: JAMES YOCHUM PHOTOGRAPHY

Units	Single
Price Code	D
Total Finished	2,038 sq. ft.
First Finished	1,213 sq. ft.
Second Finished	825 sq. ft.
Basement Unfinished	1,213 sq. ft.
Deck Unfinished	535 sq. ft.
Porch Unfinished	144 sq. ft.
Dimensions	46'4"x37'8"
Foundation	Basement
Bedrooms	3
Full Baths	1
3/4 Baths	1
Half Baths	1
First Ceiling	9'
Second Ceiling	8'
Max Ridge Height	24'8"
Roof Framing	Stick/Truss
Exterior Walls	2x6

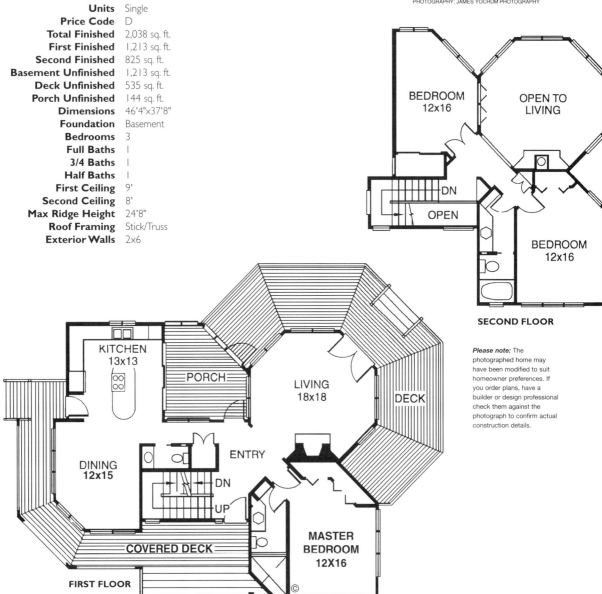

Please note: The photographed home may have been modified to suit homeowner preferences. If you order plans, have a builder or design professional check them against the photograph to confirm actual construction details.

Design 62041

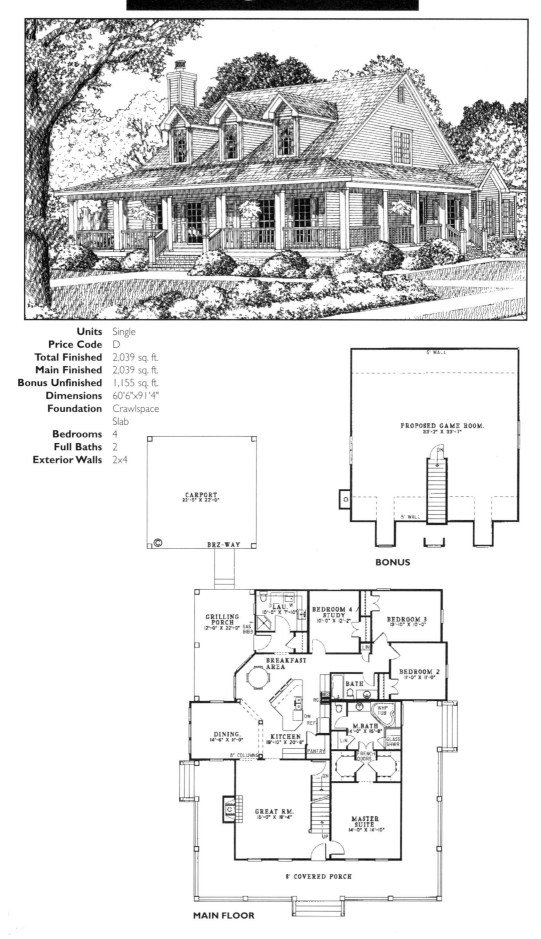

Units	Single
Price Code	D
Total Finished	2,039 sq. ft.
Main Finished	2,039 sq. ft.
Bonus Unfinished	1,155 sq. ft.
Dimensions	60'6"×91'4"
Foundation	Crawlspace
	Slab
Bedrooms	4
Full Baths	2
Exterior Walls	2x4

CARPORT
22'-0" X 22'-0"

BRZ-WAY

PROPOSED GAME ROOM.
33'-2" X 33'-7"

5' WALL

5' WALL

DN

BONUS

GRILLING PORCH
12'-0" X 22'-0"

LAU. W
10'-0" X 7'-10"

GAS BBQ

BEDROOM 4
STUDY
10'-0" X 12'-2"

BEDROOM 3
13'-10" X 10'-0"

LIN

BREAKFAST
AREA

BEDROOM 2
11'-0" X 11'-0"

BATH

DINING.
14'-6" X 11'-0"

KITCHEN
18'-10" X 20'-8"

DW
REF

RG

WHP TUB

M.BATH
14'-0" X 15'-8"

LIN.

GLASS SHWR

PANTRY

FRENCH DOORS

8" COLUMNS

DN

GREAT RM.
15'-0" X 18'-4"

UP

MASTER SUITE
14'-0" X 14'-10"

8' COVERED PORCH

MAIN FLOOR

Units	Single
Price Code	D
Total Finished	2,044 sq. ft.
First Finished	1,403 sq. ft.
Second Finished	641 sq. ft.
Basement Unfinished	1,394 sq. ft.
Garage Unfinished	680 sq. ft.
Deck Unfinished	156 sq. ft.
Porch Unfinished	231 sq. ft.
Dimensions	68'x47'
Foundation	Basement
	Crawlspace
	Slab
Bedrooms	3
Full Baths	2
Half Baths	1
First Ceiling	9'
Second Ceiling	8'
Vaulted Ceiling	12'9"
Roof Framing	Truss
Exterior Walls	2x4

OPTIONAL CRAWLSPACE/SLAB FOUNDATION

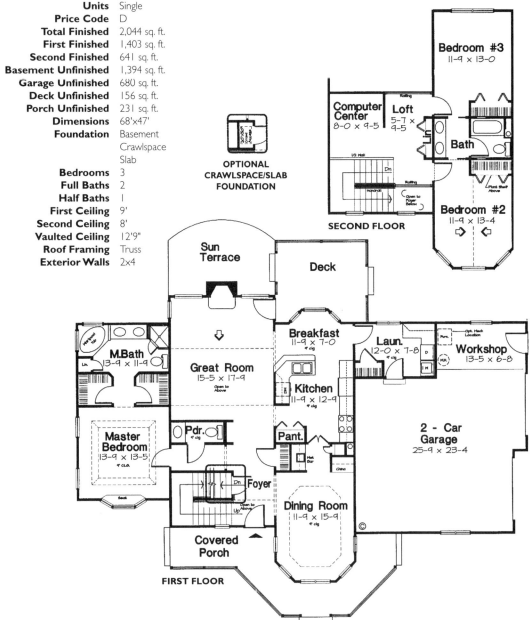

Design 67003

Units	Single
Price Code	D
Total Finished	2,044 sq. ft.
First Finished	1,203 sq. ft.
Second Finished	841 sq. ft.
Garage Unfinished	462 sq. ft.
Porch Unfinished	323 sq. ft.
Dimensions	56'x44'5"
Foundation	Slab
Bedrooms	3
Full Baths	2
Half Baths	1
First Ceiling	8'
Second Ceiling	8'
Vaulted Ceiling	16'
Max Ridge Height	28'9"
Roof Framing	Stick
Exterior Walls	2x4

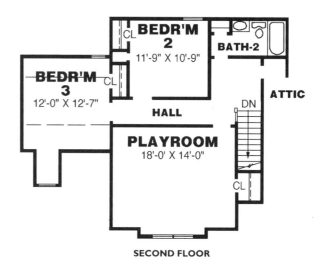

SECOND FLOOR

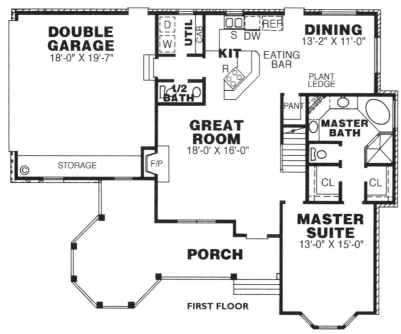

FIRST FLOOR

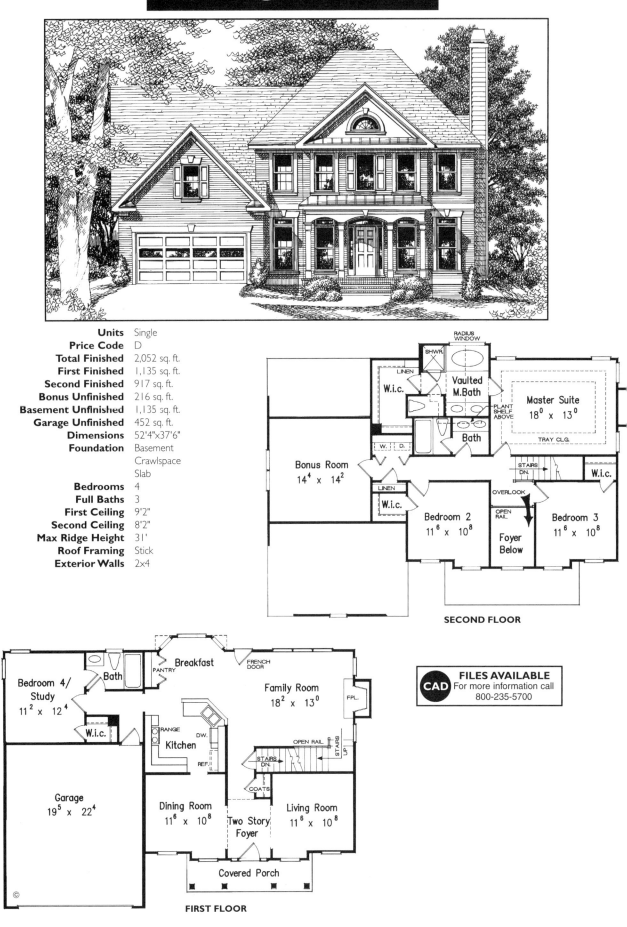

Units	Single
Price Code	D
Total Finished	2,052 sq. ft.
First Finished	1,135 sq. ft.
Second Finished	917 sq. ft.
Bonus Unfinished	216 sq. ft.
Basement Unfinished	1,135 sq. ft.
Garage Unfinished	452 sq. ft.
Dimensions	52'4"×37'6"
Foundation	Basement
	Crawlspace
	Slab
Bedrooms	4
Full Baths	3
First Ceiling	9'2"
Second Ceiling	8'2"
Max Ridge Height	31'
Roof Framing	Stick
Exterior Walls	2x4

SECOND FLOOR

- RADIUS WINDOW
- SHWR.
- LINEN
- W.i.c.
- Vaulted M.Bath
- PLANT SHELF ABOVE
- Master Suite 18⁰ x 13⁰
- Bath
- W. D.
- TRAY CLG.
- Bonus Room 14⁴ x 14²
- STAIRS DN.
- W.i.c.
- LINEN
- W.i.c.
- Bedroom 2 11⁶ x 10⁸
- OVERLOOK
- OPEN RAIL
- Foyer Below
- Bedroom 3 11⁶ x 10⁸

FIRST FLOOR

- Bedroom 4/ Study 11² x 12⁴
- Bath
- PANTRY
- Breakfast
- FRENCH DOOR
- Family Room 18² x 13⁰
- FPL.
- W.i.c.
- RANGE
- Kitchen
- DW.
- REF.
- OPEN RAIL
- STAIRS DN.
- STAIRS UP
- COATS
- Garage 19⁵ x 22⁴
- Dining Room 11⁶ x 10⁸
- Two Story Foyer
- Living Room 11⁶ x 10⁸
- Covered Porch

CAD FILES AVAILABLE
For more information call
800-235-5700

Design 94260

Units	Single
Price Code	F
Total Finished	2,068 sq. ft.
Main Finished	2,068 sq. ft.
Lower Unfinished	1,402 sq. ft.
Garage Unfinished	560 sq. ft.
Deck Unfinished	594 sq. ft.
Porch Unfinished	696 sq. ft.
Dimensions	54'x58'
Foundation	Pier/Post
Bedrooms	3
Full Baths	2
Max Ridge Height	37'
Roof Framing	Truss
Exterior Walls	2x6

* Alternate foundation options available at an additional charge.
Please call 1-800-235-5700 for more information.

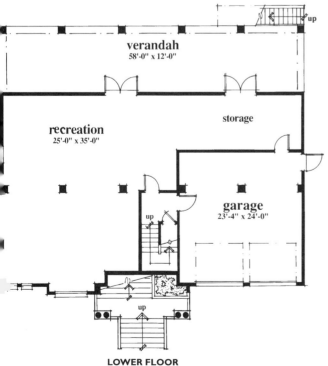

LOWER FLOOR

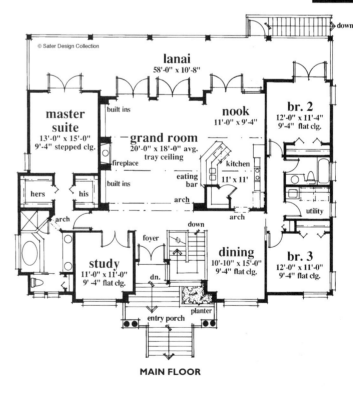

MAIN FLOOR

Units	Single
Price Code	D
Total Finished	2,069 sq. ft.
Main Finished	2,069 sq. ft.
Garage Unfinished	481 sq. ft.
Porch Unfinished	374 sq. ft.
Dimensions	70'x58'
Foundation	Crawlspace
	Slab
Bedrooms	3
Full Baths	2
Half Baths	1
Main Ceiling	9'
Max Ridge Height	23'
Exterior Walls	2x4

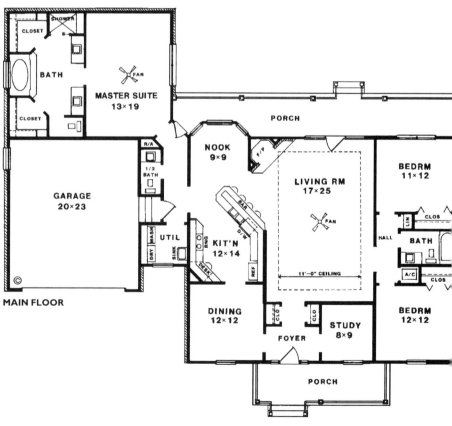

MAIN FLOOR

Design 24245

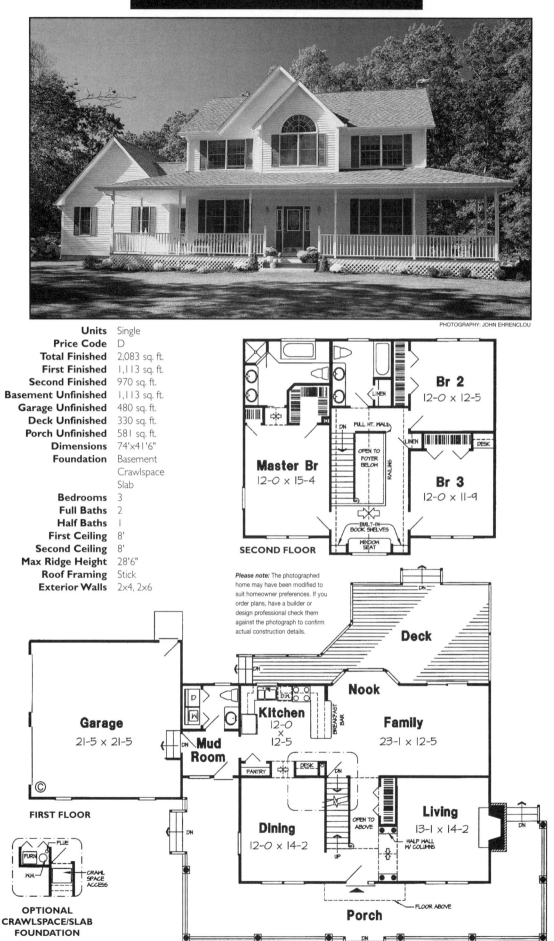

PHOTOGRAPHY: JOHN EHRENCLOU

Units	Single
Price Code	D
Total Finished	2,083 sq. ft.
First Finished	1,113 sq. ft.
Second Finished	970 sq. ft.
Basement Unfinished	1,113 sq. ft.
Garage Unfinished	480 sq. ft.
Deck Unfinished	330 sq. ft.
Porch Unfinished	581 sq. ft.
Dimensions	74'x41'6"
Foundation	Basement
	Crawlspace
	Slab
Bedrooms	3
Full Baths	2
Half Baths	1
First Ceiling	8'
Second Ceiling	8'
Max Ridge Height	28'6"
Roof Framing	Stick
Exterior Walls	2x4, 2x6

SECOND FLOOR

- Master Br 12-0 x 15-4
- Br 2 12-0 x 12-5
- Br 3 12-0 x 11-9
- OPEN TO FOYER BELOW
- FULL HT. WALL
- RAILING
- LINEN
- DESK
- BUILT-IN BOOK SHELVES
- WINDOW SEAT

Please note: The photographed home may have been modified to suit homeowner preferences. If you order plans, have a builder or design professional check them against the photograph to confirm actual construction details.

FIRST FLOOR

- Garage 21-5 x 21-5
- Mud Room
- Kitchen 12-0 x 12-5
- Nook
- Family 23-1 x 12-5
- Deck
- Dining 12-0 x 14-2
- Living 13-1 x 14-2
- Porch
- PANTRY
- DESK
- BREAKFAST BAR
- OPEN TO ABOVE
- HALF WALL W/ COLUMNS
- FLOOR ABOVE
- UP

OPTIONAL CRAWLSPACE/SLAB FOUNDATION

- FURN
- FLUE
- W.H.
- CRAWL SPACE ACCESS

Units	Single
Price Code	D
Total Finished	2,083 sq. ft.
First Finished	1,171 sq. ft.
Second Finished	912 sq. ft.
Garage Unfinished	424 sq. ft.
Dimensions	50'x42'4"
Foundation	Basement
Bedrooms	3
Full Baths	2
Half Baths	1

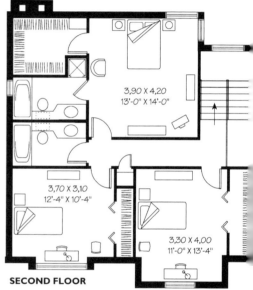

SECOND FLOOR

FIRST FLOOR

Design 65253

Units	Single
Price Code	D
Total Finished	2,089 sq. ft.
First Finished	1,204 sq. ft.
Second Finished	885 sq. ft.
Basement Unfinished	1,204 sq. ft.
Garage Unfinished	287 sq. ft.
Dimensions	43'x40'
Foundation	Basement
Bedrooms	3
Full Baths	1
Half Baths	1
First Ceiling	8'
Second Ceiling	8'
Max Ridge Height	27'10"
Roof Framing	Truss
Exterior Walls	2x6

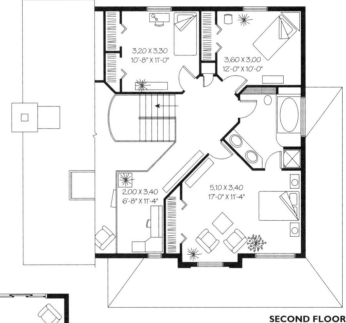

SECOND FLOOR

FIRST FLOOR

Design 96529

Units	Single
Price Code	D
Total Finished	2,089 sq. ft.
Main Finished	2,089 sq. ft.
Bonus Unfinished	497 sq. ft.
Garage Unfinished	541 sq. ft.
Dimensions	79'x52'
Foundation	Crawlspace
	Slab
Bedrooms	3
Full Baths	2
Half Baths	1
Main Ceiling	9'
Max Ridge Height	22'
Roof Framing	Stick
Exterior Walls	2x4

BONUS

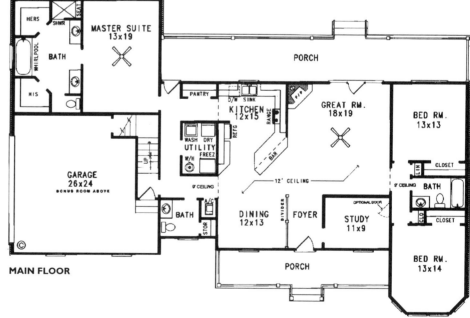

MAIN FLOOR

Units	Single
Price Code	D
Total Finished	2,091 sq. ft.
First Finished	1,362 sq. ft.
Second Finished	729 sq. ft.
Bonus Unfinished	384 sq. ft.
Basement Unfinished	988 sq. ft.
Garage Unfinished	559 sq. ft.
Porch Unfinished	396 sq. ft.
Dimensions	78'x38'
Foundation	Basement
	Crawlspace
	Slab
Bedrooms	3
Full Baths	2
Half Baths	1
Max Ridge Height	23'
Roof Framing	Stick
Exterior Walls	2x4

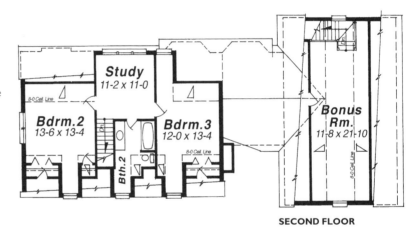

SECOND FLOOR

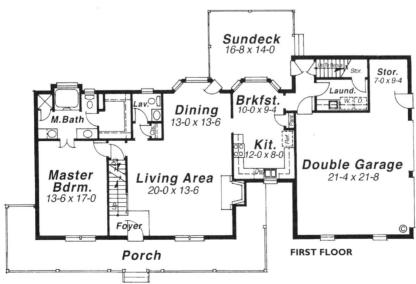

FIRST FLOOR

Units	Single
Price Code	D
Total Finished	2,094 sq. ft.
First Finished	1,713 sq. ft.
Second Finished	381 sq. ft.
Bonus Unfinished	327 sq. ft.
Garage Unfinished	400 sq. ft.
Porch Unfinished	271 sq. ft.
Dimensions	62'4"x60'
Foundation	Crawlspace Slab
Bedrooms	3
Full Baths	3
First Ceiling	8'
Second Ceiling	8'
Max Ridge Height	20'
Roof Framing	Stick
Exterior Walls	2x4

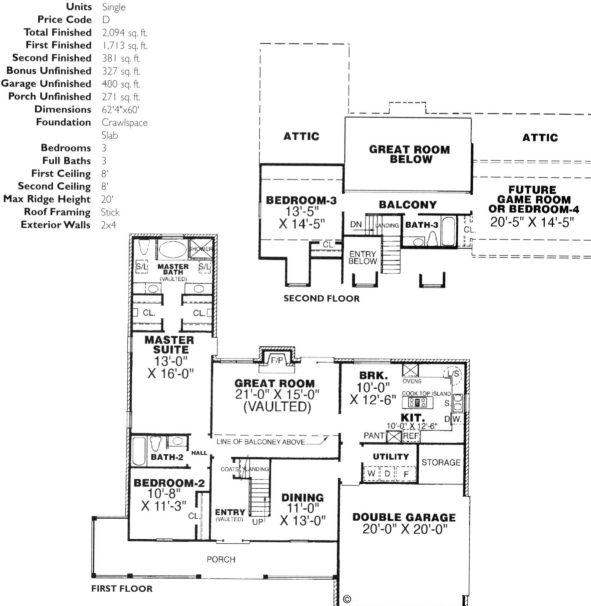

Design 91053

Units	Single
Price Code	D
Total Finished	2,099 sq. ft.
First Finished	1,150 sq. ft.
Second Finished	949 sq. ft.
Garage Unfinished	484 sq. ft.
Dimensions	59'6"x35'
Foundation	Crawlspace
Bedrooms	3
Full Baths	2
Half Baths	1
First Ceiling	8'
Max Ridge Height	26'
Roof Framing	Truss
Exterior Walls	2x6

SECOND FLOOR

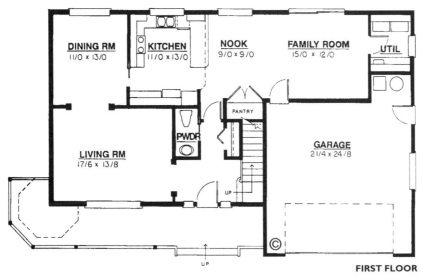

FIRST FLOOR

Design 92610

PHOTOGRAPHY: DONNA & RON KOLB, EXPOSURES UNLIMITED

Units	Single
Price Code	D
Total Finished	2,101 sq. ft.
First Finished	1,626 sq. ft.
Second Finished	475 sq. ft.
Basement Unfinished	1,512 sq. ft.
Garage Unfinished	438 sq. ft.
Dimensions	59'x60'8"
Foundation	Basement
Bedrooms	3
Full Baths	2
Half Baths	1
First Ceiling	8'
Second Ceiling	8'
Max Ridge Height	31'
Roof Framing	Truss
Exterior Walls	2x4

SECOND FLOOR

Bedroom 15x10-8

Great Room Below

Bath

Bedroom 14x10-6

Foyer Below

Please note: The photographed home may have been modified to suit homeowner preferences. If you order plans, have a builder or design professional check them against the photograph to confirm actual construction details.

FIRST FLOOR

Deck

Breakfast 9-2 x 16

Sunken Great Room 16-10 x 21

Kitchen 8 x 13-4

Bath

Walk-in closet

Dining Room 16 x 11-8

Master Bedroom 14 x 17-4
Slope ceiling Slope ceiling

Bath

Foyer

Stairs up

Hall

Laundry

Two-car Garage 21 x 20-8

Design 82082

Units	Single
Price Code	D
Total Finished	2,107 sq. ft.
Main Finished	2,107 sq. ft.
Dimensions	64'8"×62'1"
Foundation	Basement
	Slab
Bedrooms	4
Full Baths	2
Half Baths	1
Exterior Walls	2x4

MAIN FLOOR

Design 24256

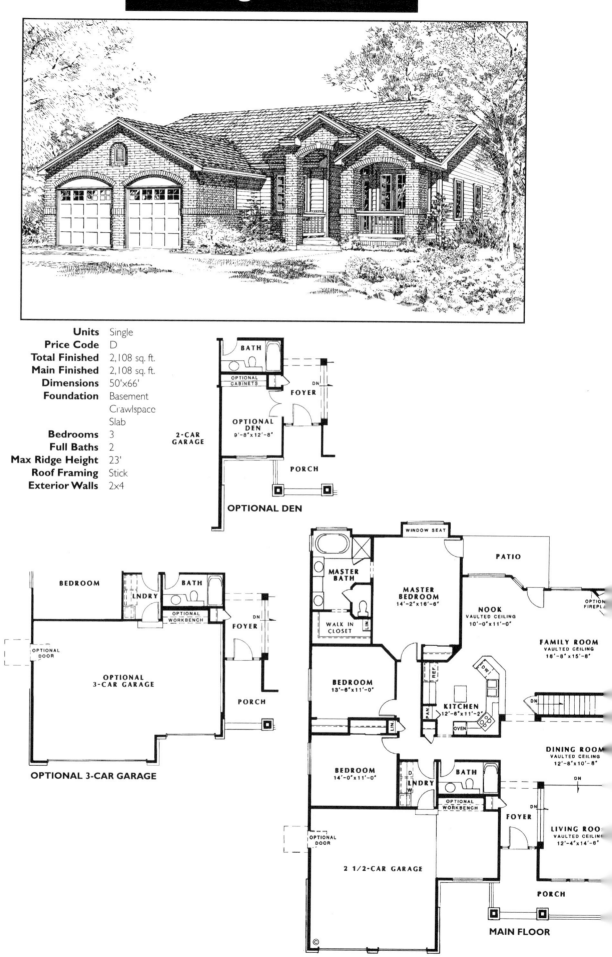

Units	Single
Price Code	D
Total Finished	2,108 sq. ft.
Main Finished	2,108 sq. ft.
Dimensions	50'x66'
Foundation	Basement
	Crawlspace
	Slab
Bedrooms	3
Full Baths	2
Max Ridge Height	23'
Roof Framing	Stick
Exterior Walls	2x4

OPTIONAL DEN

OPTIONAL 3-CAR GARAGE

MAIN FLOOR

Design 97890

Units	Single
Price Code	D
Total Finished	2,118 sq. ft.
Main Finished	2,118 sq. ft.
Garage Unfinished	660 sq. ft.
Deck Unfinished	260 sq. ft.
Porch Unfinished	304 sq. ft.
Dimensions	73'4"x49'1"
Foundation	Slab
Bedrooms	3
Full Baths	2
Half Baths	1
Main Ceiling	9'-10'
Max Ridge Height	27'
Roof Framing	Stick
Exterior Walls	2x4

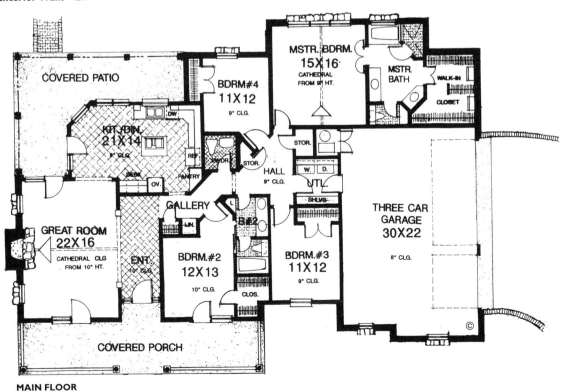

MAIN FLOOR

Units	Single
Price Code	D
Total Finished	2,126 sq. ft.
Main Finished	2,126 sq. ft.
Garage Unfinished	528 sq. ft.
Deck Unfinished	428 sq. ft.
Dimensions	66'x54'
Foundation	Basement
	Crawlspace
	Slab
Bedrooms	3
Full Baths	2
Main Ceiling	9'
Max Ridge Height	24'
Exterior Walls	2x4

* Alternate foundation options available at an additional charge.
Please call 1-800-235-5700 for more information.

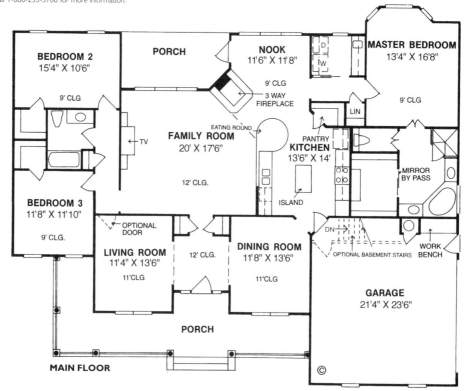

Design 97219

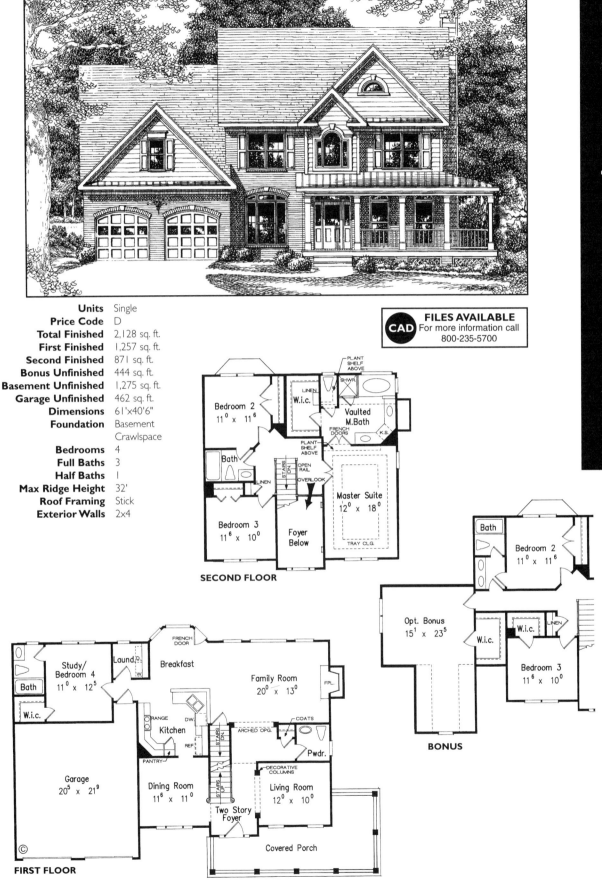

Units	Single
Price Code	D
Total Finished	2,128 sq. ft.
First Finished	1,257 sq. ft.
Second Finished	871 sq. ft.
Bonus Unfinished	444 sq. ft.
Basement Unfinished	1,275 sq. ft.
Garage Unfinished	462 sq. ft.
Dimensions	61'x40'6"
Foundation	Basement Crawlspace
Bedrooms	4
Full Baths	3
Half Baths	1
Max Ridge Height	32'
Roof Framing	Stick
Exterior Walls	2x4

CAD FILES AVAILABLE
For more information call
800-235-5700

SECOND FLOOR

Bedroom 2
11⁰ x 11⁶

LINEN
W.i.c.

PLANT SHELF ABOVE

SHWR.

Vaulted M.Bath

FRENCH DOORS

K.S.

Bath

PLANT SHELF ABOVE

OPEN RAIL OVERLOOK

Master Suite
12⁰ x 18⁰

Bedroom 3
11⁶ x 10⁰

Foyer Below

TRAY CLG.

BONUS

Bath

Bedroom 2
11⁰ x 11⁶

Opt. Bonus
15¹ x 23⁵

W.i.c.

W.i.c.

LINEN

Bedroom 3
11⁶ x 10⁰

FIRST FLOOR

Study/ Bedroom 4
11⁰ x 12⁵

Bath

W.i.c.

Laund.

FRENCH DOOR

Breakfast

Family Room
20⁰ x 13⁰

FPL.

RANGE

Kitchen

DW

COATS

ARCHED OPG.

REF.

Pwdr.

PANTRY

DECORATIVE COLUMNS

Garage
20⁵ x 21⁹

Dining Room
11⁶ x 11⁰

Two Story Foyer

Living Room
12⁰ x 10⁰

Covered Porch

Design 65214

Units	Single
Price Code	D
Total Finished	2,129 sq. ft.
First Finished	1,162 sq. ft.
Second Finished	967 sq. ft.
Garage Unfinished	317 sq. ft.
Dimensions	10'x42'
Foundation	Basement
Bedrooms	3
Full Baths	1
Half Baths	1
First Ceiling	8'
Second Ceiling	8'
Max Ridge Height	30'4"
Roof Framing	Truss

3,00 X 3,30
10'-0" X 11'-0"

3,60 X 3,30
12'-0" X 11'-0"

4,80 X 2,20
16'-0" X 7'-4"

OPEN TO BELOW

4,40 X 4,00
14'-8" X 13'-4"

SECOND FLOOR

3,30 X 3,30
11'-0" X 11'-0"

2,40 X 3,70
8'-0" X 12'-4"

4,50 X 3,30
15'-0" X 11'-0"

4,60 X 5,10
15'-4" X 17'-0"

4,40 X 6,40
14'-8" X 21'-4"

FIRST FLOOR

PHOTOGRAPHY: COURTESY OF THE DESIGNER

Units	Single
Price Code	D
Total Finished	2,131 sq. ft.
First Finished	1,093 sq. ft.
Second Finished	1,038 sq. ft.
Basement Unfinished	1,093 sq. ft.
Garage Unfinished	527 sq. ft.
Dimensions	55'4"x37'8"
Foundation	Basement
Bedrooms	4
Full Baths	2
Half Baths	1
First Ceiling	8'
Second Ceiling	8'
Max Ridge Height	27'
Roof Framing	Stick
Exterior Walls	2x4

* Alternate foundation options available at an additional charge.
Please call 1-800-235-5700 for more information.

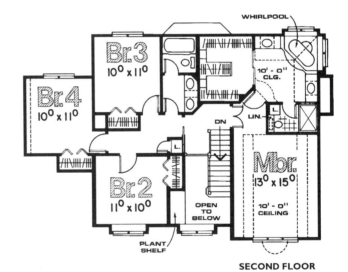

SECOND FLOOR

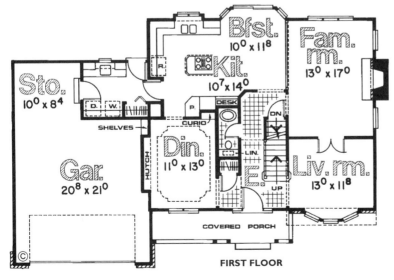

FIRST FLOOR

Please note: The photographed home may have been modified to suit homeowner preferences. If you order plans, have a builder or design professional check them against the photograph to confirm actual construction details.

Design 99124

Units	Single
Price Code	D
Total Finished	2,133 sq. ft.
First Finished	1,099 sq. ft.
Second Finished	1,034 sq. ft.
Basement Unfinished	1,099 sq. ft.
Dimensions	40'8"x44'
Foundation	Basement
Bedrooms	4
Full Baths	2
Half Baths	1
Max Ridge Height	28'
Roof Framing	Truss
Exterior Walls	2x6

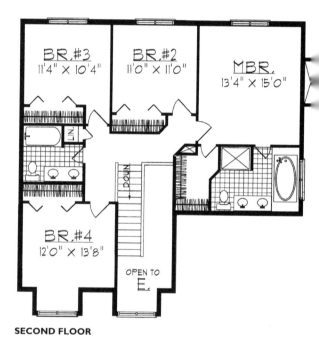

SECOND FLOOR

BR.#3 11'4" X 10'4"

BR.#2 11'0" X 11'0"

MBR. 13'4" X 15'0"

BR.#4 12'0" X 13'8"

OPEN TO E.

FIRST FLOOR

NK. 14'6" X 9'4"

GRT.RM. 21'8" X 14'0"

KIT. 14'6" X 11'6"

DIN. 12'0" X 12'6"

2 CAR GAR. 20'4" X 22'0"

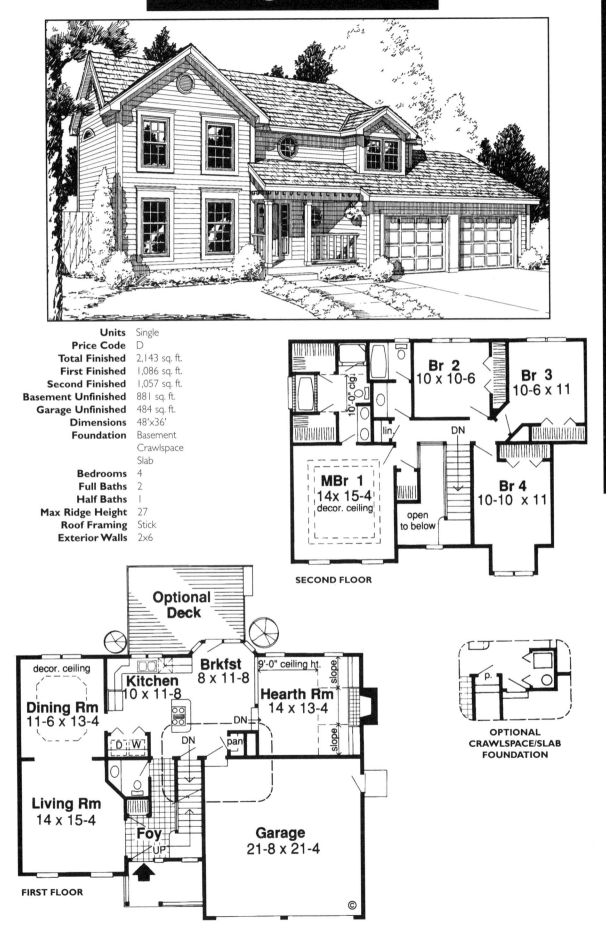

Units	Single
Price Code	D
Total Finished	2,143 sq. ft.
First Finished	1,086 sq. ft.
Second Finished	1,057 sq. ft.
Basement Unfinished	881 sq. ft.
Garage Unfinished	484 sq. ft.
Dimensions	48'x36'
Foundation	Basement
	Crawlspace
	Slab
Bedrooms	4
Full Baths	2
Half Baths	1
Max Ridge Height	27
Roof Framing	Stick
Exterior Walls	2x6

SECOND FLOOR

Br 2
10 x 10-6

Br 3
10-6 x 11

MBr 1
14x 15-4
decor. ceiling

DN

Br 4
10-10 x 11

open to below

lin.

10'-0" clg.

FIRST FLOOR

Optional Deck

Kitchen
10 x 11-8

Brkfst
8 x 11-8

9'-0" ceiling ht.

decor. ceiling

Dining Rm
11-6 x 13-4

Hearth Rm
14 x 13-4

slope

slope

DN

D W

DN

pan

Living Rm
14 x 15-4

Foy

UP

Garage
21-8 x 21-4

OPTIONAL CRAWLSPACE/SLAB FOUNDATION

p.

Units	Single
Price Code	D
Total Finished	2,144 sq. ft.
Main Finished	2,144 sq. ft.
Garage Unfinished	483 sq. ft.
Dimensions	57'4"x65'
Foundation	Slab
Bedrooms	4
Full Baths	3
Max Ridge Height	25'
Roof Framing	Stick
Exterior Walls	2x6

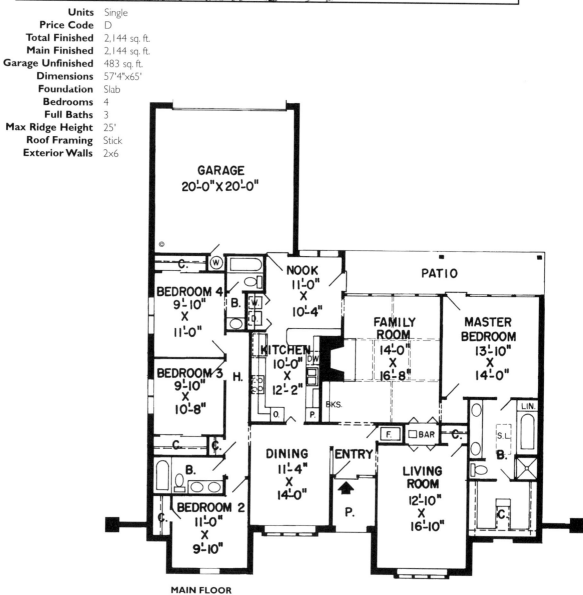

MAIN FLOOR

Design 61096

Units	Single
Price Code	D
Total Finished	2,148 sq. ft.
Main Finished	2,148 sq. ft.
Garage Unfinished	477 sq. ft.
Porch Unfinished	190 sq. ft.
Dimensions	63'x52'8"
Foundation	Crawlspace
	Slab
Bedrooms	4
Full Baths	2
Main Ceiling	9'
Roof Framing	Stick
Exterior Walls	2x4

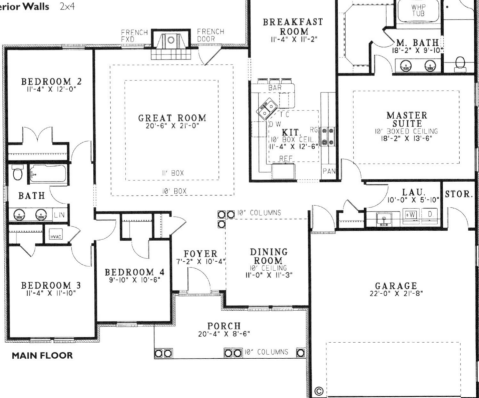

MAIN FLOOR

PHOTOGRAPHY: JOHN EHRENCLOU

Units	Single
Price Code	D
Total Finished	2,157 sq. ft.
First Finished	1,590 sq. ft.
Second Finished	567 sq. ft.
Basement Unfinished	1,576 sq. ft.
Garage Unfinished	456 sq. ft.
Dimensions	54'x46'
Foundation	Basement
	Crawlspace
	Slab
Bedrooms	3
Full Baths	2
Half Baths	1
Max Ridge Height	28'
Roof Framing	Stick
Exterior Walls	2x4, 2x6

Please note: The photographed home may have been modified to suit homeowner preferences. If you order plans, have a builder or design professional check them against the photograph to confirm actual construction details.

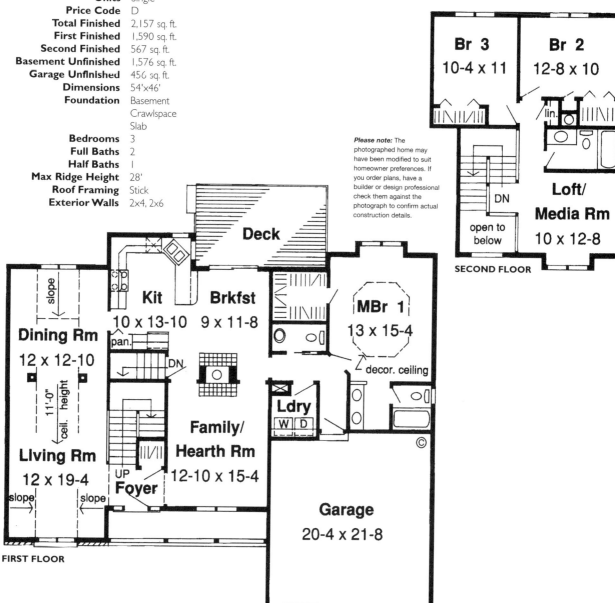

SECOND FLOOR

- Br 3 10-4 x 11
- Br 2 12-8 x 10
- Loft/ Media Rm 10 x 12-8
- lin.
- DN
- open to below

FIRST FLOOR

- Deck
- Kit 10 x 13-10
- Brkfst 9 x 11-8
- MBr 1 13 x 15-4 decor. ceiling
- Dining Rm 12 x 12-10 11'-0" ceil. height
- pan.
- DN
- Ldry W D
- Family/ Hearth Rm 12-10 x 15-4
- Living Rm 12 x 19-4
- UP
- Foyer
- Garage 20-4 x 21-8

Units	Single
Price Code	D
Total Finished	2,158 sq. ft.
Main Finished	2,158 sq. ft.
Basement Unfinished	2,190 sq. ft.
Garage Unfinished	485 sq. ft.
Dimensions	63'x63'6"
Foundation	Basement
	Crawlspace
Bedrooms	4
Full Baths	3
Max Ridge Height	25'
Roof Framing	Stick
Exterior Walls	2x4

CAD FILES AVAILABLE
For more information call
800-235-5700

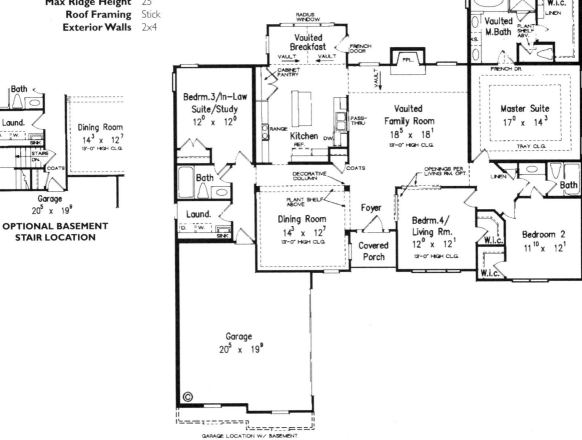

OPTIONAL BASEMENT STAIR LOCATION

MAIN FLOOR

Design 91343

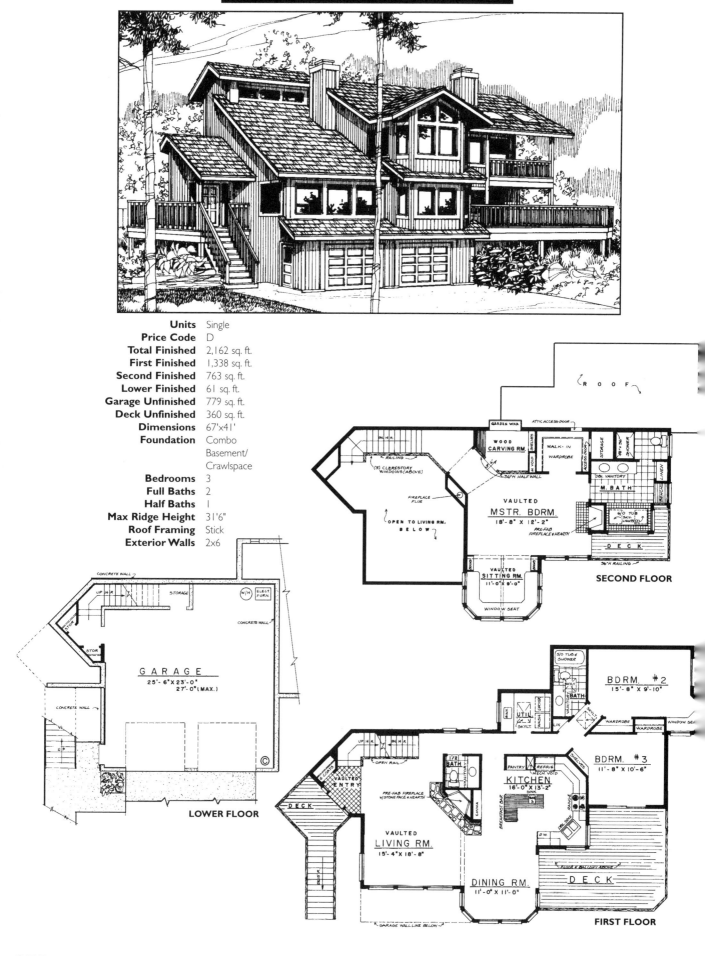

Units	Single
Price Code	D
Total Finished	2,162 sq. ft.
First Finished	1,338 sq. ft.
Second Finished	763 sq. ft.
Lower Finished	61 sq. ft.
Garage Unfinished	779 sq. ft.
Deck Unfinished	360 sq. ft.
Dimensions	67'x41'
Foundation	Combo Basement/ Crawlspace
Bedrooms	3
Full Baths	2
Half Baths	1
Max Ridge Height	31'6"
Roof Framing	Stick
Exterior Walls	2x6

SECOND FLOOR

VAULTED MSTR. BDRM. 18'-8" X 12'-2"

WOOD CARVING RM.

WALK-IN WARDROBE

M. BATH

VAULTED SITTING RM. 11'-0" X 9'-0"

WINDOW SEAT

OPEN TO LIVING RM. BELOW

DECK

LOWER FLOOR

GARAGE 25'-6" X 23'-0" 27'-0" (MAX.)

STORAGE

FIRST FLOOR

BDRM. #2 15'-8" X 9'-10"

BDRM. #3 11'-8" X 10'-6"

KITCHEN 16'-0" X 13'-2"

VAULTED LIVING RM. 15'-4" X 18'-8"

DINING RM. 11'-0" X 11'-0"

DECK

VAULTED ENTRY

Units	Single
Price Code	D
Total Finished	2,167 sq. ft.
Main Finished	2,167 sq. ft.
Garage Unfinished	690 sq. ft.
Deck Unfinished	162 sq. ft.
Porch Unfinished	22 sq. ft.
Dimensions	64'x58'1"
Foundation	Slab
Bedrooms	3
Full Baths	2
Main Ceiling	8'-10'
Max Ridge Height	26'3"
Roof Framing	Stick
Exterior Walls	2x4

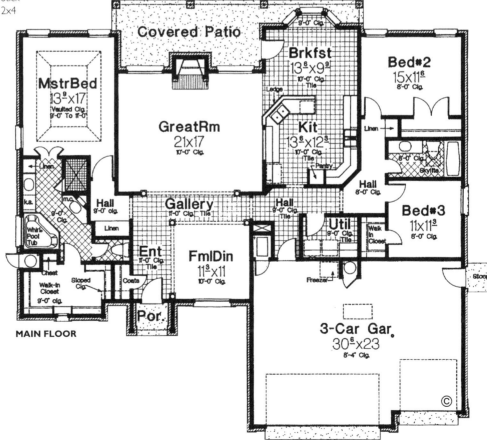

MAIN FLOOR

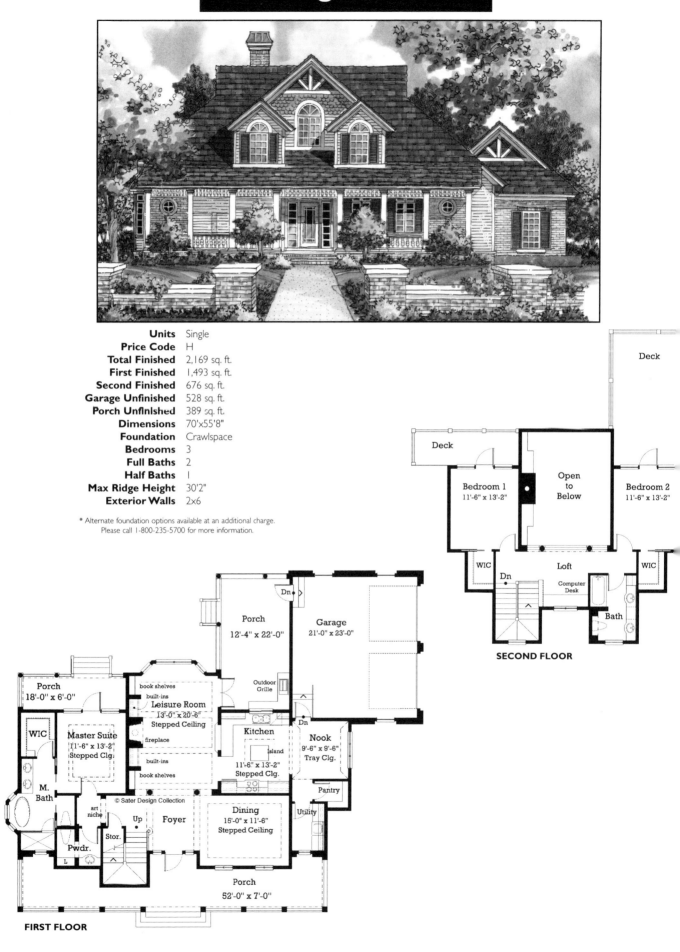

Units	Single
Price Code	H
Total Finished	2,169 sq. ft.
First Finished	1,493 sq. ft.
Second Finished	676 sq. ft.
Garage Unfinished	528 sq. ft.
Porch Unfinished	389 sq. ft.
Dimensions	70'x55'8"
Foundation	Crawlspace
Bedrooms	3
Full Baths	2
Half Baths	1
Max Ridge Height	30'2"
Exterior Walls	2x6

* Alternate foundation options available at an additional charge.
Please call 1-800-235-5700 for more information.

Deck

Deck

Bedroom 1
11'-6" x 13'-2"

Open
to
Below

Bedroom 2
11'-6" x 13'-2"

WIC

Loft

Dn

WIC

Computer
Desk

Bath

SECOND FLOOR

Porch
12'-4" x 22'-0"

Garage
21'-0" x 23'-0"

Dn

Outdoor
Grille

Kitchen
11'-6" x 13'-2"
Stepped Clg.

island

Nook
9'-6" x 9'-6"
Tray Clg.

Dn

Porch
18'-0" x 6'-0"

book shelves

built-ins

Leisure Room
13'-0" x 20'-6"
Stepped Ceiling

fireplace

built-ins

book shelves

Pantry

WIC

Master Suite
11'-6" x 13'-2"
Stepped Clg.

M.
Bath

art
niche

Up

Foyer

Dining
15'-0" x 11'-6"
Stepped Ceiling

Utility

© Sater Design Collection

Pwdr.

Stor.

Porch
52'-0" x 7'-0"

FIRST FLOOR

Design 94971

Units	Single
Price Code	D
Total Finished	2,172 sq. ft.
Main Finished	2,172 sq. ft.
Garage Unfinished	680 sq. ft.
Dimensions	76'x46'
Foundation	Basement
Bedrooms	4
Full Baths	2
3/4 Baths	1
Max Ridge Height	21'6"
Roof Framing	Stick
Exterior Walls	2x4

* Alternate foundation options available at an additional charge.
Please call 1-800-235-5700 for more information.

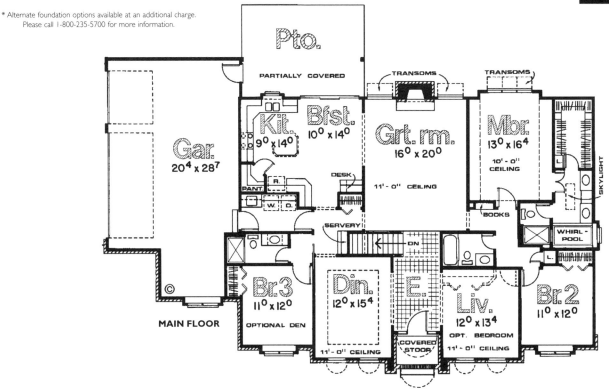

MAIN FLOOR

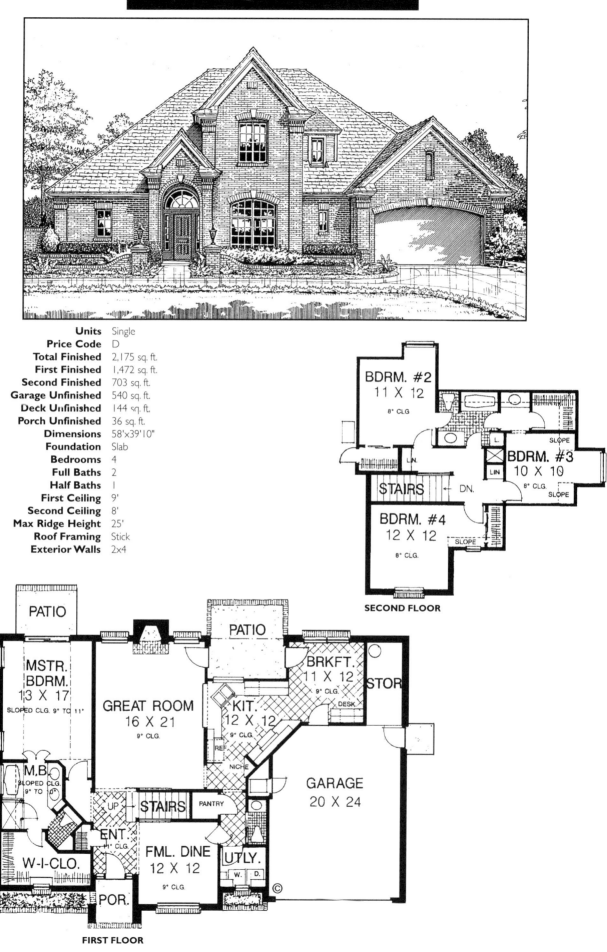

Units	Single
Price Code	D
Total Finished	2,175 sq. ft.
First Finished	1,472 sq. ft.
Second Finished	703 sq. ft.
Garage Unfinished	540 sq. ft.
Deck Unfinished	144 sq. ft.
Porch Unfinished	36 sq. ft.
Dimensions	58'x39'10"
Foundation	Slab
Bedrooms	4
Full Baths	2
Half Baths	1
First Ceiling	9'
Second Ceiling	8'
Max Ridge Height	25'
Roof Framing	Stick
Exterior Walls	2x4

BDRM. #2
11 X 12
8" CLG.

BDRM. #3
10 X 10
8" CLG.

SLOPE

L.

LIN.

LIN.

STAIRS DN.

BDRM. #4
12 X 12
8" CLG.

SLOPE

SECOND FLOOR

PATIO

PATIO

MSTR. BDRM.
13 X 17
SLOPED CLG. 9' TO 11'

GREAT ROOM
16 X 21
9" CLG.

BRKFT.
11 X 12
9" CLG.

STOR

KIT.
12 X 12
9" CLG.

DESK

REF.

NICHE

M.B.
SLOPED CLG.
9' TO 10'

GARAGE
20 X 24

W-I-CLO.

UP

STAIRS

PANTRY

ENT.
11' CLG.

FML. DINE
12 X 12
9" CLG.

UTLY.
W. D.

POR.

©

FIRST FLOOR

Design 92443

Units	Single
Price Code	D
Total Finished	2,184 sq. ft.
Main Finished	2,184 sq. ft.
Garage Unfinished	548 sq. ft.
Dimensions	71'2"x58'1"
Foundation	Basement
	Slab
Bedrooms	4
Full Baths	3
Main Ceiling	9'
Max Ridge Height	24'
Exterior Walls	2x4

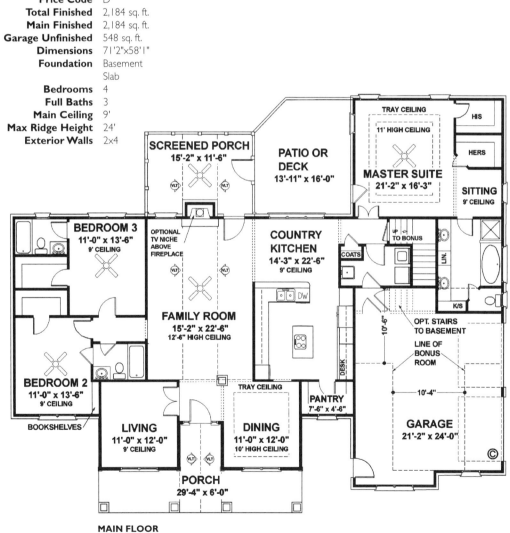

MAIN FLOOR

Units	Single
Price Code	D
Total Finished	2,188 sq. ft.
Main Finished	2,188 sq. ft.
Bonus Unfinished	674 sq. ft.
Basement Unfinished	2,188 sq. ft.
Garage Unfinished	455 sq. ft.
Dimensions	58'x64'4"
Foundation	Basement
	Crawlspace
	Slab
Bedrooms	3
Full Baths	2
Half Baths	1
Main Ceiling	9'
Second Ceiling	8'
Max Ridge Height	27'
Roof Framing	Stick
Exterior Walls	2x4

CAD FILES AVAILABLE For more information call 800-235-5700

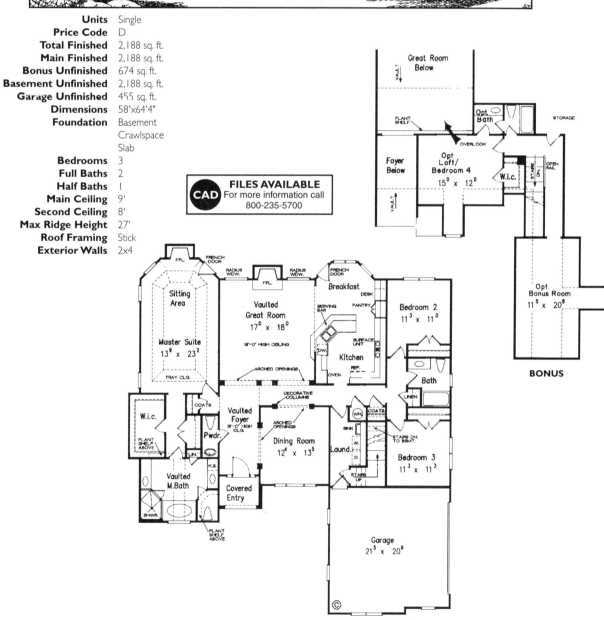

MAIN FLOOR

Design 98466

Units	Single
Price Code	D
Total Finished	2,193 sq. ft.
Main Finished	2,193 sq. ft.
Bonus Unfinished	400 sq. ft.
Basement Unfinished	2,193 sq. ft.
Garage Unfinished	522 sq. ft.
Dimensions	64'6"x59'
Foundation	Basement
	Crawlspace
	Slab
Bedrooms	4
Full Baths	2
Main Ceiling	9'
Second Ceiling	8'
Max Ridge Height	27'
Roof Framing	Stick
Exterior Walls	2x4

CAD FILES AVAILABLE
For more information call
800-235-5700

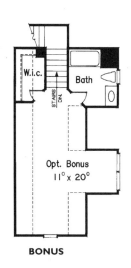

BONUS

MAIN FLOOR

Design 69100

Units	Single
Price Code	D
Total Finished	2,193 sq. ft.
First Finished	1,506 sq. ft.
Second Finished	687 sq. ft.
Garage Unfinished	703 sq. ft.
Dimensions	60'x52'
Foundation	Crawlspace
Bedrooms	4
Full Baths	2
Half Baths	1
First Ceiling	8'
Second Ceiling	8'
Max Ridge Height	26'
Roof Framing	Truss
Exterior Walls	2x6

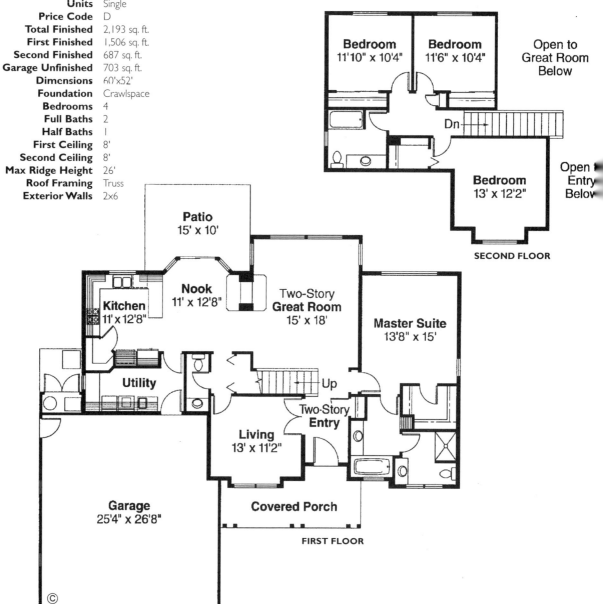

Design 91846

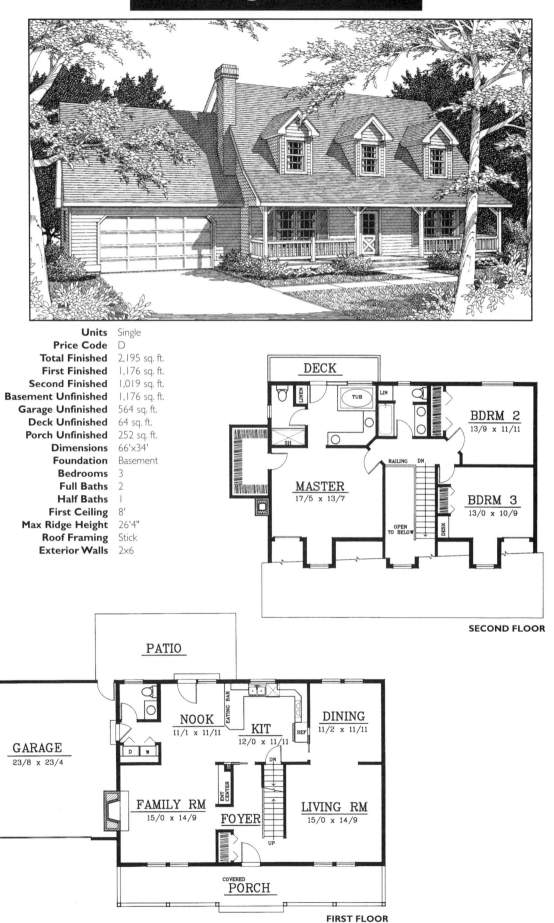

Units	Single
Price Code	D
Total Finished	2,195 sq. ft.
First Finished	1,176 sq. ft.
Second Finished	1,019 sq. ft.
Basement Unfinished	1,176 sq. ft.
Garage Unfinished	564 sq. ft.
Deck Unfinished	64 sq. ft.
Porch Unfinished	252 sq. ft.
Dimensions	66'x34'
Foundation	Basement
Bedrooms	3
Full Baths	2
Half Baths	1
First Ceiling	8'
Max Ridge Height	26'4"
Roof Framing	Stick
Exterior Walls	2x6

DECK

LINEN

TUB

LIN

SH

BDRM 2
13/9 x 11/11

RAILING   DN

MASTER
17/5 x 13/7

BDRM 3
13/0 x 10/9

OPEN
TO BELOW

DESK

SECOND FLOOR

PATIO

GARAGE
23/8 x 23/4

NOOK
11/1 x 11/11

EATING BAR

KIT
12/0 x 11/11

REF

DINING
11/2 x 11/11

D   W

ENT
CENTER

DN

FAMILY RM
15/0 x 14/9

FOYER

LIVING RM
15/0 x 14/9

UP

COVERED
PORCH

FIRST FLOOR

Units	Single
Price Code	D
Total Finished	2,200 sq. ft.
First Finished	1,688 sq. ft.
Second Finished	512 sq. ft.
Bonus Unfinished	238 sq. ft.
Basement Unfinished	1,608 sq. ft.
Garage Unfinished	471 sq. ft.
Dimensions	52'x48'
Foundation	Basement
	Crawlspace
Bedrooms	3
Full Baths	2
Half Baths	1
First Ceiling	9'
Second Ceiling	8'
Roof Framing	Stick
Exterior Walls	2x4

CAD FILES AVAILABLE
For more information call
800-235-5700

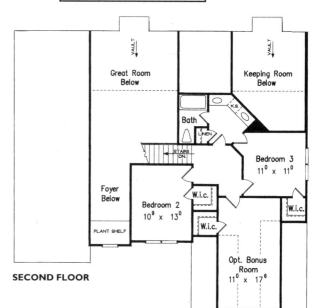

SECOND FLOOR

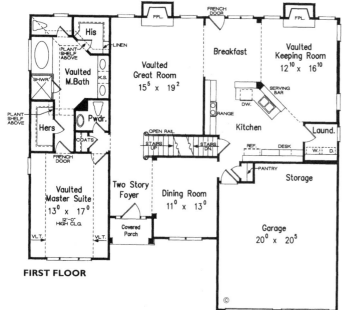

FIRST FLOOR

Design 94676

PHOTOGRAPHY: CHRIS A. LITTLE

Units	Single
Price Code	D
Total Finished	2,201 sq. ft.
Main Finished	2,201 sq. ft.
Garage Unfinished	853 sq. ft.
Deck Unfinished	222 sq. ft.
Porch Unfinished	240 sq. ft.
Dimensions	71'10"x66'10"
Foundation	Crawlspace
Bedrooms	3
Full Baths	2
Half Baths	1
Main Ceiling	9'
Max Ridge Height	30'9"
Roof Framing	Stick
Exterior Walls	2x4

Please note: The photographed home may have been modified to suit homeowner preferences. If you order plans, have a builder or design professional check them against the photograph to confirm actual construction details.

Deck
37'x 6'

Porch
21'2"x 8'

Breakfast
11'10"x 11'

Master Bath

Master Bedroom
14'6"x 18'4"

Living
22'x 17'

Kitchen
11'10"x 12'

Walk-In Closet

Utility

Bath

Bath

Bedroom
11'8"x 12'6"

Foyer

Dining
14'10"x 12'

Bedroom
11'4"x 12'

Porch

Three Car Garage
21'4"x 34'8"

Courtyard

MAIN FLOOR

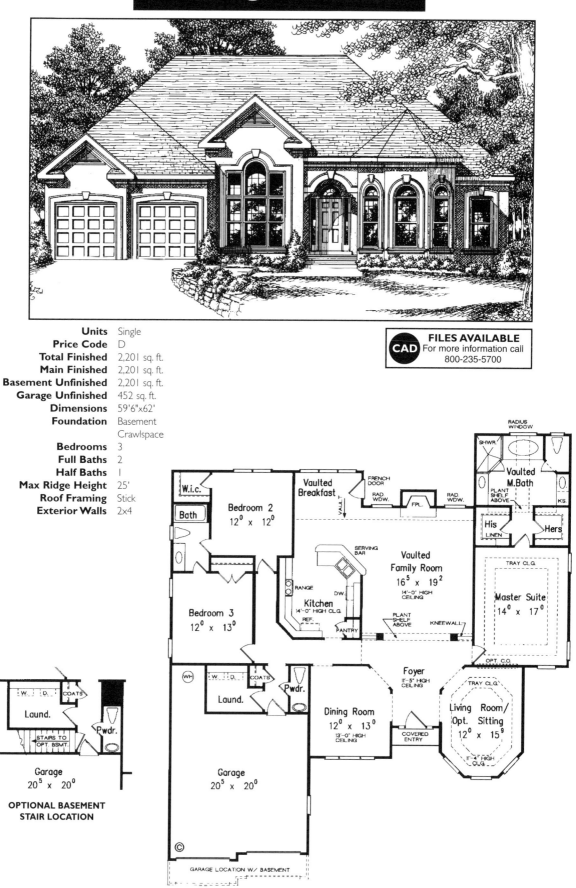

Units	Single
Price Code	D
Total Finished	2,201 sq. ft.
Main Finished	2,201 sq. ft.
Basement Unfinished	2,201 sq. ft.
Garage Unfinished	452 sq. ft.
Dimensions	59'6"x62'
Foundation	Basement
	Crawlspace
Bedrooms	3
Full Baths	2
Half Baths	I
Max Ridge Height	25'
Roof Framing	Stick
Exterior Walls	2x4

CAD FILES AVAILABLE
For more information call
800-235-5700

OPTIONAL BASEMENT
STAIR LOCATION

MAIN FLOOR

Design 52151

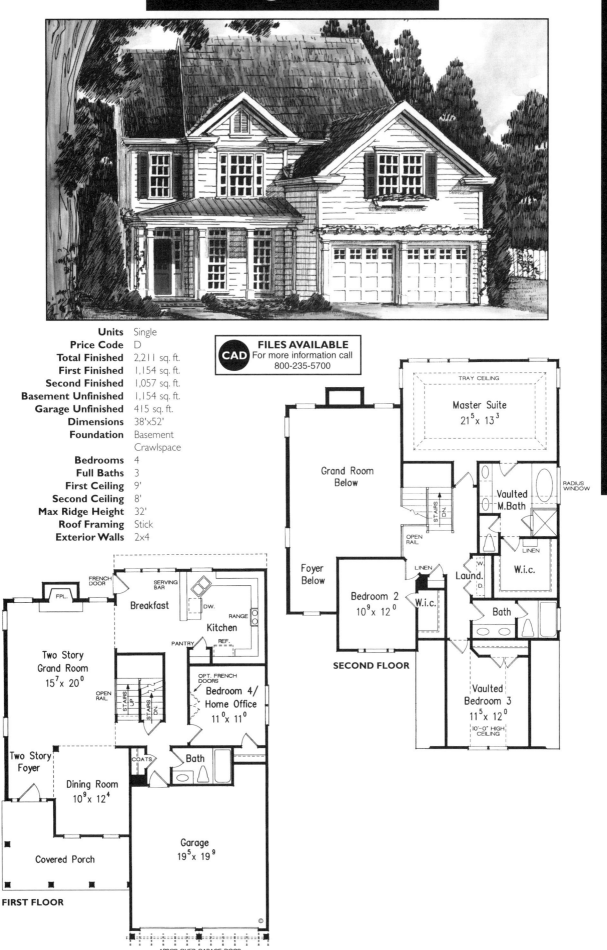

Units	Single
Price Code	D
Total Finished	2,211 sq. ft.
First Finished	1,154 sq. ft.
Second Finished	1,057 sq. ft.
Basement Unfinished	1,154 sq. ft.
Garage Unfinished	415 sq. ft.
Dimensions	38'x52'
Foundation	Basement
	Crawlspace
Bedrooms	4
Full Baths	3
First Ceiling	9'
Second Ceiling	8'
Max Ridge Height	32'
Roof Framing	Stick
Exterior Walls	2x4

CAD FILES AVAILABLE
For more information call
800-235-5700

SECOND FLOOR

TRAY CEILING

Master Suite
21⁵ x 13³

Grand Room Below

Vaulted M.Bath

RADIUS WINDOW

LINEN

OPEN RAIL

STAIRS DN.

Foyer Below

Laund.

W.i.c.

Bedroom 2
10⁹ x 12⁰

LINEN

W.i.c.

Bath

Vaulted Bedroom 3
11⁵ x 12⁰

10'-0" HIGH CEILING

FIRST FLOOR

FRENCH DOOR

FPL.

SERVING BAR

Breakfast

DW.

RANGE

Kitchen

PANTRY

REF.

Two Story Grand Room
15⁷ x 20⁰

OPEN RAIL

STAIRS UP

STAIRS DN.

OPT. FRENCH DOORS

Bedroom 4/ Home Office
11⁰ x 11⁰

COATS

Bath

Two Story Foyer

Dining Room
10⁹ x 12⁴

Covered Porch

Garage
19⁵ x 19⁹

ARBOR OVER GARAGE DOOR

Design 90454

Units	Single
Price Code	D
Total Finished	2,218 sq. ft.
Main Finished	2,218 sq. ft.
Basement Unfinished	1,658 sq. ft.
Garage Unfinished	528 sq. ft.
Deck Unfinished	342 sq. ft.
Porch Unfinished	216 sq. ft.
Dimensions	72'x64'
Foundation	Basement
	Crawlspace
Bedrooms	3
Full Baths	2
Main Ceiling	9'
Max Ridge Height	20'10"
Roof Framing	Stick
Exterior Walls	2x4

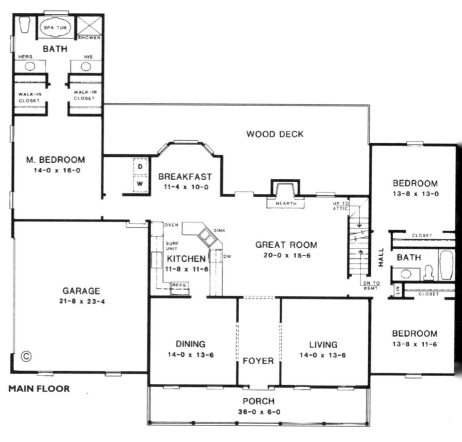

MAIN FLOOR

Design 34705

Units	Single
Price Code	D
Total Finished	2,224 sq. ft.
First Finished	1,090 sq. ft.
Second Finished	1,134 sq. ft.
Basement Unfinished	1,090 sq. ft.
Garage Unfinished	576 sq. ft.
Dimensions	66'x27'
Foundation	Basement
	Crawlspace
	Slab
Bedrooms	4
Full Baths	2
Half Baths	1
Max Ridge Height	27'
Roof Framing	Stick
Exterior Walls	2x4, 2x6

OPTIONAL BASEMENT FOUNDATION

SECOND FLOOR

Br 4
11-4 x 10-8

MBr 1
13-8 x 15-6

Br 2
11-8 x 16

Br 3
11-4 x 10-8

DN

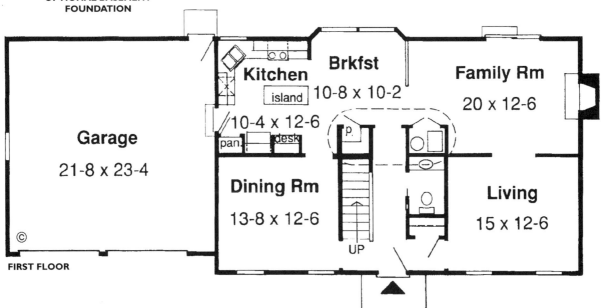

FIRST FLOOR

Garage
21-8 x 23-4

Kitchen
10-4 x 12-6

Brkfst
10-8 x 10-2

island

pan. desk

Family Rm
20 x 12-6

Dining Rm
13-8 x 12-6

Living
15 x 12-6

UP

Units	Single
Price Code	D
Total Finished	2,229 sq. ft.
Main Finished	2,229 sq. ft.
Basement Unfinished	2,229 sq. ft.
Garage Unfinished	551 sq. ft.
Dimensions	65'x56'
Foundation	Basement
Bedrooms	3
Full Baths	2
Max Ridge Height	26'
Roof Framing	Truss
Exterior Walls	2x6

MAIN FLOOR

Design 68162

Units	Single
Price Code	E
Total Finished	2,252 sq. ft.
First Finished	1,736 sq. ft.
Second Finished	516 sq. ft.
Bonus Unfinished	242 sq. ft.
Garage Unfinished	638 sq. ft.
Deck Unfinished	1,223 sq. ft.
Dimensions	80'x59'
Foundation	Slab
Bedrooms	4
Full Baths	3
First Ceiling	9'
Max Ridge Height	30'
Exterior Walls	2x4

* Alternate foundation options available at an additional charge.
Please call 1-800-235-5700 for more information.

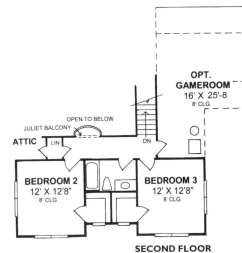

SECOND FLOOR

OPT. GAMEROOM 16' X 25'-8 8' CLG.

JULIET BALCONY
OPEN TO BELOW
ATTIC LIN DN
BEDROOM 2 12' X 12'8" 8' CLG.
BEDROOM 3 12' X 12'8" 8' CLG.

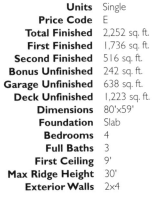

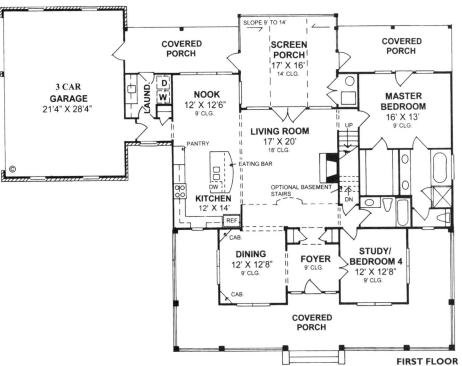

FIRST FLOOR

3 CAR GARAGE 21'4" X 28'4"

COVERED PORCH

SCREEN PORCH 17' X 16' 14' CLG.
SLOPE 9' TO 14'

COVERED PORCH

LAUND.

NOOK 12' X 12'6" 9' CLG.

MASTER BEDROOM 16' X 13' 9' CLG.

PANTRY

LIVING ROOM 17' X 20' 18' CLG.

EATING BAR

UP

OPTIONAL BASEMENT STAIRS

DN

KITCHEN 12' X 14'

REF.

CAB.

DINING 12' X 12'8" 9' CLG.

FOYER 9' CLG.

STUDY/ BEDROOM 4 12' X 12'8" 9' CLG.

CAB.

COVERED PORCH

Units	Single
Price Code	E
Total Finished	2,257 sq. ft.
Main Finished	2,257 sq. ft.
Garage Unfinished	601 sq. ft.
Porch Unfinished	325 sq. ft.
Dimensions	65'x65'10"
Foundation	Crawlspace
	Slab
Bedrooms	4
Full Baths	2
Half Baths	1
Main Ceiling	9'-11'
Max Ridge Height	25'
Roof Framing	Stick
Exterior Walls	2x4

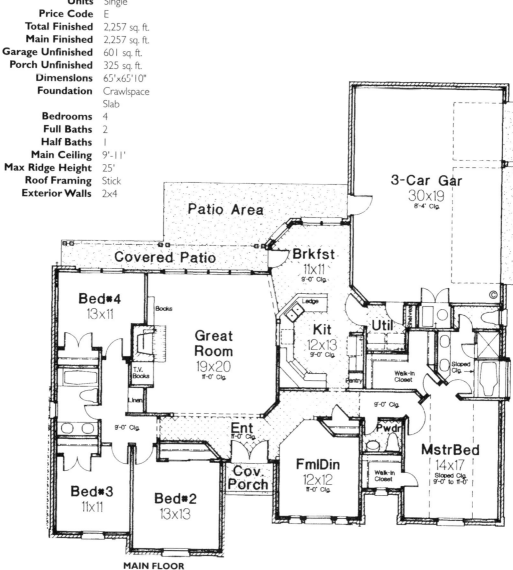

MAIN FLOOR

PHOTOGRAPHY: JOHN EHRENCLOU

Units	Single
Price Code	E
Total Finished	2,281 sq. ft.
First Finished	1,260 sq. ft.
Second Finished	1,021 sq. ft.
Basement Unfinished	1,186 sq. ft.
Garage Unfinished	851 sq. ft.
Dimensions	76'4"x45'10"
Foundation	Basement
	Crawlspace
	Slab
Bedrooms	3
Full Baths	2
Half Baths	1
First Ceiling	9'
Second Ceiling	8'
Vaulted Ceiling	10'
Max Ridge Height	29'6"
Roof Framing	Stick
Exterior Walls	2x4, 2x6

SECOND FLOOR

Attic Space (Optional)

W.P. Tub · Skylt

Br #3
11-7 x 9-10

MBr #1
12-1 x 15-10
8' Clg.

DN Railing

Plant Shelf

Br #2
11-7 x 11-10

Open to Below

Flat Clg 10'

OPTIONAL CRAWLSPACE/SLAB FOUNDATION

Please note: The photographed home may have been modified to suit homeowner preferences. If you order plans, have a builder or design professional check them against the photograph to confirm actual construction details.

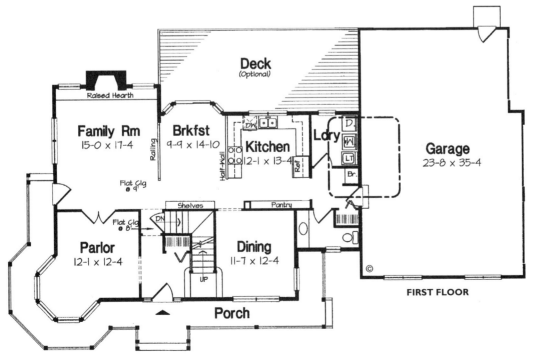

Deck (Optional)

Raised Hearth

Family Rm
15-0 x 17-4

Brkfst
9-9 x 14-10

Kitchen
12-1 x 13-4

Ldry

Garage
23-8 x 35-4

Flat Clg 9'

Shelves · Pantry

Flat Clg 8'

DN

Parlor
12-1 x 12-4

Dining
11-7 x 12-4

UP

FIRST FLOOR

Porch

Units	Single
Price Code	E
Total Finished	2,286 sq. ft.
First Finished	1,663 sq. ft.
Second Finished	623 sq. ft.
Bonus Unfinished	211 sq. ft.
Basement Unfinished	1,663 sq. ft.
Garage Unfinished	461 sq. ft.
Dimensions	54'x48'
Foundation	Basement
	Crawlspace
Bedrooms	4
Full Baths	3
Max Ridge Height	26'6"
Roof Framing	Stick
Exterior Walls	2x4

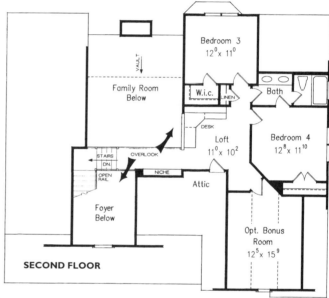

SECOND FLOOR

FIRST FLOOR

Design 65145

Units	Single
Price Code	E
Total Finished	2,292 sq. ft.
First Finished	1,246 sq. ft.
Second Finished	1,046 sq. ft.
Basement Unfinished	1,246 sq. ft.
Garage Unfinished	392 sq. ft.
Porch Unfinished	323 sq. ft.
Dimensions	58'x42'2"
Foundation	Basement
Bedrooms	3
Full Baths	1
3/4 Baths	1
Half Baths	1
First Ceiling	9'
Second Ceiling	8'
Max Ridge Height	33'1"
Roof Framing	Truss
Exterior Walls	2x6

SECOND FLOOR

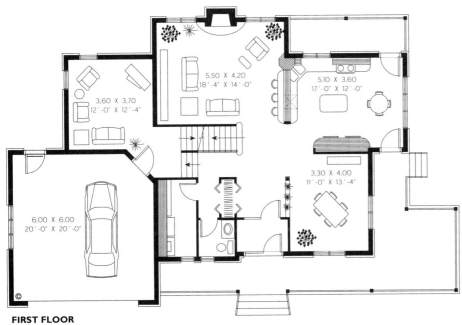

FIRST FLOOR

Design 65004

Units	Single
Price Code	E
Total Finished	2,300 sq. ft.
First Finished	1,067 sq. ft.
Second Finished	1,233 sq. ft.
Basement Unfinished	1,067 sq. ft.
Dimensions	58'x33'
Foundation	Basement
Bedrooms	3
Full Baths	2
Half Baths	1
First Ceiling	9'2"
Second Ceiling	8'2"
Max Ridge Height	24'6"
Roof Framing	Truss
Exterior Walls	2x6

SECOND FLOOR

FIRST FLOOR

Units	Single
Price Code	E
Total Finished	2,300 sq. ft.
First Finished	1,620 sq. ft.
Second Finished	680 sq. ft.
Bonus Unfinished	284 sq. ft.
Garage Unfinished	595 sq. ft.
Dimensions	56'x53'2"
Foundation	Combo Basement/ Crawlspace
Bedrooms	3
Full Baths	2
Half Baths	1
First Ceiling	9'
Second Ceiling	8'
Max Ridge Height	29'9"
Roof Framing	Truss
Exterior Walls	2x6

SECOND FLOOR

FIRST FLOOR

Design 90444

Units	Single
Price Code	E
Total Finished	2,301 sq. ft.
First Finished	1,996 sq. ft.
Second Finished	305 sq. ft.
Dimensions	63'x64'6"
Foundation	Basement
	Crawlspace
Bedrooms	3
Full Baths	3
Max Ridge Height	22'10"
Roof Framing	Stick
Exterior Walls	2x4

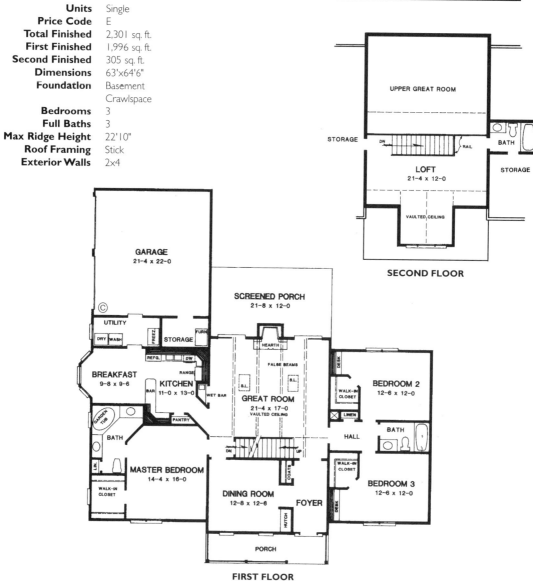

Design 98455

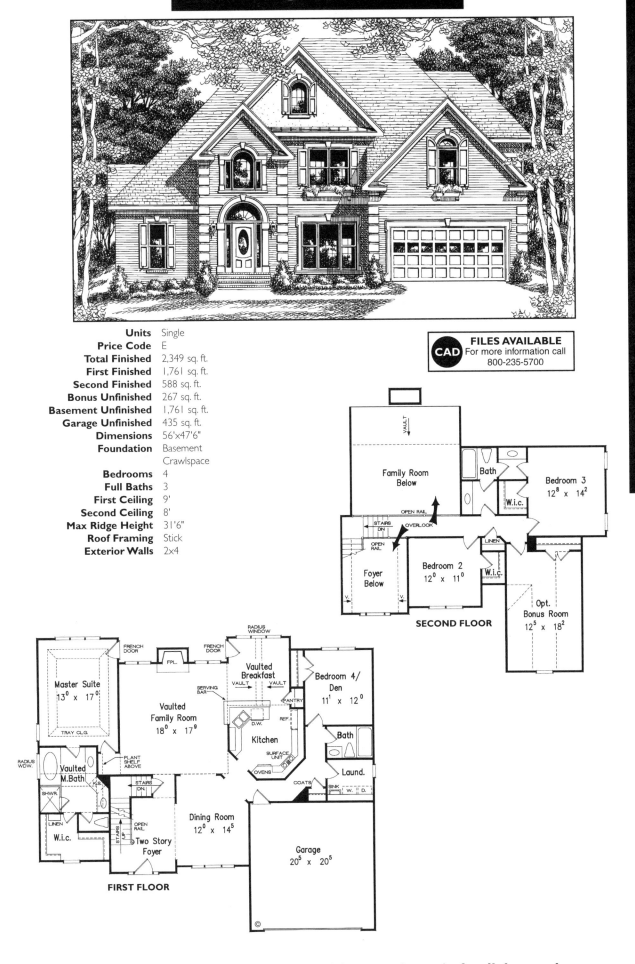

Units	Single
Price Code	E
Total Finished	2,349 sq. ft.
First Finished	1,761 sq. ft.
Second Finished	588 sq. ft.
Bonus Unfinished	267 sq. ft.
Basement Unfinished	1,761 sq. ft.
Garage Unfinished	435 sq. ft.
Dimensions	56'x47'6"
Foundation	Basement
	Crawlspace
Bedrooms	4
Full Baths	3
First Ceiling	9'
Second Ceiling	8'
Max Ridge Height	31'6"
Roof Framing	Stick
Exterior Walls	2x4

CAD **FILES AVAILABLE**
For more information call
800-235-5700

SECOND FLOOR

VAULT

Family Room Below

Bath

Bedroom 3
12^8 x 14^2

W.i.c.

OPEN RAIL

STAIRS DN

OVERLOOK

LINEN

OPEN RAIL

Foyer Below

Bedroom 2
12^0 x 11^0

W.i.c.

Opt. Bonus Room
12^5 x 18^2

FIRST FLOOR

FRENCH DOOR

FPL.

FRENCH DOOR

RADIUS WINDOW

Vaulted Breakfast

VAULT

VAULT

Master Suite
13^0 x 17^0

Vaulted Family Room
18^0 x 17^9

SERVING BAR

Bedroom 4/ Den
11^1 x 12^0

PANTRY

TRAY CLG.

D.W.

REF.

Kitchen

Bath

RADIUS WDW.

Vaulted M.Bath

PLANT SHELF ABOVE

SURFACE UNIT

OVENS

Laund.

SHWR.

STAIRS DN

COATS

SINK

W. D.

LINEN

W.i.c.

STAIRS UP

OPEN RAIL

Two Story Foyer

Dining Room
12^0 x 14^5

Garage
20^5 x 20^5

Design 10619

Units	Single
Price Code	E
Total Finished	2,352 sq. ft.
Main Finished	2,352 sq. ft.
Basement Unfinished	2,352 sq. ft.
Garage Unfinished	696 sq. ft.
Dimensions	93'6"x48'
Foundation	Basement
Bedrooms	3
Full Baths	2
3/4 Baths	1
Max Ridge Height	20'
Roof Framing	Stick
Exterior Walls	2x6

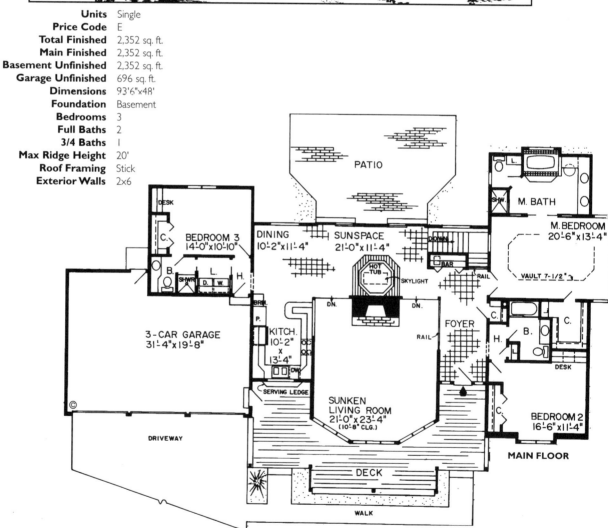

Design 24404

Units	Single
Price Code	E
Total Finished	2,356 sq. ft.
First Finished	1,236 sq. ft.
Second Finished	1,120 sq. ft.
Dimensions	68'8½"x42'
Foundation	Basement
	Crawlspace
	Slab
Bedrooms	4
Full Baths	2
3/4 Baths	I
First Ceiling	9'
Second Ceiling	8'
Max Ridge Height	28'
Roof Framing	Stick
Exterior Walls	2x4

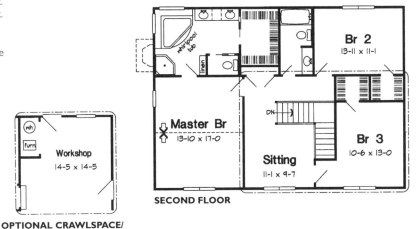

SECOND FLOOR

Workshop 14-5 x 14-5

OPTIONAL CRAWLSPACE/ SLAB FOUNDATION

Master Br 13-10 x 17-0

Br 2 13-11 x 11-1

Br 3 10-6 x 13-0

Sitting 11-1 x 9-7

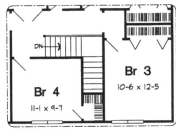

FOURTH BEDROOM OPTION

Br 4 11-1 x 9-7

Br 3 10-6 x 12-5

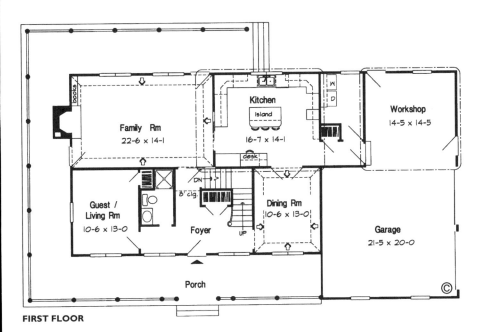

FIRST FLOOR

Family Rm 22-6 x 14-1

Kitchen island 16-7 x 14-1

Workshop 14-5 x 14-5

Guest / Living Rm 10-6 x 13-0

Foyer

Dining Rm 10-6 x 13-0

Garage 21-5 x 20-0

Porch

KITCHEN OPTION

Family Dining 8-10 x 14-1

Kit. 10-0 x 14-1

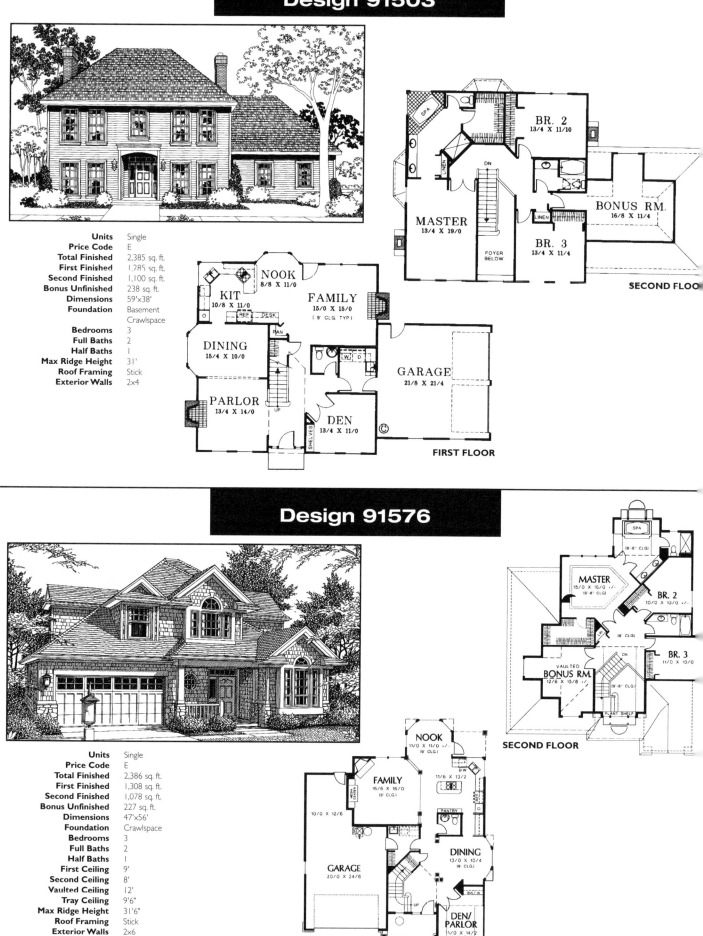

Design 91503

Units	Single
Price Code	E
Total Finished	2,385 sq. ft.
First Finished	1,285 sq. ft.
Second Finished	1,100 sq. ft.
Bonus Unfinished	238 sq. ft.
Dimensions	59'x38'
Foundation	Basement
	Crawlspace
Bedrooms	3
Full Baths	2
Half Baths	1
Max Ridge Height	31'
Roof Framing	Stick
Exterior Walls	2x4

SECOND FLOOR

BR. 2
13/4 X 11/10

SPA

MASTER
13/4 X 19/0

DN

BONUS RM.
16/8 X 11/4

LINEN

LINEN

BR. 3
13/4 X 11/4

FOYER BELOW

NOOK
8/8 X 11/0

KIT
10/8 X 11/0

FAMILY
15/0 X 15/0
(9' CLG. TYP)

REF DESK

PAN

DINING
15/4 X 10/0

W D

GARAGE
21/8 X 21/4

PARLOR
13/4 X 14/0

UP

DEN
13/4 X 11/0

SHELVES

FIRST FLOOR

Design 91576

Units	Single
Price Code	E
Total Finished	2,386 sq. ft.
First Finished	1,308 sq. ft.
Second Finished	1,078 sq. ft.
Bonus Unfinished	227 sq. ft.
Dimensions	47'x56'
Foundation	Crawlspace
Bedrooms	3
Full Baths	2
Half Baths	1
First Ceiling	9'
Second Ceiling	8'
Vaulted Ceiling	12'
Tray Ceiling	9'6"
Max Ridge Height	31'6"
Roof Framing	Stick
Exterior Walls	2x6

SPA

(9'-6" CLG.)

MASTER
15/0 X 16/0
(9'-6" CLG.)

BR. 2
10/0 X 13/0

(8' CLG.)

BR. 3
11/0 X 10/0

VAULTED
BONUS RM.
12/6 X 15/8
(9'-6" CLG.)

PLANT SHELF

SECOND FLOOR

NOOK
11/0 X 11/0 +/-
(9' CLG.)

FAMILY
16/6 X 16/0
(9' CLG.)

11/6 X 13/2

DW

10/0 X 12/6

PANTRY

GARAGE
20/0 X 24/6

DINING
13/0 X 10/4
(9' CLG.)

UP

BUILT-IN

DEN/
PARLOR
11/0 X 14/2
(9'-6" CLG.)

FIRST FLOOR

Exterior Elevations

These front, rear, and sides of the home include information pertaining to the exterior finish materials, roof pitches, and exterior height dimensions.

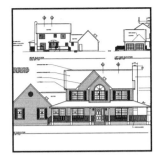

Cabinet Plans

These plans, or in some cases elevations, will detail the layout of the kitchen and bathroom cabinets at a larger scale. Available for most plans.

Typical Wall Section

This section will address insulation, roof components, and interior and exterior wall finishes. Your plans will be designed with either 2x4 or 2x6 exterior walls, but if you wish, most professional contractors can easily adapt the plans to the wall thickness you require.

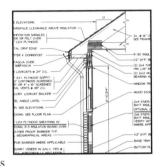

Fireplace Details

If the home you have chosen includes a fireplace, a fireplace detail will show typical methods of constructing the firebox, hearth, and flue chase for masonry units, or a wood frame chase for zero-clearance units. Available for most plans.

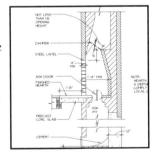

Foundation Plan

These plans will accurately show the dimensions of the footprint of your home, including load-bearing points and beam placement if applicable. The foundation style will vary from plan to plan. **(Please note: There may be an additional charge for optional foundation plan. Please call for details.)**

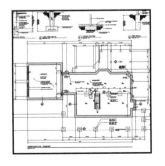

Roof Plan

The information necessary to construct the roof will be included with your home plans. Some plans will reference roof trusses, while many others contain schematic framing plans. These framing plans will indicate the lumber sizes necessary for the rafters and ridgeboards based on the designated roof loads.

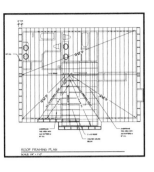

Typical Cross Section

A cut-away cross section through the entire home shows your building contractor the exact correlation of construction components at all levels of the house. It will help to clarify the load bearing points from the roof all the way down to the basement. Available for most plans.

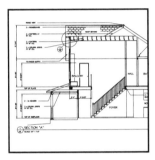

Detailed Floor Plans

The floor plans of your home accurately depict the dimensions of the positioning of all walls, doors, windows, stairs, and permanent fixtures. They will show you the relationship and dimensions of rooms, closets, and traffic patterns. The schematic of the electrical layout may be included in the plan.

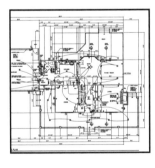

Stair Details

If the design you have chosen includes stairs, the plans will show the information that you need in order to build them—either through a stair cross section or on the floor plans.

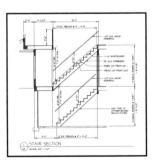

Garlinghouse Options & Extras

Reversed Plans can Make Your Dream Home Just Right!

You could have exactly the home you want by flipping it end-for-end. Simply order your plans "reversed." We'll send you one full set of mirror-image plans (with the writing backwards) as a master guide for you and your builder.

The remaining sets of your order will come as shown in this book so the dimensions and specifications are easily read on the job site. Most plans in our collection come stamped "reversed" so there is no construction confusion.

We can only send reversed plans with multiple-set orders. There is a $50 charge for this service.

Some plans in our collection are available in "Right Reading Reverse." Right Reading Reverse plans will show your home in reverse. This easy-to-read format will save you valuable time and money. Please contact our Sales Department at 800-235-5700 to check for Right Reading Reverse availability. There is a $135 charge for this service. **RRR**

Remember to Order Your Materials List

Available at a modest additional charge, the Materials List gives the quantity, dimensions, and specifications for the major materials needed to build your home. You will get faster, more accurate bids from your contractors and building suppliers—and avoid paying for unused materials and waste. **Materials Lists are available for all home plans except as otherwise indicated, but can only be ordered with a set of home plans.** Due to differences in regional requirements and homeowner or builder preferences, electrical, plumbing and heating/air conditioning equipment specifications are not designed specifically for each plan. **ML**

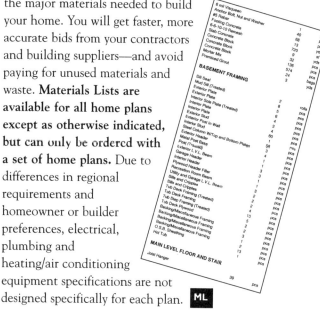

What Garlinghouse Offers

Home Plan Blueprint Package

By purchasing a multiple-set package of blueprints or a Vellum from Garlinghouse, you not only receive the physical blueprint documents necessary for construction, but you are also granted a license to build one (and only one) home. You can also make simple modifications, including minor non-structural changes and material substitutions, to our design as long as these changes are made directly on the blueprints purchased from Garlinghouse and no additional copies are made.

Home Plan Vellums

By purchasing Vellums for one of our home plans, you receive the same construction drawings found in the blueprints, but printed on vellum paper. Vellums can be erased and are perfect for making design changes. They are also semi-transparent, making them easy to duplicate. But most importantly, the purchase of home plan Vellums comes with a broader license that allows you to make changes to the design (i.e., create a hand drawn or CAD derivative work), to make copies of the plan, and to build one home from the plan.

License to Build Additional Homes

With the purchase of a blueprint package or Vellums, you automatically receive a license to build one home and only one home. If you want to build more homes than you are licensed to build through your purchase of a plan, then additional licenses must be purchased at reasonable costs from Garlinghouse. Inquire for more information.

Modifying Your Favorite Design Made Easy

#1 Modifying Your Garlinghouse Home Plan

Simple modifications to your dream home, including minor non-structural changes and material substitutions, can be made by you and your builder with the consent of your local building official, by marking the changes directly on your blueprints. However, if you are considering making significant changes to your chosen design, we recommend that you use the services of The Garlinghouse Design Staff. We will help take your ideas and turn them into a reality, just the way you want. Here's our procedure:

Call 800-235-5700 and order your modification estimate. The fee for this estimate is $50. We will review your plan changes and provide you with an estimate to draft your specific modifications before you purchase the vellums. **Please note: A vellum must be purchased to modify a home plan design.**

After you receive your estimate, if you decide to have Garlinghouse do the changes, the $50 estimate fee will be deducted from the cost of your modifications. If, however, you chose to use a different service, the $50 estimate fee is non-refundable. **(Note: Personal checks cannot be accepted for the estimate.)**

A 75% deposit is required before we begin making the actual modifications to your plans.

Once the design changes have been completed to your vellum plan, a representative will call to inform you that your modified vellum plan is complete and will be shipped as soon as the final payment has been made. For additional information, call us at 1-800-235-5700. Please refer to the Modification Pricing Guide for estimated modification costs.

#2 Reproducible Vellums for Local Modification Ease

If you decide not to use Garlinghouse for your modifications, we recommend that you follow our same procedure of purchasing vellums. You then have the option of using the services of the original designer of the plan, a local professional designer, or an architect to make the modifications.

With a vellum copy of our plans, a design professional can alter the drawings just the way you want, then you can print as many copies of the modified plans as you need to build your house. And, since you have already started with our complete detailed plans, the cost of those expensive professional services will be significantly less than starting from scratch. Refer to the price schedule for vellum costs.

How to obtain a construction cost calculation based on labor rates and building material costs in your zip code area.

What will your dream home cost? ZIP QUOTE has the answer!

How does Zip Quote actually work? When you call to order, you must choose from the options available for your specific home in order for us to process your order. Once we receive your Zip Quote order, we process your specific home plan building materials list through our Home Cost Calculator which contains up-to-date rates for all residential labor trades and building material costs in your zip code area. The result? A calculated cost to build your dream home in your zip code area. This calculation will help you (as a consumer or a builder) evaluate your building budget.

All database information for our calculations is furnished by Marshall & Swift, L.P. For over 60 years, Marshall & Swift L.P. has been a leading provider of cost data to professionals in all aspects of the construction and remodeling industries.

Zip Quote can be purchased in two separate formats, either an itemized or a bottom-line format.

Option 1 The **Itemized Zip Quote** is a detailed building materials list. Each building materials list line item will separately state the labor cost, material cost, and equipment cost (if applicable) for the use of that building material in the construction process. This building materials list will be summarized by the individual building categories and will have additional columns where you can enter data from your contractor's estimates for a cost comparison between the different suppliers and contractors who will actually quote you their products and services.

Option 2 The **Bottom-Line Zip Quote** is a one line summarized total cost for the home plan of your choice. This cost calculation is also based on the labor cost, material cost, and equipment cost (if applicable) within your zip code area. Bottom-Line Zip Quote is available for most plans. Please call for availability.

Cost The price of your Itemized Zip Quote is based upon the pricing schedule of the plan you have selected, in addition to the price of the materials list. Please refer to the pricing schedule on our order form. The price of your initial Bottom-Line Zip Quote is $29.95. Each additional Bottom-Line Zip Quote ordered in conjunction with the initial order is only $14.95. A Bottom-Line Zip Quote may be purchased separately and does NOT have to be purchased in conjunction with a home plan order.

FYI An Itemized Zip Quote Home Cost Calculation can ONLY be purchased in conjunction with a Home Plan order. The Itemized Zip Quote can not be purchased separately. If you find within 60 days of your order date that you will be unable to build this home, then you may apply the price of the plans and the materials list towards the price of a new set of plans (see order info pages for plan exchange policy). The Itemized Zip Quote and the Bottom-Line Zip Quote are NOT returnable. The price of the initial Bottom-Line Zip Quote order can be credited toward the purchase of an Itemized Zip Quote order only if available. Additional Bottom-Line Zip Quote orders within the same order can not be credited. Please call our Sales Department for more information.

An Itemized Zip Quote is available for plans where you see this symbol. **ZIP**

A Bottom-Line Zip Quote is available for all plans under 4,000 sq. ft. or where you see this symbol. **BL** Please call for current availability.

Some More Information The Itemized and Bottom-Line Zip Quotes give you approximated costs for constructing the particular house in your area. These costs are not exact and are only intended to be used as a preliminary estimate to help determine the affordability of a new home and/or as a guide to evaluate the general competitiveness of actual price quotes obtained through local suppliers and contractors. **Land, landscaping, sewer systems, site work, contractor overhead and profit, and other expenses are not included in our building cost figures. Excluding land and landscaping, you may incur an additional 20% to 40% in costs from the original estimate.** Garlinghouse and Marshall & Swift L.P. cannot guarantee any level of data accuracy or correctness in a Zip Quote and disclaim all liability for loss with respect to the same, in excess of the original purchase price of the Zip Quote product. All Zip Quote calculations are based upon the actual blueprints and do not reflect any differences or options that may be shown on the published house renderings, floor plans or photographs.

CAD Files Now Available

A CAD file is available for plans where you see this symbol. **CAD**

Cad files are available in .dc5 or .dxf format or .dwg formats (R12, R13, R14, R2000). Please specify the file format at the time of your order. You will receive one bond set along with the CAD file when you place your order. **NOTE: CAD files are NOT returnable and can not be exchanged.**

Your Blueprints Can Be Sealed By A Registered Architect

We can have your home plan blueprints sealed by an architect that is registered in most states. Please call our Order Department for details. Although an architect's seal will not guarantee approval of your home plan blueprints, a seal is sometimes required by your state local building department in order to get a building permit. Please talk to your local building officials, before you order your blueprints, determine if a seal is needed in your area. You will need to provide the county and state of your building site when ordering an architect's seal on your blueprints, and please allow additional time to process your order (an additional five to fifteen working days, at least). Seals are available for plans numbered 0-15,999, 17,000-18,999, 20,000 - 31,999, and 34,000 - 34,999.

State Energy Certificates

A few states require that an energy certificate be prepared for your new home to their specifications before a building permit can be issued. Again, your local building official can tell you if one is required in your state. You will first need to fill out the energy certificate checklist available to you when your order is placed. This list contains questions about type of heating used, siding, windows, location of home, etc. This checklist provides all the information needed to prepare your state energy certificate. **Please note: energy certificates are only available on orders for blueprints with an architect's seal.** Certificates are available for plans numbered 0-15,999, 17,000-18,999, 20,000 - 31,999, and 34,000 - 34,999.

Specifications & Contract Form

We send this form to you free of charge with your home plan order. The form is designed to be filled in by you or your contractor with the exact materials to use in the construction of your new home. Once signed by you and your contractor it will provide you with peace of mind throughout the construction process.

Detail Plans
Valuable Information About Construction Techniques

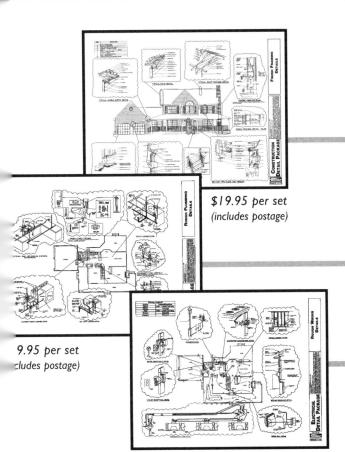

$19.95 per set
(includes postage)

9.95 per set
(includes postage)

$19.95 per set
(includes postage)

PLEASE NOTE: The detail plans are not specific to any one home plan and should be used only as a general reference guide. Because local codes and requirements vary greatly, we recommend that you obtain drawings and bids from licensed contractors to do your mechanical plans. However, if you want to know more about techniques — and deal more confidently with subcontractors — we offer these remarkably useful detail sheets. These detail sheets will aid in your understanding of these technical subjects.

RESIDENTIAL CONSTRUCTION DETAILS

Ten sheets that cover the essentials of stick-built residential home construction. Details foundation options — poured concrete basement, concrete block, or monolithic concrete slab. Shows all aspects of floor, wall and roof framing. Provides details for roof dormers, overhangs, chimneys and skylights. Conforms to requirements of Uniform Building code or BOCA code. Includes a quick index and a glossary of terms.

RESIDENTIAL PLUMBING DETAILS

Eight sheets packed with information detailing pipe installation methods, fittings, and sized. Details plumbing hook-ups for toilets, sinks, washers, sump pumps, and septic system construction. Conforms to requirements of National Plumbing code. Color coded with a glossary of terms and quick index.

RESIDENTIAL ELECTRICAL DETAILS

Eight sheets that cover all aspects of residential wiring, from simple switch wiring to service entrance connections. Details distribution panel layout with outlet and switch schematics, circuit breaker and wiring installation methods, and ground fault interrupter specifications. Conforms to requirements of National Electrical Code. Color coded with a glossary of terms.

Questions?
Call our customer service number at 1-800-235-5700.

the Garlinghouse company

Order Form

BEST PLAN VALUE IN THE INDUSTRY!

Order Code No. **H4AHP**

_____foundation

_____ set(s) of blueprints for plan #_____ $_____

_____ Vellum for plan #_____ $_____

_____ Additional set(s) @ $50 each for plan #_____ $_____
(Not available for 1 set-study set)

_____ Mirror Image Reverse @ $50 each $_____

_____ Right Reading Reverse @ $135 each $_____

_____ Materials list for plan #_____ $_____

_____ Detail Plans (Not plan specific) @ $19.95 each

    ❏ Construction ❏ Plumbing ❏ Electrical $_____

_____ Bottom-Line Zip Quote @ $29.95 for plan #_____ $_____

_____ Additional Bottom-Line Zip Quotes

    @ $14.95 for plan(s) #_____ $_____

Zip code where building _____

_____ Itemized Zip Quote for plan(s) #_____ $_____

Shipping $_____

Subtotal $_____

Sales Tax (CT residents add 6% sales tax. Not required for other states) $_____

TOTAL AMOUNT ENCLOSED $_____

Send your check, money order, or credit card information to:
(No C.O.D.'s Please)

Please submit all United States & other nations orders to:
Garlinghouse Company
174 Oakwood Drive
Glastonbury, CT. 06033
CALL: (800) 235-5700   FAX: (860) 659-5692

VISA   **MasterCard**

Please Submit all Canadian plan orders to:
Garlinghouse Company
102 Ellis Street
Penticton, BC V2A 4L5
CALL: (800) 361-7526   FAX: (250) 493-7526

ADDRESS INFORMATION:

NAME: _____

STREET: _____

CITY: _____

STATE: _____ **ZIP:** _____

DAYTIME PHONE: _____

E-MAIL ADDRESS: _____

Credit Card Information

Charge To: ❏ Visa   ❏ Mastercard

Card # |_|_|_|_|_|_|_|_|_|_|_|_|_|_|_|_|

Signature _____ Exp. _____/_____

To order your plan on-line now using our secure server, visit:
www.garlinghouse.com

CUSTOMER SERVICE	TO PLACE ORDERS
Questions on existing orders?	• To order your home plan • Questions about a plan
➡ **1-800-895-3715**	➡ **1-800-235-5700**

Privacy Statement (please read)

Dear Valued Garlinghouse Customer,

Your privacy is extremely important to us. We'd like to take a little of your time to explain our privacy policy.

As a service to you, we would like to provide your name to companies such as the following:

- Building material manufacturers that we are affiliated with, who would like to keep you current with their product line and specials.
- Building material retailers that would like to offer you competitive prices to help you save money.
- Financing companies that would like to offer you competitive mortgage rates.

In addition, as our valued customer, we would like to send you newsletters to assist in your building experience. _We_ would also appreciate _your_ feedback by filling out a customer service survey aimed to improve our operations.

You have total control over the use of your contact information. You let us know exactly how you want to be contacted. Please check all boxes that apply.
Thank you.

    ☐ Don't mail
    ☐ Don't call
    ☐ Don't E-mail
    ☐ Only send Garlinghouse newsletters
      and customer service surveys

In closing, we hope this shows Garlinghouse's firm commitment to providing superior customer service and protection of your privacy. We thank you for your time and consideration.

Sincerely,

The Garlinghouse Company

For Our **USA** Customers:
Order Toll Free: 1-800-235-5700
~~M~~onday-Friday 8:00 a.m. to 8:00 p.m. Eastern Time
~~o~~r FAX your Credit Card order to 1-860-659-5692
All foreign residents call 1-860-659-5667

CUSTOMER SERVICE	**TO PLACE ORDERS**
Questions on existing orders?	• To order your home plans • Questions about a plan
➡ **1-800-895-3715**	➡ **1-800-235-5700**

For Our **Canadian** Customers:
Order Toll Free: 1-800-361-7526
Monday-Friday 8:00 a.m. to 5:00 p.m. Pacific Time
or FAX your Credit Card order to 1-250-493-7526
Customer Service: 1-250-493-0942

Please have ready: 1. Your credit card number 2. The plan number 3. The order code number ➡ **H4AHP**

~~C~~arlinghouse 2004 Blueprint Price Code Schedule
Prices subject to change without notice.

1 Set Study Set	4 Sets	8 Sets	Vellums	ML	Bottom-Line ZIP Quote	CADD Files
$395	$435	$485	$600	$60	$29.95	$1,250
$425	$465	$515	$630	$60	$29.95	$1,300
$450	$490	$540	$665	$60	$29.95	$1,350
$490	$530	$580	$705	$60	$29.95	$1,400
$530	$570	$620	$750	$70	$29.95	$1,450
$585	$625	$675	$800	$70	$29.95	$1,500
$630	$670	$720	$850	$70	$29.95	$1,550
$675	$715	$765	$895	$70	$29.95	$1,600
$700	$740	$790	$940	$80	$29.95	$1,650
$740	$780	$830	$980	$80	$29.95	$1,700
$805	$845	$895	$1,020	$80	$29.95	$1,750
$825	$865	$915	$1,055	$80	$29.95	$1,800

Shipping — (Plans 1-35999)	1-3 Sets	4-6 Sets	7+ & Vellums
Standard Delivery (UPS 2-Day)	$25.00	$30.00	$35.00
Overnight Delivery	$35.00	$40.00	$45.00

Shipping — (Plans 36000-99999)	1-3 Sets	4-6 Sets	7+ & Vellums
Ground Delivery (7-10 Days)	$15.00	$20.00	$25.00
Express Delivery (3-5 Days)	$20.00	$25.00	$30.00

International Shipping & Handling	1-3 Sets	4-6 Sets	7+ & Vellums
Regular Delivery Canada (10-14 Days)	$30.00	$35.00	$40.00
Express Delivery Canada (7-10 Days)	$60.00	$70.00	$80.00
Overseas Delivery Airmail (3-4 Weeks)	$50.00	$60.00	$65.00

Additional sets with original order $50

IMPORTANT INFORMATION TO READ BEFORE YOU PLACE YOUR ORDER

~~H~~ow Many Sets of Plans Will You Need?

~~Th~~e Standard 8-Set Construction Package
Our experience shows that you'll speed up every step of construction and avoid costly building errors by ordering enough sets to go around. Each ~~tra~~desperson wants a set—the general contractor and all subcontractors: foundation, electrical, plumbing, heating/air conditioning, and framers. Don't forget ~~yo~~ur lending institution, building department, and, of course, a set for yourself. * Recommended For Construction *

~~Th~~e Minimum 4-Set Construction Package
If you're comfortable with arduous follow-up, this package can save you a few dollars by giving you the option of passing down plan sets as work ~~pro~~gresses. You might have enough copies to go around if work goes exactly as scheduled and no plans are lost or damaged by subcontractors. But for only ~~$4~~0 more, the 8-set package eliminates these worries. * Recommended For Bidding *

~~Th~~e 1 Set-Study Set
We offer this set so you can study the blueprints to plan your dream home in detail. They are stamped "study set only—not for construction" and you can~~not~~ build a home from them. In pursuant to copyright laws, it is _illegal_ to reproduce any blueprint. 1 set-study sets cannot be ordered in a reversed format.

~~To~~ Reorder, Call 800-235-5700
If you find after your initial purchase that you require additional sets of plans, a materials list, or other items, you may purchase them from us at special reorder prices ~~(ple~~ase call for pricing details) provided that you reorder within six months of your original order date. There is a $28 reorder processing fee that is charged on all reorders. ~~For~~ more information on reordering plans, please contact our Sales Department.

~~C~~ustomer Service/Exchanges Call 800-895-3715
If for some reason you have a question about your existing order, please call 800-895-3715. Your plans are custom printed especially for you once you place your ~~ord~~er. For that reason we cannot accept any returns. If for some reason you find that the plan you have purchased from us does not meet your needs, then you may ~~exc~~hange that plan for any other plan in our collection. We allow you 60 days from your original invoice date to make an exchange. At the time of the exchange, you will be ~~cha~~rged a processing fee of 20% of the total amount of your original order, plus the difference in price between the plans (if applicable), plus the cost to ship the new ~~plan~~s to you. Call our Customer Service Department for more information. Please Note: Reproducible Vellums can only be exchanged if they are unopened.

~~Im~~portant Shipping Information
Please refer to the shipping charts on the order form for service availability for your specific plan number. Our delivery service must have a street address or ~~Rur~~al Route Box number—never a post office box. (PLEASE NOTE: Supplying a P.O. Box number will _only_ will delay the shipping of your order.) Use a work address if ~~no~~ one is home during the day. Orders being shipped to APO or FPO must go via First Class Mail. Please include the proper postage.
For our International Customers, only Certified bank checks and money orders are accepted and must be payable in U.S. currency. For speed, we ship interna~~tion~~al orders Air Parcel Post. Please refer to the chart for the correct shipping cost.

~~Im~~portant Canadian Shipping Information
To our friends in Canada, we have a plan design affiliate in Penticton, BC. This relationship will help you avoid the delays and charges associated with ship~~me~~nts from the United States. Moreover, our affiliate is familiar with the building requirements in your community and country. We prefer payments in U.S. currency. ~~If y~~ou however are sending Canadian funds, please add 45% to the prices of the plans and shipping fees.

~~A~~ Important Note About Building Code Requirements
All plans are drawn to conform to one or more of the industry's major national building standards. However, due to the variety of local building regulations, your ~~plan~~ may need to be modified to comply with local requirements—snow loads, energy loads, seismic zones, etc. Do check them fully and consult your local building ~~offi~~cials.
A few states require that all building plans used be drawn by an architect registered in that state. While having your plans reviewed and stamped by such an ~~arch~~itect may be prudent, laws requiring non-conforming plans like ours to be completely redrawn forces you to unnecessarily pay very large fees. If your state has ~~suc~~h a law, we strongly recommend you contact your state representative to protest.
The rendering, floor plans, and technical information contained within this publication are not guaranteed to be totally accurate. Consequently, no information ~~in~~ this publication should be used either as a guide to constructing a home or for estimating the cost of building a home. Complete blueprints must be purchased ~~for~~ such purposes.

Index

Option Key

BL Bottom-Line Zip Quote **ML** Materials List BL/ML **ZIP** Itemized Zip Quote **RRR** Right Reading Reverse **DUP** Duplex

Index

Option Key

BL Bottom-Line Zip Quote   **ML** Materials List BL/ML   **ZIP** Itemized Zip Quote   **RRR** Right Reading Reverse   **DUP** Duplex

TOP SELLING
GARAGE PLANS

Save money by Doing-It-Yourself using our Easy-To-Follow plans. Whether you intend to build your own garage or contract it out to a building professional, the Garlinghouse garage plans provide you with everything you need to price out your project and get started. Put our 90+ years of experience to work for you. Order now!!

No. 06016C $24.95
Cape Cod Style Apartment Garage With One Bedroom

- 28' x 24' Overall Dimensions
- 544 Square Foot Apartment
- 12/12 Gable Roof with Dormers
- Slab or Stem Wall Foundation Options

No. 06015C $24.95
Apartment Garage With Two Bedrooms

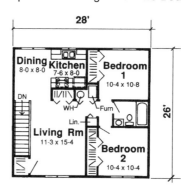

- 28' x 26' Overall Dimensions
- 728 Square Foot Apartment
- 4/12 Pitch Gable Roof
- Slab or Stem Wall Foundation Options

No. 06012C $16.95
30' Deep Gable &/or Eave Entry Jumbo Garages

- 4/12 Pitch Gable Roof
- Available Options for Extra Tall Walls, Garage & Personnel Doors, Foundation, Window, & Sidings
- Package contains 4 Different Sizes
- 30' x 28'   • 30' x 32'   • 30' x 36'   • 30' x 40'

No. 06013C $16.95
Two-Car Eave Entry Garage With Mudroom/Breezeway

- Attaches to Any House
- 36' x 24' Eave Entry
- Available Options for Utility Room with Bath, Mudroom, Screened-In Breezeway, Roof, Foundation, Garage & Personnel Doors, Window, & Sidings

No. 06001C $14.95

12', 14' & 16' Wide-Gable Entry 1-Car Garages

- Available Options for Roof, Foundation, Window, Door, & Sidings
- Package contains 8 Different Sizes
- 12' x 20' Mini-Garage   • 14' x 22'   • 16' x 20'   • 16' x 24'
- 14' x 20'   • 14' x 24'   • 16' x 22'   • 16' x 26'

No. 06003C $14.95

24' Wide-Gable Entry 2-Car Garages

- Available Options for Side Shed, Roof, Foundation, Garage & Personnel Doors, Window, & Sidings
- Package contains 5 Different Sizes
- 24' x 22'   • 24' x 28'   • 24' x 36'
- 24' x 24'   • 24' x 32'

No. 06007C $16.95

Gable 2-Car Gable Entry Gambrel Roof Garages

- Rear Stairs to Loft Workshop
- Front Loft Cargo Door With Pulley Lift
- Available Options for Foundation, Garage & Personnel Doors, Window, & Sidings
- Package contains 5 Different Sizes
- 22' x 26'   • 22' x 28'   • 24' x 28'   • 24' x 30'   • 24' x 32'

No. 06006C $16.95

22' & 24' Deep Eave Entry 2 & 3-Car Garages

- Can Be Built Stand-Alone or Attached to House
- Available Options for Roof, Foundation, Garage & Personnel Doors, Window, & Sidings
- Package contains 6 Different Sizes
- 22' x 28'   • 22' x 32'   • 24' x 32'
- 22' x 30'   • 24' x 30'   • 24' x 36'

No. 06002C $14.95

20' & 22' Wide-Gable Entry 2-Car Garages

- Available Options for Roof, Foundation, Garage & Personnel Doors, Window, & Sidings
- Package contains 7 Different Sizes
- 20' x 20'   • 20' x 24'   • 22' x 22'   • 22' x 28'
- 20' x 22'   • 20' x 28'   • 22' x 24'

No. 06008C $16.95

Eave Entry 2 & 3-Car Clerestory Roof Garages

- Interior Side Stairs to Loft Workshop
- Available Options for Engine Lift, Foundation, Garage & Personnel Doors, Window, & Sidings
- Package contains 4 Different Sizes
- 24' x 26'   • 24' x 28'   • 24' x 32'   • 24' x 36'

Order Code No: **H4AHP**

Here's What You Ge

- One complete set of drawings for each plan ordere
- Detailed step-by-step instructions with easy-to-follo diagrams on how to build your garage (not available with apartment garages)
- For each garage style, a variety of size and garage door configuration options
- Variety of roof styles and/or pitch options for most garages
- Complete materials list
- Choice between three foundation options: Monolith Slab, Concrete Stem Wall or Concrete Block Stem W
- Full framing plans, elevations and cross-sectionals f each garage size and configuration

Garage Plan Blueprints

All blueprint garage plan orders contain one complete of drawings with instructions and are priced as listed n to the illustration. **These blueprint garage plans can be modified.** Additional sets of plans may be obtained $10.00 each with your original order. UPS shipping used unless otherwise requested. Please include proper amount for shipping.

Garage Plan Vellums

By purchasing vellums for one of our garage plans, receive one vellum set of the same construction drawi found in the blueprints, but printed on vellum pa Vellums can be erased and are perfect for making des changes. They are also semi-transparent making th easy to duplicate. But most importantly, the purchase garage plan vellums comes with a broader license allows you to make changes to the design (ie, creat hand drawn or CAD derivative work), to make copies the plan and to build one garage from the plan.

Send your order to:
(With check or money order payable in U.S. funds only)

The Garlinghouse Company
174 Oakwood Drive
Glastonbury, CT 06033

No C.O.D. orders accepted; U.S. funds only. UPS will not ship to Po
Office boxes, FPO boxes, APO boxes, Alaska or Hawaii.

Canadian orders:
UPS Ground (5-10 days within Canada)
1-3 plans $15.95
4-6 plans $17.95
7-10 plans $19.95
11 or more plans $24.95
Prices subject to change without notice.